7 Sqn.

9 Sqn.

10 Sqn.

15 Sqn.

18 Sqn.

35 Sqn.

27 Sqn.

27 Sqn.

49 Sqn.

55 Sqn.

83 Sqn.

138 Sqn.

90 Sqn.

100 Sqn.

100 Sqn.
Wittering

V·BOMBER FIN MARKINGS

bombing
colours

bombing colours

RAF bombers, their markings and operations 1937–1973

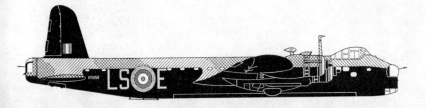

MICHAEL J F BOWYER

Patrick Stephens
Cambridge

ISBN 0 85059 128 7
First edition—October 1973

Text set in 9 on 10pt Times Roman type.
Printed in Great Britain
for Patrick Stephens Ltd, Viking Way, Bar Hill, Cambridge CB3 8EL
by Blackfriras Press, Leicester and
bound by Hunter & Foulis Ltd, Edinburgh.

introduction

author's preface

BOMBING COLOURS first appeared as a series of articles in *Airfix Magazine*. Now it has been put into book form as a companion volume to *Bombing Colours—British bomber camouflage and markings, 1914-1937* by Bruce Robertson. Like *Fighting Colours*, the first volume in the series, Bruce Robertson's book is still available. Additional text, drawings and photographs have been added to the second *Bombing Colours* which, in *Airfix Magazine*, covered only the period 1937-1945. This volume extends the story to the present day.

The reason why the series was split at 1937 was conditioned solely by the subject matter; that year saw the introduction of the aircraft resulting from the expansion and re-equipment of the Royal Air Force in the mid-1930s which largely brought to an end the biplane era.

The dual authorship of Michael J. F. Bowyer and Bruce Robertson is not a case of two writers being commissioned independently, for they have worked closely together on publishing ventures for over 20 years. Continuity of presentation is maintained by the services of expert artists Alfred M. Alderson and David Dean. The former was responsible for all the drawings except those of the V-bombers, the Washington and the Lincoln.

Thanks are due to the contributors of photographs who are all credited in the captions. The authors and publishers are also grateful to the British Aircraft Corporation, Hawker Siddeley Ltd, Jack Bushby, Eric Rhodes, Eric Watts, Leonard Clarke, Gerrit Zwanenburg and all others who contributed so readily both to the original articles and to this volume. The author extends his thanks to Keith Braybrooke who gave valuable assistance with proof-reading the book.

author's preface

THIS BOOK relates not merely how the aircraft were camouflaged and marked over the period 1937-1973. It also simply outlines the bomber offensive, 1939-1945, considers the requirements for aircraft and discusses those built in answer to the needs. In this manner it follows the pattern set by *Fighting Colours*.

The field covered is therefore wide, but no account is taken of fighter-bombers which, from 1941, played an ever-increasing part in the bomber offensive. These were referred to in *Fighting Colours*.

In the case of aircraft markings they are generally quoted as they were recorded, the notes being largely based upon personal records made at the time by the author and others. Thus, the notes record the aircraft markings as they actually were, not how they might or should have been. Markings clearly did not necessarily accord in detail or dating with official dictums, and often it will be seen that changes took place over lengthy periods. It is usually impossible to date changes precisely. Equally, it is impossible to lay down blanketing statements affording any reality where markings are concerned. Every machine had some individuality, which has made the study of aircraft markings such a vast and fascinating pastime.

Cambridge, October 1973   **Michael J. F. Bowyer**

contents

illustrations

diagrams in text

The front end papers show Avro Lancaster tail markings, 1944-45 and V-bomber fin markings. The rear end papers show more V-bomber fin markings and Canberra fin markings. Captions for the drawings on both the front and rear end papers appear on pages 282-284.

Chapter I

The colours from expansion

HEAVY BOMBERS had long worn camouflage of a sort, the Nivo finish. This was intended as a night disguise. By the 1930s there was no firm decision that bomber operations should be only by night, but it seemed possible. What was more certain was that, in the event of war, air attack upon aircraft and airfields would come and both would need to wear maximum camouflage coupled with aircraft dispersal. Thus, there came into being a basic colour scheme that, with relatively few variations, was to last on home-based bombers almost to the 1950s.

From April 1 1937, camouflage consisting of irregular patterns of Dark Green and Dark Earth to tone with the grass and bare land was ordered to be applied to all fighters and bombers leaving the aircraft factories, the under surfaces of bombers being Night, ie Black, up to the 60 degree tangent line. Air Ministry prescribed basic patterns to be followed in planning aircraft finishes. Light and medium bombers would have patterns akin to those applied to fighters, whereas heavy bombers—particularly the Whitley—would carry more elaborate designs. Serial numbers would be black on the fuselage sides and rudders—on fins in the case of many Whitleys—in 8-inch digits 5 inches wide in 1¼-inch strokes usually spaced 1½ inches apart. Under the wings the serials were repeated in large white digits. When the war came, white serials passed into memory until after hostilities in Europe had ceased. This scheme was virtually unaltered until April 16 1946, when the post-war grey/black finish was promulgated. Within these confines there were a number of variations mentioned within the chapters of this volume of *Bombing Colours* which concerns itself with the period 1937-1973.

The scope and aims of the book

It differs somewhat from its predecessor in this series in that it concerns itself with aspects of the Royal Air Force's use of bombers, rather than just markings. It sets these against an outline of the bombing campaigns, and discusses the considerable range of aircraft types and marks employed at home and overseas, and instances markings known to have been worn by the aircraft. For the most part the markings referred to were observed in use and were not necessarily in accord with official dictums. It is, of course, unrealistic to issue firm dates for the changes of markings and virtually impossible to produce a dependable account by basing it mainly upon official instructions periodically promulgated and not always rescinded. Quite often markings changed to accord with new orders over a lengthy period running to weeks and sometimes months. Nor is it possible to lay down precise shades of colours used—indeed, had one accumulated dope samples and pieces of aircraft either aged or almost direct from production lines the shades would immediately be seen to vary quite considerably. Dope used was that available and sometimes it did not accord in tone with any of the colour chips supplied by the Ministries. Sometimes it was mixed on stations and this without doubt was the cause of such variations that existed among the shades used for squadron identity letters. Accuracy in model finishes is highly desirable, yet achieving it on models of aircraft of the past is exceedingly difficult, unless the model maker has colour samples of the particular machines, or is fortunate enough to be able to refer to paintings made of the aircraft at the time. Repairs undertaken by front-line units often resulted in patching using varying shades of dope, this being particularly true when various standards of Night finish were applied. The very matt Special Night often appeared in conjuction with other specifications; sometimes it appeared almost as a grey wash. All these points made in the preamble should be borne in mind when reading this book.

Enter disruptive camouflage

From April 1937, bomber aircraft in Britain were ordered to have Dark Green-Dark Earth-Night finish, although this was evident months before this date upon the emergence of the first Handley Page Harrows, as mentioned later. A major change at this time concerned the introduction of a new roundel for peacetime use on camouflaged aircraft, the Type A1 with its yellow surround to the Bright blue-white-red roundel that had lasted so long. It made, and was intended to make, aircraft very conspicuous for reasons of safety. For use in the event of mobilisation a Secret Document (SD109) was passed to stations prescribing special markings then to be applied.

Identifying the squadrons – and roundel changes

Unit markings on the new types consisted of the squadron number, usually ahead of the roundel, with an individual letter aft. Generally these markings were medium to dark grey, but some aircraft are known to have carried yellow squadron markings. Squadron badges, or some unit crests, were sometimes to be seen—114 Squadron had them on the standard 'bomber' grenade marking (see Chapter 4) on the fin for instance, and some of the Whitleys had them on the nose.

About September 25 1938, a new feature appeared. With the autumn crisis upon them some bomber squadrons painted out all unit markings and in their place came unit code letters, two letters identifying the squadron and one letter for the individual machine. The letters were grey. Some units did not apply code letters until March-April 1939.

Another change seen at this time of serious crisis was the application of Type B roundels in place of the Type A. The red-blue roundels were of smaller diameter than those previously carried and on many aircraft one could see very visible traces of the former brilliance. No rules can really be laid down about these new markings for they were introduced at different times and in differing manner by the stations. Suffice to say that some units adopted them in the September crisis, while others held their hand until the war clouds gathered in March 1939, when some Battles seem to have adopted them. But the official date for their general adoption on all operational aircraft was April 27 1939. On this date all roundels on the fuselage and upper surfaces of operational aircraft were ordered to be Type B, whilst under the wing tips Type A were prescribed. Again the order does not seem to accord

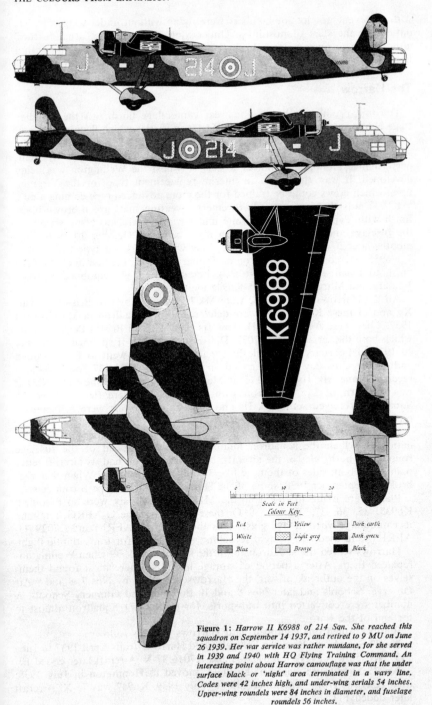

Figure 1: *Harrow II K6988 of 214 Sqn. She reached this squadron on September 14 1937, and retired to 9 MU on June 26 1939. Her war service was rather mundane, for she served in 1939 and 1940 with HQ Flying Training Command. An interesting point about Harrow camouflage was that the under surface black or 'night' area terminated in a wavy line. Codes were 42 inches high, and under-wing serials 54 inches. Upper-wing roundels were 84 inches in diameter, and fuselage roundels 56 inches.*

with the event, for lots of bombers were flying without under-wing roundels until after the start of hostilities. Under-wing serials were a usual feature, although again on some squadrons these were painted out, sometimes with a light wash, such a change also applying to other serials on some aircraft.

The Harrow

The first production bomber to wear camouflage finish was the Handley Page Harrow. Its origin lay in the HP51 troop carrier which flew in 1935 and from which the Harrow emerged via Specification 29/35. Behind this lay the idea that the Harrow should be built quickly providing a relatively high-performance monoplane bomber in service whilst the Wellington was being developed. It was, therefore, an interim replacement type for the Virginia, upon which crews could be trained for the more advanced type coming along.

K6933 was the first example to emerge wearing matt green-brown-black finish with Type A1 roundels, white under-wing serials and black serials on the fuselage and rudders. Its maiden flight came on October 10 1936. Two months later it went to Martlesham, along with K6934, for type trials.

K6935 arrived on 214 Squadron on January 13 1937, the first in camouflage finish to reach a squadron. No 214, based at Feltwell, equipped between January and March with K6936-K6945 inclusive.

All the Harrows up to K6952 were Mk Is, powered by two Bristol Pegasus Xs, and of these K6946-6952 were delivered to 37 Squadron in March-April 1937. They were followed by Harrow IIs (2 × 925 hp Bristol Pegasus XXs) which bore the serials K6953-7032. Delivery of the Mk II spanned from May 10 1937 to February 1938. The first machine, K6953, went to Farnborough and on the same day K6954 arrived on 214 Squadron. No 37 Squadron also received some Mk IIs; then 115 at Marham equipped in June-July. Next it was the turn of 215 Squadron with K6975-6982. Thereafter 214 and 75 Squadrons received some Mk IIs and some other aircraft were delivered as replacements for earlier aeroplanes.

In service, Harrows generally adopted the usual grey number-letter combination of which the squadron number was placed ahead of the fuselage roundel on both sides of the aircraft. No 214 Squadron had its aircraft letter painted on both sides of the nose like 37 and 115 Squadrons. When the crisis broke in September 1938, some of the Harrows acquired Type B roundels.

Plans were made to re-engine the Mk Is but only six were so modified, K6933, '35, '36, '37, '38, and '39. Of these K6933 became G-AFRG, retaining its camouflage when in civil guise. This and K7027 (G-AFRL) and K7029 (G-AFRH) were used for in-flight refuelling experiments for transatlantic flight.

Harrows served the squadrons until the summer of 1939 when Wellingtons replaced them. After a period of storage in MUs, where most found themselves on the outbreak of war, the Harrows were used by Nos 7, 8 and 9 Air Observer Schools and later Nos 8 and 10 Bombing and Gunnery Schools. A number were converted into transports, for use by 271 Squadron almost to the end of the war.

Bomber squadrons equipped with Harrows were as follows:

No 37 Squadron: Based at Feltwell; used Harrows from April 1937 to June 1939. K6956 was 37-V, K7001:37-S and K7016:37-X. Aircraft later coded FJ.

No 75 Squadron: Based at Driffield; moved to Honington in July 1938; used Harrows from September 1937 to July 1939. K6947 was 75-X. Aircraft later coded FO.

No 115 Squadron: Based at Marham; used Harrows from June 1937 to June 1939. K6962, in use June 1937 to April 1939, was 115-M. Squadron had a repeat of the aircraft letter on the nose. Aircraft later coded BK.

No 214 Squadron: Based at Feltwell; was equipped from January 1937 to July 1939. K6987 was 214-L, K6989:214-K, and K6996:214-H. Squadron had a repeat of the aircraft letter on the nose. Aircraft later coded UX.

No 215 Squadron: Based at Driffield; moved to Honington in July 1938. Was equipped with Harrows from August 1937 to June 1938. K6974 was 215-Y, later 215-G; K6975 was 215-H, later 215-R. Aircraft later coded BH of which K6980:BH-D is an example.

Enter the Wellesley

The second type to emerge in camouflage was the Vickers Wellesley. Its origin lay in Specification G.4/31 for a general purpose bomber to which Vickers produced two designs, a biplane and a monoplane of geodetic construction. The latter was very successful and in September 1935 an order for production aircraft was placed. Following an accident the G.4/31 monoplane was rebuilt as K7556, the all-silver prototype Wellesley.

K7713, the first production machine, flew on January 30 1937 in Dark Green-Dark Earth-Black camouflage with white under-wing serials and Type A1 roundels. It had the typical bronze-coloured exhaust collector ring of those days. Like the Harrows, Wellesleys left the production line in A and B camouflage patterns, one the mirror image of the other and applied to alternate machines. On March 18, K7713 passed to Martlesham for type trials. K7714 was delivered to 76 Squadron at Finningley on March 25 and gradually that squadron was equipped. As with the Harrow the Wellesleys' service—at home at least—was brief and they had left the squadrons before the war commenced, by which time they were in storage or in the Middle East.

Three batches were built: K7713-7791, delivered to squadrons between March and October 30 1937; K8520-8536, delivered October-November 1937; and L2637-2716 delivered February-May 1938.

The best-known Wellesleys were without doubt those used by the Long Range Development Unit. In July 1938, four of them (L2638, L2639, L2680 and L2681) flew from Cranwell to the Persian Gulf, then landed at Ismailia. Their most famous flight was one from Ismailia to Australia. L2638, L2639 and L2680 took off in November, the first and third reaching Darwin after 48 hours' flying, a record non-stop flight which stood for years.

Home-based Wellesley squadrons were as follows:

No 35 Squadron: Based at Worthy Down; equipped July-September 1937 to May 1938. Examples used: K7736, '38, '47-52, '54-55, '68 and '70. K8530 was 35-G; squadron marking applied, number forward in flight colour (red) outlined black with white 'G' aft. Re-equipped May 1938.

No 76 Squadron: Based at Finningley; equipped March-July 1937. Examples used: K7714-20, K7735, '52, '67, K8522, K8531 and L2641. '76' aft in flight colour outlined yellow. Aircraft later coded NM, eg, NM-H:K7748. Re-equipped April 1939.

No 77 Squadron: Based at Honington; moved to Driffield July 1938; equipped October-December 1937. Examples used: K7787, '89, K8524, '25, '34-36, '47-48, L2642, L2679, L2682 and L2688. Later coded ZL.

No 148 Squadron: Based at Scampton; moved to Stradishall March 1938;

B

equipped June-September 1937. Examples used: K7720, '21, '25-28 and '32-35. Most carried '148' aft in yellow. Re-equipped November 1938.

No 207 Squadron : Based at Worthy Down; equipped August-September 1937. Examples used included K7756-66. Carried squadron number in flight colour with white identity letter aft. Re-equipped April 1938. It will be noted that the Wellesleys did not have the usual grey lettering, but had flight markings, until code letters were introduced.

Three overseas squadrons were equipped with them before the war. They were:

No 14 Squadron : Based at Amman; equipped June-August 1938. Examples used: K7755, '59, L2649, L2692-2700, L2650-2659 and L2697. They had the squadron motif on the fin and an individual letter aft in white, eg, L2766:W.

No 45 Squadron: Based at Helwan; moved to Ismailia January 1939, and equipped at the end of 1937. Examples used: K7776-83, K7756, '57, '60 and K7784-86. Carried '45' in grey ahead of roundel with individual letter aft in grey, as on K7742:45-T. Re-equipped June 1939.

No 223 Squadron : Based at Nairobi; equipped May 1938. Examples used: L2701-2709 and L2660-70.

Chapter 2

The Fairey Battle, 1936 - 39

THE ONLY LIGHT BOMBER to emerge in the new camouflage scheme was the Fairey Battle. This design to Specification P.27/32 was planned as the Hart replacement. Terms of the requirement led to a rather mediocre machine when compared with other bombers coming along, but it was too late to improve it much. Replacement needs were urgent and, as the Battle was the only light bomber available, production went forward with an order for 155, subsequently stepped up to 655 under production specification 23/35, in May 1936. These aircraft were allocated the serials K7558-7712, K9176-9486. N2020-2066, N2082-2131, N2147-2190 and N2211-2258. A new factory was built at Heaton Chapel to produce them.

All-silver, the prototype K4303 first flew on March 10 1936. It proceeded to Martlesham for trials on October 31. Here a top speed of 257 mph was recorded. Wearing Dark Green-Dark Earth-Black camouflage, the first production Battle flew early in 1937. It passed to Martlesham in July. Here it showed a disappointing top speed of only 241 mph.

Production Battles had A and B mirror image paint schemes like other aircraft, but photographs which have survived of early Battles show that mirror patterns were not necessarily applied to alternate aircraft. Type A1 roundels with yellow outer rings were painted on the fuselage sides and above the wings, 70 inches outside diameter above the wings and 35 inches on the fuselage. Eight-inch black fuselage and rudder serials were applied, but the digits were spaced further apart than usual, being 2 inches apart and making the serial total length about 33 inches instead of the usual 29. Under the wings white serials were 42 inches high, and in 6-inch thick strokes.

Because the Battle bomber did not meet requirements it was decided to cancel those which had not been delivered by March 31 1939. It then became apparent that production of later types of bomber was lagging so Battle production was re-instated. Indeed, further orders of a stop-gap nature were placed with Fairey and also Austin Motors, who set up a new airframe shadow factory, and were under contract to build 500. Austin's order soon stood at 863 (L4935-5797).

Fairey production became quite rapid and to keep the production lines intact, also the labour force, another 400 were ordered, serials: P2155-2204, P2233-2278, P2300-2336, P2353-2369, P5228-5252, P5270-5294, P6480-6509, P6523-6572, P6596-6645, P6663-6692, P6718-6737 and P6750-6769.

Delivery began with K7559 to 63 Squadron at Upwood on May 20 1937. It became '63-A' ('63' forward on both sides). The number-letter combination was applied in light grey. After 63 Squadron was equipped, 105 Squadron began to receive Battles, which wore '105' well ahead of the roundels in smaller digits—and in varying positions—applied in grey. The individual letter was painted aft, as on 105-D:K7576. Later the squadron's aircraft carried the 'battleaxe' unit badge on the fins. There was little uniformity in 'coding' styles, as can be seen from the drawings on page 21.

The first 136 Battles powered by the Merlin I were designated Mk I. From K7695 the Merlin II was fitted and such aircraft were known as Battle IIs. Fairey's second batch had Merlin IIs, also L4935-4993. Most of the Austin machines then left their lines fitted with Merlin IIIs, and were called Battle Mk IIIs. In the 'N2' series, those to N2109 had Merlin IIs and the rest IIIs. R3922-4045 were Battle IIIs. But the Battle mark is complicated further by the fact that many aircraft had engine changes.

Battle markings remained largely unchanged until March 1939. It is certain that some changes to squadron markings came with the autumn crisis of 1938, but the main alterations were ordered on March 24 1939. B Type roundels now replaced the A1, their outer yellow rings being usually painted over, leaving the new roundels to be applied over the remaining area. On the same day all unit markings were ordered to be removed and replaced by grey squadron letters. An interesting anomaly here is that some squadrons had these much earlier alongside Type A1 roundels, XV Squadron for instance. Many Battles had their serial numbers painted out except under the wings—and even here there were some overpainted. This had been done on bombers in September 1938, but on some they were re-instated.

There were the usual anomalies. Some units carried code letters *and* the unit badge on the fin, this being true of 103 and 142 Squadrons. Nos 105 and 226 Squadrons at Harwell retained fuselage, tail and wing serials between May and August 1939, during which period they certainly had Type B roundels. A member of the squadron, Mr L. R. Clarke recalls that at no time did these two units wear pre-war codes; instead the aircraft merely carried a grey individual letter in a large size. When he returned to his unit on August 28 1939, the Battles of both squadrons were already displaying their wartime codes.

A feature which became common was the carrying of a Type A roundel beneath each wing tip. But again, there were anomalies and this roundel was not always applied.

When war began, deliveries had reached about P2310 and L5320.

All the Battle squadrons were home-based. Their squadrons and equipment, in order of being equipped, were as follows :

No 63 Squadron: Based at Upwood and equipped between May and August 1937 with Mk Is. Aircraft used included K7559-7570. K7649 became 63-B. Replaced by Battle IIs in December 1938, eg, K9412-9423 inclusive. Code letters used were NE.

No 105 Squadron : Based at Harwell and equipped between August and October 1937 with Mk Is. Aircraft used included K7571-7576 and K7578-7585. K7576 became 105-D. Mk IIs arrived October 1938, eg, K9338-9342. Mk IIIs in use August 1939 included P2258-2261. Code letters allocated were MT.

No 226 Squadron : Based at Harwell and equipped October-November 1937 with Mk Is. Aircraft used included K7588-7590 and K7592-7598. K7596 became 226-C. Mk IIs arrived October 1938, eg, K9343-9347. Mk IIIs in use August 1939 included P2250-2257. Code letters allocated were KP.

No 52 Squadron : Based at Upwood and equipped November 1937 to January 1938 with Mk Is. Aircraft used included K7602-7612. K7602 became 52-B. Mk IIs arrived in November 1938, eg, K9395-9401. Mk IIIs arrived August 1939, eg, P2267-2269. Code letters used were MB.

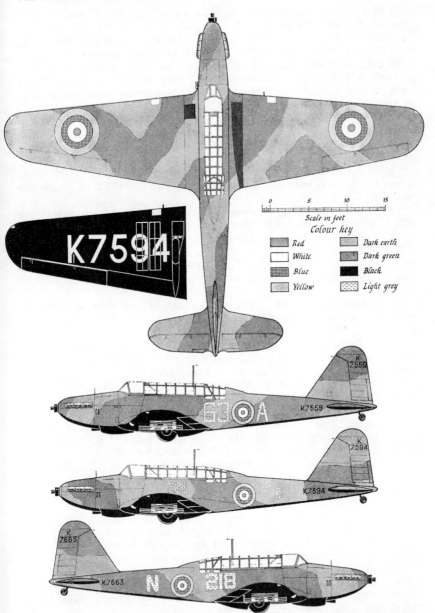

Figure 2: (*Top*) *Battle K7594 wearing the B paint scheme. Although the instructions for camouflage application explicitly required alternate aircraft in alternate patterns this policy was not adhered to with the Fairey Battle. A most unusual feature of some Battles was that they had the colours reversed in the scheme; thus Battle K9322 had the A Pattern, but green where dark earth would normally have been. (Above) The three Battles depicted here show how the size and style of the 1938 squadron marking varied. K7559, in scheme A, had bold unit numbering; 226 Sqn like 88 adopted small markings as on K7594 illustrated here and 218 Sqn went for thick numbering on K7663, wearing pattern B. Similar variations were to be seen where squadron codes were concerned. 142 Sqn had minute letters whereas XV Sqn wore EF in large letters. Usually the unit letters were aft of the roundels on both sides of the aircraft—and the colour of the letters varied in tones of grey. Type B roundels also varied in diameter.*

No 88 Squadron : Based at Boscombe Down and equipped December 1937-January 1938 with Mk Is. Aircraft used included K7629-7644. They carried '88' ahead of the roundel and later adopted the code letters HY. Mk IIs arrived October 1938, eg, K9348-9352. Mk IIIs came in July 1939.

No 218 Squadron : Based at Upper Heyford but moved to Boscombe Down in April 1938. Equipped January-February 1938 with Mk Is. Aircraft used included K7651-7661. K7655 became 218-F. Code letters used were SV. Mk IIs arrived October 1938, eg, K9353-9357. Mk IIIs came in July 1939.

No 12 Squadron : Based at Andover; moved to Bicester May 1939. Equipped February-March 1938 with Mk Is. Aircraft used included K7667-7675. Mk IIs received at the end of 1938 included K9485 and K9486. Code letters used were QE.

No 142 Squadron : Based at Andover. Equipped March-April 1938 with Mk Is and IIs. Aircraft used included K7683-7689 and K7700-7704. Code letters used were KB.

No 35 Squadron : Based at Cottesmore. Equipped April-May 1938 with Mk I/II. Aircraft used included K7705-7712, all of which passed to 226 Squadron in October 1938. Code letters used were WT.

No 207 Squadron: Based at Cottesmore. Equipped May 1938 with Mk IIs. Aircraft used included K9185-9197, all of which passed to 105 Squadron in October 1938. Mk IIIs used August 1939 included K5274-5284. Code letters used were WJ.

No 98 Squadron : Based at Hucknall. Equipped June 1938 with Mk IIs. Aircraft used included K9201-9206 and K9209-9219. Code letters used were QF.

No XV Squadron: Based at Abingdon. Equipped June 1938 with Mk IIs. Aircraft used included K9224-9229 and K9300-9304. Mk IIIs used from July 1939 included L5227-5239. Code letters used were EF.

No 40 Squadron : Based at Abingdon. Equipped July 1938 with Mk IIs. Aircraft used included K9234-9239 and K9306-9310. Mk IIIs in use by July 1939 included L5240-5250. Code letters used were OX.

No 106 Squadron : Based at Abingdon; moved to Thornaby in September 1938. Equipped July 1938 with Mk IIs. Aircraft included K9247-9250 and K9262. Re-equipped May 1939. Code letters used were XS.

No 185 Squadron : Based at Abingdon; moved to Thornaby in September 1938. Equipped July-August 1938 with Mk IIs. Aircraft used included K9251-9256 and K9259-9260. Re-equipped June 1939. Code letters used were ZM.

No 103 Squadron : Based at Usworth but moved to Abingdon in September 1938, and to Benson in April 1939. Equipped July-August 1938 with Mk IIs including K9263-9271 and received Mk IIIs by July 1939, including L5204-5214. Code letters used were GV.

No 150 Squadron: Based at Boscombe Down; moved to Benson in April 1939. Equipped August 1938 with Mk IIs. Aircraft used included K9274-9277, K9279, K9280 and K9282-9288. Mk IIIs in use by July 1939, included L5215-5225. Code letters used were DG.

Chapter 3

The Armstrong Whitworth Whitley, 1936 - 39

IN THE SUMMER of 1934 the agreed disarmament restriction on bomber aircraft weight had been abandoned by Britain, since other countries were clearly not interested in adhering to it. The Air Ministry was then able to shop around for a larger, heavier bomber than previously. Armstrong Whitworth had designed a bomber for the Czech Government in the spring of 1934. Interested, the Ministry asked the company to adapt it for possible RAF use, under Specification B.3/34 of July.

On September 14 1934, two prototypes were ordered with a proviso that the whole development programme must be rapid. Speedy production was also a feature of the basic design, and it led to an aeroplane with a very angular appearance. Nevertheless, the new bomber was the first heavy with retractable undercarriage and turreted armament to enter service.

From the start it had an unmistakable trade mark, a very 'nose down' attitude in flight owing to the wing incidence being set at 8.5 degrees in an attempt to cut the landing run. The latter, and the take-off run, were expected to be lengthy with the new monoplanes of those days. Considerable acquisition of land for airfields even then could have had awkward political repercussions, irrespective of the obvious need for massive defence commitments. It was still hoped to operate the bombers from grass fields to spare the expense of runways or some form of assisted take-off.

On August 23 1935, the Ministry ordered 80 of the new Armstrong Whitworth bombers 'off the drawing board' (ie, even before the prototype had flown). But this quantity was soon deemed insufficient, so on May 13 1936 the order was increased to 240.

The all-silver prototype, K4586, first flew on March 17 1936. It had black serials on the fuselage sides and under the mainplanes, beneath the tips of which were Type A roundels, also carried above the wings and on the fuselage sides.

It was soon apparent that the machine, whose performance was far from glittering, would be obsolete even before it entered service, for 1936 saw the decision to go for four-engined bombers and the high-performance multipurpose machine to Specification P.13/36 of which so much was expected. The Armstrong Whitworth machine was now seen not as a heavy, but as a medium bomber. Nevertheless, more orders were placed for aircraft looked upon to maintain front-line strength, and in 1936 production orders called for 320 B.3/34s, all to be complete by March 31 1939. By this time the second all-silver prototype, K4587, was flying.

Thirty-four of the first type, the Mk I (K7183-7216), were laid down, powered by Tiger IXs of 795 HP. A feature of the early machines was that they had no dihedral—about 18 of them—but later machines had 4 degree outer wing dihedral and earlier ones seem all to have been modified retrospectively.

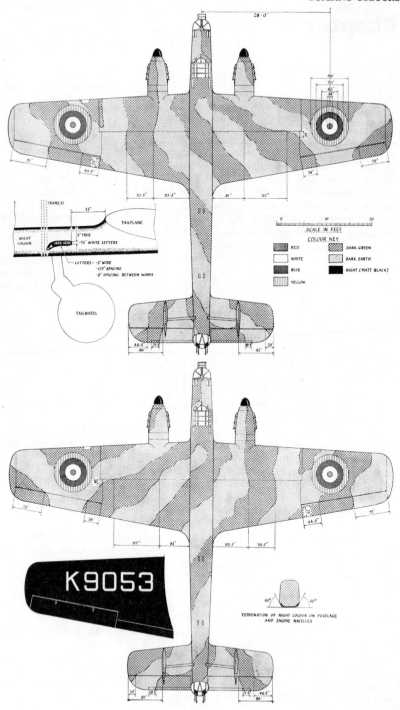

28'·0"

FRAME 51

13"

TAILPLANE

NIGHT
COLOUR

JACK HERE

5" TRUE
·75" WHITE LETTERS

LETTERS : ·5" WIDE
·125" SPACING
·3" SPACING BETWEEN WORDS

TAILWHEEL

SCALE IN FEET

0   10   20

COLOUR KEY

RED   DARK GREEN

WHITE   DARK EARTH

BLUE   NIGHT (MATT BLACK)

YELLOW

K9053

TERMINATION OF NIGHT COLOUR ON FUSELAGE
AND ENGINE NACELLES

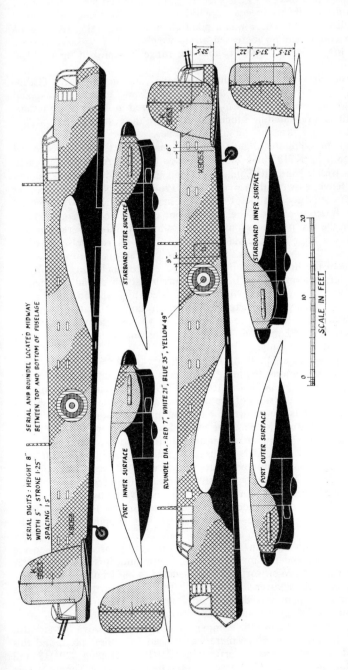

SERIAL DIGITS : HEIGHT 8"
WIDTH 5" , STROKE 1·25"
SPACING 1·5"

SERIAL AND ROUNDEL LOCATED MIDWAY
BETWEEN TOP AND BOTTOM OF FUSELAGE

STARBOARD OUTER SURFACE

PORT INNER SURFACE

ROUNDEL DIA.- RED 7", WHITE 21", BLUE 35", YELLOW 49"

STARBOARD INNER SURFACE

PORT OUTER SURFACE

SCALE IN FEET

0   10   20

32.5"

22"   31.5"   32.5"

6"

9"

K9053

Figure 3: *Depicted here is Whitley IVA K9053 in drawings based upon the Armstrong Whitworth works scheme. Note that the machine did not emerge in this exact style, but had Type B roundels. Colour key is given on opposite page. In the plan views opposite the pattern applicable to K9053 is shown, also the mirror image pattern for the next aircraft. The drawings upon which these are based were dated May 8 1938*

The Whitley I had one .303 inch Vickers gun in nose and tail turrets and a bomb load of 3,365 lb. Its speeds were 192 mph at 7,000 ft and 186 mph at 15,000 ft with full load. There was a good chance of increasing its range if the structure could bear an increased all-up weight. K7208 was accordingly modified to lift an extra 10,000 lb, and the range was pushed up to 1,940 miles.

Four Whitley Is were delivered in March 1937, all wearing Dark Green-Dark Earth-Night camouflage, the texture of which was extremely matt and very rough to the touch. Under-wing serials appeared in 4-feet white letters, the numbers being repeated in 8-inch characters on the rear fuselage and, unusually, on the outer faces of the aircraft's fins.

K7184 came first, going straight to No 10 Squadron at Dishforth, followed the same month by K7185 and '86. K7183 was the A & AEE trials aircraft.

Whitley Is trickled into 10 Squadron which had K7184-95 by the end of June 1937. Deliveries were then made of K7196-7207 to No 78 Squadron at Dishforth between July and October 1937. Finally came K7209-7216 for 58 Squadron at Boscombe Down, delivered from October to November 1937.

Apart from the two prototypes, production Whitley bombers were delivered camouflaged. On their fuselage sides they had Type A1 roundels, the outer diameter being 49 inches. Above the wing tips, centred one-third of the half wing span from the tip, they again wore Type A1 roundels, this time of 98 inches diameter. Alternate aircraft were in mirror pattern A and B Schemes. Under their wings they carried white serials 4-feet high spaced much more widely than might have been expected. Another unusual feature was that 8-inch fin serials were planned to be applied to all four faces. Photographs show that few featured this, but it was more customary for them to carry serials on the outer fins only.

In 1937-38 service the Mk Is of 10 Squadron wore 4-foot Medium Grey number-letter combinations, the number forward of the roundel, letter aft, eg, K7185:H-10, K7189:L-10, K7192:C-10 and K7194:E-10. Usually the aircraft letter was repeated on the sides of the nose, too. No 58 Squadron had similar markings, but its Mk Is are known to have had an adaptation of its squadron badge, an owl painted on quite a large white disc on the extreme front of the sides of the nose. No 78 Squadron had unit number and letter applied on the rear fuselage, 78-R being K7207. An unusual machine used by this squadron was K4587, the second prototype camouflaged, which it was flying in 1939.

Early in 1937, the Air Ministry considered that at the present rate of production there would still be about 120 Whitleys undelivered by March 31 1939, and so on April 30 it was decided to cancel these. But by February 1938 it was obvious that the schedule for the P.13/36 was slipping badly so the Ministry decided to order an additional 148 Whitleys on May 4 1938. Armstrong Whitworth's production rate was still very poor and by then the Wellington had become the main 'stop gap' type and was a much better performer. Armstrong Whitworth, it was decided, would build Wellingtons, 164 of them. The changeover in production was then seen to cause serious dislocation and the plan was dropped in favour of Armstrong Whitworth building another 64 Whitleys and keeping its labour force intact.

The urgent problem facing the company was how to improve the aircraft. Apart from increasing the range there was a need for more speed, and this led to the Mk II with more powerful Tiger VIIIs developing 920 HP and answering Specification 21/35. These engines had two-speed superchargers and the speed rose to 215 mph at 15,000 feet. Range with full load was 1,315 miles. Forty-six Mk IIs were built as K7217-7262, thus completing the original order for 80 aircraft.

First deliveries of the Whitley II were made in January 1938, when four (K7218-21) passed into RAF hands. But there were production hold-ups and delivery was erratic. By the end of May it had reached K7260 and was completed in June.

No 58 Squadron was first to receive the Mk II for whom K7218 arrived on January 13 1938, K7217 having gone to Martlesham five days previously. K7219-21 also went to 58 Squadron in January and K7222 to 10 Squadron the same month. Next came K7223-32, all for No 51 Squadron at Boscombe Down. Then came the turn of No 7 Squadron, based at Finningley, which was equipped between March and May with K7233, '36-42, '44-47 and '53. Equipment of 58 Squadron then continued, with K7254-60 replacing its Mk Is which were put into temporary storage.

Again these aircraft had the now customary Dark Green and Dark Earth camouflage with Night under surfaces, and Type A1 roundels and serials as on the Mk Is. K7228 was initially marked 51-K in the usual style but, when seen in September 1938, she was 51-T. K7232 at this time was 51-K. K7253:7-E was something of an oddity for her lettering (E repeated on the nose) in August 1938 was in pale blue after the manner of some fighter squadrons. She was the only Whitley of the period noted by the author that did not have the same Medium Grey shade of lettering. The bombers—unlike the fighters whereon, despite recent comments to the contrary, codes varied enormously in colour from light blue to dark grey—usually opted for Medium Grey.

By September 1938, 412 Whitleys were on order, of which 100 had been delivered. Under Scheme L of October 1938, 5,500 aircraft of existing types were ordered, this including 164 more Whitleys on November 29 1938.

The Whitley III figured under the inventory from the second order. It also had Tiger VIIIs, but in the nose was a Nash & Thompson power-operated turret mounting a single Vickers .303 inch machine gun. The old AWA turret was retained in the tail, but armament was supplemented by a ventral dustbin turret, retractable and mounting two Browning .303s. This was a heavy addition and, when lowered, cut the speed considerably. Turret supply was not good, and many Whitleys entered squadron service with fairings in place of the turrets which were later fitted. New bomb racks in the Mk III were also featured to permit carriage of larger bombs.

The 80 Mk IIIs were K8936-9015 and they answered Specification 20/36. K8937, the first taken on RAF charge, in August 1938, went to 51 Squadron which received K8938 the same month. K8939-41 reached that squadron early in September. Thereafter came Mk IIIs for 102 Squadron at Driffield, eg, K8943-58, delivered by November 1938, of which K8945 became 102-V. A quota was delivered to 77 Squadron, Driffield, between November and February 1939, including K8959, '60, '61 and K8991-98. Examples for 7 Squadron were delivered between November and December 1938, and included K8964 and K8978-75. No 7 Squadron also received earlier machines transferred from 51 and 102 Squadrons, such as K8942, '45 and '49. Still the Whitleys left the production line in the familiar finish.

A change for the better in the Whitley's fortunes came when it was decided to fit Merlin engines, again conferring additional power. This was first done in the Mk IV which had Merlin IVs offering 1,030 HP. It also had a power-operated four-gun Nash & Thompson tail turret in place of the manually operated one, a great step forward.

In May 1939, the Mk IV came into service when K9018 passed to 10 Squadron. In a few weeks K9017-9037 were all with No 10 at Dishforth, K9026 becoming PB-0. This released Mk Is for a new squadron, No 166, at Leconfield, which served as a 4 Group Pool training squadron and used amongst others K7184-88 and K7191, and some from other squadrons, also supplanted by later marks.

By July 1939, the Mk IVA was on the production lines differing by having 1,145 HP Merlin Xs. Most of the Mk IVs had the four-gun tail turret but a few started life with the old AWA type. The Mk IV also had extra fuel tankage and it was the first to feature a fixed chin bomb aimer's perspex canopy. Extra power in the Mk IV gave it a top speed of 245 mph at 16,250 feet; it cruised at 215 mph at 15,000 feet and its range of 1,250 miles—considerable by any standard at this time—could rise to 1,800 miles by fitting additional long-range tanks. Thirty-three Mk IVs were built (K9016-9048) and seven Mk IVAs (K9049-9055). The IVAs were delivered in July and August 1939 to 78 Squadron, beginning with K9049 on August 3. K9050-9055 all went to No 78 at Dishforth.

All the IVs and IVAs were delivered in the standard 'brown and green' finish, and in service acquired Type B roundels of much-reduced diameter on the fuselage and Type B roundels above the wings of the same outer diameter as previous roundels. Fin serials were retained.

Final bomber variant of the Whitley was the Mk V (Merlin X) which had its fuselage length increased by 15 inches at the extreme rear and was the first mark to feature straight fin leading edges. A total of 302 was ordered in 1938, but only five had reached the RAF by the start of hostilities. The first of these, N1345, went to A & AEE for trials on August 28 1939, where N1346 and N1349 joined it. On August 27, N1347 and 1348 went to 78 Squadron. Pre-war Whitley equipment was complete.

By the summer of 1939 one other squadron had received Whitleys. This was No 97 at Leconfield which was the second Group Pool Squadron for 4 Group. In July-August 1939 it received Mk IIs including K7219, K7221 and K7248, and Mk IIIs in February-March 1939, including K8999 and K9014. There were six front-line Whitley squadrons when the war started, Nos 10 and 78 at Dishforth, Nos 51 and 58 at Linton-on-Ouse and Nos 77 and 102 at Driffield. Nos 97 and 166 were training squadrons at Leconfield. On the night of September 3/4, ten Whitleys of 51 and 58 Squadrons left on the first night operation of the war, dropping 13 tons of leaflets on the Ruhr, Hamburg and Bremen. Between them the squadrons used: K8938, K8941, K8982 (51 Squadron) and K8964, '69, '73, K8990, K9006, K9009 and K9013 (58 Squadron). From the start Whitley squadrons specialised in night operations.

The Whitleys had passed through three phases of marking styles before the war. First came the green-brown-black finish with Type A1 roundels on fuselage and wings with fuselage, fin and wing serials. There was a change in the spacing of those under the wings and on the Mk IVs and Vs the digits were closely spaced, as they were on some earlier aircraft. Number-letter combinations about 4 feet high were carried and some squadrons wore their badges on the nose. There was also an interim stage when machines with Type A1 roundels were carrying code letters.

By the spring of 1939 many Whitleys had Type B roundels, and even in late 1938 some were recorded wearing them. The first coded aircraft recorded by the author were those of 7 Squadron in April 1939, with Medium Grey codes—LT-A, D and E—with Type B roundels and shorn unfortunately of their serials. Some of No 7 Squadron's aircraft had worn codes and Type A1 roundels early in 1939, but they were soon changed to Type B.

It used to be generally thought that codes were applied at a specific date but the latest reliable evidence indicates that this occurred between September 1938 and March 1939. This also seems to be true of Type B roundels. A possible explanation is that codes and 'night flying' roundels were applied by some squadrons during the crisis in September 1938, and not removed from some aircraft after it had abated. Others then appear to have gradually come into line in the following winter. Firm dates sometimes listed bear little relation to these events, unfortunately.

Code letters for the Whitley squadrons before the war were: 7(LT), 10(PB), 51(UT), 58(BW), 77(ZL), 78(YY), 97(MR), 102(TQ) and 166(GB). Examples of coded machines with Type B roundels include BW-D:K8967, BW-H:K8979 and BW-G:K8969. BW-L was K8970 and K7228 was UT-T.

An interesting feature of the Mk IV and IVA was that when their markings were originally planned in May 1938, it was proposed that they wore inner and outer fin stripes for certain identity, red leading followed by a 14½-inch white stripe and a 14-inch blue stripe, taking the striping to the rudder post. This never emerged on any aircraft, since markings changed to war standard before the IVs left the production line.

Chapter 4

The Bristol Blenheim, 1936 - 39

NUMERICALLY THE BRISTOL BLENHEIM was the most important pre-war expansion type. Additionally, it was a pacemaker destined to play a significant part in the air war at home and overseas, serving to the end of hostilities. It was the first all-metal monoplane monocoque type to be ordered under the expansion programme of the mid-1930s. The ease with which it outran biplane fighters of that era brought their death knell, but the bomber, which attracted wide interest on account of its speed, was simply not fast enough by the time war came. It had then become the mainstay of the re-equipment programme, eventually serving all Commands, truly a multi-rôle machine.

Its origin lay in two-engined fast transports designed by Bristol. Of these the Type 135 of 1933 was still-born, no suitable engine being available. A year later, after re-design around the Bristol Mercury VI, it was schemed as the Bristol Type 142 to requirements of Lord Rothermere, who was anxious to acquire a high-speed aeroplane for business purposes. Alongside came the Type 143 which was less advanced in concept.

As R-12, the silver Type 142 flew on April 12 1935, and was soon at Martlesham for official C of A trials. Here it showed an excellent performance and reached 285 mph at maximum loaded weight. Thus, it was faster than the new Gladiator fighter.

The Air Ministry asked Lord Rothermere for loan of the aircraft for further trials. In his reply he went one better—he presented the machine to the Air Council and it became K7557, well known as *Britain First*. Bristol looked at the design's military potential. With a crew of two, twin Mercury or Aquila engines, a 1,000 lb bomb load and a range of 1,000 miles, it was an attractive proposition. To accommodate the bombs the mainplane needed to be placed higher, unfortunately, spoiling the pilot's view. A turret was placed amidships and in July 1935 the scheme was discussed. A specification was drawn up based on the Bristol ideas and agreed in August 1935. On August 22, 150 examples of the new machine, Type 142M to B.28/35, were ordered 'off the drawing board' for it would be some time before any example flew.

During the following winter, consideration was given to expanding requirements for the type. Under re-armament Scheme F it was decided to order large numbers of Bristol 142M Blenheims and Fairey Battles. The other two important bombers to B.9/32—the Hampden and Wellington—had yet to prove themselves, but the Battle and Blenheim at this time looked quite good and large orders were placed. Scheme F brought into play the Shadow Scheme whereby non-aircraft manufacturers would begin to build aircraft for the RAF. Austins, the motor car firm, were to build Battles and Rootes were to build Blenheims.

By April 1936, the Air Ministry had decided to acquire 1,320 Blenheims of which 620 would be built by a shadow factory. But Rootes seemingly could not fulfil this order so it was decided later that year to bring A. V. Roe into the scheme. By the end of 1936, 1,568 Blenheims were on order. Of these, 568 were ordered from Bristol on June 11 1936; Rootes were to produce 600 and A. V. Roe 250.

The first all-silver Blenheim, K7033, flew on June 25 1936. It had the usual fuselage, rudder and under-wing serials with Type A roundels above and below the wing tips and on the fuselage. On trials it reached a top speed of 281 mph at 12,000 feet at a weight of 11,000 lb. Very few modifications were required before late in 1936 the go-ahead for full production was given. The first batch, K7033-7182, were well under way by the start of 1937 and as soon as turrets were available delivery to squadrons began. In its contemporary state the Blenheim Mk I had a top speed of 285 mph at 15,000 ft, weighed 12,500 lb loaded and had a range of 1,250 miles when cruising at 225 mph. Its crew numbered three, a pilot, an observer, and a gunner situated in the B.I. Mk I turret using a Lewis gun, later replaced by a Vickers K in the Mk III turret. The pilot had a .303 inch gun in the port wing.

By March, the first Blenheims were ready for delivery to 114 Squadron at Wyton. On March 10, K7036 set out for its new home but, alas, the pilot braked too hard. It whipped on to its back and was a write-off. Thus, the first to join the squadron were K7035 and '38 which arrived a few days later. No 114 Squadron equipped in March and April, the new machines representing a vast improvement over its Audax bombers. With their twin-engine safety, flaps, variable pitch propellers and retractable undercarriages, they were quite a novelty, since all these things had to be mastered, often after only a few minutes' conversion. Little wonder that as well as equipping new squadrons the Filton line was constantly delivering aircraft as replacements for those written off in service. Deliveries were next made to 90 Squadron at Bicester and by August to 139 Squadron at Wyton. Then it was the turn of 144 Squadron.

Something had to be done to update the RAF in the Middle East where biplanes had soldiered on so long. So, with four Metropolitan Air Force squadrons equipped with Blenheims, it was decided to equip No 30 Squadron at the turn of the year, by which time Nos 44 and 110 Squadrons at home had Blenheim Is. Before the first 150 were flying, Nos 61 and 62 Squadrons also had equipped.

Machines in this first batch were all finished in the customary rough matt Dark Green and Dark Earth with Night under surfaces upon which were painted white serial numbers. On the first 12 aircraft these appeared in 30-inch high strokes placed at the wing tips and hyphenated like K-7041. From K7045 they took on a more conventional look, being placed further inwards. Another variation on later machines was to have much wider strokes in the wing serials. On the rudder and fuselage the black serials were of the usual size and form.

When 114 Squadron equipped with Blenheims it was customary to apply the squadron number to the aircraft's fuselage and on their machines 114 was placed aft. All those recorded by the author had yellow numbers, but it is likely some had them in other Flight colours. No 139 Squadron certainly adopted this policy.

Individual letters were applied in the same colour ahead of the fuselage roundel and on 114 and 139 repeated on the side of the nose in the same colours, although for a time 114 Squadron wore theirs in white. Some of the later squadrons had only grey squadron numbers on their aircraft which superseded the yellow and Flight colours on earlier ones.

Delivery of the second batch began in March 1938, and deliveries followed to Nos 82, 57, 18, 104, 108, 101, 34, 21, 107 and 44 Squadrons during 1938, in that order. Of these, 44, 104 and 108 Squadrons all had grey unit numbering and letters for certain. In October, examples were despatched to 84 Squadron overseas and later 45, 55, 60, 211, 113 and 8 Squadrons abroad all received Blenheim Is. Many of the machines in the second batch were, incidentally, Mk IF fighters. Overseas the Blenheims wore the usual Dark Green-Dark Earth-Night finish with Type A1 roundels. It seems some carried unit number-letter combinations in the normal style and they certainly wore grey individual letters.

When the autumn crisis of 1938 broke, war seemed imminent and orders were given that home-based Blenheims should have their unit identity markings removed, leaving only the roundels. Some squadrons, including 114 and 139, then applied grey squadron codes. Apparently not all received codes then and a number of Blenheims flying some weeks later were without any unit identity. Another point in which they varied was in roundels. Wyton's seemed all to have Type B blue and red night flying roundels, while at Bassingbourn the old Type A1 were in use into 1939. As with the Battles it seems likely that a reversion to pre-crisis state was never made. At the time of the March 1939 crisis, Type B roundels were certainly ordained as a general feature along with code letters, but it would be very wrong to imagine consistency during this period where roundels and code letters were concerned. Additionally, some Blenheims at this time had Type A roundels beneath their wing tips, but again these were not featured by them all. Some also had their squadron motif on a grenade shape on the fin at this time as well as code letters, and underwing serials which, in time of crisis, were overpainted on some machines, yet were seen on others to the outbreak of war.

During 1938, re-armament Scheme L accelerated production, although the Air Council was not too happy about ordering vast quantities of Blenheims, for their showing against the new monoplane fighters was not so good. Bristol had the Beaufort under way; therefore few extra orders were placed with the parent company. Rootes production was to expand and another hundred were ordered from A. V. Roe. By May 1938, order books stood as follows : Bristol, 818; Rootes, 600; and Avro, 350—total 1,768. Production reached a peak in September 1938 with 45 aircraft built. The production pattern was altered somewhat when the Blackburn Botha general reconnaissance machine began to look troublesome, and additional orders were placed with Bristol. Although its output was not rapid, Avro had its order book boosted to 600. On January 24 1939, 62 more were ordered from Filton to fill the gap prior to the delivery of Beauforts, and in April 1939, 250 more from Rootes. By the outbreak of war all but 50 had been delivered from Filton; 147 had left the Avro works and of the 850 then on order from Rootes, 240 had been built. Orders placed with the parent company before the war may be summarised as follows : 150 on August 2 1935, 568 on June 11 1936, 100 on May 12 1938, 70 on November 23 1938 and 62 on February 25 1939 (cut by 12 later). A total of 250 were ordered from Avro on December 22 1936, 100 on May 12 1938 and 250 on August 18 1939, on which date 250 were also ordered from Rootes. This was far from the end of Blenheim orders, many following after the start of the war. By this time another major version of the Blenheim was in service.

There was an urgent need for a reconnaissance bomber, an interim type

1 Harrow K6962 joined 115 Sqn on June 14 1937, and passed to 75 Sqn on April 13 1939. After early war service with 9 AGS she passed to 271 Sqn with whom she flew from October 1940 until March 1944. The photograph was taken at Marham, now the home of Strike Command's Victor tanker force (Ministry of Defence).

2 Harrow K6952 before delivery to 37 Sqn on May 4 1937, where she served until November 1937, when she became '215:N'. After early war service with 10 BGS she flew with 271 Sqn as a transport from October 1940 until March 1941.

3 (Right) Wellesleys of 45 Sqn over Cairo on May 11 1938. The 'A' and 'B' camouflage patterns are in evidence and the aircraft include K7783 nearest, K7772 and K7777 (Ministry of Defence).

4 (Below) Vickers Wellesley K7718 with '76' in red aft of the roundel—the 'Flight' colour.

34

5 (Upper) Fairey Battle K7558 as new, wearing the A pattern scheme, very carefully applied. 6 (Lower left) K4303, the Battle prototype, in silver finish. After type trials it was used at Farnborough for drag research. It was grounded in May 1939, as 1475M. 7 (Lower right) A formation of 142 Sqn Battles with K9335 nearest, then K7704, K9292, K9293 and farthest away a machine coded KB, very small, and wearing Type B roundels (possibly K9295).

8 (*Above*) *Battles of 226 Sqn in August 1939. Note the absence of squadron letters. 'G' is K9176* (Ron Clark).

9 (*Right*) *Fairey Battle K7602 of 52 Sqn, wearing grey unit markings and in paint scheme B* (Ministry of Defence).

10 *K4586, the first prototype Whitley. It soldiered on into the war being used at 1 AAS and by the Airborne Forces in 1943.*

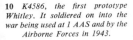

11 *K7183, the first production Whitley I, in Scheme 'A'. Used for official acceptance trials at Martlesham and for development work at Armstrong Whitworth. Turret trials carried out on this aircraft included those of the four-gun tail turret for the Whitley V, also the tail turret for the Halifax I. Ultimately became 2181M.*

12 *Whitley K7194:E of 10 Sqn with enlarged lettering* (Ministry of Defence).

36

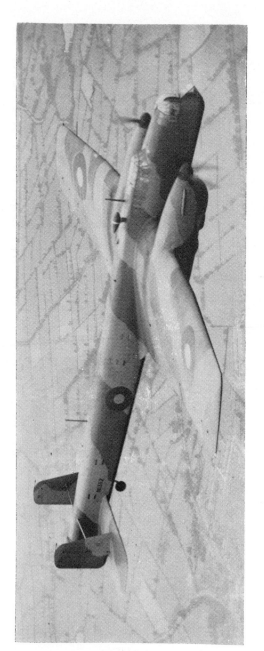

13 (Upper) Whitley N1352 was delivered just as war had commenced and wears the factory finish of the Mk V, being first flown in August 1939. Note the absence of fin serials. 14 (Lower left) Whitley K7244:LT-G of 7 Sqn at Finningley. It had Type B roundels overpainted on Type A1. It appears to have very light-grey codes and under-wing serials (via Bruce Robertson). 15 (Lower right) Whitley N1349, delivered last before the war, was a Mk V with closely spaced serial. Type A under-wing roundels and light under surface finish forward on the nacelles (Ministry of Defence).

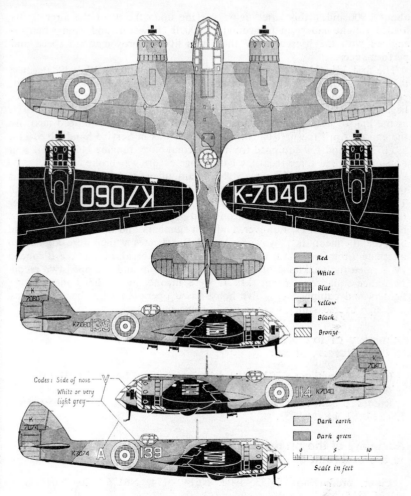

Figure 4: *Blenheim Is of the Wyton-based squadrons. The top view shows camouflage pattern A which the other also wear. K7060 has 3-foot serials under the wing; on K7040 they are 2½ feet high. Fuselage roundels have an outside diameter of 49 inches, and those above the wings measure 70 inches across. K7060 has red '139' on the side outlined black; K7040 has a red '114' in 18-inch digits like K7060. K7074-A:139 has numbering very slightly off white, a colour also used by 104 and 108 Sqns at Bassingbourn. K7060 served with 139 Sqn from July 1937 until February 1938. K7040 arrived on 114 Sqn in March 1937 and served the unit for a year. K7074 is shown in the markings it was carrying when it crashed on April 8 1938.*

before the Beaufort and Botha entered service. Bristol looked into the need and came up with the Bolingbroke. K7072 had its nose lengthened, but the view without moving the pilot's seat forward was poor. In September 1937, the first flight of K7072 with its forward nose lowered took place. Still the view over the nose navigation station was not good so the port side of the new nose was scooped to improve the pilot's view. This version, after other changes, emerged as the Type 149 Blenheim IV, production of which commenced late in 1938. Soon the production of the Mk I ceased and the Mk IV was produced in great quantity, after 1,457 Mk Is had been built. The new type had a top speed of about 280 mph, a ceiling of 31,500 ft and a range of about 1,900 miles, this latter figure varying upon the fit of the aircraft. Its loaded weight had risen to around 13,800 lb, however, and even when re-engined with the Mercury XV there was little improvement in speed and performance.

The first Mk IV was delivered from Filton on January 19 1939. Because this new variant was, from the outset, a reconnaissance bomber, it first equipped Nos 53 and 59 Squadrons. It was March 1939 before the first examples began to replace Blenheim Is. L4865 reached 90 Squadron on March 22 1939, as the first to join a bomber squadron. No 101 Squadron equipped next. By the end of April the first batch, L4835-4902, was in Service hands. Nos 114, 59, 107, 110 and 139 equipped from the second batch ranging N6140-6242 and 82 Squadron had some from the P48.. range before war broke out.

Early Mk IVs wore the same style of camouflage and Type A1 roundels as the Mk Is, and not until the summer of 1939 were they leaving the works with Type B roundels, apparently introduced on factory aircraft some time after they appeared on those in squadron hands, as was the case with the Whitley. None of the Mk IVs, however, had unit numbers and all wore codes. And like the Blenheim Is they wore A and B Schemes which were applied to alternate aircraft in the usual manner. At the outbreak of war the Blenheim IV formed the backbone of No 2 (Bomber) Group and equipped two recon-naissance squadrons. Many Mk Is were then being modified into Mk IF fighters and equipped only five home-based operational bomber squadrons, although overseas they were in use in some numbers.

Summary of the production of the Blenheim I to the outbreak of war

Filton production : K7033-7182, L1097-1546, L4817-4834, L4903-4934.
A. V. Roe production : L6594-6739.
Rootes production : L8362-8407, L8433-8482, L8500-8549, L8597-8632, L8652-8701, L8714-8731.

Summary of the production of the Blenheim IV to the outbreak of war

Filton production: L4835-4902, N6140-6174, N6176-6220, N6223-6242, P4825-4855.

Pre-war home-based Blenheim bomber squadrons

No 18 Squadron : Equipped April-May 1938, and based at Upper Heyford. Examples : L1171 and L1177:GU-K.

No 21 Squadron: Equipped August 1938, and based at Eastchurch, later Watton. Examples : L1280, L1269. Code letters JP. L1279 was JP-L.

No 34 Squadron : Equipped July 1938, and based at Upper Heyford, moved to Watton, then to Tengah in August 1939. Examples : L1252 with '34' ahead of the roundels and a much larger 'H' aft, all in yellow; squadron motif on a grenade on the fin. L1247 was 34-T and L1243: 34-V. Code letters later used were LB.

No 44 Squadron : Equipped December 1937-January 1938, and based at Waddington. Re-equipped with Hampden, February 1939. Examples used : 44-M:K7138, 44-E:K7133, 44-F:K7113; letters, etc, in grey, '44' aft. Code letters allocated to this squadron were JW, and were possibly not used.

No 57 Squadron : Equipped April 1938, and based at Upper Heyford. Examples used: L1146:G and L1171:K, both with unit crests on fin grenades. Believed not to have used any number. Code letters allocated were EQ.

No 61 Squadron : Equipped January 1938, and based at Hemswell. Re-equipped with Hampden in February 1939. Examples used: K7170:61-V ('61' aft in grey, individual letter in grey on outer sides of cowlings as on K7163: 61-X and K7160:61-U). Code letters allocated were LS, possibly not used.

No 62 Squadron : Equipped February-March 1938, and based at Cranfield; to Far East, August 1939. Examples used: L1108:62 ahead W aft in grey, as on L1113:62-W and L1101:62-R; K7174 was coded JO-L.

No 82 Squadron : Equipped March 1938, and based at Cranfield and later Watton. Examples used : L1112 : A-82 and L1333 : OZ-S. Received Mk IV in August 1939, such as P4829 and P4830, coded OZ.

No 90 Squadron : Equipped May-June 1937, and based at Bicester; moved to West Raynham later. K7050 : 90-C and K7054 : 90-F used yellow and later grey codes. K7113 : 90-D and K7092 : 90-K. Later coded TW as on L1283:TW-H and L1285:TW-F. Received Mk IV May-June 1939, for example L4865.

No 101 Squadron : Equipped June-July 1938, and based at Bicester, later West Raynham. Examples used: L1244, L1225. Began to receive Mk IV in May 1939, such as N6165. Code letters LU.

No 104 Squadron : Equipped May 1938, and based at Bassingbourn. Examples included L1188 and L1195. The aircraft carried '104' ahead of roundels in grey and were later coded PO.

No 107 Squadron : Equipped August 1938, and based at Harwell, later at Wattisham. Examples used : L1290 and L1291. Received Mk IV in May-June 1939, including N6174 and N6166. Coded BZ.

No 108 Squadron : Equipped June 1938, and based at Bassingbourn. Examples included L1202 with '108' ahead of roundels and 'J' aft in light grey. Later coded MF.

No 110 Squadron : Equipped January 1938, and based at Waddington, later at Watton. Examples K7150,K7157,L1204. Received Mk IV in June-July 1939, including N6198 : AY-B (AY aft).

No 114 Squadron : Equipped March-May 1937, and based at Wyton. Examples: K7040:V on the nose with '114' aft, also K7041:114-K and K7122 : 114-E. Initially this and 139 Squadron opted for unit markings and letter in flight colours, then appeared to favour yellow, and in 1938 switched to grey. Code letters were FD as on L1206:FD-H (FD aft). Received Mk IV in April-May 1939, including N6152, N6153 and N6155 : FD-F.

No 139 Squadron : Equipped July-August 1937, and based at Wyton. Examples : K7078 : 139 aft with 'J' ahead; and in 1938, K7074 : 139-A in very light grey. Mk IV received July 1939, including N6216 and N6217. Code letters SY.

No 144 Squadron : Equipped September-October 1937; based at Hemswell; re-equipped with Hampden, March 1939. Examples included L1321 and L1322. Code letters if carried were NV.

Bomber squadrons based overseas and equipped with Blenheim I pre-war

No 8 Squadron: Equipped May-June 1939; based at Khormaksar. Ex·

amples included L1479. Code letters YO, possibly never carried.

No 11 Squadron : Equipped July 1938; based at Risalpur; moved to Tengah, August 1939. Example : L4914. Coded OY pre-war.

No 30 Squadron : Equipped January-April 1938, and based at Habbaniya. Examples: K7107:B, L4917:B and K7180:V, with grey letter aft. Later coded DP.

No 45 Squadron : Equipped June-July 1939, and based at Ismailia. Examples : L6628, L6629 and L8472. Later coded DD.

No 55 Squadron : Equipped May-June 1939, and based at Habbaniya; to Ismailia, August 1939. Example : L1540. Later coded GM.

No 60 Squadron : Equipped June 1939, and based at Ambala. Example : L8448. Later coded AD.

No 84 Squadron : Equipped February-March 1939, and based at Shaibah. Example : L4833. Later coded UR.

No 113 Squadron : Equipped May-June 1939, and based at Heliopolis. Example : L1527 and L8447.

No 211 Squadron : Equipped May-June 1939, and based at Ismailia. Examples: L1480 and L8460.

Chapter 5

The pre-war Wellingtons and Hampdens

NOWADAYS IT IS CUSTOMARY for the design stage of a major military aircraft to span as much as a decade—which means that the basic concept needs to correspond with requirements a long time ahead. Thus, the new MRCA, the culmination of years of consideration, needs to be suitable for front line service in the 1980s. This, of course, was less true in the past, although such a trend was appearing in the 1930s. Then, the Ministry was looking some five or six years ahead. Once the mould for a new project has been cast it is, and always will be, difficult and time consuming to radically alter it. This was true of bomber specification B.9/32, one of the most important of all, which was nevertheless basically changed after it was first promulgated.

In October 1931, requirements were formulated for a bomber ultimately to replace the new biplane heavies and the Sidestrand/Overstrand series. It was to be a high-performance long-range twin-engined monoplane carrying a goodly load at high speed. And before details of the specification were circulated, plans were agreed for a single-engined equivalent, the P.27/32 which evolved as the luckless Fairey Battle.

B.9/32 was put out to tender in October 1932. Resultant schemes were delivered from Vickers, Handley Page, Gloster and Bristol in February 1933. All were radically different designs and, following the tender conference of May 29 1933, the Vickers and Handley Page designs were accepted. In September the firms were told to proceed with prototypes.

There was one feature of the specification which displeased the manufacturers. It prescribed an empty airframe weight of 6,000 lb, thus severely limiting the designs, particularly where the choice of engines and fuel load was concerned. In the chosen prototypes these were to be Rolls-Royce Goshawks, with the Bristol Pegasus as an alternative.

A 6,000 lb basic weight was the top limit laid down for bomber aircraft by the Geneva Disarmament Convention, but by 1934 the British Government was aware that other powers were not keeping to the agreement. Therefore, the way was clear for heavier, larger British aircraft, and in the summer of 1934 Britain, too, reluctantly disregarded the agreement. Vickers and Handley Page could now proceed on a better basis. Both companies chose more powerful engines, submitting plans for machines powered by Pegasus or Perseus radials. These changes delayed the designs, but in both cases led to much superior aeroplanes.

Once the weight ban was lifted, the Ministry, too, began to think along other lines and issued a new specification for a heavier bomber, B.1/35, which attracted many projects and threw a shadow over B.9/32. The latter, which was well under way, proceeded, and in 1936—by which time major rearmament schemes were in being—had assumed great importance. Both chosen designs were, under Scheme F, to form the backbone of the new

Bomber Command. In June 1936, prototypes of each made their first flights, the Vickers machine on the 15th and the HP 52 five days later. Four and a half crowded years had elapsed since the original plans were laid for them.

K4049, the Vickers B.9/32, Pegasus-powered and in all-silver finish with Type A roundels and far removed from the original design which featured a high wing and fixed undercarriage, was seen to be a graceful machine with long tapering wings akin to those of the Wellesley. It had another feature in common—it was of geodetic construction composed of criss-cross strong metal members devised by the ever-ingenious Barnes Wallis. It was this feature as much as any that, since 1933, had allowed the load and range of the design to be much increased.

K4240, the Handley Page B.9/32, emerged as a much more curious machine, and in a glossy olive green. It had little in common with the Vickers aircraft apart from its engines. The wing was massive and greatly tapered, but the astonishing feature was a slender boom upon which dangled the tail unit after the manner of the earlier HP 47, whose layout was to a certain extent reflected in the HP 52. This had been introduced to the company by Dr G. V. Lachmann, its German influence stemming from work which the Messerschmitt company had undertaken, and which was to some extent reflected in the Messerschmitt 110 and the Dornier 17. It proved an unfortunate decision to adopt an extremely slender and cramped forward fuselage deep in side elevation and terminating amidships in dorsal and ventral gun positions. The narrow fuselage with its belly bomb bay permitted virtually no increase in weapons load and restricted the addition of special equipment.

On August 15 1936, two months from the day when the Vickers bomber first flew, the Ministry placed contracts with the two firms for 180 aircraft each (for the Vickers 29/36 L4212-4391 and the HP 30/36 L4032-L4211 production versions) under Scheme F, with an additional 100 of each to be built in shadow factories. In the case of the Vickers aircraft this was to be done by Gloster, but in the event the aircraft came from a new Vickers factory at Chester. Fearing a possible bottleneck in the building of Bristol Pegasus engines (now in great demand) it was decided that the shadow factory building the Handley Page design should fit Napier Dagger engines into the aircraft, L6002-6101. Into the shadow-built Vickers machines could go the Merlin X. Thus, the HP Hereford and the Wellington Mk II were originated.

In September, both the B.9/32 types were named, the Vickers aircraft becoming the Wellington and the HP 52, the Hampden. When they rolled from the production lines both types were to differ considerably from their prototypes. These latter were accepted for official trials at Martlesham in November 1936. In performance they differed surprisingly little.

Already modern gun turrets were to hand, which neither machine had, although the Vickers B.9/32 had been fitted with a rudimentary nose and tail type. The Ministry now wanted effective turrets installed in the nose and tail of the Wellington, which necessitated redesign and alteration to the rear fuselage which was deepened and its waisting discarded.

In the case of the Hampden it was clear that no power-operated turret could easily be fitted, an unfortunate event. The planned fixed nose gun was considered to be of little value, and it was realised that dorsal and ventral guns would have only limited traverse. At Martelsham, the accommodation was considered cramped, and it was seen to be well nigh impossible for the crew to exchange positions. But the view for the pilot was excellent and on the second prototype, L7271, which appeared in 1937 in natural finish, the nose transparency was much enlarged. The Hampden's performance was considered good, and another point in its favour was a scheme for split assembly to speed building. Its fuselage would be made in two halves, each fully fitted out before being brought together for assembly as with the Mosquito of later years. So, with modifications to the defensive armament required, both types went ahead—with official provisos that one Wellington would be fitted with Merlins and that the second prototype Hampden would be re-engined with Daggers. It first flew thus fitted on July 1 1937, and the troublesome career of the Hereford was inaugurated.

The Wellington suffered a set-back when K4049 was destroyed in a crash in April 1937. Its tailplane gave trouble and soon the aircraft inverted and crashed to its doom. Production and development had to proceed without the useful prototype.

It had been estimated at the production conference that the first Wellington I would be delivered in June 1937 and the Hampden two months later. In fact it was not until December 23 1937 that L4212 first flew, finished in Dark Green-Dark Earth-Night camouflage with Type A1 roundels and under-wing serials. The Mk I was a complete re-design of the first version, having nose and tail twin-gun turrets of Vickers design, and a retractable twin-gun dustbin turret. Pegasus XVIII engines were scheduled for production Wellingtons and were first fitted to L4212 in 1938. Doubts harboured after trials with L4212 at Martlesham that the turrets might not be effective against fast, manoeuvrable fighters led to the Mk IA fitted with superior power-operated two-gun Nash & Thompson nose and tail turrets. Three Mk IAs, N2865, '66, '67, were delivered only hours before the war commenced. Bombing trials were undertaken in 1939 with L4221, and L4302 was tested from Wattisham at take-off weights up to 27,000 lb—far removed from the originally considered take-off weight.

K4240 underwent handling trials at Martlesham between November 9 1937 and May 1938, in which month the first production Hampden, L4032, was flown, powered by Pegasus XVIIIs. Its nose transparency was still more rounded and the dorsal gun position had a rounded canopy, presenting a very streamlined top line. After initial maker's trials it proceeded to Martlesham on August 19, where further trials revealed a top speed of 254 mph with full load, and an estimated range with a 2,000 lb bomb load of 1,900 miles. Its Handley Page slots cut its landing speed to 73 mph, useful because as recounted in Chapter 3, it was still a fear that high landing speeds would plague the new bomber force and bring problems with new airfield sites which might need long runways.

In many respects the Hampden was now seen as a compromise bomber wherein moderate load and high speed were set against the need for long range. The Wellington was really a much better proposition, and when repeat orders were given for these machines, those for the Wellington were greater and its production was almost to span the war years. Nevertheless, the Hampden was to give excellent war service despite its unsuitability for much improvement. Its place on the production lines in any case would be taken by the Halifax. Its service career was nevertheless lengthened by the failure of the Manchester and in more than one sense it proved a very useful 'stop gap' aeroplane.

In 1938 and 1939, orders for the two types came fast, for 120 Wellingtons ranging N2865-3019, and for 100 to be 'shadow built' in the series N2735-2859. Another 50 Herefords were ordered as N9055-9081 and N9084-9106,

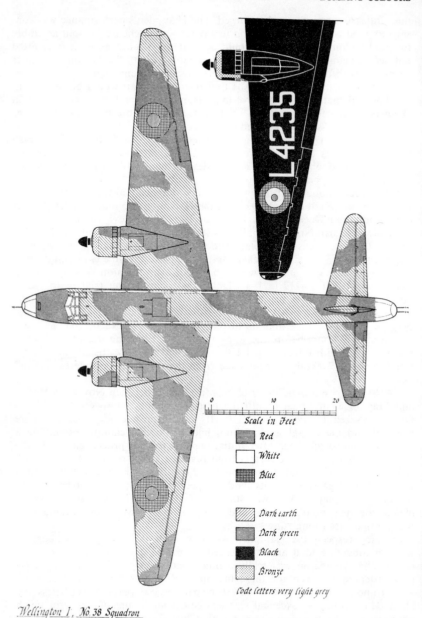

Scale in Feet

Red

White

Blue

Dark earth

Dark green

Black

Bronze

Code letters very light grey

Wellington I, No. 38 Squadron

Figure 5: (*Above and opposite*) *Wellington I L4235 in her original squadron finish, with unusually large diameter fuselage roundels, very pale grey codes and under-wing roundels. Above the wings the Wellington Is originally had 63-inch diameter roundels with 4-foot wing serials. Fuselage Type A1 roundels were 49 inches in diameter. The under-wing roundel Type A was of 60 inches diameter. The Hampden had Type A1 fuselage roundels of 35 inches diameter; those above the wings were 63 inches. Code letters seem to have been about 2 feet high, whereas on the Wellington they appear to have been 4 feet and sometimes slightly larger—possibly 4 feet 6 inches.*

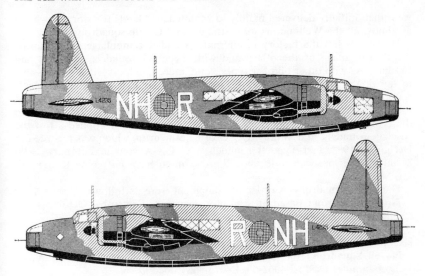

and 200 Hampdens in the range P1145-1356, of which P1145-1189 and P1194-1198 had been delivered by the commencement of hostilities. On August 8 1938, the first shadow factory contract for Hampdens was confirmed with English Electric at Preston where 75 (P2062-2100 and P2110-2145) were to be built. At the same time another 120 were ordered from the parent firm ranging P4285-4418 and a Canadian concern, Canadian Associated Aircraft Ltd, was to produce an initial 80, range P5298-5436, this contract being signed in November 1938. On April 21 1939, a second Hampden order was placed with English Electric and building of tarmac runways for flight test began at Salmesbury on August 14 1939. On August 26, an aircraft design and experimental building was begun at Salmesbury, but few could then have foreseen the day when this company would one day produce the RAF's leading fighter and bomber aircraft. Their first Hampden was delivered on March 30 1940.

Eighteen replacement Wellingtons were ordered as P2515-2532, and 82 more, on April 13 1939, ranging P9205-9300, bringing the total to 100. Six hundred and fifty more were on order by September 1939. In the case of the Wellington, the first one, L4212, was delivered to Martlesham on January 25 1938, and L4391, the last Mk I, to 38 Squadron on August 8 1939. Apart from the three IAs, the only other pre-war deliveries were of L7770 on August 14 1939, and R2699-2703 which were replacements for L4312-4316 undelivered, and all Mk Is. L4250 was set aside to become the Mk II prototype, first flown on March 3 1939, and L4251 was fitted with early Hercules engines to become the Mk III, prototype of a variant not introduced for a long time, and first flown on May 19 1939.

Entry into front-line service by the two types was almost simultaneous with the Hampden making it a few weeks ahead of the Wellington, when L4034, which had been at CFS for handling trials, passed to 49 Squadron on September 20 1938, leaving L4032 and '33 to serve their time as development aircraft. Wellington L4215 was the first to reach a squadron, No 99 at Mildenhall, on October 10 1938. Ten squadrons were flying Hampdens by June 1939, when L4206 was in 185 Squadron's hands. P-serialled Hampdens were then initially delivered mainly to Maintenance Units for storage, whereas almost all the Wellingtons went straight to 3 Group squadrons.

Hampdens left the factory in alternate A and B camouflage schemes, one the mirror image of the other, and with Type A1 roundels on wings and fuselage. As with other bomber types—and, indeed, fighters—it is not possible to lay down specific dates for the introduction of unit codes and Type B roundels, but it is certain that Hampdens never wore any unit numbers, and some were certainly wearing code letters in the winter of 1938/39 before these were ordered as obligatory. Unit letters were usually applied aft of the fuselage roundels, and in grey. QQ-G of 83 Squadron, which was recorded in December 1938, had Type B roundels, like QX-A seen in February 1939. Serial number/pre-war code allocations seem to have not come to light so far.

Hampden squadrons in order of equipment were as follows:

No 49 Squadron: Based at Scampton; equipped September-October 1938. Examples used: L4039-45, P1174. Coded XU.

No 83 Squadron: Based at Scampton; equipped October-November 1938. Examples used: L4048-59. Coded QQ.

No 50 Squadron: Based Waddington; equipped December 1938-January 1939. Examples used: L4062-65, L4073-84. Coded QX.

No 44 Squadron: Based Waddington; equipped January-February 1939. Examples used: L4085-91. Coded JW.

No 61 Squadron: Based Hemswell; equipped February-March 1939. Examples used: L4103-4116, P1170. Coded LS.

No 144 Squadron: Based Hemswell; equipped March 1939. Examples used: L4124-36, L4141:NV-P.

No 76 Squadron: Based Finningley; equipped March-April 1939. Examples used: L4137-52, P1182. Coded NM.

No 7 Squadron: Based Finningley; equipped April-May 1939. Examples used: L4155-69. Coded LT.

No 106 Squadron: Based Thornaby; equipped May 1939. Examples used: L4174-90. Coded XS.

No 185 Squadron: Based Thornaby; moved to Cottesmore, August 1939; equipped June 1939. Examples used: L4191-4206. Coded ZM.

Like the Hampdens, Wellingtons left the factory in alternate A and B camouflage schemes with Type A1 roundels on wings and fuselage. From the start of 1939, Type B roundels were in vogue on the VF coded examples of 99 Squadron aircraft. These early aircraft were to be seen at Mildenhall with Type A1 roundels initially, but none are known to have worn code letters with these roundels. During 1939, Wellingtons became increasingly common over East Anglia, and all that the author recorded had grey codes with squadron letters aft on both sides of the fuselage.

By the spring it was usual to find that they had a Type A roundel beneath each wing tip, alongside the usual white serial. Rudder serials were not carried. The style of presentation of code letters varied from units, and the tone of grey extended from very pale on 38 Squadron aircraft to dark on 149 Squadron. Between May and August 1939, the following aircraft were recorded, all with Type B roundels with Type A under the wings: L4230:NH-O, L4231:NH-P, L4242:NH-S and L4245:NH-G (reputedly not of 38 Squadron but certainly wearing its markings), all with very pale codes; L4259:LY-R, L4253:LY-P and L4257:LY-M, all with dark grey codes; L4261:KA-B and L4275:KA-H, with medium grey codes, also L4388:

BH-B, L4354 : UX-U and L4371 : FO-Q. As a general rule the aircraft retained their original camouflage pattern but again it is wrong to maintain categorically that this was so.

An unusual but very temporary breakaway from standard markings was evident in August 1939, when Wellingtons of 37 and 214 Squadrons at Feltwell had white crosses painted over their roundels for exercise purposes.

Squadrons equipped with Wellingtons prior to the war were as follows :

No 99 Squadron : Based Mildenhall; equipped October-November 1938. Examples used : L4215-20, '22, '27-29, R2701-02, L7770. Coded VF.

No 38 Squadron : Based Marham; equipped November 1938-January 1939. Examples used: L4230, '31, '34-43, '85, '86, L4235 : NH-R.

No 149 Squadron : Based Mildenhall; equipped January-February 1939. Examples used : L4249, '52-58, '63-66, '70-72, L4272 : LY-G. Even serialled aircraft to 'A' Flt, odd to 'B' Flt.

No 9 Squadron : Based Stradishall, to Honington, July 1939; equipped January-March 1939. Examples used : L4260, '61, '73-78, '86-88, L4276 : KA-M.

No 148 Squadron : Based Stradishall; equipped March-April 1939. Examples used : L4280-84, '89-94, L4303-4. Coded BS.

No 115 Squadron : Based Marham; equipped March-April 1939. Examples used: L4289, L4300-1, L4305-7, '17-19, '21-22. Coded BK.

No 37 Squadron : Based Feltwell; equipped May-June 1939. Examples used : L4326-29, '31, '32, '36-39, '47-53. Coded FJ.

No 214 Squadron : Based Feltwell; equipped May-June 1939. Examples used: L4341-43, '44-46, '56-65, R2699; L4345 : UX-L with exercise markings.

No 75 Squadron : Based Stradishall; equipped June-July 1939. Examples used : L4366-73. Coded FO.

No 215 Squadron : Based Honington; equipped July-August 1939. Examples used : L4375-90. Coded BH.

Chapter 6

The Phoney War?

OVER 47,000 MEN of Bomber Command, gifted, capable people of high calibre, were killed in action during the Second World War. Their value to our nation in peace cannot ever be overestimated. This seems an apt moment to remember those fallen. The total represented one eighth of the total casualties, Service and civilian, incurred by the nation, and half the loss of the Royal Air Force. Added to this nearly 5,000 were seriously wounded. Additionally, there was a sizeable number killed and injured during training flights; the total killed or injured was approaching 60,000—a frightening figure. Young or old, we should never forget the appalling sacrifice and horror behind those ghastly days.

The opening months of the Second World War are usually referred to as the 'Phoney War'. For Bomber Command there was nothing phoney about it. From the moment Neville Chamberlain made his grim broadcast, Bomber Command was virtually in action. Full mobilisation was publicly proclaimed on September 1 1939, and squadrons began to move to war stations and aircraft to receive their wartime squadron codes. Fearing all-out attack, and reprisals for any operations carried out, many squadrons followed very elaborate plans and scattered westwards, in part to civilian airfields.

On the afternoon of September 2 watchers on the South Coast witnessed a host of Fairey Battles—ten squadrons totalling 149 aircraft—heading for France. The Battle's range was too short to permit operations over Germany from England, so No 1 Group (known now as First Echelon Advanced Air Striking Force) moved to forward bases.

Bomber Command's strength on September 3 was 55 squadrons. Additional to the Battles there were at readiness 79 Blenheims of 2 Group, 69 Wellingtons of 3 Group, 50 Whitleys of 4 Group, 81 Hampdens of 5 Group and a handful of Battles and Blenheims in 6 Training Group. It was the largest Command, but not big enough, and by September 30 operational strength had fallen to 33 squadrons as others went to France or took on training commitments.

Numerically too small for a sustained hefty offensive the Command at least had aircraft mainly superior to enemy bombers, and there was the prospect of four-engined heavies to come. On September 1 approval had been given to two plans, (1) an all-out offensive if the enemy attacked in strength and, (2) a limited offensive against the German Navy and the dropping of propaganda leaflets. No German onslaught came, and plan 2 was enacted.

Since September 1 Blenheim IV N6215 of 139 Squadron, Wyton, had been at standby to reconnoitre German ports and assess the position and strength of the German fleet and sundry military targets. At noon on September 3 it set off and secured photographs.

When war commenced home-based bomber aircraft were all basically coloured alike—Dark Green-Dark Earth-Night. When mobilisation reached a high state at the end of August, orders promulgated earlier came into force and within a few days all units changed their squadron identity letters for security reasons. Since they did not move immediately to war stations it was quite clear which unit was which! At the same time under-wing serials were removed and most remaining rudder or fin serials were overpainted. Some units painted out serial numbers altogether, whereas some of the Battles which had gone to France retained fin serials for many months.

My own recollection of the first afternoon of war was the amazing stillness and sense of foreboding. Nothing seemed to move, and in my diary I noted only the passage of a solitary Blenheim IV of 82 Squadron, already coded UX. During an afternoon tour around the airfields—in retrospect unwise—I noted that on Newmarket Heath 'LN' coded Wellingtons presented a most unexpected sight. At Mildenhall, Wellington Is of 149 Squadron coded OJ were already dispersed around the airfield. Some had been pushed among the trees on the perimeter and this, too, was an unusual sight in those days. At Bassingbourn, already a training camp, the Blenheims and the black under-surfaced Ansons were partly squatting amongst the trees in Wimpole Park. All that I noted were still wearing pre-war letters.

In the late afternoon, Wellingtons of 37 Squadron (L4328, L4352, L4347, L4332, L4326 and L4349) with a similar force from 149 Squadron, also Hampdens L4050, L4054, L4055, L4071 and L4094, all of 83 Squadron, searched the North Sea for enemy warships.

The earlier Blenheim reconnaissance had revealed ships and it was decided during the following night—despite a bad weather forecast—to attack those in the roads off Wilhelmshaven and Brunsbuttel. Accordingly, three squadrons of long-range Blenheims, Nos 107, 110 and 139, were despatched.

No success came to 139 Squadron's Blenheims, N6216, N6217, N6218, N6224 and N6225, which failed to locate their target. No 110 Squadron, which despatched N6204, N6201, N6198, N6197 and N6199, lost the latter aeroplane when it attacked enemy warships. No 107 Squadron lost N6184, N6188, N6240 and N6189. Only N6195 returned and little had been achieved against capital ships. The weather was extremely bad and when the Wellingtons of 9 Squadron (L4320, L4278, L4287 and L4262, and two which failed to return—L4268 and L4275) and 149 Squadron (L4265, L4263, L4270, L4271, L4272 : OJ-A, L4229, L4302 and L4374) tried to bomb ships off Brunsbuttel, conditions were appalling and they had to face fierce flak.

All the Wellingtons were Mk Is, but already the Mk IA with its superior turrets was becoming available. The first two Mk IAs to join a squadron, N2866 and N2867, were delivered to No 149 on September 1, and on September 9 No 99 Squadron received its first example. During that month the six front-line squadrons all received some IAs. Very few sorties were flown by the Mk Is whose armament, 3 Group considered, was simply not good enough for safe operations.

The scene and activity in Yorkshire on that first night of the war was quite different from that on the 2 and 3 Group stations. Whitley IIIs of Nos 51 and 58 Squadrons were ordered to operate on September 3/4 scattering leaflets over Hamburg, Bremen and the Ruhr and gathering useful information about night operations. They encountered storms and icing conditions, and one crashed in France. Although they had the longest endurance of the bombers the five squadrons of Whitley III/IVs were the slowest and from the start of hostilities were relegated to night operations. In use in

October 1939 were K8984 : MH-A and K8989 : MH-M of 51 Squadron. Mk Vs entered squadron service at a trickle, 78, 77 and 102 Squadrons having them by the end of 1939. They included N1355 : KN-X (in use October 1939), N1378 : DY-Q (in use November 1939) and N1380 : DY-R (in use December 1939). Into mid-1940 the Tiger-engined Whitleys were on operations.

No 5 Group's Hampdens, despite their poor armament, were committed to operations at once and undertook daylight patrols over the North Sea searching for warships. In France the Battle squadrons took a fortnight to settle, then began daylight lone reconnaissance flights over the German lines and their hinterland. On September 20 the gunner of Battle K9243 of 88 Squadron shot down a Bf 109, the first to fall to an aircraft of Bomber Command in the war. At this time Battles were making daylight reconnaissance flights over the Western Front. For example, on September 26 K9250, K9348, K9318, K9321, K9322 and K9242 reconnoitred the Saarbrucken area.

Every effort was ordered to avoid attacking any civilian target. Now came the order to attack warships at sea using formations of armed bombers. From September 26 sizeable forces would fly over the North Sea and on the 29th eleven Hampdens of 144 Squadron attempted to attack two destroyers. Off the Frisians, Bf 109s swept in and downed five of the bombers, including L4121, L4126, L4132 and L4134.

The markings change

Already a noticeable change had come in bomber roundels. When I took myself to view the Wellingtons Mk I/IA of 99 Squadron on Newmarket Heath on October 1 1939, I was surprised to find them all wearing Type A red-white-blue fuselage roundels, and about half had under-wing roundels. The new side roundels had also been applied to some of 149's aircraft. Otherwise there was no change, and serials were only worn on the fuselage. The authorised date for a complete introduction of the new roundels was December 7, but my diary shows that quite a number of bombers seen in October had them.

For daylight operations black under surfaces on Blenheims penetrating high and quite deeply into Germany were deemed unsuitable. There was also dissatisfaction with the rough paintwork which reduced the aircraft's speed at a time when even a marginal increase was worthwhile. A series of special shades for reconnaissance aircraft had been under consideration for some months and these were collectively then known as Sky shades. The work was being undertaken at Heston. On October 27 a Blenheim left Wyton for Heston, there to be camouflaged by Titanine on its under surfaces in a new shade from the series, the chosen one being then known as Light Sea Green, later *officially* as Duck Egg Green.

In view of some erroneous comments which have appeared on the subject of 'Sky' it is interesting to know what the manufacturers responsible for the chosen shade comment : 'The colour Sky originated just prior to the war from a shade devised by Titanine and called Camotint. This was a greenish blue shade. "Type S" referred to a standard of finish. At the start of the war matt camouflage paints were very rough and as speeds of aircraft increased, it was found that significant advantages in drag could be obtained by using smoother finishes while retaining an adequately non-reflecting surface. "S" thus stood for "smooth".'

As to the colour of the paint, the manufacturers record : 'the SBOAC

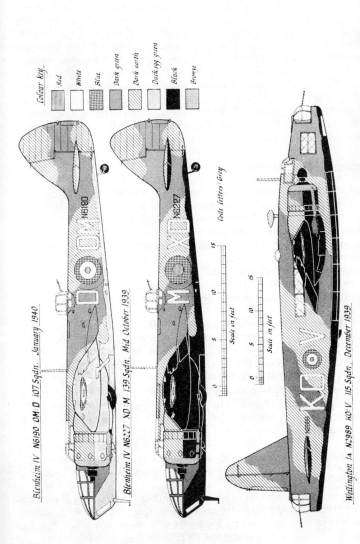

Blenheim IV N6190 OM:D 107 Sqdn. January 1940

Blenheim IV N6227 XD:M 139 Sqdn. Mid October 1939

Wellington IA N2989 KO:V 115 Sqdn. December 1939

Colour key: Red, White, Blue, Dark green, Dark earth, Duck egg green, Black, Bronze

Code letters: Grey

Scale in feet

Figure 6: The two Blenheims show schemes in use in 1939. N6190 wears the late 1939 scheme and was recorded in the markings shown in early January 1940. Squadron codes were light grey. The machine was 'polished' and traces of the old pre-war roundel were visible. N6227 was recorded at Wyton on October 16 1939, and also wears light grey codes. No fuel jettison pipes were in evidence, but the machine is believed to have been a long-range aircraft—perhaps not then fully modified. Again traces of pre-war roundels were in evidence. Note that in both cases the under surface colour ends in an irregular line at the 60-degree tangent point. Both have under-wing roundels, probably because they were used for daylight operations. Wellington N2989 was seen at Newmarket on December 3 1939 in the markings shown. Her codes appeared to be about 4 feet high, whereas those on the Blenheims were about 30 inches high. An interesting point about Blenheims is that, although they were alternately produced machines, their camouflage patterns were similar.

formulation in use during the war consisted of White tinted with about 4% Yellow Oxide and a trace of Prussian Blue. The white pigment varied with the type of paint—NC paints used Zinc Oxide while Synthetic Resin paints used Titanium Dioxide, Antimony Oxide and some Zinc Oxide.'

In addition to the new under surface shade the first Blenheim thus treated had its paintwork polished, and various cracks were filled. But it was a lengthy job consuming many man hours. On the other hand it afforded an increase in aircraft speed. It was therefore decided to apply the new paint scheme to Blenheim IVs at Wyton, soon to be transferred to France, and to a few selected aircraft in other squadrons which would be fully treated to become what were known as 'polished' aircraft. By late November both 114 and 139 Squadrons had on charge specially treated machines wearing what were still known as 'Light Sea Green' under surfaces. Two uncoded specimens I noted on November 29 were L8859 and N6227. But it was February 1940 before many Blenheims were to be seen with the new under surface colour referred to, in contemporary records, as 'Duck Egg Green'.

Limited operations continue

Meanwhile the general level of operations had continued at low key. On October 1/2 three Whitleys of 10 Squadron had ventured to Berlin to bombard the city with paper. They did so in conditions of appalling cold for the Whitleys were unheated, and many were the astonishing stories that circulated about their operations. For the Wellingtons and Hampdens North Sea Sweeps were a frequent feature. There was a general need for more positive action, if only to maintain morale, and so on November 19 it was decided to attack ships close in harbour and still avoid civilian casualties. For many crews there were long standbys usually resulting in the cancellation of operations at this time.

Eventually a suitable day came, December 3, when 24 Wellingtons drawn from 38 Squadron (HD-Y : N2878, W : N2880 and Z : N2879), 115 Squadron (N2876, N2877, N2875, N2899, N2900, N2989, N2947, N2949 and N2950) and 149 Squadron (N2960, N2945, N2892, N2946, N2867, N2984, N2893, N2944, N2866, N2894, N2943 and N2980) set out to bomb two cruisers. They met 5/10 cloud and Bf 109s engaged the bombers. LAC Copley, the rear gunner of HD : Z, destroyed one. The three turrets of each Wellington IA, good station keeping and the use of cloud cover had, it seemed, saved the day. Only a minesweeper was, by luck, sunk.

Whitleys now began their 'security patrols' over bases from which enemy aircraft had been setting out to sow magnetic mines around the eastern shores of Britain. Nos 77 and 102 Squadrons commenced such sorties on December 12.

Enemy warships were reported at sea on December 13. Next day Hampdens made an abortive early search and then 12 Wellington IAs of 99 Squadron were despatched to Schillig Roads. Cloud was low; there was much flak and fighters engaged them. Five Wellingtons (N2870, N2886, N2986, N2911 and N2956) were shot down and N2957 crashed near base. Those that survived were N2991, N2914, N2999, N2887, N2913 and N2958.

On December 18 another armed reconnaissance was flown, to the Schillig Roads and Wilhelmshaven. Twenty-four aircraft of Nos 9 (N2964 : WS-D, N2941*, N2981 : F, N2983*, N2940*, N2873 : C, N2872*, N2871 : B and N2939*), 37 (N2904 : B*, N2935 : H, N2936 : J*, N2903, N2888 : A and

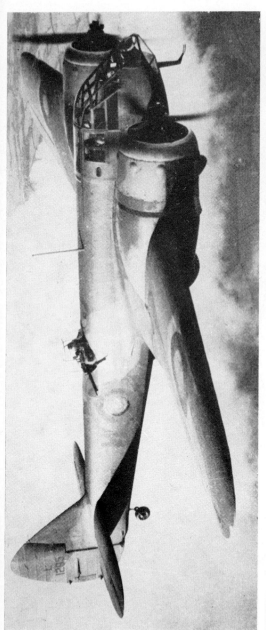

16 (Upper) Blenheim I L1295 in the markings it carried in the summer of 1939. Its roundels are all Type B, and there are clear traces of the old Type A1. Also visible is the fuselage unit marking H-107, the aircraft having been used by 107 Sqn between August 1938 and July 1939. After conversion into a fighter it served with 600 Sqn and 54 OTU (Ministry of Defence). 17 (Lower left) Blenheim I K7078 in the A camouflage pattern has '139' in green outlined black aft of its roundel and 'J' is the same colour on the nose. Photo taken in the autumn of 1937. 18 (Lower right) Blenheim I K7074 after a flying accident near Wyton on April 8 1938. Identity lettering is light grey.

19   *Wellington I L4288: KA-Z at the Evere display in July 1939. She had by then acquired an under-wing roundel (Guy Destrebecq).*

20   *Wellington I L4235 after a heavy landing. Her fuselage roundel is much larger than on the 9 Sqn aircraft, the blue extending to cover the area of the old Type A1. When her paintwork was changed so was the style of the letter R* (Ron Clark).

21   *Hereford L6006 with Type B fuselage roundels, but with Type A under the wing tips. An unusual feature is the wavy line demarcation of the black under surfaces.*

22   *Hampden L4074 of 44 Sqn at Drem after a North Sea Sweep early in 1940. The outer surround to the fuselage roundel has been over-painted and the under-wing roundel too appears to have a grey wash over it. The KM coding is in the thin style of stroke that characterised aircraft of the squadron. The under-wing serial is still visible despite over-painting. The nose bears a white inscription. Individual letter was 'O'* (via P. Scott).

23   *Whitley V N1357 was initially delivered to 78 Sqn. Here it is seen early in its career with 77 Sqn. It was later interned.*

24 (*Above*) *Blenheim IV XD-M: N6227 of 139 Sqn. Sky under surfaces and Medium Grey codes (XD aft). Aircraft served in the squadron from July 1939 until its loss in June 1940* (Imperial War Museum). **25** (*Right*) *K8985 DY-J of 102 Sqn. a Whitley III which lost its way and landed in Belgium on September 9 1939. All her roundels carry traces of the former yellow ringed type, and she has a fin serial in Whitley style. Roundels are Type B. Photograph taken at Nivelles* (Guy Destrebecq).

26 (*Right*) *Wellington IA L7779: LF-P of 37 Sqn wears the small fin flash and narrow yellow ring carried by many Wellingtons circa May-July 1940. The under surface black terminates in a wavy line and does not sweep up to the wing.*

27 *Three Battles of 88 Sqn with pre-war service seen over France. RH-K is interesting in that it was one of the machines with colours reversed. Type B roundels have been applied over the old Type A1* (Imperial War Museum).

28 (Upper) After serving with 99 Sqn, Wellington IA N2912 passed to 215 Sqn at Bassingbourn in April 1940. Previously LN-H, she acquired the LG coding in April and the photograph is believed to have been taken in June 1940. By this time she was part of 11 OTU whose Wellingtons were certainly wearing KJ and OP coding in that month. Note the enlarged red centre to the roundel and the broad fin striping. Both aircraft have under-wing roundels and appear to have differing colour codes. **29** (Lower) Wellington II W5379 prior to serving 12 Sqn as PH-O. Note the wavy line along the starboard wing leading edge and the larger diameter fuselage roundel. She completed 15 sorties and was lost on October 10 1941 (Imperial War Museum).

N2889 : P*) and 149 (N2960, N2984, N2866, N2892, N2894, N2962*, N2980, N2943 and N2961*) Squadrons were despatched. Twenty-two of them pressed on, avoiding flak ships. East of Heligoland they ran into a swarm of 109s of JG 1. A long battle ensued without any bombing, fighters attacking from above on the beam, a blind spot for the Wellington gunners. Ten bombers were shot down, two ditched through loss of fuel from unprotected tanks and three forced landed. Four fighters had been destroyed for the loss of a fair proportion of the force. N2871 : WS-B and N2873 : WS-C crashed, and those marked with an asterisk above were missing. Reluctantly it had to be concluded that Wellingtons and Hampdens were unsuitable for daylight operations, although on a few occasions later in the war they made cloud cover attacks in daylight. Nevertheless, Hampdens of 83 and 49 Squadrons searched for the *Deutschland* on the 21st, but the warning was clear – it must be night operations for the present heavies from now on. It was a grim note upon which to close the year.

Examples of aircraft in squadron service between September 3 1939, and the end of December :

Fairey Battle	12 Sqn	PH-X: L4952 in use October
	88 Sqn	RH-L: L9244 in use September
	105 Sqn	GB-W: K9191 in use September
	218 Sqn	HA-J: K9353 in use September
	226 Sqn	MQ-W: K9330 in use September
Blenheim IV	21 Sqn	YH-F: L9837 in use December
	82 Sqn	UX-O: P4852 in use October
	114 Sqn	RT-J: N6161 in use September
	139 Sqn	XD-R: N6217 in use October
	139 Sqn	XD-R: N6227 in use December
Wellington	9 Sqn	WS-B: N2871 in use October
	38 Sqn	HD-Z: N2879 in use September-December
	99 Sqn	LN-J: N2887 in use October
	149 Sqn	OJ-C: L4272 in use September
Whitley	51 Sqn	MH-J: K9008 in use October
	58 Sqn	GE-G: K8969 in use September
	102 Sqn	DY-E: K8976 in use September
Hampden	44 Sqn	KM-A: L4085 in use December
	83 Sqn	OL-L: L4050 in use September
	106 Sqn	ZN-B: L4175 in use September

D

Chapter 7

The fight in earnest

WHEN 1940 OPENED Bomber Command was flying sweeps in force over the North Sea, and sending Blenheims on reconnaissance flights to Germany and adjacent waters. Leaflet dropping continued and soon Hampdens and Wellingtons were taking part. Whitleys of 77 Squadron probed as far as Prague and Vienna on the night of January 12/13, a journey made possible by their very long range. In March, Poznan was reached, again from an advanced base in France, and even Warsaw was visited on the 15th/16th. But, between late January and mid February, there were no operations for the weather was so bad.

Whitley Vs slowly replaced the Tiger-engined versions in 1939, 78 then 77 and 102 Squadrons having them by the end of the year. In January No 51 Squadron began to equip, N1405-1408 being the first batch which joined the squadron in that month. Delivery to 58 Squadron also commenced, early machines including N1424 : GE-P and N1427 : GE-K. It was March before 58's Mk IIIs were phased out, and as late as June 1940, Mk IIIs were still being used by 51 Squadron. The last squadron to receive Mk Vs was No 10 which acquired its first three in March. Mk IIIs released from front-line service subsequently flew with 97 and 166 reserve training squadrons. Later they were used by Nos 7, 9 and 10 BGS; 8, 9 and 10 AOS; 2 BAT Flight; and the Parachute Training School. Such machines were re-painted Dark Green-Dark Earth-Training Yellow.

The most important type to enter service at this time was the Wellington IC which followed the phase-out of Mk IA delivery in February 1940. Over 2,500 Mk ICs were ultimately produced, many of them for front-line Bomber Command squadrons. Externally the IC differed little from the IA. Its special features included a 24-volt electrical system and re-designed hydraulics, both the result of the Wellington's service career so far. But the main difference lay in armament. The retractable dustbin turret on the IA was replaced by two hand-manipulated .303 inch Browning guns, one of which could be fired from a mounting in the rear of each long side window affording protection from beam attacks. Some Mk IAs later carried this feature, their dustbin turrets being removed. Mk IAs remained operational alongside ICs until late 1940. Equipment with these later Wellingtons meant that Mk Is could be released to reserve squadrons like 75, 148 and 215.

The first batches of Wellington ICs were P9237-9250 and P9265-9300. They began to join the squadrons in some numbers during March 1940. Delivery began of Mk ICs in the R serial range in April 1940, and all had left the makers by early June. These aircraft were R3150-3179, R3195-3220, R3222-3239 and R3275-3297. They filtered into the 3 Group squadrons, R3151-3159 going to No 115, R3166-3169 to No 75 and R3170-3175 to No 148. Prior to May 1940, the ICs appeared to wear alternate A and B paint schemes, but a small point of interest was that the black under surfaces terminated in an irregular manner on many aircraft. Type A roundels on the fuselage sides, which had recently varied dimensionally, were now of uniform size, and were still carried under the wings of most aircraft. Mid-grey codes appeared on the many examples I saw at this time. It seems that few, if any, of the bombers were yet carrying any artistry on their noses.

With the return of better weather, Battles of the Advanced Air Striking Force (AASF) commenced leaflet dropping by night over the Rhineland. Blenheims were by then attacking heavily armed German flak ships, sometimes meeting enemy fighters, and often a hail of flak from armed trawlers.

Success of the enemy minelaying campaign gave added weight to a plan to mine inland German waterways. Long flights over enemy territory provided useful data on this account. The annoyance enemy minelaying aircraft had been causing led to the first Bomber Command night bombing raid of the war on an island target. This was directed against Hornum, on Sylt, as a reply to German bombing of Hoy on the Orkneys, on the night of March 19/20. It was opened by 30 out of 31 Whitleys despatched (K9036, K9028, K9033, K9035, K9034, K9025, K9037 and K9023 of 10 Squadron; N1405 (missing), K9043, N1408, K9041, K9048, K9040 and N1407 of 51 Squadron; eight aircraft of 77 Squadron; N1380, N1382, N1379, N1421, N1386 : P, N1415 : D, N1381 and N1386 (abortive) of 102 Squadron, followed by Hampdens L4171, L4074, L4100, L4087 and P1137 of 44 Squadron; L4064, L4076, L4075, L4077 and L4065 of 50 Squadron; L4106, L4103, L4119, L4105 and P1323 of 61 Squadron; and L4124, L4133 and L4137 of 144 Squadron. Forty-one crews claimed to attack and the only Hampden missing was L4105.

A pressing need now was for a large number of air and ground crews for the expansion of Bomber Command. Second line squadrons were presently training flying personnel who, it was found, really needed to form up as a crew before joining operational squadrons. In peacetime these could readily train their own crews, but when hostilities became more hectic—as it was expected they soon must—operational squadrons would have little time for crew training. Therefore it was decided to replace Reserve Squadrons with special Operational Training Units which would initially consume them. They were to expand into very large formations, each comprising a number of squadrons or flights, and equip with first-line aircraft. They therefore offered excellent training and could, if the need arose, become fully operational.

The first eight bomber OTUs, formed early April 1940 as Nos 10-17, were as follows :

No 10 (formed from Nos 97 and 166 Squadrons): Based at Abingdon; used Whitley II, III, IV coded ZG and later also RK, and Ansons coded UY. Example in use in 1940: Whitley III ZG-X:K9013, with white code letters, white band encircling rear fuselage.

No 11 (formed basically from 215 Squadron): Based at Bassingbourn; used Wellington I/IA coded KJ and OP, also Ansons coded TX. Wellingtons used in 1940 : N2750 : OP-J, L4391 : KJ-A. Anson used : N5173 : TX-F (Ansons camouflaged dark green-dark earth-black).

No 12 (formed from 52, 63 and 270 Squadrons): Based at Benson; used Battles coded JP. Examples used in 1940 : L5061, L5079.

No 13 (formed from 104 and 108 Squadrons): Based at Bicester; used Blenheim I/IV coded FV and XJ and Ansons. Examples used in 1940 : L1269 : XJ-R, L1188 and Anson N5174.

No 14 (formed from 185 Squadron): Based at Cottesmore with detachments at Pembrey; used Hampdens, Herefords and Ansons. Hampdens and Herefords coded GL and AM. Examples used in 1940 : Hampdens GL-M1 : P1276, GL-T : L4201; Herefords L6011, L6012; Anson N5211.

No 15 (formed from 75 and 148 Squadrons): Based at Harwell; used Wellington I/IA and Ansons. Wellingtons coded FH and KK. Examples used in 1940 : FH-W : L7853, KK-W : L7793, L4231, Anson N5020.

No 16 (formed from 7 and 76 Squadrons): Based at Upper Heyford; used Hampdens, Herefords and also Ansons. Examples used in 1940 : XG-D : P5310, JS-G : P1174 and Anson N5000. Herefords used: L6026, L6040.

No 17 (formed from 35 and 90 Squadrons): Based at Upwood; used Blenheim I/IV coded JG and WJ, also Ansons coded AY. Examples used in 1940 : Blenheims L4891 and L1264. Anson used : N5179 : AY-A.

Aircraft in OTUs wore the usual operational camouflage, and Ansons normally had black under surfaces at this time.

Just as the OTUs were forming, the expected extension of hostilities broke upon Europe. Daily reports had suggested important enemy shipping movements off Denmark, and on April 9 the enemy invaded Norway. Germany had been receiving considerable quantities of iron ore from Sweden, some from the ice-free northern port of Narvik. Various schemes to halt this flow had been discussed by the British Cabinet, such as sending a force to help the Finns fight the Russians and at the same time conveniently cut ore supplies. Eventually it was decided to mine two areas off Norway using surface ships. Before the Finnish war ended, some Blenheims were despatched from Bicester, flown by civilian-clothed crews, as a gesture of support to the Finns

On April 7 enemy ships had sailed for Norway. They were seen by Hudson crews, and 107 Squadron's Blenheims (L8777, N6190, N6192, P4906, N6183, P4914, P4956, P4905, P4952, L9041, P4924 and N6191) were despatched to bomb them, and were later aided by two Wellington squadrons. As often happened bad weather interfered and the attacks achieved nothing. The enemy force sailed on and in the early hours of April 9 the landings in Norway were made. Ports and airfields quickly fell and Denmark, too, was overrun.

At this time Nos 9 and 115 Squadrons, equipped with Wellingtons, were on detachment at Lossiemouth for operations against shipping forced out to sea from the planned minefields off Norway. It fell to 115 Squadron to make the first RAF bombing attack on a mainland target, when six Wellingtons raided Stavanger/Sola airfield by day, with a small escort of 254 Squadron Blenheims, on April 11. The same day both squadrons sent their aircraft to attempt to sink two cruisers in Bergen harbour, but their bombs fell wide and one ship promptly sailed for safety. Next day Hampdens of 44 and 50 Squadrons were despatched to bomb a warship at Kristiansund. Bf 109s raced in from the beam and soon half the force had been destroyed, including L4064 of 44 Squadron and L4073, L4081 and L4083 of 50 Squadron. Daylight bombing by the heavies was clearly impossible.

By now the enemy was securely installed in Norway, although British forces were to land and courageously hold the north for some weeks. To aid them it was decided to attack airfields constantly. Only the Whitleys, like K9048 : MH-P missing from a raid on Oslo on April 24, really had sufficient range to do this comfortably, but in an endeavour to maintain round-the-clock bombing some Blenheims were moved to Lossiemouth. From here, for three weeks, they kept day and night sorties mainly to Stavanger/Sola. Heavy bombers still made night raids, but airfields proved to be difficult targets.

Already another campaign, that of minelaying, had been launched. It was

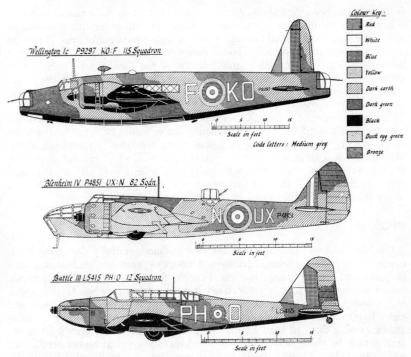

Figure 7: *Three styles of fuselage roundels and fin stripes are depicted here on aircraft seen in May 1940. The Wellington IC was used for operations over Norway and later over the Continent. The Blenheim P4851 was lost on May 17 1940, when 82 Sqn suffered a crippling loss, and is drawn as recorded a few days earlier flying near Watton. Battle L5415 served 12 Sqn for a few operations from its French base. It had very striking fin striping but a narrow yellow surround to the fuselage roundel.*

to pay good dividends in the years ahead. On April 13/14 fifteen Hampdens of Nos 44, 49, 50, 61 and 144 Squadrons set out to lay mines off Denmark in an attempt to interfere with German shipping movements from Norway. Hampdens were chosen because at this time they were the only aircraft available capable of carrying suitable weapons. On the night of April 14/15 50 Squadron despatched L4164, L4097, L4062 and L4079 on the task.

During the Norwegian campaign bomber aircraft markings were basically unchanged from those in use at the end of 1939, but most of 2 Group's Blenheims now had Duck Egg Green under surfaces. Early in May the Norwegian campaign came to its disastrous end. Hitler now had a long coastline facing Britain.

Early March 1940, Battles in France began appearing with a yellow surround to the fuselage Type A roundel, and had wide band red-white-blue fin stripes which to some extent brought them into line with the rudder striping on French aircraft. Rudder striping might seem more logical, but already this was known to have some effect upon control balance. As with the new roundels, fin striping was introduced over a period of some weeks, and in great profusion of size and style. The surge of intense fighting about to come highlighted the need for the new markings to be used, and hasty provision led to a wide assortment of stylings evident even on the aircraft of any one squadron. In this respect 2 Group's Blenheims were no exception, with narrow or broad fin stripes and narrow or wide yellow surrounds to roundels.

In the weeks ahead they showed another new feature in some cases. This was a single gun mounted in a transparent blister placed under the nose escape hatch, the gun being aimed through a mirror sight to fire backwards. It proved of limited use and few victory claims were ever made using it. As a scare gun it played a useful part. Only a small portion of the Blenheim force had such guns by the end of May 1940. Thus the Blenheims depended upon the single gun in the dorsal turret for defence against fighter attack—and this was soon seen to be quite inadequate.

An attack upon the Low Countries and France had been expected for months. The rôle of the bombers, when it came, would be three-fold. Battles of the AASF would attack enemy forces in the southern sector ahead of the Maginot Line. Blenheims based in East Anglia would go for any advance in the northern areas, and the 16 squadrons of heavies would attack oil targets and factories in the Ruhr in an attempt to cut oil supplies to the invaders and tempt the Luftwaffe into retaining aircraft for home defence.

Blitzkreig

On May 10 1940, the Germans invaded Holland, skilfully deploying paratroops to capture airfields. Mechanised columns were soon advancing into Belgium and Luxembourg, but the French, fearful of reprisal air attacks, would not agree at first to operations from their territory where the AASF was situated. At mid-day the British took things into their own hands and eight Battles went into action over Luxembourg making low-level strafing attacks, losing three of their number to ground fire. It was a grim start. Low-level attack by these slow machines was hazardous, yet at higher levels they were very vulnerable to attacks from below, since no really effective under-gun mounting was ever devised. Blenheims from England tackled the Dutch airfields, suffering losses for limited results. At night 36 Wellingtons of 3 Group continued with an attack on Waalhaven airfield whilst Whitleys were despatched to communications targets in Germany near the Dutch border. Among the aircraft despatched were Wellingtons P9280, P9222, P9243, P9275, R3170 and P9277 of 99 Squadron and Whitleys N1372, N1367, N1373 and N1355 of 77 Squadron with N1382:DY-A, N1415:D, N1417:B, N1380 : R and N1375 : N of 102 Squadron.

The enemy advance continued seemingly unimpeded. Again the Battles went into action and suffered heavy losses. Of eight drawn from 88 and 218 Squadrons attacking near the Luxembourg border seven were shot down. One line of enemy advance particularly worrying was that via Maastricht. Blenheims attacked the bridges in the area but with little effect. Next morning 139 Squadron of the AASF sent nine Blenheims to raid the same area. Fighters swarmed in and only two bombers escaped. This virtually brought an end to the two AASF Blenheim squadrons, since No 114 had already been all but wiped out on the ground. The French operated later in the area and again the losses were heavy. It was imperative that the bridges should be destroyed. Blenheims from England had another go and ten out of 24 were shot down. Two bridges over the Albert Canal were seen to be vital targets and, whilst the Blenheims were dealing with Maastricht, a formation of Battles went to the Albert Canal.

Chosen for the dangerous task of bringing down the Vroenhoven and Veldwezelt bridges was No 12 Squadron. Clearly it would be a perilous operation and so it was decided to call for volunteers. At once the entire squadron volunteered, so it was decided to take the first six crews on the duty roster. Only five took off, the sixth making two attempts before abandoning their sortie. Flg Off N. M. Thomas and Plt Off T. D. H. Davy dive bombed Vroenhoven doing slight damage. Flak was heavy and enemy fighters were around. One Battle was soon a smoking ruin. Flg Off D. E. Garland (in PH-K : P2204) led his section to Veldwezelt where the attack was delivered at low level. Flak was murderous again and all three machines were soon brought down—after the bridge was severely damaged. As a mark of respect for courage of the highest standard both Garland and his observer, Sgt T. Gray, were awarded Victoria Crosses posthumously, this being the first occasion when the award was made to the RAF in the war.

Leonard Clarke was with 12 Squadron at this time and recalls that 'up to May 14 1940, all the squadron's aircraft displayed fin flashes of equal height and yellow roundel surrounds in width the equal of the other roundel bands. Replacement aircraft may well have worn roundels with narrower yellow bands. One point of interest is that some of the Battle squadrons in France painted over much of the long cockpit canopy.

'In listing aircraft which participated in the famous raid on the bridges the serial number of PH-F of 'A' Flight is often given erroneously as P2322. It should be P2332. The former machine, P2322, was a 'B' Flight aircraft, PH-J, shot down by Bf 109s on May 14. Neither is it true to say, as is often quoted, that all the Battles on that raid were shot down. Plt Off Davy in L5241 : PH-G ran out of fuel and landed about two miles short of Amifontaine, his crew having baled out soon after leaving the target. After being re-fuelled an intrepid crew flew L5241 back to base. It was abandoned in France.'

More Battle sorties were flown on May 12. Losses all round were so severe that no operations took place next day in order to conserve strength. Meanwhile the enemy crossed the River Meuse at two points. The position was now very serious, and whilst the RAF's bombers rested the Luftwaffe delivered a savage attack on the centre of Rotterdam destroying the old city and killing over 1,000 civilians. The British Government decided, following this raid, that the Germans were not respecting civilian life, and gave the go ahead for RAF operations against targets in the Ruhr, which had been held off until then. If, as was expected, these led the Luftwaffe into attacking Britain, it would at least take some of the pressure off Continental targets.

But before Bomber Command struck its first blow against German industry the AASF was called upon to make a supreme effort to halt the German advance, at Sedan. Nos 103 and 150 Squadrons made a morning raid on the 14th to little avail, then a large operation followed in mid-afternoon using eight Blenheims and 63 Battles. Forty bombers were shot down, bringing the highest loss ever in any operation of comparable size by Bomber Command. Among the Battles lost during the operation were L4950 : PH-V, L4952 : PH-X and L5188 : PH-C of 12 Squadron; L5581, L5422 of 88 Squadron; K9485 of 105 Squadron; N2333 and L5517 of 142 Squadron; and K9343, L5438 and P2267 of 226 Squadron.

In the evening, 28 Blenheims attacked the area and seven were lost. The net result was a slight hold up of the enemy, but in a matter of hours the German army crossed into France and an even more dangerous situation presented itself. The AASF had been dealt a powerful blow, so it was now left largely to the Blenheims of 2 Group to do all possible to impede the enemy. In the face of heavy flak, as well as swarms of Bf 109s, it was asking crews to face certain death, and, in fact, casualties over the next fortnight were appalling.

On May 15/16 the nightly campaign against the Ruhr opened. A force of 96 Wellingtons, Whitleys, and Hampdens was despatched, 78 of them to oil refinery targets. Among the aircraft in use at the time were Whitleys N1424 : GE-P, N1433 : GE-D and N1436 : GE-F of 58 Squadron. Only 24 claimed to find their targets through the haze on this first raid, an inauspicious start. The crying need was to halt the German thrusts into France and so the Ruhr campaign was seen to appear irrelevant. Effort in the nights ahead was therefore divided—bombs were aimed through the Ruhr haze or the mist over river crossings; neither were easy targets. The German advance soon threatened the AASF bases. Its battered squadrons were reduced in number and it retreated to bases around Troyes. Six Battle squadrons now operated mainly by night and their losses fell to almost nil, but bombing results were poor. To the north, despite the valiant effort of the Bomber Command Blenheims, the Germans hurried to the Channel ports and the encirclement of the British Expeditionary Force. Sometimes there were Hurricanes to sweep the area ahead of the Blenheims; occasionally fighters gave them a small measure of close support. But the loss rate was high and on May 17, 11/12 crews of 82 Squadron were lost and the squadron all but wiped out. In these squadrons every man was a hero—the situation was such that he had little choice to be otherwise.

Eventually the BEF was surrounded at Dunkirk by which time its evacuation was under way. By day and night Bomber Command hammered at the German forces on the perimeter and gave the troops therein some relief by attacking guns pounding the beach areas. Further behind the lines heavy bombers attempted by night to halt supplies and reinforcements. When the last troops left Dunkirk's beaches on June 4 the bombers, after a brief rest, turned to aid the French in their desperate fight against impossible odds.

The final nail driven into the French coffin was the declaration of war by Italy on June 10. British response led to direct disagreement with the French. It was to hit the Italians as hard as possible with air raids on their northern cities from advanced French bases. Nos 99 and 149 Squadrons left Newmarket and Mildenhall and flew to Salon. At first the French, again fearing retaliation, stopped the Wellingtons from operating, but on June 15 the first raids on Italy were made. From 149 Squadron's detachment P9248, R3160, R3163, R3164, P9272 and P9268 operated. Only '68 claimed to bomb the target in Genoa. Additional strength to the operation was afforded by 36 Whitleys operating from the Channel Islands where they had arrived at mid-day. Aircraft of Nos 10, 51, 58, 77 and 102 Squadrons faced for the first time the difficult task of crossing the Alps and 23 were forced back through storms. When one so easily crosses the Alps in a jet-liner of today it is always, I think, worth sparing a thought for the wartime bomber crews who, in pitch darkness, sometimes threaded their ways between those inspiring peaks, or flew just a few feet above them with full bomb and heavy fuel loads.

The operations by 77 Squadron on June 15 typified what was demanded of the Whitley crews. The target was Turin and they operated from Jersey, their aircraft in the standard Dark Green-Dark Earth-Night finish with rather pale grey codes at this time and tall narrow fin striping. No under-wing roundels were borne by any of the Whitleys. Over France they ran into electrical storms and above 10,000 feet the icing was severe. Plt Off Eno in N1473 had engine trouble and his radio froze. In the target area there was plenty of flak and N1365 returned well iced and with one engine almost out of action. The

same troubles affected N1508 flown by the well-known S/L Mahaddie. N1367
never returned.

In France the situation was now at its worst. On June 15 the remaining
Battles of the AASF flew home and two days later the Wellingtons returned
from Salon. When the reckoning was made it was found that, between May
10 and June 20, 115 Battles had been lost and Bomber Command had lost 162
aircraft. Little had been achieved at a fearful cost.

Chapter 8

Survival in the balance

THE FIGHTING OVER FRANCE mercifully left Bomber Command fairly intact, although 2 Group's Blenheim squadrons had suffered sorely, whilst the Battles of the AASF had been decimated. Remnants of the latter struggled home and lodged on stations from Stradishall to Lincolnshire. They were either subsequently absorbed into 2 Group—like 105 Squadron—or joined a new No 1 Group and continued to use Battles, including some which survived the fighting in France. Heavy bomber squadrons, less affected by the recent slaughter, continued the new offensive under way against Germany.

Basically Bomber Command was now raiding three types of targets—oil refineries and synthetic oil plants, power installations and the rail network. Hampdens, Wellingtons and Whitleys were engaged, whilst by day small numbers of Blenheims, relying on cloud cover for protection, set out for similar targets.

By night the heavies were despatched to Germany in relatively small numbers, and found difficulty in locating targets on dark nights and in the hazy conditions met over industrial areas. Operations by No 77 Squadron flying Whitley Vs were typical. In June the squadron attempted to bomb oil targets at Gelsenkirchen, Sterkrade and Hanover, installations which were to attract Bomber Command almost to the end of the war. The infamous marshalling yards at Hamm, such a feature of the 1940 BBC news reports, were frequently raided, particularly by Hampdens of 5 Group. Duisburg and Friedrichshafen also figured on 77's target list which, in July, included Wilhelmshaven, Kassal and Bottrop.

The battle cruiser *Scharnhorst* presently lay in Kiel. On July 1/2 a Hampden of 83 Squadron dropped the first 2,000 lb bomb there, the heaviest weapon yet used by the Command. On this operation the squadron despatched L4053, L4070, L4066, L4058, L4049, L4124, L4106, L4057, L4051, P1355, P1171 and P1334.

Hampdens of 5 Group were, on August 12/13, despatched against another target that was to be attacked frequently, the Dortmund-Ems Canal. Flying P4403 of 49 Squadron was Flt-Lt A. B. Learoyd, who bombed from a very low level in the face of intense flak which seriously damaged his aircraft. He pressed home his attack 'with the greatest resolution and skill', being subsequently awarded the Victoria Cross.

During August, Whitley squadrons made some deep penetrations of enemy air space. On the 18/19th the Caproni factory and Pirelli tyre works at Milan were raided, 77 Squadron despatching N1365, P5004, N1474 and N1373. On the 24/25th Milan and Augsburg were targets. But the climax came on the 25/26th with the first raid on Berlin. Eighty-one bombers were despatched but only 29 claimed to attack the primary. Twenty-seven crews reached Berlin but could not locate their targets and 21 brought their bombs back.

Eighteen crews bombed alternative targets. Wellingtons R3228, P9242, P9243, P9277, L7802, R3289, R3222, T2461 and R3203 of 99 Squadron took part in the raid in which Whitleys and Hampdens (including L4062, L4076, P2124, P4417 and P4416 of 49 Squadron) also participated. Among the missing were Hampdens P2070 (50 Squadron), P4314 (61 Squadron), and P1354 (83 Squadron) being one of three which came down in the sea. The whole operation emphasised the difficulty which faced bomber crews at that time when they had great distances to cover in utmost discomfort, without much radio aid and lacking radar.

Bombs had fallen on London the previous night—possibly by chance—and the Cabinet's reaction was that Berlin should be bombed immediately in retaliation. The Air Staff was not keen to do this. Berlin involved a very long journey, and they considered there were more worthwhile strategic targets. But the politicians had their way, discarding professional advice and Berlin was also placed higher on the bombing priority listing. Berlin was raided again on August 30/31 when Hampdens X2894, X2906, P4399, P4405 and P4378 were part of the force despatched.

Early in September a new threat had clearly developed. Many large and some motorised barges were massing in the captured ports of Belgium, France and Holland intended for the transport of an army to invade Britain. It was decided to launch an all-out attack upon these, employing all Groups of Bomber Command.

Since their mauling in France, the Battle squadrons had largely been rested. but on August 13 Nos 12 and 142 moved from Binbrook to Eastchurch for possible anti-invasion operations. Battles L5391, L5404, L5359, P2331 and L5495 of No 12 Squadron went bravely into action during the late evening of August 17 with a Blenheim escort. A follow-up raid was made by L5569, L5501, L5566, L5503, L5582, L5586, L5560, L5456, L5569, and three other aircraft of No 142 Squadron.

In September the Battles flew a few more operations against Channel ports by night and soon the Command was directing half its offensive sorties against this dangerous development so close at hand.

Even these operations were fraught with risks. On the night of September 15/16, which we now celebrate as Battle of Britain Day, Hampden P1355: OL-W of 83 Squadron was ordered to bomb Antwerp. A shell apparently burst in the bomb bay and soon a fire had started. Young Sgt John Hannah fought it with fire extinguishers and later his log book, whilst ammunition exploded around him. Heat and flames all but blinded him. The floor of the aircraft burnt away, leaving only the main frames. Although badly burnt, John Hannah succeeded in putting out the fire and then, discovering that the navigator had left the aircraft, passed maps to the pilot who brought the crippled machine back to base. Although Hannah reached home he was subsequently ill for many months in Papworth Hospital. Some time after, he died, a fourth Bomber Command recipient of the Victoria Cross.

The intensity of the German attacks on Britain brought more clamour for retaliation raids. This was one of the reasons why the Whitleys were taken off the attacks on the barges in September. It led also to 119 Whitley-Wellington-Hampden sorties being despatched to Berlin on September 23/24 once again to specified targets. This time 84 aircraft claimed to attack. Raids on Berlin by smaller forces had been taking place earlier that month, 77 Squadron, for instance, sending its Whitleys there on the 10/11, 12/13 and 15/16th. Some of the aircraft that were used at the time included Whitleys

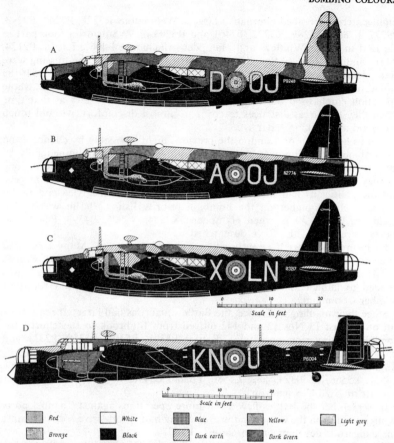

Figure 8: **(A)** *Wellington IC P9248: D-OJ of 149 Sqn as recorded at the end of July 1940 at Mildenhall. Its black under surfaces have begun to 'creep' up the fuselage sides; the roundel has been 'doctored', its white over-painted by what appeared to be a grey wash and the fin stripe remains minute—something favoured by the operational Wellington squadrons.* **(B)** *By the end of August 1940 the black on the Wellingtons terminated higher on the fuselage. Codes and serial remained grey, but the fin stripe is now more conventional like the roundel. This particular example was seen in the depicted markings much later—November 1940. She failed to return from an operation on November 20 1940.* **(C)** *LN-X : R3217 served with 99 Sqn at Newmarket Heath in late 1940, and was seen wearing the illustrated scheme at the end of November. National identity markings, codes and roundels are conventional but note that the black extends over the rear fuselage and the wavy line termination has been tidied. It would be wrong to think all the aircraft had such a finish or indeed the wavy line, for some had a straight line and even an almost indeterminate shadow area where the colours met. Missing from these three Wellingtons are the sometimes numerous red fabric patches where shrapnel had entered the covering. It was always a feature of the aircraft in those days.* **(D)** *Whitley V P5004 : KN-U of 77 Sqn in November 1940. She had quite a lengthy career, particularly with No 10 OTU with whom she served until 1942.*

P4988 : GE-L, P5008 : GE-M and T4137 : GE-K.

Early in October, more bombers were taken off operations against the barges, for these had been progressing well. In their place came raids of a strategic nature and on October 5/6 Whitleys crossed the Alps again, this time going to Turin. Soon the *Scharnhorst* and *Gneisenau* at Kiel were receiving such attention, and one of the types upon which Bomber Command's 1940 strength had rested was withdrawn. This was the luckless Fairey Battle.

Shortage of front-line aircraft had led to some new Polish squadrons forming with Battles at Bramcote. They were then placed in 1 Group and later equipped with Wellingtons. Rumour rife at the time suggested that the reason the Poles had Battles was that had they been given longer-range aircraft they might have taken the conduct of the war more into their own hands and struck at German cities in retribution for the rape of their homeland—but rumours abounded in those days.

Few operations were flown by the Battles in October. On the 15/16th they flew their last operational sorties in Bomber Command. Nos 12 and 142 Squadrons each sent two aircraft to Calais, L5399 with L5076 and L5240 with L5259 respectively. Later No 301 Squadron continued the operations with a mixed assortment of aircraft, JN-K:L5448, JN-R:L5545, GR-P:L5549, GR-E:P6567, GR-G:P6556 and GR-D:P6569. The squadrons then withdrew from operations and prepared themselves to operate Wellingtons.

It will be recalled that when the Wellington was ordered into production a proviso was made that machines from the shadow factory would be powered by Merlin Xs to ease any production bottleneck concerning the much-needed Bristol Pegasus. No real emergency in engine production ever arose, but the great demand on the Rolls-Royce Merlin lines for the three principal fighters was such that few could be spared for any bomber aircraft. It was indeed one reason why the Mosquito was never adopted when first mooted.

Design work on the Merlin-engined Wellington had been initiated in January 1938, and on March 3 1939, the prototype of the Mk II, L4250, a modified Mk I airframe, made its initial flight. It differed from the Mk I in other important aspects. It had Frazer-Nash turrets like the Mk IA, and the superior 24-volt electrical system. Its more powerful engines in heavier units than the radials had an unfortunate aspect. They forced the centre of gravity forward, this considerably upsetting the trim as well as being linked with increased all-up weight. A solution was eventually found in a larger tailplane and stronger undercarriage with slightly larger diameter wheels. These requirements, the results of trials, and the great demands on the Merlin in 1940, delayed the aircraft, which in its production form proved superior to the Mk IC on several counts. Increased power improved take-off characteristics and allowed an increased all-up weight. This afforded either a heavier bomb load or more fuel. The Mk II was faster and it had a higher ceiling. Against this the availability of engines had to be set, whilst in service the new Mk II suffered from engine overheating on numerous occasions and was not popular with those squadrons which operated only a handful. Others more fully equipped encountered much less trouble with an aircraft which had one great advantage. In the autumn of 1940 the possibility of increased bomb load was considered and it was decided to adapt the Mk II to carry the new 4,000 lb bomb. There were problems with the weapon and it was March 1941 before it was cleared for service. No Mk IIs had yet flown on operations.

An initial order was agreed for 200 Wellington IIs which materialised as T2545 (an experimental machine) and production aircraft W5353-5401, W5414-5463, W5476-5500, W5513-5537, W5550-5598 and W5611. First to receive them was No 12 Squadron at Binbrook, which took W5353 and '54 on strength on November 10 1940. The next two aircraft went to 142 Squadron at Driffield. But it was April 1941 before they commenced operations, the long conversion period being due to slow operational development of the type and crew shortages, since front-line squadrons were making great demands on the output from OTUs.

The Wellington II was little more than an interesting addition to squadron strength. Much more important and larger shapes had joined, or were about to join, Bomber Command. The first of these aircraft was the giant four-engined Short Stirling whose origins lay in Specification B.12/36 and upon which great hopes were pinned. Suffice at the moment to say that it entered production in July 1940. The first to join No 7 Squadron at Leeming, N3640, is reputed to have come on strength on August 2. No proof that this actually happened seems yet to have been forthcoming and so it would be interesting to hear from any readers who then served with 7 Squadron, or who can throw some light on this aspect.

Initially it was planned to equip the squadron with eight aircraft for trials, as this new exciting large four-engined bomber was the herald of the force with which Bomber Command was to destroy the German industrial machine. Stirlings in their early days attracted much undesired attention. Oft-pictured N3641 was fired upon over the Isle of Man in September, being an unfamiliar shape to the AA gunners. Over the Thames Estuary on their test flights from Shorts at Rochester, Stirlings aroused much suspicion amongst fighter pilots despite their 'trainer' camouflage and, at one time, their 'Sky' under surfaces. Late in October the squadron moved to its operational station, Oakington. But it was December 20 before one of the huge machines, N3637, moved in.

Another new type had by then made its debut in Bomber Command. Great things were also expected of this machine, the Avro Manchester. It, too, was conceived to a 1936 specification, as a bomber for world-wide service and the latest in the changing chain of 'general purpose' aircraft. It stemmed from a most exacting requirement which made almost impossible demands upon the aircraft industry. On November 6, L7279, the fourth production example, touched down at Boscombe Down where No 207 Squadron was to receive several before taking them to its war station, Waddington. By the end of November, L7278, '7283 and '7284 were on strength, by which time another important new aircraft was in RAF hands. This was the Handley-Page Halifax whose origins lay in the same specification as the Manchester but which, in the project stage, had been re-planned as a four-engined bomber. No 35 Squadron was the first recipient and on November 13, L9486 passed into its hands, also at the experimental station on Salisbury Plain. But these were merely beginnings of a new era still really far off. Upon the Wellington IC, the Hampden, Blenheim IV and the Whitley V, Bomber Command had to rely for a very long time.

Against the searchlights

Apart from the introduction of revised roundels and fin stripes on the night bombers, and the painting of Blenheims and some Battles in the day bomber scheme, there was little change in bomber markings until the strategic offensive got fully under way in summer 1940. By then very few Wellingtons and Hampdens had under-wing roundels; exceptionally one could see Hampdens wearing them as late as 1941. Blenheims and the repainted Battles also wore them at this time.

The addition of the yellow outer ring to fuselage roundels, ideal for identification purposes, brought misgivings amongst bomber crews. Visible signs of this appeared, certainly in 3 and 4 Groups, in July 1940. Wellingtons and Whitleys had either a grey wash over the white of the fuselage roundels, black paint over these areas, and/or 'doctoring' of the wide yellow ring. There was never any consistency of these features on any of the many bombers I recorded, nor among those of any one unit. Whilst this change was manifest-

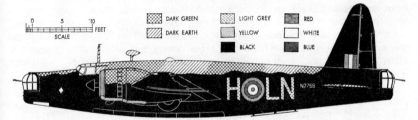

Figure 9: *Vickers Wellington IC, N2768, 'H' of 99 Sqn. Code letters and serials very light grey. Exhaust collector ring on some Mk IC aircraft were a reddish colour, but on this aircraft were a shade of mid-grey. Exhaust pipes were bronze-grey. Recorded at Waterbeach, March 22 1941.*

ing itself there was at the other extreme 11 OTU where Wellingtons acquired pale blue KJ and OP letters of a tone I never saw on any other bombers.

Blenheims of 2 Group usually wore grey codes but an interesting exception concerned those of Nos 15 and 40 Squadrons at Wyton. They applied red codes to their aircraft and outlined them in white, a colour retained until they received Wellingtons. I first noted this change early in August 1940. At no time did they ever wear grey codes outlined white, as erroneously depicted elsewhere.

On July 9, I first recorded a quite different feature. A passing Wellington had a most unusual extension of its matt black under surfaces from wing root up the sides of the fuselage rear and sweeping down to the tailplane leading edge. Within a few days I had noted others similarly but never identically marked. Some Wellingtons retained such markings well into 1941. P9248, recorded at Mildenhall at the end of July 1940, is illustrated from a sketch then made (see page 68). Grey codes remained and the serial number was either re-applied in grey or left in black on a 'box' of the old camouflage. From Wellington crews it soon emerged that these markings were to defeat the searchlights for which reason the white roundel had been overpainted and some yellow rings reduced to narrow bands.

By August 1940, the black sides were common, soon extending higher up the fuselage and terminating in irregular wavy lines, the number of wave tops varying in size and style from aircraft to aircraft. An extension of the black finish which assumed a super-matt texture had meanwhile appeared on the fins and rudders of many bombers, and by November the black had been extended on some Wellingtons to cover the entire rear fuselage from the fin leading edge aft, but many aircraft, even late in 1941, retained some upper surface camouflage in this area. The ultimate in Wellington markings (which included extension of the black on the nose from about August 1940) was the overpainting in black of the long side windows. Although these had a gun station aft, it was felt that any means of reducing the very troublesome searchlight glare in the aircraft was worth seizing, hence the overpainting. Beam guns were often not fitted.

For operations on winter nights in 1940/41, Blenheims also acquired black under surfaces and tails, to a limited extent. Since these squadrons formed basically a day force, only a portion of each squadron had black aircraft.

Grey codes and serials on the black were the norm, but some early Stirlings, Manchesters and Halifaxes had red serials on their Dark Green and Dark Earth finish, the extension of the black not appearing until March 1941 on these.

This, then, was a period of flux where markings were concerned. Only a basic outline can really be given, for precise camouflage varied from aircraft to aircraft and the usual A and B camouflage patterns were still in vogue.

October in many respects represented a watershed where squadron equipment was concerned. The following table covers the end of an era and the birth of a new one, and indicates equipment state on November 30 1940.

Sqn	Base	Aircraft	Sqn identity letters	Example in use
7	Oakington/Leeming	Stirling I	none	N3636
9	Honington	Wellington IC	WS	L7799:D
10	Leeming	Whitley V	ZA	T4265:J
12	Binbrook	Wellington II	PH	W5395:T
15	Wyton	Wellington IC	LS	T2702:H
18	Gt Massingham	Blenheim IV	WV	T1862
21	Watton	Blenheim IV	YH	R3675:A
35	Leeming	Halifax I	none	L7244
40	Wyton	Wellington IC	BL	R1166:M
44	Waddington	Hampden	KM	X3026:R
49	Scampton	Hampden	EA	X2900:S
50	Lindholme	Hampden	VN	P3004
51	Dishforth	Whitley V	MH	P5027:H
57	Feltwell	Wellington IC	DX	T2713:Q
58	Linton-on-Ouse	Whitley V	GE	P5058:F
61	Hemswell	Hampden	QR	P4339:H
75	Feltwell	Wellington IC	AA	R1177:F
77	Topcliffe	Whitley V	KN	N1524:G
78	Dishforth	Whitley V	EY	T4209:W
82	Watton	Blenheim IV	UX	R3594:F
83	Scampton	Hampden	OL	X2978:K
99	Newmarket	Wellington IC	LN	R3199:S
101	West Raynham	Blenheim IV	SR	P6908:D
102	Topcliffe	Whitley V	DY	T4135:K
103	Newton	Wellington IC	PM	R1043
105	Swanton Morley	Blenheim IV	GB	L8788:N
106	Finningley	Hampden	ZN	P1320:B
107	Wattisham	Blenheim IV	OM	N3575
110	Wattisham	Blenheim IV	VE	T1993
114	Oulton	Blenheim IV	RT	T1830
115	Marham	Wellington IC	KO	R1084:Q
139	Horsham	Blenheim IV	XD	R3611:N
142	Waltham	Wellington II	QT	W5364
144	Hemswell	Hampden	PL	X3007
149	Mildenhall	Wellington IC	OJ	P9247:M
150	Newton	Wellington IC	JN	R1042:A
207	Waddington	Manchester	EM	L7279
214	Stradishall	Wellington IC	BU	N2778:R
218	Marham	Wellington IC	HA	R1009:L
300	Swinderby	Wellington IC	BH	R1183:B
301	Swinderby	Wellington IC	GR	R1006:H
304	Syerston	Wellington IC	NZ	R1215
305	Syerston	Wellington IC	SM	R1213
311	East Wretham	Wellington IC	KX	R1021:W

Chapter 9

The Short Stirling

LONG BEFORE the bombers of the pre-war expansion were hardware the Air Ministry had formulated plans for successors. In 1935 they issued a requirement for an enlarged twin-engined machine. Then, somewhat influenced by American thought, they considered the possibility of a well-defended four-engined long-range bomber carrying a very much-increased bomb load. The Air Staff had already commissioned papers outlining an 'Ideal Bomber' but its contributors did not agree. Eventually, an extensive requirement, B12/36, was issued on July 15 1936 for a bomber for world-wide use whose speed was not less than 230 mph at 15,000 feet, and whose range would be over 3,000 miles. It was to be highly manoeuvrable and have 2-gun nose, 4-gun tail and 2-gun ventral turrets, giving it good protection since it was not to be confined to night operations. Its maximum bomb load was to be 14,000 lb; it should have rest facilities for a spare crew and be capable of carrying 24 troops for whom windows serving also as emergency exits were to be fitted. A crew of six included a co-pilot. On 2/3 power its effective range must be at least 1,500 miles. A good take-off and landing performance was required permitting operations from standard grass fields to obviate expensive runway construction programmes. In retrospect, the most regrettable demands were for provisioning to carry weapons increasing in size to the new 2000 lb AP bomb, and a restriction on wing span to 100 feet to allow the aircraft to fit existing hangars. Additionally, components had to break down small enough to fit standard packing cases for transport by rail. It was these three latter points that eventually damned the aeroplane chosen in answer to the need.

Early in 1937 all the usual contenders to bomber design contributed their schemes—Armstrong Whitworth, Avro, Bristol, Handley Page, Shorts, Supermarine and Vickers. Most of them already had large major projects in hand or would soon have—except for Supermarine and Shorts. Their tenders were closely considered and accepted in February 1937. Both received prototype contracts in September of that year. Although very elegant, the two Supermarine designs dragged behind Shorts' contender. Both Supermarine prototypes were destroyed in a 1940 attack on their works. Only the Short B12/36 was left.

To answer all the needs of the specification required no mean feat. To equate speed, bomb load, range and troop-carrying requirement with the limitation on size could only lead to a less effective aeroplane than might have been the case. Shorts drew up a project which offered a good performance—particularly at higher altitudes—and submitted it, complete with 112-foot wing span. The Air Ministry would not agree to this. Accordingly the span was cut to 99 feet; from then onwards the design began to suffer.

To achieve maximum load-carrying characteristics a low-aspect ratio wing was chosen somewhat akin to that of the Sunderland. With its thick section

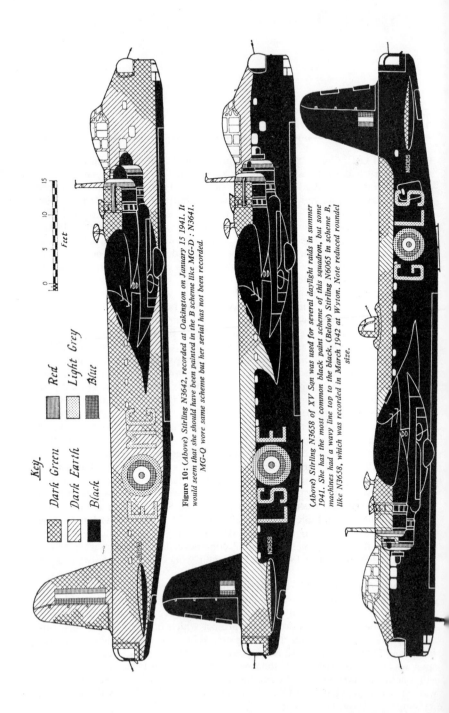

Key.

Dark Green

Dark Earth

Black

Red

Light Grey

Blue

Figure 10: *(Above) Stirling N3642, recorded at Oakington on January 15 1941. It would seem that she should have been painted in the B scheme like MG-D : N3641. MG-Q wore same scheme but her serial has not been recorded.*

(Above) Stirling N3658 of XV Sqn was used for several daylight raids in summer 1941. She has the most common black paint scheme of this squadron, but some machines had a wavy line top to the black. (Below) Stirling N6065 in scheme B, like N3658, which was recorded in March 1942 at Wyton. Note reduced roundel size.

and high drag it was set midway on the long 87-foot fuselage. Huge Gouge flaps which slid out of the wing in stately style were incorporated in a wing whose angle of attack needed careful thought to achieve good take-off performance. Like so many designs the bomber suffered from increasing all-up weight which rapidly climbed from 48,000 to 55,000 lb. By the time the aircraft entered squadron service its all-up weight was nearly 60,000 lb, allowing a maximum take-off weight of 70,000 lb. Performance suffered. Increased load and high drag from the wing all affected its characteristics, drastically reducing its service ceiling below the stipulated 28,000 feet.

Influenced by their small-scale Scion which tested ideas for a larger flying boat, Shorts decided to build a half-scale Stirling powered by Pobjoy Niagaras and designated S31. In all-silver finish the model first flew on September 9 1938, proving useful early in the bomber development programme.

Other events had meanwhile occurred. Increased German belligerence prompted a massive up-to-date re-armament programme. On April 11 1938, 100 production Short bombers were ordered and the type was soon named Stirling. Under programme L, 1,500 Stirlings were to be built by Shorts, by Short and Harland, Belfast, to follow the Hereford line there, and by Austins who would commence production once their Battle order was complete, and also by Rootes. A production line in Canada was also a popular notion, but this was never established because of the complexity of the aeroplane and the likely need to ship engines to Canada.

Brief trials with S31 prompted the Ministry to ask for a greater wing angle of attack. This could be achieved only by lengthening the undercarriage struts. It resulted in a long, lanky undercarriage which, although ingenious, gave trouble on the squadrons and particularly at training units.

The prototype, L7600, first flew May 14 1939. On landing it suffered brake binding, the pressure set up causing the undercarriage to fail after which the aircraft was wrecked. The undercarriage was simply not strong enough. Also finished in Dark Green-Dark Earth-Night camouflage, the second prototype had Type B roundels. Its undercarriage was re-worked and strengthened. Basically the huge 6-foot diameter wheel retracted backwards into a crate which swung forward into the nacelle as fairing doors closed around the wheel and leaving it partially exposed.

The second Stirling, L7605, first flew on December 3 1939. It was powered by four Hercules HE1 Mas and passed to Boscombe Down for trials on April 22 1940. Meanwhile, production had slowly come under way. On May 7 1940, the first aircraft (N3635) was flown. It had distinctive yellow under surfaces and wore Type A fuselage roundels early in its career, along with tall fin striping. Five hundred Stirlings were now on order and like other early examples the first one had Hercules II engines. Other early machines had Hercules Is, IIIs and XIs.

Now the cry was for fully operational aircraft from the industry and production schedules for new types slipped. N3638 emerged as a second production machine, held for development work. Three are believed to have been completed in July 1940, one in August and two in September, the slow production rate due partially to constant air raid warnings and the bombing of Shorts' Rochester factory on August 15. Six machines on the line, N3645 and 3647-51, were destroyed. At this time some of the early Stirlings were flying with Sky under surfaces apparently as an aid to their safety in a zone where British fighters were active. Flight trials were quite dangerous and there were several occasions when anti-aircraft guns around the Thames Estuary area fired upon the strange new machines which flew escorted by fighters.

Far away in relative safety at Leeming, near Northallerton, No 7 Squadron re-formed under Wg Cdr P. I. Harris, DFC, on August 1. Establishment of an intensive trials flight of eight Stirlings was intended. N3640 was allotted to the squadron on August 2.

Certain aspects of the exciting new bomber were readily apparent. It was extremely stable, and amazingly manoeuvrable for it could be thrown around in a most memorable manner. Engines were suffering teething troubles, and pronounced swing on take-off needed care. A run of about 1,400 yards was needed to clear 50 feet. On landing, care was also needed and the unusual undercarriage caused trouble throughout the Stirling's career. Too much braking, a difficult cross wind—not to mention any battle damage— all could and did bring trouble, and a visit to a Stirling base often revealed one of these huge machines with one undercarriage unit bent or retracted.

Six months shake-in was required, for the Stirling was, by 1940 standards, a highly complex piece of machinery. Many modifications were needed and by the end of the year only 15 production machines had been completed. Four had joined 7 Squadron when N3640 crashed in Lincolnshire at the end of September. No doubts were expressed about the excellent defensive armament, but the retractable ventral dustbin, which later became troublesome, was removed before operations commenced. Immense strength was a feature of the Stirling. It was well made and whilst favoured of course by the crews this actually impeded high-speed production.

In bad weather and when carrying a heavy load, it was soon apparent that all was not well, and the Stirling's ceiling was considerably below that expected in such conditions. Its lengthy fuselage had required longitudinal stiffening. In consequence the bomb bay was divided into long narrow cells able only to accommodate weapons in size up to the 2,000 lb bomb. Again in months ahead this was most unfortunate for, although the machine was able to lift a 14,000 lb offensive load, it could not carry the 4,000 lb blockbuster. This restricted the Stirling to operating with a 500 lb or 1,000 lb load, frequently mines and huge incendiary loads. A typical load was 18 × 500 lb in the bomb bay and three 500 pounders in each wing's cells and some extra tankage. With a full load of 14,000 lb range was 690 miles, 1,390 miles with 5,000 lb load. Maximum range was 2,330 miles and top speed about 260 mph at 10,500 feet. Weight empty was 44,000 lb, all-up weight 59,400 lb.

One hundred Stirlings were to be built at Belfast as N6000-6049, 6065-6104 and 6120-6129. The first of these flew on October 18 and was delivered from Belfast on October 25 1940. It differed from the Rochester-built aircraft in that its black camouflage terminated in a straight line high upon the fuselage and swept up to the all-black fin. Serials were grey.

Existence of the Stirling was by now barely secret. Many had seen the small handbook of silhouettes of British aircraft that circulated around the ROC posts and to the Home Guard. I well remember how excited our local band of enthusiasts was when word passed around that those weird coloured reconnaissance Spitfires at Oakington and the Blenheims of 218 Squadron stationed there were to be joined by a secret four-engined bomber. It remained to be seen which it would be. Officially 7 Squadron moved to Oakington on October 29 but there were no Stirlings there for many weeks. I caught my first glimpse of one on December 12 as it circled Cambridge before lowering its curious undercarriage and turning for Oakington. It was in standard bomber colours, but the black underside terminated at the 60 degree tangent and the tail was in upper surface colours. The aircraft carried no code letters.

In the first week of January 1941, squadron letters were applied on the aircraft in dark grey, N3636 becoming MG-A. Mingling with those in standard colours were three Stirlings with yellow under surfaces, one of which was N3637. None of these wore codes. N6003 : MG-V ('MG' forward of the fuselage roundels on both sides of the aircraft in standard style) was set aside for intensive flying. On February 9 one of her undercarriage legs would not lower. She droned round and round whilst the crew threw out as much load as possible. This went on for five hours until a belly landing was made. The crew survived the ordeal. Next day, following some postponements, three Stirlings (N3642, N3644 and the oft-pictured N3641 : MG-D) were prepared for operations. A small point of interest was that they all wore red serials. On the evening of February 10 they set off led by Sqn Ldr Griffiths-Jones for a successful attack on oil tanks at Rotterdam. Four days after the raid I had a close look at N3641 and N3642 : MG-E being bombed up for the evening's operation against Ostend. Both machines now had black areas extended up the fuselage to terminate in an irregular wavy line. Codes remained grey and a strip of camouflage continued along the rear fuselage above which soared the black tail now sporting smaller fin striping. Oakington was now a sea of mud. PRU Spitfires based there were operating from Alconbury and the Stirlings transferred to Newmarket Heath. Operations were being made with a handful of aircraft. On March 17 N3652 set off for Bremen to make the first Stirling sortie to Germany. Although Newmarket had only a grass runway and failure to get airborne meant a crash into the Devil's Dyke, it afforded a useful long run and a number of raids were flown from here before 7 Squadron's aircraft returned to Oakington. On April 9 the target was, for the first time, Berlin. But this was asking too much and N6009 returned with engine trouble; N6005 bombed Hanover instead and of N6011 nothing more was heard. The first bombing of Berlin took place on April 17 when N6010 reached the city and N6009 raided Cologne.

The first daylight raid by Stirlings was attempted on April 29 with Wilhelmshaven the target for N6010. Cloud cover ran out so the bombs were directed at a convoy instead.

The first Stirlings from the Austin Longbridge production line were delivered in April by which time some crews were at Wyton where XV Squadron had begun converting to fly Stirlings. Their first aircraft, N3644, arrived April 11 1941. During April, flying was intensive and on the 30th, XV's first raid was optimistically launched against Berlin, but none of the aircraft despatched (LS-B : N3654, LS-A : N6015, LS-F : N6004 and LS-C : N6018) was able to penetrate so far. Early 'W' serialled aircraft used by XV Squadron included W7427 : LS-B and W7429 : LS-J.

A memorable night was May 2. N6012 was returning to Oakington from Hamburg when an intruder—probably a Ju 88c—caught it and shot it down in a mass of flames visible for miles around. Its remnants fell near Dry Drayton village. Spasmodic day raids were now flown, five aircraft attempting to bomb Cologne on May 25 1941. Near hits were later scored on a ship off Holland and on June 9 N6020 returned from Dunkirk peppered with over 200 holes from intercepting Bf 109s. The Stirling always showed an amazing ability to absorb punishment. Already it was apparent that for daylight operations beam defence was essential. At Oakington in the early months of 1941 several Stirlings appeared with a gun poking from a side window and eventually two beam guns were standard. This was insufficient and replaced by a dorsal FN7 turret like that for the Botha, which appeared on aircraft supplied to 7 Squadron in June 1941. Its introduction was timely for in July small formations of Stirlings heavily escorted by fighters were launched on *Circus* operations over France to entice enemy fighters to battle. Both 7 and XV Squadrons took part, finding few fighters but the flak formidable. Into July the raids continued and then came an abrupt ending. A large-scale operation against the *Scharnhorst* and *Gneisenau* had been planned in July 1941. When all was ready *Scharnhorst* sailed. Hurriedly, five Stirlings (W7434, N6037 and N6035 of 7 Squadron and LS-F:W7428 with LS-R:N6038 of XV Squadron) set off to attack her at La Pallice using 2,000 lb AP bombs. N6038 was shot down, but one crew claimed a hit on the ship.

No more daylight raids were flown until late in 1941. By August 1941, a sprinkling of Stirlings had FN7 dorsal turrets, including W7444: MG-L and W7447: MG-V. N6006: MG-G, with a Donald Duck motif on the port side of her nose, settled for beam guns, and the black paintwork on her sides terminated in a wavy line, swept up to the fin. W7429: LS-J was XV Squadron's only dorsal turreted aircraft on August 5. LS-S: N3665 and LS-H: N3656, without dorsal turrets at this time, had their black areas ending in a straight line along the fuselage, again with an upswept area to the fin. Whereas XV Squadron had its unit letters placed aft of the roundels, 7 Squadron carried its letters ahead.

On September 10 thirteen Stirlings set off for the first Stirling venture to Italy, the only one in 1941. Among the force were N3667: LS-T and W7440 of 7 Squadron. Turin was a long way to fly and the aircraft's poor ceiling meant a journey fraught with grave dangers. In some cases the crews threaded their way between the mountains in terrifying darkness. Some of the aircraft now in use were Mk I series ii fitted with Hercules XI engines.

Berlin, Magdeburg, Kiel, Karlsruhe, Duisburg, Cologne—all had figured in the operational order for the squadrons by now. On October 28 nine Stirlings of the two squadrons were despatched to distant Pilsen, but it was a fruitless venture.

Relying upon cloud cover some daylight operations were mounted in November. The most memorable came on the 24th when N6095: MG-K (the machine the Airfix model is based upon) and W7449: MG-J set off to attack shipping off Borkum. Bf 109s intercepted them and a running fight followed. Two fighters were claimed but MG-K was shot down in flames into the sea.

During November 149 Squadron at Mildenhall began to equip with Stirlings. One of its early machines was N6009: OJ-C, fitted with a dorsal turret. At this time Stirlings began to arrive at Waterbeach, gathered partly from Conversion Flights attached to squadrons. Additionally, some 'war weary' Stirlings were flown in and a training unit was soon under way. It became No 1651 Conversion Unit on January 2 1942. Many of its aircraft bore traces of previous squadron letters but for a long time 1651 CU possessed no unit identity letters of its own. N3652: M had been MG-M and N3676: LS-S, both without dorsal turrets.

On December 18 nineteen Stirlings (N3669: MG-E, W7436: D, N3668: B, N6089: L, MG-K, W7449, N3700: A, N3680, N6121 and W7454 of 7 Squadron, and LS-F: N6086, C: N6093, N6098: G, N6092: O, N3673: D, N6088: Q, N3676: U, N3665: B and W7428: Z of XV Squadron) participated in a major operation. A large number of bombers under a fighter escort was despatched to Brest in daylight. The flight was fierce and four Stirlings were shot down. Seven 109s latched on to LS-G: N6098 but it survived, and was not once hit by enemy fire. Others were less fortunate and on passing Bourn two days after the operation I saw MG-L looking forlorn with a burst main tyre, both tailwheel tyres burst and in pathetically shot-up state. No dorsal turret was fitted. It was at this time that small squadron letters were introduced on the Stirlings of 7 Squadron. I first recorded such a serial-letter tie up on December 29 on W7436 : MG-D. Both 7 and XV Squadrons were also concerned with another innovation, the introduction of Trinity Oboe for limited trial attacks on Brest. This was a special radar bombing device from which the highly effective Oboe gear stemmed in late 1942. N3668 : B-MG and W7454 : S-MG had it fitted. Undoubtedly the best-known 1941 Stirling was *MacRoberts Reply*, LS-F : N6086 which, between October 1941 and January 1942, flew about a dozen sorties. A Stirling that flew a sizeable number of missions in 1941 was N3669, successively MG-H, MG-E, MG-D and later LS-H, and which ultimately managed over 60 sorties.

Chapter 10

The Avro Manchester

THE REQUIREMENT is 'for a twin-engined medium bomber for world-wide use ... that can exploit the alternatives between long-range and very heavy bomb load ... the highest cruising speed is necessary'. These were the basic points of Specification P 13/36 for the bomber to replace the new interim types and to operate alongside the Stirling in the 1940s. It was to lead to a disastrous failure, to a bomber of fine and rather unsung qualities, and to the two most efficient bombers of the war years. Ironically the machine which seemed originally to meet the specification's needs was a costly failure.

The Air Ministry developed during 1935 two specifications for bombers for the 1940s, one tipping the scales at 45,000 lb, the other at 55,000 lb. The former, P 13/36, was to have a top speed of 275 mph at 15,000 ft and a range of 3,000 miles when carrying a 4,000 lb bomb load. Nose and tail turrets were needed and bombs could, if necessary, be accommodated in tiers in foreign style. Mindful of overseas needs the specification read, 'there is a possibility of combining medium-bomber, general reconnaissance and general purpose classes in one basic design', and suggested that provision also be made for two 18-inch torpedoes. A more novel possibility was the use of remotely controlled guns. It was in all a tough requirement.

On September 8 1936 the Specification letter was passed to the industry. Here was a need for a high-performance bomber accommodating an 8,000 lb bomb load and up to 12 armed troops. It needed to break down into components which would fit standard packing cases; at the other extreme, short field take-off and landing performance from grass fields was expected, qualified by remarks about the possibility of 'frictionless take-off' implying catapult launching of some sort. In essence, P 13/36 was a smaller two-motor edition of B 12/36 (the Stirling's spec), and it interested a number of contractors.

Three basically similar projects eventually evolved. From Hawker there came a twin-Vulture layout with low-set wings; Handley Page opted for a mid-wing and twin-fin form not unlike the tender from A. V. Roe which also had two Rolls-Royce Vulture engines. Tenders were submitted in January 1937.

A few months later, prototypes of the HP 56 and Avro 679 were ordered, as L7244/45 and L7246/47 respectively. The new Rolls-Royce Vulture engine which was to power them was, in effect, two 12-cylinder engines based upon the highly successful Kestrel, one of them inverted leading to an 'X' cross section around a central crankcase. Early promise was shown and the engine was to develop over 1,500 hp— half as much again as the Merlin was then delivering. But soon some basic troubles arose and the engine was in jeopardy. This prompted the Air Ministry to take out an insurance policy on P 13/36 and begin prodding Handley Page to re-design its project to take four Merlin engines, lifting increased all-up weight. Reluctantly the firm agreed to this—

and the famous Handley Page Halifax bomber was under way.

Avro, however, persevered with their plans. With considerable foresight Roy Chadwick, the chief designer, had begun his project around a bomb bay of proportions which would allow the carrying of far larger bombs than generally envisaged at this time. He had to provide for the torpedo load, too, which meant a combination of wide capacious bomb bay and long doors. He carefully watched the undercarriage design, determined to avoid the complication Shorts had encountered with the Stirling. Thus, two unfortunate features of the Stirling were avoided, narrow bomb cells with small doors and a lanky troublesome undercarriage. With the Avro 679 as the only accepted tender, a production schedule was drawn up in Specification 19/37. Early in 1938 the first production order was placed, for 200 aircraft, L7276-7325, L7373-7402, L7453-7497 and L7515-7526. Although the Vulture engine was still in trouble the two prototypes went forward and initial production plans were laid. Repeated adjustments were being made to the whole bomber programme. In the Expansion Scheme of October 1938, it was proposed to build 1,500 Short B 12/36s, 1,500 Avro 679s and 500 of the Handley Page design. Following the completion of Battle production Fairey Aviation would build 150 Avro 679s. Another 150 would come from Armstrong Whitworth once Whitley production was completed. At Manchester another 100 would be built by Metropolitan-Vickers and flown from Avro's field. Contracts were placed with all these sub-contractors under the Shadow Scheme.

Departure from the original Avro design had already been made. The company had designed a 72-foot span aeroplane to carry an 8,000 lb load 2,000 miles at a top speed of 289 mph. By now it was a heavier machine, its span increased to 82 feet 2 inches. Top speed was accordingly reduced. Increased all-up weight without extra power was the first big nail in its coffin

No agreement had yet been made as to whether any special take-off scheme would be needed, but eventually it was to be completely conventional, although catapult and tracked take-off experiments were performed in a venture into the fantastic. Fear lingered that the heavy bomber would require a very long take-off run, preferably from a runway when only grass fields were available. Special provision was therefore made on the early production machines for assisted take-off.

On July 25 1939, L7246, the first prototype of the 679 for which the name Manchester was chosen, made its initial flight. High wing loading made it a difficult aeroplane to handle, particularly as it was immediately apparent that it was under-powered and depended on two unreliable engines. It had no turrets which, when installed, would add considerably to the weight. During the summer of 1939, in its Dark Green-Dark Earth-Night finish with white under-wing serials and Type A1 roundels, it made a few flights between bouts of unserviceability. After the outbreak of war, L7246 was flying with under-wing serials overpainted, and Type B fuselage and wing roundels. It passed then to A & AEE at Boscombe Down for initial trials. Stability left much to be desired, and so an unusual third fin was fitted for tests at Farnborough. L7246 then returned to Boscombe Down. Engine trouble struck during an approach on December 12, as a result of which it slithered to an ignominious halt in a cabbage field. Repairs were effected and further handling work went ahead, whilst at Manchester L7247 was nearing completion. This, too, had short span wings and for a time featured a 'shark's fin' third tail. From the start it was armed, with nose and tail FN turrets and a retractable FN21A dustbin turret, and first flew on May 26 1940. Both Manchesters went to

82

Code letters were light
grey

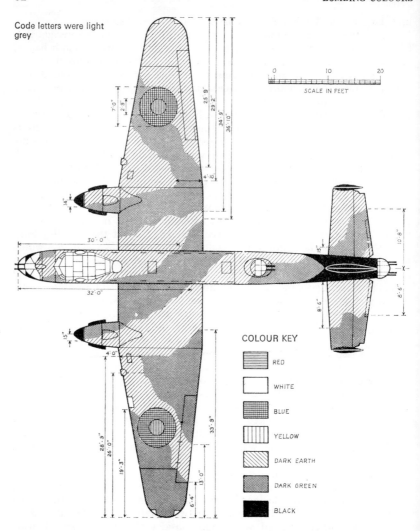

SCALE IN FEET

COLOUR KEY

RED

WHITE

BLUE

YELLOW

DARK EARTH

DARK GREEN

BLACK

Figure 11: (*Above and top on facing page*) *Manchester R5771 wearing camouflage pattern A. When the scheme for alternate patterns was dropped at the beginning of 1941, pattern A was used on all subsequent aircraft. In the drawings issued by the manufacturer, upon which these are based, instructions were that the aircraft be finished in the very rough matt 'Special Night'. This finish crept slowly into use early in 1940, and reproducing it on a model would be very difficult since, although it resembled a layer of soot, it dried out to form light and dark patches—in short, it looked a horrible mess! Not all bombers in front-line service had it, but it was common and was the norm. Often an undercoat layer of the earlier Night finish showed through. The very large diameter fuselage roundels on the early Manchesters were 5 feet 6½ inches in diameter (9½-inch bands); the smaller were the more standard 49-inch with 7-inch bands. Prior to the introduction of Type C1 roundels a further reduction to 42 inches was made on some aircraft. The camouflage measurements given by A. V. Roe, and repeated on the drawing, must be taken as a guide; they were of course not slavishly repeated on each aircraft. R5771 was built in 1941 and delivered to 25 OTU in March 1942, to 83 Sqn on April 13 1942, to 49 Sqn on April 15 1942, to 420 Sqn on May 23 1942, to 57 Sqn on September 6 1942, and joined No 50 Con Flight for Lancaster training on September 23 1942. She then settled at 1654 Conversion Unit from October 10 1942 until moving to 2 AGS on May 27 1943, where she became 3746M. She survived the war being struck off charge on December 6 1945. Her only operations, with 49 Sqn, were mining and leaflet dropping sorties. (Beneath R5771 on facing page) Manchester L7417 : ZN-V (codes 4-feet high) was held a long time in storage and eventually joined 106 Sqn in March 1942. As a trainer she subsequently served in 106 Con Flt and for a few days was with 1660 Con Unit in October 1942*

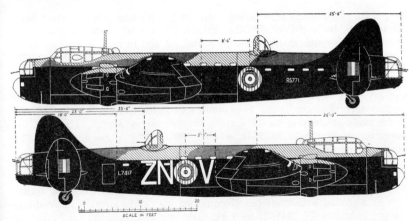

Boscombe for tests on July 9, 7246 returning to Woodford six weeks later. Neither were viewed with much enthusiasm. Stability problems, over-weight, engine snags—all were quite serious; but the aircraft had one redeeming feature, that huge bomb bay. If only it could reliably lift the possible load for a useful distance! Production was in any case under way. In July, L7276 was flying and it passed to Boscombe for acceptance trials on August 8. By September the first production machines were well advanced.

There was still much development work required to bring out that Standard Manchester I to which the following details apply. All the production aircraft had a further span increase, to 90 ft 1 in. The Vulture engine was rated at 1,760 hp. Two pilots, a navigator, wireless operator and three gunners formed the usual crew. In the nose was fitted an FN5 turret; the tail turret was the FN20 and in about the first 20 aircraft a retractable dustbin turret was fitted. Subsequently, from early 1941, this was replaced by the FN7 'Botha type' dorsal turret. A maximum bomb load of 10,350 lb could be carried, but a more usual load was 8 × 1,000 lb bombs. Its empty weight was 29,432 lb, mean weight 41,315 lb, but the loaded weight could be up to 50,000 lb. With an 8,000 lb load the range was 1,630 miles, or 1,200 with a 10,350 lb load. On trials a top speed of 265 mph at 17,000 feet was recorded, with the best cruise as 185 mph at 15,000 ft. Take-off to clear 50 feet in calm conditions needed a 1,300-yard run and the average landing run was 1,050 yards. Maximum speed recorded on one aircraft at mean weight was 258 mph at 7,000 ft, or 273 mph at 17,000 ft. Service ceiling was none too good at 19,200 feet (the Stirling's was 17,000). Naturally, this was based on the assumption that both engines were working—which unfortunately was not always so.

On August 29 it had been decided to re-form No 207 Squadron at Lind-holme to operate Manchesters. Plans were revised and on October 19 the basic elements of the squadron moved to Waddington. Flying personnel gathered at Boscombe Down and on November 1 the squadron officially re-formed. A week later the whole unit gathered at Waddington in 5 Group where the intention was to replace the Hampden with the Manchester. L7277, '78 and '79 were now in RAF hands. On November 6, 207 Squadron received its first machine, L7279, joined by '78 on the 10th and '80 on December 2. With these 207 Squadron began intensive flight trials. They were soon joined by L7283, '84 and '86. By the end of the year, 25 production aircraft were flying, and 207 Squadron was also using Coleby Grange. It was far from happy, for the engines were giving constant trouble and exhausts were burning through. By mid-February the squadron had worked up sufficiently for operations, although many problems remained, and to raise morale six crews were briefed on the 24th to bomb the *Hipper* at Brest. They set off in L7279, '84, '86, '88, '94 and L7300—and '84 crash landed on return with undercarriage trouble. Further problems were associated with the hydraulic system and oil leaks were occurring. There were other teething troubles, too, but limited operations continued. Five crews set out for Cologne on the 26th and seven raids amounting to 21 sorties were flown in March. The first loss occurred on March 27/28 1941, when L7303 : EM-P came down at Bakel, north-east of Eindhoven in Holland.

Production by sub-contractors had trod a varied path since 1938 and only Metropolitan-Vickers was building Manchesters. Their first aircraft, R5768, flew in February 1941. Sufficient Manchesters were available for the formation of a second squadron; No 97 equipped with eight aircraft, at Waddington on February 27 1941. It took up residence at Coningsby on March 11. On April 8/9, No 97 Squadron despatched its first raid, four aircraft, L7290, '91, '94 and 7308, being sent to Kiel with eight of 207 Squadron. With engine troubles abounding—they included engine seizure and faulty bearings—it was hardly surprising that Manchesters should be coming to grief. A flight on one engine was not unusual, but none the less frightening for that. On April 13, after 15 raids had been flown, it was decided to ground all Manchesters to sort out some of the increasing problems. So far they had been dropping 500 and 1,000 lb bombs and one of the modifications now made to some aircraft was the fitting of shackles for 4,000 pounders.

Operations were resumed on May 2 with a raid on Hamburg—immediately there was a loss, L7379 : EM-T. No 97 Squadron resumed operations on the 6th. On May 9 the first Berlin raid was attempted by 207 Squadron, and next night it was the target for six Manchesters from the two squadrons. Bremen and Mannheim were also bombed, Berlin on the 15th again by both squadrons. Then came another grounding. The aircraft would not climb at all well when loaded, and there were associated engine cooling and cabin heating problems. Resumption of operations came on June 21/22 and by now a third squadron, No 61, was involved. With Boulogne as target, 16 aircraft set forth, the largest force yet. Within a week four more operations were attempted and some 4,000 lb bombs dropped. Dusseldorf, Kiel and Hamburg were bombed—and on July 1 came yet another grounding, for all except six aircraft. Engines were too troublesome to permit operational flights. This time a concentrated attempt was to be made to cure the problems. One aircraft was to be supplied to each squadron fitted with engines specially overhauled by Rolls-Royce, and intensively flown. L7427 was placed in 97 Squadron, and L7389 : QR-J soon ended up in a wheatfield near Fowlmere, the subject of engine failure. This was a relatively lucky machine and crew, for often crashes resulted in complete write-offs. So troublesome was the Manchester that some squadrons, including No 97, were temporarily equipped with Hampdens for operations whilst the problems were looked into. For a month intensive investigation into engine failure proceeded; then on August 7/8 L7381 : EM-K and L7422 : EM-V were despatched to Essen and EM-T : L7373 to Duisburg. On August 12, 97 and 207 Squadrons attacked Berlin: but 61 Squadron proved a more effective force with its Hampdens. No 207 Squadron lost two aircraft, L7381 : R and L7377 : G. The cause of this was at the time unknown, but now it is established that L7381 crashed at 00.15 hrs on August 13 between Kolham and Sappemeer, not far from Groningen in north-east Holland. The reason? Engine trouble.

A more successful period was struck, although aerodynamic characteristics, were far from satisfactory. There was tail flutter to contend with and buffeting on the climb. Avro looked into these complaints. A redesigned tail unit seemed the answer. Tailplane span was increased from 28 to 33 feet and two much-enlarged fins replaced the triple tail. L7489 was 97's first modified aircraft, reaching the unit on September 20, when only 207 was operational. As if there had not been enough ill fortune, trouble with propeller feathering now occurred, and there were numerous crashes due to varying causes.

In the latter part of October, 97 Squadron resumed operations with some of the new aircraft and 207 received a few of the twin-tailed variety commonly called the Mk IA. These never entirely replaced the triple fin machines, which soldiered on to the end of the Manchester's days. Mine-laying was now being undertaken, and with somewhat improved reliability. The second largest Manchester operation so far, by 17 aircraft, was flown against Cologne on November 1. At the end of the year, two more major daylight raids were attempted against Brest, where the German battlecruisers lay. On the first of these, Operation *Sunrise I*, flown on December 18 1941, 97 Squadron despatched ten Manchesters (L7453:OF-X, L7489:K, L7463:P, L7492:A, R5795:W, L7460:J, L7525:D, L7491:C, L7475:G and L7488:F) and 207 Squadron sent ten as well (L7490:EM-U, L7453, L7489:K, L7463:P, L7492:O, L7406:J, L7525:D, L7491:C, L7425:G and L7488:F). R5795 was shot down by fighters and L7490 crashed on return. Only once again did Manchesters operate in daylight, on February 12 during the frantic attempt to sink the *Scharnhorst* and *Gneisenau* during their Channel dash.

With the basic snags fewer it was decided at the end of 1941 to issue Manchesters to four more squadrons. No 83 equipped in December, 106 in February and 50 in March. It was considered this would be for a very limited period. When a decision to halt the Vulture development programme was taken in 1940 the initial reaction of the Ministry of Aircraft Production was to cancel the Manchester, too, despite its advanced state of production. Sabre engines were mercifully rejected. In July 1940, satisfied that the basic layout of the aircraft was good, and in particular its load potential, Avro had begun to think in terms of a four-engined development. The company was determined that improvement should be along these lines, and the Manchester III, later renamed Lancaster, was born, the four-engined derivative of an unlucky parent. Seeing the similarity between the two aircraft, and considering the Manchester a stop gap now, 5 Group agreed to its squadrons equipping with them for use virtually as crew trainers.

In January 1942, Manchesters flew 121 sorties, all of them against maritime targets, including Bremen, Brest and Hamburg. On February 4/5, 83 Squadron commenced operations, sending four aircraft—OL-F:R5790, I:R5831, N:R5833 and G:R5779—on a mining operation. For the heavy raid on the Renault works near Paris on March 3, 5 Group mustered 47 Hampdens and 25 Manchesters. On March 8, for the first big operation relying on the *Gee* navigation aid, 34 Hampdens and 21 Manchesters formed part of the force despatched to Essen. On March 28, 20 Manchesters drawn from 61, 83 and 106 Squadrons were among the 234 aircraft sent to Lübeck. On nine nights in April, Manchester bombers operated, including amongst their targets Rostock, Essen, Hamburg and Cologne. On April 9, north-west of the Frisian Isle of Vlieland, a night fighter of II/NJG.2 destroyed L7427 of 83 Squadron.

Two new Manchester squadrons were now introduced to operations, No 50 on April 8/9 when L7432, L7489 and L7455 dropped leaflets in the Paris area, and No 49 Squadron on May 2/3 when L7496, L7386, L7484, L7287 and R5771 distributed leaflets around Rennes.

The highwater mark of Manchester operations was reached on the night of May 30/31 1942, when 35 out of 46 despatched attacked Cologne during Operation *Millenium*. Included were these aircraft: 49 Squadron—L7287, L7479, L7290, L7389, L7429, L7526, L7524, L7421, L7493, L7398, R5775 and R5794; 50 Squadron—R5784, L7471, R5796, L7319, L7468, L7432, L7525, L7491, L7476, L7460, L7301, L7475, L7456, L7419 and R5833; 61 Squadron—L7415, L7425, L7473 and L7427; 83 Squadron—L7293, L7397, R5768 and one other; 106 Squadron—R5841, L7434, R5796, R5780, L7391 and L7488; 408 Squadron—L7401 : $\overline{A}$; and 44 Squadron—L7430 : $\overline{N}$ and L7480 : $\overline{A}$.

Four Manchesters were lost. Two, L7290 and L7429, were from 49 Squadron, and another was L7301 of 50 Squadron piloted by Flg Off L. T. Manser. Over Mannheim his aircraft ran into heavy flak and was hit. The port engine caught fire and part of the wing was burnt. As the crippled bomber flew homewards it slowly lost height. All the crew except Manser baled out over Holland even though the aircraft was flying very low. The last to go handed Manser's parachute to him, but he remained at the controls of the machine, still presumably hoping to nurse it home. It crashed and he was killed. For his courage he was posthumously awarded the Victoria Cross, a mark of tribute to all who bravely took the Manchester into action.

In the Essen thousand bomber raid of June 1, 27 Manchesters took part. Only a few more operational sorties were flown, mainly mining. Final sorties were flown on June 25/26 during the third thousand bomber raid, this time on Bremen. The five participants were L7453, R5772, R5788 and R5850 of 49 Squadron and L7477 of 61 Squadron.

Nearly 1,000 operational bombing sorties had been flown by Manchesters, about 220 mining and another 60 or so dropping leaflets over France. The total number of sorties flown is said to be 1,269—the Lancaster was to fly over 156,000. On operations, 63 Manchesters were missing and three more were damaged beyond repair. No 61 Squadron incurred the highest loss rate, 13 aircraft out of the 47 used. No 207 Squadron lost 14 of its 65 machines. Peak months for losses were August 1941 (7), March 1942 (11), and May 1942 (12). In addition, 59 Manchesters are believed to have been lost in accidents.

Training for the squadrons was undertaken by 25 OTU at Finningley and four-aircraft Conversion Flights attached to each squadron in 1941-42. These were kept largely intact, and as the Manchester squadrons re-equipped some of them were also used by squadrons switching to the Lancaster, such as Nos 9, 44 and 57 Squadrons wherein they equipped Conversion Flights in the summer and autumn of 1942. No 1654 Conversion Unit at Swinderby began using Manchesters in May 1942, but it was October before the Manchesters were all withdrawn from 5 Group squadrons, in part to equip three more Conversion Units at Swinderby, Winthorpe and Lindholme. A few percolated into 1485 Gunnery Flight. In November 1943, Manchesters of 1660 CU retired. With this ended the service life of the Manchester. But there were some sequels. Most obvious was the Lancaster, for this remarkable bomber would never have existed but for the failure of the Manchester. Less apparent is the fact that it was the P 13/36 specification which sowed the seed that developed years later as the Mosquito, surely the most outstanding military aeroplane of all time.

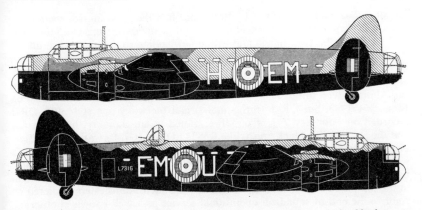

Figure 12: (Top) Manchester L7288 : EM-H is depicted in the paint scheme applied to the first Manchesters to join squadron service. She had red serials, and joined 207 Sqn on December 7 1940. She was transferred to 97 Sqn on February 26 1941, but before operating passed to 61 Sqn in April 1941. From June 1942 until May 1943, she was used by 1654 Con Unit. (Above) Manchester L7316 : EM-U served with 207 Sqn from April 13 1941 until she failed to return on August 31 1941. (For colour key ,see drawing on page 82.)

Manchester markings

Markings passed through three basic stages. In each instance upper surfaces were Dark Green and Dark Earth. As far as L7300 alternate mirror image camouflage patterns were applied, a system abandoned early in 1941. To this time Manchesters were delivered with black under surfaces terminating in a straight line joining the tailplane and the wing root, and extending straight forward from the wing leading edge. L7300 (Pattern A) wore this style in January 1941, when recorded coded EM-S (EM aft on both sides of the fuselage). Roundels on the fuselage at this time were 63 inches in diameter, as on L7288 : EM-H, which also wore camouflage Pattern A. Both aircraft had Dull Red fuselage serials. By late February 1941 all the Manchesters in 207 Squadron had the black area extended up the fuselage side and terminated in a wavy line, the style varying on each machine. Codes remained grey, and serials were grey too. On the aircraft of 207 and 97 Squadrons that I saw, the codes were quite a dark shade of grey—darker, for instance, than those of the 3 Group Wellingtons. L7311 : EM-F was wearing this scheme in March 1941, also L7302 : EM-R.

When I observed L7389 at Fowlmere in July 1941, it had wavy line camouflage and was the first Manchester I saw with a dorsal turret. When the revised black camouflage came into vogue, fuselage roundel size was cut to 42 inches, and another interesting feature noticed on L7389 was her starboard fuselage roundel sited further forward than the port one. This was also the first Manchester that I saw with the squadron codes ahead of the roundel on the port side, aft on the starboard, and since I had of late been recording them in the old style it suggests that the changes were made about this time, when dorsal turrets were being added. From about this time, other squadrons wore this pattern of coding, including L7319 : EM-X and L7321 : EM-D—both late June recordings and both fitted with dorsal turrets. Code letters were now usually 3 feet tall, those of 97 Squadron looking curious on account of the thin strokes of the letters applied throughout the time they had Manchesters. It was October 1941 when I recorded twin-finned machines,

L7489 : OF-T and L7490 : OF-U. Both once had the third fin, for their wavy line camouflage swept up to meet its position in standard trim. On November 25 I noted QR-M, twin-finned and with a new ending to the black camouflage, which terminated in a straight line as featured by the drawing reproduced on page 87 dated September 1941. An interesting feature was that the black area swept up to where a third fin would have been and continued to do so on Manchesters until their withdrawal. Twin-finned QR-G had this on January 1 1942, but QR-T (three-finned) had the wavy line style, like QR-J recorded on February 7. L7476 : OF-K, noted in late January, had twin fins and the straight line black finish, like R5833 : OL-N (OL forward on port side, aft on starboard). L7378 : EM-A and R5837 : OL-R, both seen in March 1942, were similar and had twin fins. It was well into 1942 before the wavy line finish was absent on all twin-finned aircraft, and the black line was straight at the top on all aircraft thus modified. Three-finned Manchesters soldiered on right to the end of squadron operational service as a well-known photograph of L7453 : EA-T shows. This aircraft, like others in use in June 1942, had Dull Red codes and serials and Type C1 roundels, but wavy line black top. Other red-coded machines recorded with three fins were QR-I on July 9 and EA-M on August 20 1942. A red-coded two-fin aircraft was EA-J seen on June 19, also VN-C which, too, had straight line black top. The last Manchester I saw flying was three-finned GP-E on November 4 1943— and she had straight line top to her black camouflage.

Manchester squadrons

Sqn	Code letters	Example	Equipped date (approx)	Bases, notes
49	EA	T: L7453	4.42 - 8.42	Scampton. Operational 2.5.42 to 25.6.42
50	VN	R5833	3.42 - 8.42	Skellingthorpe. Operational 8.4.42 to 25.6.42
61	QR	J: L7389	4.41 - 6.42	Syerston. Operational 7.12.41 2nd phase
83	OL	N: R5833	12.41 - 6.42	Scampton. Operational 4.2.42 to 29.5.42
97	OF	H: L7473	2.41 - 5.42	Waddington then Coningsby. Operational 8.4.41 to 17.1.42. To Woodhall 3.42.
106	ZN	L7463	2.42 - 6.42	Coningsby. Operational 20.3.42 to 25.6.42
207	EM	V: R5791	11.40 - 8.42	Waddington to Bottesford 11.41. Operational 24.2.41 to 10.3.42
408	EQ	A: L7401	5.42 - 7.42	Balderton
420	PT	L7291	5.42 - 7.42	Waddington

NB: Conversion Flights on the squadrons kept aircraft after the operational flights had given theirs up, eg 50 Squadron had L7319 in 10.42; 83 Squadron had L7277 in 10.42 and 57 Con Flt L7325 in 10.42.

Conversion and training units which used Manchesters were: 1654 CU (example L7419:UG-B, used 5.42-7.43), at Swinderby 5.42, to Wigsley 15.6.42; 1660 CU (example L7280:TV used 10.42-11.43), formed Swinderby from 61, 97 and 106 Con Flts; 1661 CU (example L7281:GP) at Winthorpe 11.42-11.43; 1656 CU (example L7467:BL-Y) at Lindholme 10.42-4.43; 1668 CU (example L7307:CE) 9.43-10.43; 25 OTU (example L7283, possibly coded PP) at Finningley 10.41-8.42; No 5 LFS (example L7307); and 1485 TTF (example L7401 used 8.42 to 4.43).

30 *Wellington IC GR-W of 301 Sqn wears her serial in a camouflaged 'box' and can be seen to have the camouflage on only part of the rear fuselage, even in 1941* (Imperial War Museum).

31 *Whitley V N1434:GE-E of 58 Sqn under inspection in the Channel Islands prior to the first raid on Italy* (V. W. Clarkson).

32 *An early Stirling of XV Sqn exhibits unusual black finish terminating in a very wavy line. Note too that 'LS' appears ahead of the roundel, a most unusual feature, positioning possibly influenced by previous MG coding visible on the print* (Imperial War Museum).

33 *An early production Belfast Stirling with yet another style of camouflage, with the black sweeping up to the cockpit and also terminating in a downward sweep to the rear of the wing. This machine has the large roundel applicable to early aircraft; possibly N6001.*

34 *Photographed in the winter of 1941-42, Stirling W7455 of 149 Sqn at Mildenhall. Her paintwork again is ragged, codes grey like the serial and her collector rings are in the other frequently seen style of light and dark grey.* ('Aeroplane')

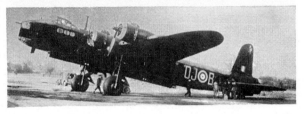

35 (Above) Stirling R9147:U of 1651 Conversion Unit at Water-beach, early 1943, where she had arrived in January, and became BS-U.

36 (Left) Stirling W7459 had a varied career, serving with 149 Sqn 26 Conversion Flt, 218 Sqn, and finally 1651 Conversion Unit, in whose marking she is seen here. Note the FN7 dorsal turret.

37 Stirling I W7447, in atrocious state, was a very popular aircraft at 1651 Conversion Unit, Water-beach, and seemed to be flying every day. She began life on XV Sqn and ended her days with 1651 Conversion Unit.

38 Manchester L7288 of 207 Sqn. Even after a short length of service her finish looks quite tatty, as the aircraft in Special Night always did. Code letters were 3 ft 6 in high. (Imperial War Museum).

39 Manchester L7287 was used by Avro for turret installation trials and general development work. This photograph clearly shows a special markings feature, the asymmetric siting of the fuselage roundels, which is also depicted with the stipulated measurements on the drawings of R5771 and L7417 (see page 83). On April 1 1942 she joined 49 Sqn and failed to return from Emden on the night of June 6/7 1942. L7287 crashed in a deep canal near Den Osse, Isle of Schouwen, south-west of Rotterdam.

40 (*Upper*) *L7279, one of the Manchesters used on the first operation by the type. It was later operated by 61 Sqn and then used, in 1943, by RAE (Imperial War Museum).* **41** (*Lower left*) *The second prototype Manchester, L7247, with shark's fin and ventral turret lowered.* **42** (*Lower right*) *The short-span wings can be seen in this photograph of Manchester L7247 in the summer of 1940, by which time she had yellow under surfaces denoting a prototype*

43 and 44 *German airmen inspect the battered remains of Manchester L7380:EM-W which came down at Schiermonikoog, one of the Frisian Isles, on September 8 1941, after a Berlin raid. No enemy claims were made that night, so possibly the machine had engine failure (via G. J. Zwanenburg).*

45 *L7244, the first Halifax prototype, in her initial finish with Type B fuselage roundels.*

46 *L7245, the second Halifax prototype, in 1941 finish with full armament and with under-wing serials (Real Photographs).*

47 *Halifax I L9601, photographed in September 1941 at Radlett. It became MP-F of 7 Sqn and was later used by 78 Sqn in 1942, mainly for training purposes ('Flight International').*

Chapter II

The early Halifaxes

HANDLEY PAGE, whose recent liquidation brought an inglorious ending to an illustrious firm, supplied the Royal Air Force with long-range bombers for nearly 50 years. It was natural for the company to tender designs to pre-war heavy bomber specifications. Its Hampden proved successful and the firm viewed with interest Specification B.1/35 for a large two-motor heavy bomber. This specification had evolved after lengthy discussion but was soon eclipsed by two important 1936 requirements, B.12/36 for a four-engined bomber and P.13/36 for a high-performance aircraft powered by two engines. Handley Page tendered to the B.1/35 but before proceeding adapted its design, the HP 55, to P.13/36 which consequently became the HP 56. Two Bristol Hercules engines had been originally chosen, but greater power seemed likely to be available from the new Rolls-Royce Vulture.

Handley Page planned the '56 with an all-up weight of 45,000 lb around two of these engines to carry a greater load further than would the HP 55. In April 1937, two prototypes were ordered by the Air Ministry along with two of the competitor, the Avro 679. Serials L7244/45 were allotted.

As work advanced a mock-up was built. It soon became obvious that the Vulture programme was in difficulties. The Air Ministry suggested to Handley Page that, as an insurance against the failure of the Vulture, and indeed the Avro design, the HP 56 should be re-thought, enlarged and powered by four Rolls-Royce Merlins. Handley Page were reluctant to do this. Eventually, seeing the official demand more like an ultimatum, they gave way and re-designed the machine around four engines. Basically its shape was unaltered, the bulky fuselage stemming from the need for the aircraft to be a possible troop carrier, which eventually it became. Enlargement of the design, however, pushed the weight to around 50,000 lb.

Two prototypes of the new aircraft, the HP 57, were ordered on September 3 1937. On January 7 1938, the first production order for 100 machines to Specification 32/37 was placed. Construction of the first prototype began the same month. To speed and ease production the machine was built to a split assembly system.

Fear that the aircraft would require a long take-off run led to its component parts (the machine was easily broken down, as in the case of other bombers of this period, to fit the standard packing cases) being taken to Bicester just as the war commenced. Here the parts were re-assembled and on October 25 1939 L7244, in Dark Green, Dark Earth, and Night finish with Type B roundels, made its first flight. As with the Manchester, no turrets were fitted, for this was an aerodynamic trials aircraft powered by four Merlin Xs. It also had wing leading edge slots, a popular feature with the firm, and slotted flaps. Slots were never featured on production aircraft for they proved to be unnecessary and in any case they were deleted to make room for anti-

F

aircraft balloon cable cutters which, in the event, proved of little real value.

The prototype flew from Bicester, Boscombe and Radlett whilst L7245 was being completed. This aircraft, fully armed, first flew on August 17 1940, and from the start was in the new prototype colours of Dark Green and Dark Earth with Yellow under surfaces. Unusual were the bold black serials under the mainplane in trainer style. After initial handling it was passed to Boscombe Down, where it stayed for most of its time, used for general development work until November 1941, when it crashed on take-off.

Already Handley Page production lines had swung over to the Halifax, as the new bomber was named. On April 30 1940, English Electric had received an order for 400 Halifaxes and other production lines were to be established by the London Aircraft Production Group led by the London Passenger Transport Board, by Fairey at Stockport, and by Rootes Group at Speke.

On October 11 1940, the first production aircraft, L9485 (Merlin X), made its first flight painted in Dark Green and Dark Earth finish with its Special Night under surfaces terminating in a wavy line roughly mid-way up the fuselage sides, a feature of all the Mk Is when they left the factory. Like the Manchester and Stirling, the Halifaxes had red serials which were still being applied when the Mk I was phased out, and these serials appear to have been retained into 1942. Its maximum take-off weight was now 55,000 lb—a further increase which could only detract from its performance. Two days after its flight, L9485 passed to Boscombe for trials which continued into December, by which time L9486 had joined her. Both machines had the standardised armament of two nose and four tail guns in Boulton Paul turrets. Boscombe's trials revealed a top speed of 262 mph at 18,000 ft on 50,000 lb. Bomb load/range assessment was 1,740 miles with 8,500 lb load or 1,000 miles with 13,000 lb. Take-off run at 55,000 lb was 1,020 yards, initial climb 750 ft/min, and service ceiling 22,800 ft. Dimensions were span 98 ft 10 in, length 70 ft 1 in and wing area 1,250 sq ft.

Under the review of current projects in May 1940, Handley Page were ordered to stop work on their B.1/39 'super bomber'. All effort was to be concentrated on the Halifax in view of the Manchester's troubles. Now the firm was so keen on the initially less promising machine that they adamantly maintained there was no need for any other four-engined bomber, especially when rumours circulated that Avro were planning a four-engined Manchester development.

On November 5 1940, No 35 Squadron re-formed attached to A & AEE Boscombe Down under Wing Commander R. W. P. Collings, there to become acquainted with the first production machine and L7245. Production was slow and, when the squadron moved to more permament quarters at Leeming, it took L9486 on loan. On November 23, L7244 was attached to the squadron, a very useful addition for it had dual control.

The squadron moved to Linton-on-Ouse on December 5 and further handling and fuel consumption trials were held, along with conversion training. Before the squadron could operate, flight engineers needed to be trained. This could only be done on the squadron, which now had three aircraft assigned to it, L9486, '87 and '89. Further deliveries took place in February and the aircraft were now wearing 'TL' coding in a dark shade of grey. TL was painted forward of the port side, and aft on the starboard, as on L9486 : TL-M and L9489 : TL-F.

By early March 1941, six crews were operationally fit and on the night of March 10/11 1941, the first operation was laid on with Le Havre docks as target. Despatched were TL-B:L9486, F:L9489, N:L9496, G:L9493, L: L9490 and M:L9488. It was a cloudy night and finding the target was difficult. Flak damaged 'G' which limped home with an undercarriage leg dangling and one engine out of use. Another fell to a more unlucky fate over Surrey, for a night fighter mis-identified L9489 and shot it down. Next night L9496, L9488 and L9490 attempted the first raid on Germany, with Hamburg as their target.

In mid-April, news broke that a second Halifax squadron would form, No 76, which began to rise from a third flight of 35 Squadron. On May 1, No 76 Squadron came into being at Linton. On May 12, the enemy, doubtless aware of the lair of the new bombers, attacked their airfield, damaging some aircraft in hangars and on dispersals.

No 76 Squadron took six weeks to work itself up for action, despatching its first sorties on June 12 to the oil refinery at Huls, when L9516, L9514 and L9518 were operated. Kiel, Duisburg and Hanover had now felt the weight of Halifax bombs. The two squadrons were not operating alongside.

Daylight attack by heavy bombers was a cherished idea to the Air Staff who considered this quite feasible if fighters flew diversions and the Blenheims of 2 Group could pave the way. The first day raid by Halifaxes was mounted on June 30 when six crews of 35 Squadron flying L9500:H, L9508:F, L9509:C, L9499:Q, L9503:P and L9501:Y set off to attack Kiel from 18,000 feet, the height at which the Halifax I best performed. To increase their fire power the bombers now had beam guns, but this did not save two of them falling to enemy fire. Although 35 Squadron expected more daylight raids these were still considered too costly, so night raids on targets such as Frankfurt and Magdeburg followed.

Main parts of the first English Electric Halifax reached the flight shed at Salmesbury on June 24 and on July 9 a second order was placed with that company for 250 machines. V9976, their first aircraft, flew on August 15 and was ready for delivery on September 20. At Cricklewood and Radlett, Handley Page had not wasted time. The result was a refinement of the first version of the Halifax. Early machines were designated Mk I Series I, and before the production type had even flown it had been decided to re-stress the aircraft to 60,000 lb, a feature of the Series II. An increase in fuel load from 1,392 to 1,636 gallons and maximum possible fuel load from 2,242 to 2,363 gallons resulted in the Mk I Series III. A few of the latter aircraft are believed to have had 1,390 hp Merlin XX engines, but these were more a feature of the HP 59 Halifax II Series I which had increased power to combat the extra load. This version also had greater fuel capacity, 1,882 gallons (2,572 in overload state), but the most distinctive item of the Mk II was its two-gun 'Hudson-like' Boulton Paul dorsal turret. L9515 was set aside as prototype, completed in June 1941 and first flown on July 3 1941. It was much superior to the Mk I, production of which terminated in September 1941 with L9608. The first production Mk II was V9976 and the first from the parent company was L9609 which flew in September 1941.

Meanwhile, operations by both squadrons were well under way. The most spectacular as yet had been on July 24 1941. A large-scale daylight raid on Brest had been planned for all the medium and heavy bombers in an attempt to sink or disable the *Scharnhorst* and *Gneisenau*. Failings of the Manchester caused these machines to be withdrawn. Then, the day before the raid, *Scharnhorst* sailed. Stirlings were immediately despatched to attack her and, although their operation was gallantly flown, little was achieved. Next day,

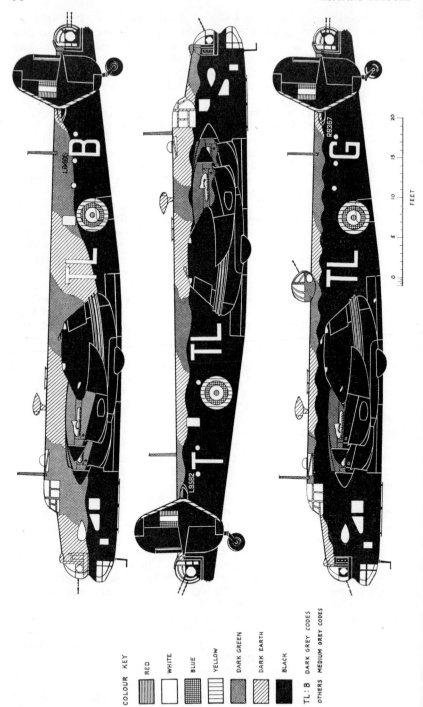

COLOUR KEY

RED

WHITE

BLUE

YELLOW

DARK GREEN

DARK EARTH

BLACK

TL: B   DARK GREY CODES

OTHERS   MEDIUM GREY CODES

FEET

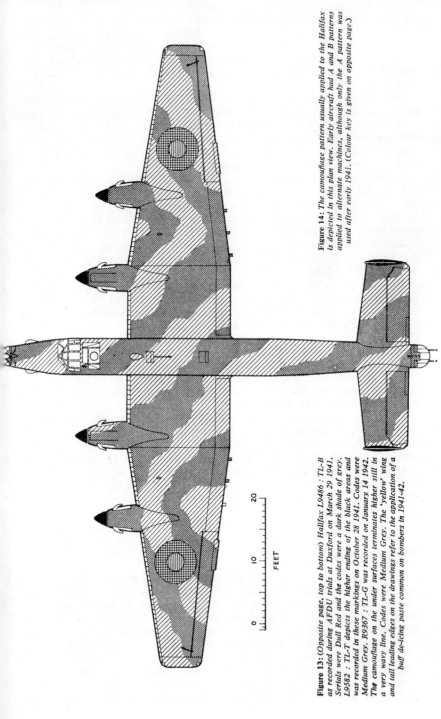

Figure 13: *(Opposite page, top to bottom) Halifax L9486 : TL-B as recorded during AFDU trials at Duxford on March 29 1941. Serials were Dull Red and the codes were a dark shade of grey. L9582 : TL-T depicts the higher ending of the black areas and was recorded in these markings on October 28 1941. Codes were Medium Grey. R9367 : TL-G was recorded on January 14 1942. The camouflage on the under surfaces terminates higher still in a very wavy line. Codes were Medium Grey. The 'yellow' wing and tail leading edges on the drawings refer to the application of a buff de-icing paste common on bombers in 1941-42.*

Figure 14: *The camouflage pattern usually applied to the Halifax is depicted in this plan view. Early aircraft had A and B patterns applied to alternate machines, although only the A pattern was used after early 1941. (Colour key is given on opposite page.)*

FEET

0   10   20

the two squadrons despatched Halifaxes L9524:V, L9512:U (missing), L9500 : H, L9501 : Y, L9507 : W, L9527 (missing), L9511 : D, L9491 : J and L9508 : X (all of 35 Squadron), and L9496, L9516, L9529, L9494, L9531 and L9517 (of 76 Squadron) to raid her at La Pallice. Under-armed, the Halifaxes were clearly unsuited for day raids and not until the end of 1941 did they operate by day again.

The first Berlin raid was mounted on July 25/26 and on September 10/11 Halifaxes, using Stradishall as a forward base, set off for Turin. It was a long, long journey, taxing to the extreme as the bombers laboured over or between the high Alps. When they came back from their long journeys, three of the aircraft crashed from fuel shortage, one of them being hopelessly lost. In 1941, Bomber Command still had much to learn.

Production Mk IIs began to leave the Handley Page works in October 1941, by which time the second production source, English Electric Preston, was a fully going concern and made its first squadron delivery of V9979 on October 25 to No 35 Squadron on the day when another Mk II, R9364, from Handley Page's second batch also joined 35 Squadron. L9611 had joined 76 Squadron the previous day, and Mk IIs slowly replaced the Is. The Mk II first operated on November 25/26, when V9979 : TL-E and V9980 : MP-B were part of the force.

Training for the Halifax crews had hitherto taken place on squadrons, but an operational formation is ill-placed if it has major training duty to perform. In October, by which time Halifax deliveries were sufficient, No 28 Halifax Conversion Flight was established using, amongst others, L9486, '91, '96 and L9509.

Berlin, Essen, Hamburg and Stettin—all were attacked in the closing weeks of the year. Production was building up and a third Halifax squadron, No 10, formed at Leeming. It received its first aircraft, R9367, on October 24 and, although it used few Mk Is, had mainly Mk II aircraft from the start. It flew its first operation on December 18.

The German battlecruisers were both at Brest and there was constant fear lest they put to sea to sink vital British merchant shipping in the North Atlantic. Therefore it was decided to attempt another day raid, for night attacks were achieving little. On December 18 a force of Stirlings, Manchesters and 18 Halifaxes (six from each squadron) set off for the raid and, although the fighters came in, only one Halifax was lost. The raid was nevertheless not very successful and so another attack was launched by Halifaxes only on December 30, when, of the 18 despatched (L9617:MP-A, L9780: B, 9379:L, L9620:O, L9583:M and L9615:X of 76 Squadron; R9386: TL-A, V9979 : E, R9372 : O, R9364 : N, R9367 : G and R9377 : B of 35 Squadron; and L9619, L9368, L9369, V9984, L9370 and L9371 of 10 Squadron), three were shot down.

Nevertheless, all was not well with the Halifax. Additional all-up weight had resulted in an under-powered machine, and the massive dorsal turret coupled with the nose contours and the six striking fuel jettison pipes were excrescences which led to excessive drag. Another unhappy feature of the aircraft was its tendency to spin when heavily loaded. All these features needed urgent attention, particularly the spinning characteristic. R9534, on the line in March 1942, was set aside as a trial installations aircraft and was stripped of many items. A new nose of curved streamlined form was fitted, a metal nose for aerodynamic tests reproduced in Perspex for trials in DG276. A flatter Boulton Paul dorsal turret was fitted. Fuel jettison pipes

were removed; exhaust shrouds modified; Merlin 22 engines with reduced
radiator area were installed; bomb doors were modified to allow carriage of
larger weapons; and much internal gear stemming from the original specification was removed. But the arrival of production aircraft featuring these
points came months later.

In the meantime, a new variant appeared, the Mk II Series I (Special).
From these aircraft the nose turret and bomb aimer's canopy were replaced
with a so-called 'Z Fairing'. Dorsal turrets were removed, as were the jettison
pipes. Exhaust shrouds were modified, but the triangular fins were retained. It
was discovered that the spinning troubles arose from these. Air flow around
the fins and rudders was found to cause rudder stalling which put the aircraft
on to its back in a dive. 'Square' fins were tried on R9534 but it was 1943
before Halifaxes appeared on the squadrons with them.

Modifications were also made to the undercarriage on L9520 between April
and May 1941 by Dowty which led to the Mk V. Rotol experimented with
fluid de-icers and three-bladed wooden propellers.

Ventral turrets attracted the armament experts throughout the war. Trials
were conducted in 1942 with W7650 but few other aircraft appear to have
had them at this time. V9977 was fitted with a large plastic cupola and it
arrived at the TFU Hurn on March 27 1942. Here the first H2S blind bombing equipment was installed and the machine began trials in April 1942.
V9985 was used for dummy drops of 4,000 lb bombs.

About June 1941, Halifaxes on the squadrons began to appear with the
Night areas of the paintwork extended high on the fuselage side, terminating
in a wavy line in common style. Codes remained grey and serials positioned
further aft were also grey. The straight line ending to the black was a 1942
feature. There were very few changes in markings, and by 1942 the Halifax
was very much a going concern.

Halifax production, 1940/early 1942

Mk I: L9485-9534, L9560-9684, L9600-9608.
Mk II: L9609-9624, R9363-9392, R9418-9457, R9482-9498, R9528-9540, V9976-
       9994, W1002-1021, W1035-1067, W1090-1177, W1141-1190, W1211-1253,
       W1270-1276.

Halifax squadrons, 1941/early 1942

No	Identity letters	Example	Bases
10	ZA	C: L9624	Leeming
35	TL	P: L9511	Leeming, Linton-on-Ouse
76	MP	B: L9565	Linton; to Middleton June 1941
102	DY	T: R9449	Dalton; equipped at end of 1941

Chapter 12

Hostilities begin in the Middle East

WHEN ITALY DECLARED WAR on June 10 1940, there were 29 RAF squadrons around the Mediterranean. They were stationed in Egypt, Jordan, Palestine, Malta, Aden and East Africa. Fourteen were bomber squadrons—nine of them equipped with Blenheims, mostly short-range Mk Is. In the Sudan were three long-range Wellesley squadrons. Including Blenheims, about 85 bombers were there, in addition to nine general-purpose aircraft and units of the SAAF facing the Italian East African possessions. Strength of the bomber squadrons in Egypt was nominally 96 aircraft (Blenheim Is), about a dozen Bombay bomber transports and a handful of Valentias of 70 Squadron which, at a hard push, could drop a variety of objects but which could not be truly counted as bombers.

Aden increased in strategic importance now that the war was going so badly for the British. On this arid site there were two squadrons of Blenheims, some Vincents and a flight of Blenheim IV fighters of 203 Squadron which were among the very few Mk IVs on squadrons in the Middle East at this time.

Blenheim Is had been delivered to squadrons in the same style of camouflage as worn in England before the war, ie, Dark Green, Dark Earth and Black. During the winter of 1938-39, grey squadron codes were in some cases applied and by March 1939 some of the Blenheims had Type B roundels and some had lost their under-wing serials. In the Middle East there were still quite a number of uncamouflaged aircraft including the stately Valentias, some of which wore Type B roundels and Medium Grey codes on their silver finish. In Britain there was never a completely rapid implementation of a change of markings and camouflage, or rarely so; in the Middle East the time lags were even more lengthy.

When war in Europe began, squadrons took up war stations in the Middle East and there was quite a rapid changeover to wartime codings, and an interesting feature was that some squadrons changed theirs again in 1940, a useful ruse. A point not generally realised is that code letters became allocated on a 'theatre of operations' basis. It meant that two squadrons might simultaneously carry identical coding, and that squadrons sometimes needed to change theirs on transfer from one theatre to another. When the American squadrons in Britain from 1942 adopted codes, these were part of the British system. Whilst on the subject of codes, it is interesting to note that some squadrons in the Middle East wore codes from 1940 for only a short period, and some seem never to have worn them. For some units, code letters never seem to have come to light and if any readers who served in that theatre during the war can shed light upon the 'missing' ones they would be doing a very useful service.

The line-up of squadrons in the area able to carry out bomber operations were :

Sqn No	Codes	Equipment	Dates	Notes/Examples
8	unknown	Blenheim I	5.39 - 9.41	L8433
		Blenheim IV	8.41 - 5.42	R3894
11	unknown	Blenheim I	7.38 - 1.41	L8383
		Blenheim IV	1.41 - 3.42	
14	unknown	Wellesley	8.38 - 12.40	L2693
		Blenheim IV	.40 - 8.42	Z7893: U
30	unknown	Blenheim I	4.38 - 3.41	L4917: B. Changed to fighter rôle 3.41
39	unknown	Blenheim I	.39 - 1.41	L8384
		Maryland	1.41 - 5.41	
45	OB	Blenheim I	6.39 - .41	L8502
		Blenheim IV	.41 - .42	T2318
47	KU	Wellesley	6.39 - 12.41	L2699
55	unknown	Blenheim I	6.39 - 12.40	L8664
		Blenheim IV	12.40 - 3.42	V5951
70	unknown	Valentia	11.35 - 10.40	K8062
		Wellington IC	equipped 9 - 10.40	R1029: A
84	VT	Blenheim I	2.39 - 3.41	L4833
		Blenheim IV	3.41 - 1.42	V5579
113	AD	Blenheim I	6.39 - 6.40	L4823
		Blenheim IV	3.40 - 12.42	T2177: AD-V
211	UO	Blenheim I	5.39 - 6.41	L6670
		Blenheim IV	6.41 - 2.42	?
216	SH	Bombay	10.39 - .43	L5857: C
223	AO	Wellesley	6.38 - 4.41	L2704
		Maryland	5.41 - 4.42	AR723
		Baltimore I	1.42 et seq	AG732

One style of 1939-40 bomber markings in the Middle East was portrayed by the Wellesley Wing at Khartoum, which comprised Nos 47 and 223 Squadrons. In the summer of 1939 both were equipped with aircraft wearing the usual Dark Green-Dark Earth-Night finish. On the wings and fuselage they wore Type B roundels, and each had a red identity letter aft of the roundel. Under-wing serials were still carried in white and Type A roundels were worn beneath the extreme wing tips. All the aircraft still had rudder serials as on L2663 : Y and L2713 : Z of 223 Squadron. Early letters of the alphabet were allotted to 47 Squadron, later ones to 223 Squadron.

Unit codes were not adopted until the war broke out, when L2668 of 223 Squadron became AO-B (AO aft on the starboard side, forward on the port). Under-wing serials were at the same time deleted, but rudder serials were retained.

Shortly after the outbreak of war an interesting change took place at Khartoum, when the Dark Green areas in the camouflage were over-painted in a light tan shade of dope locally devised. Unit codes were applied in Medium Grey, as they had been at the start of the war. Squadron letters were positioned as before, and the Type B roundels were retained, as on KU-N and AO-W. Type A roundels remained on the under surfaces, but all other serials were over-painted when this scheme came into vogue. No 47 Squadron still held a few Gordons, one coded 2:KU, and these were cam-ouflaged in the new manner, except that their under surfaces acquired a pale blue shade. These aircraft, too, had over-painted serials, and Type A under-wing roundels.

It seems likely that not all of the Wellesleys of the squadrons had the special finish. AO-A : L2714 was flying later in 1939 in Dark Green-Dark

Earth-Night finish with Type A fuselage roundels and Medium Grey codes. L2674 was similarly marked at this time, except that this aircraft still had rudder serials

When hostilities commenced in the Middle East probably all aircraft of both squadrons were wearing the Dark Green-Dark Earth-Night scheme and Type A1 roundels of 35 inches diameter on their fuselages. AO-K (letters placed as before) wore 2-foot codes, also 5-inch wide fin stripes placed close to the rudder post. This aircraft, badly shot up in action, had an extended 'glasshouse' terminating just ahead of the rear canopy immediately ahead of which was a D/F loop.

Another aircraft in use in the late summer of 1940 was K7760 which, like K7733, had wide red-white-blue stripes covering the fin. K7760 had the more usual cockpit canopy, but the red centre of the pre-war wing roundel was evident through the red of the Type B.

The final stage in Wellesley markings came in late 1940 when under surfaces were changed to Sky and fuselage roundels slightly enlarged, as on K7759. Details of these markings are evident on photographs which suggest that the 1940 colour schemes differed from unit to unit.

In Aden, even after the fighting had broken out, some of the Vincents (like K4143 : J of 203 Squadron) were still in silver finish. Blenheim Is of 8 Squadron still wore the camouflage and Type A1 roundels in which, like L1479, they had been ferried from England before the war. The photograph on page 147 of one of 8 Squadron's aircraft damaged by Italian air attack shows it to have Type A1 roundels. On the other hand Valentia bomber-transports were generally camouflaged like K3604.

When battle commenced in the Middle East, fuselage roundels were being revised to have the yellow outer ring, for already the white ring had appeared on the fuselage roundel, albeit later than on home-based aircraft. Fin striping, too, appeared later, possibly because there was less likelihood of confusion with Italian aircraft if no stripes were carried. This can be seen, for instance, on the Bombay photograph on page 148. But within a few weeks of the fighting, fin stripes were added.

The campaign opened for the bombers on June 11 1940 with an attack by 26 Blenheims of Nos 45, 55 and 113 Squadrons on El Adem airfield, and it set a pattern for early operations over the desert. Participating in the first raid were Blenheim Is L8476, L4923, L8519, L8466, L8524, L8478, L8469 and L8481 of 45 Squadron. Later in the day Wellesleys L2647, L2652, K7743, K7225, L2645, K7741, K7723, L2647 and L2710 of 14 Squadron attacked Italian installations at Otumlo in East Africa. Then came a raid on Tobruk, a name which was later to be heard almost daily. On the night of June 14-15, Bombays of 216 Squadron in a finish of Dark Earth and Dark Green with hastily applied black under surfaces, commenced lone night operations, which continued until January 1/2 1941, by bombing airfields at El Adem and Tobruk. By day, Blenheim raids followed, against airfields and troop concentrations, carried out by aircraft which mostly had black under surfaces, although it is known that some of 45's machines had pale blue under surfaces in a shade akin to the azure blue of later years. Such information that has come to hand suggests that Sky under surfaces on the Mk Is came into vogue at a trickle during the summer months, and that Mk IV replacement aircraft which soon began to arrive had them.

After the initial skirmishes in the desert died down, both sides realised they had serious supply problems. The Italians were not really ready for the fight, and began to build up their forces in Libya with a view to an autumn offensive.

For the British, the rapid turn in the fortunes of war brought grave problems. With Italy in the war and France lost, supply of the Mediterranean force was faced with difficult problems. One answer was to take supplies round the Cape, affording them strong cover as they passed Italian East Africa. The other, which paid handsome dividends, was to transport aircraft to West Africa by sea—Takoradi was the port chosen—and after erection fly them almost straight across Africa, bringing them to Egypt along the Nile Valley. Wellingtons for a night bombing force could be flown via Gibraltar and Malta, a route already used by crews of 2 Group squadrons which ferried out a considerable number of Blenheim IVs during the autumn months. These arrived in Dark Green-Dark Earth-Sky finish with Type A under-wing roundels which were retained on some aircraft—those of 55 Squadron, for instance—well into 1941. First aircraft to arrive by sea at Takoradi were six Blenheims which reached the port on September 5 1940. The first of the Takoradi-erected machines arrived at Abu Sueir on September 26. Then there was much to do after their long torturous flight. Added to all this, handling equipment was in short supply despite the fact that they were at bases Britain had held for many a year, albeit on a shoestring budget. Clearly it was important that the Italian holding in East Africa should be neutralised. Italy's forces there were fortunately completely cut off from their sources of supply, so the prospects looked quite good.

The war was only hours old when Wellesleys of 14 Squadron had made the first bombing raid on the large fuel depot near Massawa. Within the next four days there were eight raids by Nos 8 and 39 Squadrons on the airfields at Assab and Diredawa. Wellesleys of Nos 14, 47 and 223 Squadrons were also engaged upon the campaign, but Italian land attacks began to drive our forces back from British Somaliland. Fighting was very fierce and the strange sailplane-like Wellesleys took quite a pasting from enemy flak but somehow seemed to survive. Blenheims of 45 Squadron were brought in to assist them. Several such squadron moves came about to improve general dispositions. No 11 Squadron joined the fight in East Africa and on August 14 the forces at Aden were reinforced by 223 Squadron and a flight of 84 Squadron from Iraq. During the first six months of war, 54 convoys were escorted safely through the Red Sea by Blenheims and Wellesleys.

From Egypt and the desert beyond, the Blenheims were keeping up small-scale attacks, giving some escort to convoys which ran the Mediterranean gauntlet and flying many reconnaissance flights over the Italian positions observing the enemy build-up. It was considered that the RAF numerical strength in the desert was satisfactory, matching the enemy well. As soon as the land forces were in good order the British forestalled the Italians, opening an offensive on September 9. Blenheims hammered Tobruk and enemy landing grounds. By now, Mk IVs were in squadron hands, and the usual camouflage was the same as worn by the aircraft based in Britain. A steady advance into enemy territory began on September 19.

All was going quite well when, on October 28, Italy struck at Greece and soon the desert air forces became depleted, 84 and 211 Squadrons moving to Eleusis and Menidi near Athens. These ill-prepared airfields were quagmires in winter and some 30 miles away over mountain ranges from the area of battle. Most of their operational effort, beginning on November 11 1940, was against airfields, supply posts, communications in Albania, and on tactical

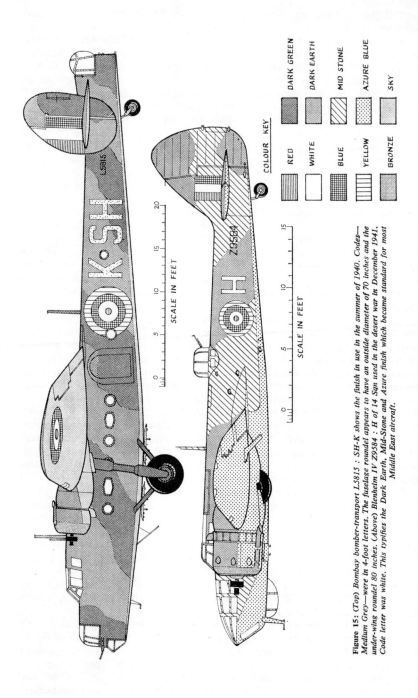

Figure 15: *(Top) Bombay bomber-transport L5815 : SH-K shows the finish in use in the summer of 1940. Codes— Medium Grey—were in 4-foot letters. The fuselage roundel appears to have an outside diameter of 70 inches and the under-wing roundel 80 inches. (Above) Blenheim IV Z9584 : H of 14 Sqn used in the desert war in December 1941. Code letter was white. This typifies the Dark Earth, Mid-Stone and Azure finish which became standard for most Middle East aircraft.*

targets for which there was so little information available.

In mid-summer 1940 the first Wellingtons flew to the Middle East, staging through Malta. They were a precious commodity and were soon positioned in the Canal Zone. No 70 Squadron had them and No 148 Squadron re-formed at Luqa on December 14 to operate them. On October 28, small-scale Wellington operations began from Malta and were directed against supply ports in Southern Italy to aid forces in the desert. Luqa was an ideal site from which to mount these raids but it was obvious that the enemy would retaliate, bringing another headache to the area.

A steady trickle of Blenheim IVs was now arriving by air from Britain. An interesting feature was that during their preparation for the Middle East theatre they were now being repainted to have Dark Earth and Middle Stone upper surfaces. This led to several incidents over Britain in the autumn of 1940 where the Blenheims in strange camouflage attracted the attention of defending fighters.

One of the essentials was good reconnaissance. What seemed an ideal air-craft was the Martin Maryland reconnaissance bomber, the first example of which, AR705, arrived in Britain in July 1940. Initial intention was that it should be used as a bomber. Instead, the first batch was put aside for the reconnaissance rôle. Indeed, No 22 Squadron operating Beauforts from Britain began to equip with Marylands in August 1940. About the same time, No 431 Flight formed at Andover, receiving Marylands. These it took to Malta in September, AR705, '707 and '712, all having the cumbersome Armstrong Whitworth dorsal turret. An interesting feature of these aircraft, and indeed other Marylands later used in Britain, was that their camouflage was Dark Green and Dark Earth with silver under-sides and not Sky as might be assumed. They wore no under-wing roundels.

During October, Wellingtons trickled through Malta from where, as their ferry crews rested, the bombers made operational flights. These Wellingtons wore black side areas to the fuselage, had grey serials and carried only in-dividual letters. By the end of October, 70 Squadron's aircraft included T2813, '2814, '2816 and '2832.

The situation in Greece boded ill and led to a complete shake-up of squadron dispositions. It was decided to mount a December offensive in the Western Desert, for which Blenheims of 55 and 113 Squadrons were sup-ported by a detachment from 45 Squadron brought from the Sudan by 11 and 39 Squadrons. To replace Nos 84 and 211 which had moved to Greece, Nos 37 and 38 Wellington squadrons were flown in from Britain in Nov-ember, supplementing No 70 and the bomber Bombays of 216. These Welling-tons retained their home coding and included LF-B : R1182 of 37 Squadron and HD-T : R1018 of 38 Squadron. Wellington IC LF-K (LF aft) was typical in its finish of Dark Earth and Middle Stone upper surfaces and Night under surfaces which terminated high on the sides in a wavy line which did not sweep up to the fin. Codes and serials W5746 were Medium Grey. Periodically some of 70 Squadron's aircraft operated from Eleusis in Greece. No 257 Heavy Bomber Wing was formed in the Canal Zone on December 20 1940.

On December 7 the air offensive began with an attack by 11 Malta-based Wellingtons on Castel Benito. Next day, 29 Wellingtons and Blenheims at-tacked Benina and 216 Squadron bombed army camps. The land forces ad-vanced on December 9 and by the 16th had pushed the enemy out of Egypt. For Operation *Compass,* 116 bombers had been available and of these the Blenheims operated by day attacking camps and airfields, and Wellingtons from the Canal Zone made night raids on Tobruk and Benghazi—both major supply bases—whilst from Malta, Wellingtons bombed Tripoli and Castel Benito. Meanwhile, the supply of aircraft was gathering momentum with the arrival between September and December of 41 Wellingtons and 85 Blenheim IVs, fortunate because aircraft were deteriorating at an alarming rate at forward bases.

After a brief rest, land forces re-opened the attack on January 3 1941, after Wellington and Bombay night raids. Bombays of 216 Squadron were, on January 1, making their last night raids, participants being L5811, L5854 and L5858. By day, Blenheims hammered the Bardia-Tobruk road and Bardia was soon captured.

It was known that units of the Luftwaffe had moved on to Sicilian airfields in late December. This dreaded event had been expected and bombing operations from Malta were bound to attract enemy reaction. On January 9, Stukas attacked shipping at Malta and the following day, HMS *Illustrious* was bombed off Sicily. A long, fearful and vicious onslaught on anything British was now unleashed. Twenty Wellingtons of 148 Squadron were presently based on Malta and they soon replied with night attacks on the Luftwaffe bases. Usually there were two bomber squadrons on Malta, supported by a handful of reconnaissance aircraft and a squadron of fighters—about 60 aircraft.

Meanwhile, the desert offensive continued, Blenheims of 45, 55 and 113 Squadrons led the assault on Tobruk on January 21; the town fell on the 22nd, and then with the Blenheims battering the retreating Italians, the army assault pressed on to Derna. Next came the encirclement of Benghazi and the capture of many troops—and with all going well came the order from London to despatch more squadrons to Greece. The fear was that the enemy might push into Turkey and on to the oilfields beyond.

In a short time only 55 Squadron was left in the desert, using Blenheims including R3919, T2175, T2429, V5579 and T2381. Blenheims sent to Greece included L1381 : VA-G, L1378 : VA-F, L6630 : VA-G and UO-R : L6670 of 211 Squadron. Reserves were getting low and the lines into the desert were long. And now the worst happened, German troops under Rommel landed at Tripoli; the advance elements of the Afrika Korps had reached the desert.

Owing to the distance involved the only response could come from the four Wellington squadrons. They could not prevent the build-up which was fast, so fast that on March 3 the enemy counter-attacked. Reinforcements in the form of a flight of 45 Squadron Blenheims flew back from Greece but could do little to stem the German advance to regain Libya, despite many attacks by day—later by night—on landing grounds and vehicles. Soon, all the Wellingtons had to be moved to Egypt owing to the intensity of enemy attacks on Malta.

As the British withdrawal from Libya continued, in April there came the German onslaught on Yugoslavia and Eastern Macedonia. What had been an unpleasant campaign immediately took on a more fearsome aspect as the Germans smashed the RAF bases in Greece. Within two weeks they were as good as destroyed. On April 17 the few Wellingtons in Greece withdrew and six days later remnants of the Blenheim force fell back to Crete. Bombays of 216 were now employed in their transport purpose, snatching what could be gathered and brought out of the chaos.

It was fortunate that the Takoradi route was flourishing. In February, for instance, there were 19 Blenheims and 23 Marylands (mostly intended for the

SAAF) ready to make the trans-Africa journey. Seventy-nine Blenheims and six Marylands were safely there in crates so that if the enemy could be held in the desert, reinforcements would soon be to hand.

In East Africa it was a different story. The Wellesleys and later Blenheims hammered away at the Italians, and land forces began an offensive on December 16 1940. This was so effective that Addis Ababa was entered on April 6 and the Italians capitulated in May 1941, releasing troops for the desert war.

Build-up of German forces in North Africa was now reaching very serious proportions. Their most vital need was a good fuel supply which could only be brought to them by tankers from Italy or Greece. To halt this it was decided to detach squadrons of 2 Group from Britain. No 21 Squadron was chosen to try out the possibility, its first detachment of six aircraft leaving in April. In June the next crews flew out drawn from 82 Squadron, a very experienced anti-shipping formation and including UX-Y : V6435 in the usual Dark Green-Dark Earth-Sky finish with grey codes. Next month, detachments from 110 Squadron (including V6523) and 105 (including V6014 : GB-J) followed, and a very tough campaign developed using aircraft which a few weeks ago were operating over the North Sea and which retained their home-style markings. Oil tankers and ammunition ships were the prime targets, calling for steel nerves and great courage during the low-level attacks from a clear blue sky. Losses were high, the campaign terrifying, and very few who flew to the Mediterranean ever returned. These detachments continued until early 1942, and they all but halted Rommel's oil supply in 1941.

On August 2 1941 a major change in aircraft colouring in the Middle East was ordered. Hitherto, the Dark Earth and Dark Green had sufficed, although many aircraft already wore other colours. It was quite acceptable for East Africa and for Greece, and 55 Squadron even considered that the colours were satisfactory for some areas in the desert war. But the deep blue sky suggested the adoption of deep blue under surfaces and the sand wastes for shades of brown. So it was that during the summer, aircraft being delivered to the area arrived wearing Dark Earth and Middle Stone camouflage with Azure Blue under surfaces. Some of these aircraft had these colours sprayed upon them before leaving England and at the preparation units there. Doubtless there was a time lag on operational units at advanced bases, but during August the major change seems finally to have been implemented. Wellingtons had the new two-tone brown finish but retained their black under surfaces and grey codes. Usually the codes were white on the Blenheims, initially at least, but a change to red came in 1942. Two aircraft, which in August had the two-tone brown camouflage, were Wellingtons X9937 : S and X9948 : G of 108 Squadron formed at the time. Blenheims with two-tone brown camouflage and white individual letters aft included V5582 : R and Z9576 : E, both used by 14 Squadron in autumn 1941, and Z9601 : H of 55 Squadron, also with white individual letters and black serials.

Rommel continued his advance towards the Egyptian border, but Tobruk did not fall and soon the Afrika Korps commander wisely halted to organise his supply lines. The respite for the British was welcomed and they too used their time very wisely. In the desert the air force was reorganised as the Desert Air Force which was formed on October 9 1941, with 16 squadrons, including six with medium bombers. They were placed in highly mobile Wings, ready to support any rapid advance. Operational Training Units were formed or expanded, whilst day and night raids continued. The heavy bomber force in the Canal Zone, No 257 Wing, was expanded to Group strength, becoming No 205 Group. From Malta, despite the shattering air attacks, the raids continued against Naples and Tripoli, whilst Wellingtons from the Canal Zone area hit at Greece, African targets and routes in and from Southern Italy. In use at this time were T2508, Z8987 : B and DV508 : G of 37 Squadron. Nightly attacks took place on Benghazi. But the main task was to build up the forces for a heavy counter-attack, Operation *Crusader*, the prelude to which opened on October 14 when Blenheims attacked airfields and dumps, and the force of Wellingtons raided Benghazi, so much so that the enemy had to use Tripoli as the supply port. It was at this time that No 104 Squadron brought its Wellington IIs to Malta, including W5531 : EP-S, which wore the two-tone brown camouflage and had grey codes. Squadron letters were later deleted from their aircraft.

Work-up of the mobile elements continued and the offensive opened on November 18, by which time there were nine bomber squadrons in the Desert Air Force. Soon a tangled battle developed, for the Germans were far tougher than the Italians had ever been. The fight flowed to and fro, with Blenheims and Marylands heavily engaged in tactical bombing. FAA Albacores of 826 Squadron acted as pathfinders at night, on account of the good view from their cockpits and their slow-flying qualities. It was not easy using the mobile bomber force, however, since the fighting was so fluid. As in the French campaign of May 1940, the Blenheims were outclassed and when six crews of 45 Squadron operated on November 21, four were shot down. Fighter escorts were always provided subsequently. By December the enemy was all but surrounded, only to escape at Gazala. On Christmas Eve, Benghazi was entered, by which time the advance was straining supply lines. Then another major blow struck the Desert Air Force. Its ranks had to be depleted again, for the war in the Far East made a desperate call on the bomber squadrons. The first six Blenheims left for the Far East on December 9 and six more left 113 Squadron on the 30th. In January and February 1942, Nos 45, 84 and 211 Squadrons were all sent to the Far East. Left were Blenheim IVs of 55 Squadron, like Z9614 : W and Z9601 : H, in two-tone brown/blue finish with white aircraft letter aft. None had under-wing roundels.

Fortunately, aircraft of more advanced types were now arriving in the theatre. Boston IIIs were coming to replace Marylands in SAAF squadrons, whereas the replacement type for the RAF Blenheim was the Martin Baltimore. The first of these to be accepted by the RAF was AG688 which reached Burtonwood on September 27 1941, and was used for service trials, and as a TI aircraft for subsequent modification programmes. AG689 arrived in Britain in October, and was soon joined by AG690 and '691, the latter in the usual 'P outlined with a ring' prototype marking. AG708 was, on October 31 1941, the first to arrive in the Middle East, and was quickly followed by AG 714, '715 and '724. On November 21 1941, the first Mk II, AG735, joined them. The first squadron to be equipped with Baltimores was No 223, which worked up with Mk Is and IIs like AG716 and AG728, the first machines joining the unit in March 1942.

Before operations commenced Mk IIIs were being delivered, with AG837 reaching Britain in March 1942 for armament trials and followed on April 10 by AG836. During the latter month the first Mk IIIs arrived in the Middle East. No 55 Squadron began to equip with Baltimores in May and on the 23rd of that month 223 Squadron attempted the first Baltimore bombing operations. Ill defended, its four machines soon ran into trouble with fighters. Unfortunately, three of the aircraft, including AG717 and '762, were shot

48 An unusual Halifax was L9619, a Mk II seen here without a dorsal turret and in the hands of 10 Sqn. She joined 10 Sqn in November 1941 and crashed on the night of February 15/16. Note the camouflage patterning and an almost invisible red serial ahead of the 'E' and on the upper surface colouring. Other early Halifaxes of 10 Sqn included L9614, L9621, L9622, L96.:-3, L9624, R9367, R9368, R9369, R9370, R9371, R9373, R9374 and R9376 (Imperial War Museum).

49 Halifax R9941 joined 35 Squadron in February 1942 and was a Mk II. This photograph, probably taken in February 1942, shows her roundels and fin striping with their white areas covered in what appears to be a grey wash. Later she served with 76 Sqn and No 1652 Conversion unit.

50 (*Above*) *Halifax L9530:MP-L of 76 Sqn, frequently flown by Pilot Officer Christopher Cheshire, brother of the famed Leonard Cheshire, VC. Delivered to 76 Sqn in June 1941, she was lost during a Berlin raid of August 12/13 1941. The aircraft is wearing Medium Grey codes and has an extension of the black finish much in evidence, while the grey serial has been repositioned* (Imperial War Museum).

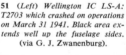

51 (*Left*) *Wellington IC LS-A: T2703 which crashed on operations on March 31 1941. Black area extends well up the fuselage sides.* (via G. J. Zwanenburg).

52 *A very rare picture of a Battle of 98 Sqn in Iceland. Note the very narrow fin striping and black under surfaces. Squadron flew reconnaissance missions around Iceland.*

53 *Wellington IC KO-P made an emergency landing at Schiermonikoog at 21.05 hrs on October 31 1941, after being attacked by German fighters. Codes and roundels appear standard, sited aft of the triangular window. All side windows have been overpainted. On the starboard side of the nose appears the 'Saint' carrying a bomb. Such artistry was not all that common at any time on RAF bombers, although some publications might tend to give a contrary impression in this respect* (via Gerrit J. Zwanenburg).

54 *R1220, the Wellington Mk IV prototype, externally identifiable by its engine cowling shape and long tail exhaust pipes emerging from the collector ring position. It had a Dark Earth-Dark Green-Yellow finish. Wellington IVs were used by the following squadrons (examples used are given in parentheses): 142 Sqn (Z1207, missing January 20 1942); 300 Sqn (Z1213, missing April 12/13 1942); 301 Sqn (Z1217, missing October 21/22 1941); 305 Sqn (Z1245, missing August 27 1942); 458 Sqn (Z1204); and 460 Sqn (Z1212, missing August 27 1942). A few like Z1275 also served with 104 OTU.*

55 *A fine view of Hampden UB-C of 455 Sqn photographed in 1942 when operating from Leuchars with Coastal Command. It retains standard Bomber Command finish with light grey codes (Ron Skidmore).*

56 *W5795, the first prototype Wellington VI, in prototype colours of Dark Green and Dark Earth upper surfaces, with yellow undersides. No ringed 'P' is carried.*

57 *Hampdens of 49 Sqn in early summer 1941. EA-V:AD980 nearest has wavy line finish and EA-S:AE354 has straight line ending to the black area. Note alternate camouflage patterns. EA-P completes the trio. Hampdens used by 49 Sqn included X3021, X3027 missing October 28 1940, X3048, X3052 missing November 25 1940, X3054, X3057, P2111, P2134, P2135, P2144, AD909, AD934, AD935, AE368, AE203, AE224 missing November 11/12 1941, AE241 and AE262 (V. W. Howland).*

58 *Mosquito IVs of 105 Sqn at Marham, setting off for a training flight in December 1942. GB-J is DZ367. She was lost on the Berlin raid of January 31 1943, when flying with 139 Sqn, and it seems possible that the aircraft was still coded GB-J and on loan to the squadron. This was her tenth sortie ('Flight International').*

59 *Lancaster KM-C of 44 Sqn seen here at AFDU Duxford. The small 'C' may have been an attempt to avoid the letters being painted over the slit windows which were a hang-over from the time when these new bombers were envisaged as transports. When I saw her at Duxford she had a red serial. She was later used by 1661 Conversion Unit and was destroyed in a crash on March 13 1943. Photograph taken on May 6 1942.*

down; and the survivor, AG703, limped home to a crash landing.

All the Baltimores despatched to the Middle East at this time wore, from the start, the Dark Earth-Middle Stone-Azure Blue finish with a white individual letter usually aft, as on A:AG832 of 55 Squadron which, with AG787 and AG773, participated in 55 Squadron's first operation on July 2 1942. Early Mk IIIs used by 223 Squadron included AG843, AG846, AG881 and AG887, all in use by August 1942.

The Far East war now snatched some of the supplies destined for Egypt, and reduced strength and the power of the Luftwaffe combined to get some convoys through to Rommel. As skilful as he was cunning, Rommel re-established his position, and on January 21 1942 he attacked, catching the British unawares, although his offensive was halted at Gazala. Supplies were still limited to both sides, but at the end of May, Rommel resumed the offensive.

Since January 1, the Kittyhawk fighter had been in action and was now escorting RAF Baltimores and SAAF Boston operations, and sometimes dropping bombs on the same sorties. Attacks on enemy troop concentrations were daily events, sometimes as many as four raids being flown. Rommel's offensive, re-opened May 26, managed to make a breakthrough in the south and the way was open for him to attack the rear of the British. A rapid retreat was the only solution. Tobruk fell and on June 24 the Germans crossed into Egypt. They were held at El Alamein on July 1 1942.

One thing was apparent. The Desert Air Force was clearly tactically superior to the Luftwaffe which had hitherto been upheld as the model to be copied. Now it was excelled. During the withdrawal phase RAF bombers had been very active and skilfully directed. Bostons and Baltimores attacked enemy positions daily from advanced bases since they were now stationed in the Canal Zone.

In December 1941 the first Liberator IIs, AL530, AL574 and AL591, arrived in the Middle East, and on January 11 1942, the first operation was flown, against Tripoli. Apart from these, only 21 Squadron's Blenheims and the Malta-based Wellingtons could reach this target, so the Liberators were a useful addition. During May, crews of 159 Squadron arrived and were followed by 160 Squadron in July. The intention was that they should stage a long-distance raid on the Ploesti oilfields, but the Americans did this and the Liberators stayed on in the Middle East until January 1943, whereas it had been intended they would be there only briefly.

By July 5 1942, 32 Halifaxes had arrived in Palestine, 16 each from Nos 10 and 76 Squadrons, on a mobility exercise. Before leaving Britain they had their upper camouflage colours changed to Dark Earth and Middle Stone. Those of 76 Squadron included MP-F : W7752, W1144 : Q, W1177 : G, W1148 : P, W7671 : H, W7672 : E, W1156 : Y, W7754 : F, W1161 : A, W1169 : S, W7655 : C and W7762 : D.

One of 10 Squadron's aircraft made the first sortie, to Tobruk, on July 11. Six days later came the first Liberator day raid, also on Tobruk.

Between November 1941 and September 1942, 308 Baltimores had reached Egypt; 488 Blenheims came in from Takoradi, and 21 Bostons. Twenty-nine Liberators arrived by air from the USA. The first Marauders were in the hands of 14 Squadron for training and the first Mitchell, too, had arrived. And behind the scenes the planners were busy, and that grand figure of victory, General Montgomery, made preparations for an offensive that was to sweep Rommel's Afrika Korps into dust.

Chapter 13

The massive offensive is prepared

SQUADRONS OF STIRLINGS, Manchesters and Halifaxes gave Bomber Command greatly enhanced striking power, but their numbers remained small until 1942. Upon the Blenheim IV, Whitley V, Hampden and in particular the Wellington IC, the Command depended. It was therefore still using aircraft types with which it entered the war.

When the three new types were entering operational service, Command's night offensive was mainly directed against maritime targets. Much of the daylight effort by the Blenheim squadrons was against shipping and fringe targets on an increasingly wide front, eventually extending from Brittany to Norway. These raids called for immense courage, as the enemy increased defences for coastal convoys until each was accompanied by an array of flak-ships, whilst overhead Bf 109s flew standing patrols. Against these, the Blenheims were gallantly flown in the face of appalling losses. At this time the Blenheims were wearing one of three colour schemes : (1) Dark Earth and Dark Green with Sky under surfaces with Medium Grey codes, which was the most common; (2) Dark Earth and Dark Green with black under surfaces which sometimes extended up the fuselage sides and even over the fin and rudder; and (3) Dark Green and a dark shade of grey with Sky under surfaces, a scheme worn certainly by some of 105 Squadron's aircraft and adopted by some aircraft of other squadrons engaged on the shipping raids. These latter operations continued until November, by which time the Hurri-bomber was available for daylight short range 'Roadstead' operations and Hudsons of Coastal Command for longer range sorties.

Since 2 Group's Blenheims were also engaged on high-level Circus opera-tions (raids by boxes of six aircraft escorted by large numbers of fighters and designed to bring enemy fighters into battle on unfavourable terms for them), most of the Blenheims continued to wear scheme (1) given above. Examples of such machines were WV-N : V6431 of 18 Squadron, YH-M : V6027 of 21 Squadron, and RT-N : Z7276. As the formations flew off to battle quite often some of the black under surface machines were among them.

On July 24 1941, for instance, when the Blenheims flew diversion opera-tions for the main attack on Brest, one aircraft could be seen to have black under surfaces. The first formation consisted of nine Blenheim IVs of 139 Squadron (V6249, V6176, V6456, Z7431, V5826, V6439, V5681, V6332 and Z7448) which operated with three of 18 Squadron (V6431 : N, V6519 : X and V6497 : U). This black paintwork was applied to give the aircraft added pro-tection during operations at night against enemy airfields and Main Force targets in Germany. UX-V : T1828, in use in February 1941, had the black finish extending high on the fuselage side and over the fin and rudder. Another Blenheim scheme, somewhat an oddity, was that carried by Mk Is and IVs of No 17 OTU at Upwood, many of whose aircraft acquired yellow under surfaces in June 1941, upon which their serials appeared in black as on Training Command aircraft. It was unusual for OTU first-line aircraft to have other than the standard operational colours, although Blenheims of the fighter OTU at Twinwood also adopted a similar finish. No rule was evident with this scheme for quite a number of the 17 OTU Blenheims still had Sky under surfaces in September 1941, and many, like WJ-A, had Sky codes instead of the usual grey ones.

From Easter 1941, a new shape was seen flying over England, the vaunted Boeing Fortress I. The first example, AN521, touched down at Watton on Easter Monday. A fortnight later it was wearing Dark Green-Dark Earth-Sky finish which the Fortresses retained until late June 1941. Before they commenced operations on July 8 their colouring had partly changed, the Dark Earth being replaced by a darkish shade of grey similar to that of some of the 2 Group Blenheims. Squadron codes changed at the same time from Medium Grey to Sky. At the start of August, I first noticed, during a visit to Polebrook, that some of them were wearing a new shade on their under surfaces. It was Azure Blue, which became the standard colour until their withdrawal from European operations. There was at least one exception, for in October I recorded in my diary the colour of WP-D as 'dark green, dark grey with black under surfaces sweeping up the fuselage sides but not covering the tail, and terminating in wide sweeps. Its codes were pure white, there wasn't a trace of grey.' For me the Fortresses were a daily and memorable sight, for they were the first aircraft I had seen streaming four broad contrails which proved a great nuisance on their lone operational flights. Although over their period of service I managed to see all of 90 Squadron's aircraft, I never at any time saw any in the supposed Deep Sky finish, and none after July 1941 wearing brown-green camouflage. WP-B:AN518 and WP-M : AN536 had the Grey-Green-Azure finish in August 1941.

By July 1941, Bomber Command had a strength of 49 squadrons in theory, giving it a strength of about 1,000 aircraft. Eight squadrons had Blenheims and a further eight had heavies, although only half of these latter units were operational. The former were usually depleted since they maintained detachments in Malta, where some retained the same colours as home-based Blenheims.

Part of Bomber Command's strength was put to use on July 24, for a large-scale daylight raid on Brest opened by three Fortresses followed by 18 Hampdens and a large force of Wellingtons. Among the latter were some Mk IIs. These were already proving extremely useful with their Type 423 provisioning equipment allowing them to carry a 4,000 lb bomb, first used on the night of March 31/April 1, when OJ-X : W5439 and an aircraft of 9 Squadron each dropped a 'cookie' on Emden. Neither of these two squadrons was fully equipped with the Mk II, 3 Group squadrons usually having about three each on strength. It was usual to allocate to them one of the last letters of the alphabet as an individual identity, as for example LN-Z:W5460 used by 99 Squadron from May 1941 until the end of the year. HA-C:W5447 was in use on 218 in September 1941. They gave to 3 Group useful load flexibility. In their markings the Mk IIs resembled other Wellingtons of the period with their wavy top line to the Special Night finish and pale grey codes which varied considerably in shade.

A few day raids were mounted in mid-1941 using Stirlings on *Circus* operations. Defensive armament of the three new types was considered inadequate and Stirlings were appearing during the summer, albeit at a trickle,

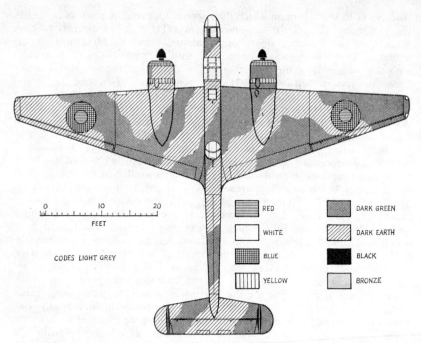

0   10   20
FEET

CODES LIGHT GREY

RED
WHITE
BLUE
YELLOW

DARK GREEN
DARK EARTH
BLACK
BRONZE

Figure 16: *Plan view of a typical late-production Hampden. Engine collector rings and gills were differing shades of bronze on the machine illustrated in this drawing.*

with dorsal turrets. But even in August they were very much the exception, and on August 3, No 7 Squadron had only MG-L:W7444 and MG-V:W7447 thus fitted. Another modification in mid-1941 of special interest to model makers was the large triangular window fitted aft on both sides of the fuse-lage of Wellingtons from which a machine gun sometimes poked for beam defence. This FN56 beam gun mounting was introduced on 214 Squadron in July 1941, but production was at a very slow rate. Some Wellingtons thus modified retained the long window strip. Others, like those of 99 Squadron, had a long strip of window painted over black. None of 99's aircraft seems ever to have been modified to have the additional triangular window, and the squadron had very few such machines even late in 1941. For the most part it was the later production ICs which presently featured it, such as OJ-B : X9817 and OJ-G : X9890 recorded at Mildenhall on September 6 alongside OJ-F : R1802 and OJ-H : R1514 which had the long window strip over-painted. Machines with the triangular windows had their serials re-sited high on the fuselage above the tailplane, their roundels reduced in diameter and their codes repositioned aft.

A highlight of August was the low-level 2 Group Blenheim raid on the power stations at Knapsack and Quadrath. Fifty-four Blenheims participated on this daring low-level penetration almost to Cologne, by any standards a remarkable achievement, costing 12 aircraft. Aircraft which took part and which are known to have had Green-Brown-Sky finish with Medium Grey codes include YH-X : V5580 and WV-Q : Z7495. These had single-gun chin blister turrets and two-gun dorsal turrets. Squadron letters were sited aft of the roundels.

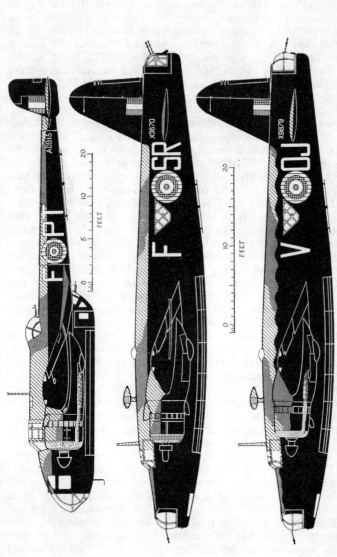

Figure 17: *(Top to bottom)* Hampden PT-F of 420 Sqn was wrecked almost beyond recognition when she was shot down on February 18 1942. On both sides of the fuselage her codes were aft in Medium Grey. Camouflage was in a straight line from slightly above the tailplane to the nose. Wellington SR-F as recorded at Bourn in March 1942. The 4-foot codes have been rather squashed to fit the area aft of the roundel: serial has been shifted on to the rear fuselage. Fuselage roundel has an outer diameter of 49 inches. Note the red portion of the collector rings, and the usual red area on the D/F fairings. Her markings are typical of a 1942 Mk III. OJ-V, a Mk IC, as recorded at Mildenhall on September 6 1941. Side and nose windows were all over-painted; codes and serials were repositioned because she had the newer window. The wavy line is depicted correctly for this aircraft but there were anything between about 10 to 15 'wave tops' aft of the cockpit on many Wellingtons which were noted. (See opposite page for Colour Key.)

Already the Blenheims' days were numbered, for Douglas Boston IIIs were arriving for their squadrons. They wore Dark Earth-Dark Green-Sky finish already seen on some Mk Is and IIs which served as trainers and trials aircraft, but never operationally with Bomber Command. During the winter months, Nos 88, 107 and 226 Squadrons equipped with Mk IIIs and a small problem was evident. Long nacelles obscured the sides of the aircraft and so the roundel was set well aft. There was then really insufficient room for the individual letter, which was accordingly painted on the aircraft's nose in Medium Grey. Early examples in use included RH-A : Z2216 and RH-N : Z2260. These were noted in March 1942. Prior to this I had recorded possibly the earliest applications of this style on Boston III AF-Z : W8286 used for tactical trials at AFDU. This machine was more of an oddity since it wore Sky codes.

A new variant which was to give valiant service to the Command and which appeared on the squadrons slowly in the summer and autumn of 1941 was the Wellington III. Its presence was most obvious from its engine note, the two Hercules producing a whispering sound akin to that of an ambling Beaufighter. One could quickly spot it, too, by its unfaired propeller hubs and 'red' and grey exhaust collector rings. No rule can really be laid down about the ending of the wavy line finish to black areas on the bombers, but from the start, Wellington IIIs in service had a straight top line to their smoother matt black paintwork. Wavy line finish was somewhat surprisingly still to be seen as late as 1943, however, and quite often the black line was far from straight, even when it was intended to be so! Although the prototype Mk III, L4251 with Hercules engines, had flown on May 19 1939, its engines were unsatisfactory. Many months passed before refinements justified production of what was intended to become the principal Wellington variant pending the introduction of the heavy bombers. Passing months enabled many refinements to be incorporated in the Mk III, all production examples of which had the triangular window aft. An important item was a four-gun Frazer-Nash tail gun turret. X3222, the first production line Mk III, was delivered to the RAF on May 22 1941, and it joined 9 Squadron at Honington on June 22. The next in squadron hands was WS-B : X3226, which reached 9 Squadron on July 24 1941. Thereafter, Mk IIIs were slowly posted into 3 Group, and 9 Squadron flew them into action for the first time on September 12. Other early examples included WS-K : X3353 and WS-L : X3354. Production rapidly built up and during the winter deliveries were made to Nos 57, 75, 101 and 115 Squadrons who worked up on them for the 1942 offensive. Examples used included DX-P : X3658 of 57 Squadron in use February 1942, AA-D : X3667 recorded March 1942, and SR-B : X3650 seen in January 1942.

At the outbreak of war a new source for engines for the Wellington was sought, and found in the American Pratt & Whitney Company. This led to the Mk IV being fitted with Twin Wasps. After various vicissitudes the prototype R1220 appeared at the end of 1940. Teething troubles were encountered with the engines but after clearance in the spring of 1941, production rapidly mounted and the first machine was delivered on June 2. Squadron deliveries began in August to Nos 300, 301 and 458 Squadrons and thereafter to Nos 142 and 460, with a few going to 305 Squadron some months later. It is believed that 142 Squadron was the first to operate them, on October 16 1941. Examples used late in 1941 included QT-B : Z1821 and QT-F : Z1206 of 142 Squadron, BH-J : Z1183 of 300 Squadron and UV-X : Z1251 of 460 Squadron.

As the Wellington IV was settling into operational service an entirely new machine joined Bomber Command. It was the de Havilland Mosquito, the most versatile and effective aeroplane of the war years. The story of its development, surprisingly based upon the same specification that produced the Manchester and Halifax and stemming from the DH 88 Comet racer and the DH 91 Albatross airliner, has often been told, and is related in detail in the book *Mosquito* available as a Faber Paper Covered Edition. Disbelief that a small unarmed wooden bomber with a crew of only two could outpace enemy fighters and carry a sizeable load even to distant Berlin was rampant among the Air Staff. Repeatedly it was rejected, an idealistic dream. It would, it was argued, use two of the precious Rolls-Royce Merlin engines and committing it to production would take them from the fighter programme. Performance estimates were carefully considered and, whilst the evidence suggested de Havilland and his team could be right, it needed some courage to sanction another bomber believed to be faster than the fighters. The Blenheim was supposed to fulfil this idea—it did not, but at least it had defensive armament. Yet Bomber Command lacked a reconnaissance aeroplane and in December 1939 the Air Staff took a chance and ordered a prototype of the DH 98 reconnaissance bomber. Throughout the summer of 1940 building proceeded even when cuts were ordered in development programmes of various new types. De Havilland, once they had the chance, were determined to prove that their aeroplane could do all they claimed it could. Construction of the prototype proceeded in great secrecy at Salisbury Hall, a historic site near St Albans, well away from uninvited observation. By November the machine was complete and was transferred to Hatfield where, on November 25, the all-yellow prototype, temporarily registered E-0234, made its first flight. When it taxied to a halt it was clear from the smile on young Geoffrey de Havilland's face that all was well. It was fast indeed, a bomber with fighter speed. In February it was flown at Boscombe Down to prove itself. At first there was disbelief of its performance, so much so that the instrumentation was ordered to be checked and initial speed trials repeated. When they were, and a speed of over 380 mph was recorded, proving it faster than even the Spitfire, the result was considered astounding. High-placed officials hurried to Boscombe to see the wonder plane, among them many who had been so sceptical. Then—disaster. Taxying over a rough patch, W4050, as the machine was now serialled, broke her back. In a matter of hours a second fuselage was rushed to the airfield and fitted. De Havilland had always maintained how easy repair and modification would be to a wooden aeroplane, and right from the start there was proof. Required modifications were few and the final production bomber Mosquito, some 7,000 examples away, differed little from the prototype. This can clearly be seen now at Salisbury Hall where the prototype W4050 rests in the hangar where she was built, whilst close at hand is TA634, one of the last B35s.

The first Mosquitoes to enter RAF service were Photo-Reconnaissance machines, then on November 15 1941, W4064 was delivered to Swanton Morley. In Dark Green-Dark Earth-Sky finish, the RAF's first Mosquito bomber, a conversion from the PR production run, had arrived. The future line of British bombers would from this time prove to be never quite the same. Speed, not heavy defensive armament, would come to be first priority, as evidenced by the Canberra and the V-bombers. But in 1941 much needed to be done before the Mosquito was ready for operations.

Meanwhile, another success story was being worked out. The sad saga of the Manchester has already been related. When the Rolls-Royce Vulture engine was really in trouble the Ministry of Aircraft Production (MAP) cancelled it and the Manchester was in danger of cancellation too. Seeing this, A. V. Roe determined something should be done to save the basically good design. If Handley Page could produce a four-engined bomber from their two-motor design, so could Avro. So the design team set about it, but MAP did not believe their design capable of effective development. Rather like de Havilland, Avro scraped together the materials for a prototype of the four-engined Manchester Mk III and gradually MAP relented and on November 15 1940 awarded a contract for a prototype. Triple-finned, it first flew as BT308 on January 9 1941, and was clearly a winner from the start. Named the Lancaster, it was so successful that orders were given to complete many Manchesters as Lancasters, a contract for 450 Lancasters being awarded on June 6 1941. A second Lancaster flew as DG595 on May 13 and this, like the first production machine L7527, flown in late October 1941, had a Dark Green-Dark Earth-Yellow finish with under-wing roundels. Meanwhile, 44 Squadron at Waddington had been informed that it would be the first to receive the Lancaster. On December 24, L7537, L7538 and L7541 joined the Waddington circuit. The magnificent Lancaster had arrived.

Thus, during the winter of 1941/42, Bomber Command worked up on three entirely new types—the Boston, Mosquito and Lancaster—whilst the Wellington III operated in increasing numbers. All were to be ready for a new round in the bomber offensive timed for March 1942. To guide them they would have the special radio aid *Gee* and the outlook for the enemy was considered to be grim.

Chapter 14

The 1942 scene

ONE OF THE MOST EXCITING aspects of being interested in aircraft during the war years was that you never knew what might come into view next. Nevertheless, I never cease to be amazed how much the keener members of that then small brotherhood knew of what was about and where it was to be seen. Even so, wherever you lived in Britain, unexpected sights abounded and interest reached fever pitch if you travelled—as I frequently did—to other parts of the country. In eastern England there were plenty of unusual aircraft ranging from the hefty and slow Folland test beds up from Luton to the ever-astonishing assortment of aeroplanes and squadrons that passed through AFDU Duxford. One of the not-to-be-forgotten moments came to me on January 2 1942. It was a dull, cold day. I had made myself a 'height finder' and determined to try it out whatever the weather. Soon I had noted Stirling I 'T' of 1651 Conversion Unit which was formed that day at Waterbeach from No 26 Conversion Flight. 'T' was an interesting sight for she had the large propeller fairing spinners that were fitted to early Training Stirlings. MG-L : N6089, complete with FN7 'Botha' turret and the small unit codes 7 Squadron carried, was busy on air test, preparatory for her part in the next night's raid on Brest. By mid-morning I had logged 21 Stirlings in the usual Dark Green-Dark Earth finish with grey codes. Modelling any of these would have been a tough task even if you could get hold of the Scalecraft kit of those days, complete with its nicely moulded transparencies. The difficulty came with the black finish which seemed to vary in its state from aircraft to aircraft. Some still had the Special Night finish whereas on others the black was a thin coat or even a very smooth finish which one associated more with the early Lancasters.

The morning progressed, highlighted by a low pass by Blenheim IV UX-B : V5856 of 82 Squadron wearing Dark Green and a shade of dark grey camouflage with Medium Grey under surfaces and Sky codes. A grey-green-blue Fortress I with an affiliated Blenheim IVF in Dark Green-Dark Earth-Sky finish passed into my 'height finder', and then ... here indeed was a new sound quite unlike anything I had heard before. The aircraft was quite low; it resolved itself as a Liberator II and to my utter delight banked sharply, revealing its upper surfaces in Dark Grey and Dark Green. The rest of it was black and as it passed its Dull Red codes came into view as MX-X. This was indeed a new sight and I determined to find its lair, suspecting it had strayed from afar. In a few days I had traced its home as Polebrook where 90 Squadron's Fortresses were based. But, alas, I was never able to 'tie up' the coding with 1653 Conversion Unit based there from January 9 until June 2 when it moved to Burn. I had to content myself with some red serials of other similarly finished uncoded Liberators including AL540, AL588 and AL616. Rumour quickly spread that other Liberators were in the area. No 159

Squadron formed at Molesworth on January 2 1942 to operate them, and
160 Squadron, which received AL551, AL552, AL520, AL542 and AL555 at
Thurleigh a week later. But these soon went overseas with crews trained at
Polebrook. The unit there had principally formed to train Liberator crews
for the squadrons of 1 Group which it was planned would operate this type.
Indeed, AL516 reached the Group, joining 150 Squadron at the end of
November 1941. Plans were altered early in 1942 and most of the Liberators
passed from Bomber Command to the Middle East where their long range
was of greater use.

By night the 3 Group Wellingtons were on the 'milk run' to Brest but a
slow change was taking place as these squadrons received the Mk III in
plenty. I noted Mk IIIs DX-C and DX-K of 57 Squadron on January 17, both
with their squadron codes well aft. Mk IC DX-G with the fuselage triangular
window also passed by the same day. There was never any real pattern as to
the placing of unit codes, however, and Hampden KM-M seen on January 13
had its squadron letters forward on both sides of the fuselage. Usually the
Wellingtons had theirs aft as on Mk ICs YR-O, TX-G and KX-T. There
were still some old Mk Is at 11 OTU and like OP-F they had now opted for
Medium Grey lettering. Two Mk IIIs noted at this time were coded YR-N
and OH-N from units apparently still unidentified.

Four-engined bombers were still comparatively rare and when a Halifax
coded NF-W appeared on February 14 (probably one of those Mk IIs without a dorsal turret that looked like Mk Is), interest was high, for it was known
that its squadron had operated Whitleys from Newmarket and Stradishall on
some special agent work. Four days later a Mk II with dorsal turret, NF-J,
was seen. An unusual Stirling seen at this time had its upper camouflage extended down to the 60° tangent line and its under side was Sky.

Bomber Command had just come through one of its most humiliating
experiences, its failure to sink the *Scharnhorst* and *Gneisenau* on their Channel dash of February 12. A massive operation had been hurriedly mounted
during which some of the Wellington III squadrons introduced their new
equipment to operations. Among the swarm of bombers despatched were
Halifaxes TL-G : R9367 and MP-K : R9391. For the most part the crews
saw nothing, but a few had glimpses of the enemy.

It was on this occasion that the Douglas Boston III went into action. The
squadrons were still under training, preparing for the opening of the 1942
daylight offensive, when the call for Operation *Fuller* came. RH-B : Z2229
was one of the aircraft used and was finished in the usual Dark Earth-
Dark Green-Sky finish with Medium Sea Grey codes.

On February 20, Bomber Command came under new, dynamic leadership
when Air Marshal Arthur Harris took command. He had at his disposal 44
squadrons—38 of them operational—and about 200 aircraft equipped with
Gee, the new radio aid which it was hoped would much improve bombing
accuracy. Policy now was three pronged: aim one was to destroy the German
industrial war machine; aim two was to pave the way for the Second Front;
and aim three was that the bombers should aid the Russians. Attacks would
be made within the range of *Gee*, about 400 miles. The latter's accuracy was
realised as being far from precise and so attacks were to be directed against
large targets.

By March, 11 squadrons (Nos 7, 10, 15, 35, 44, 76, 78, 97, 102, 149 and
218) were available for operations with four-engined bombers. There were
five squadrons of light bombers whose strength had been depleted by the

need to rush some overseas. Expansion was slow but on April 29/30 the last operations were flown by the Whitleys of Bomber Command in front-line service when 58 Squadron attacked Ostend. The Blenheim was withdrawn in August and Hampdens flew their final Bomber Command sorties on September 14/15. In their places came the Lancaster, which first flew overland sorties on March 10/11, the Mosquito and other older four-engined aircraft.

With *Gee* available, large-scale raids against towns in occupied territory had been sanctioned on February 2. On March 3/4, the large Renault works at Billancourt was the target for the 225 bombers despatched. First came Wellingtons with 4,000 lb bombs, then the other bombers including Halifax MP-R : R9447, Stirlings LS-T : N3674 and MG-P : R9297, and Whitley V KN-M : BD195.

Krupp's huge munitions factory at Essen had long been an attractive target but was still unscathed. It was the next to be attacked in force. Two hundred and eleven bombers—82 fitted with *Gee*—were despatched, 168 claiming to bomb the primary target, but bombing was scattered. Next night the raid was repeated and this time the bombs strayed on to Hamborn. *Gee* only took the crews to the approximate target area and the bombing had still to be done visually.

The next major raid (in which Stirlings MG-J : W7471 and MG-W : W7468 participated) was against the port of Lübeck on March 28/29. From here the Germans could support their invasion of Russian territory. Lightly defended and with many wooden buildings, it was soon set ablaze. Rostock, too, suffered badly. It was clear that many of the most valuable objectives could only still be attacked effectively in daylight, but to do this in Germany was easier said than done. Fighter protection for the bombers was impossible and so the best that could be done was to make the flight one way by daylight, attack at dusk and return under cover of darkness. Large-scale fighter and light bomber diversions would be laid on to confuse the defenders. On April 17 the theory was put to the test using the fastest heavy bomber, the Lancaster, which it was hoped could readily defend itself.

Selected as the target amid some controversy was the MAN diesel engine factory at Augsburg, deep in enemy territory. The force was to consist of 12 Lancasters, six each from Nos 44 and 97 Squadrons. In mid-afternoon they left for a hazardous low-level penetration across France, over which Bostons and Spitfires were operating diversionary operations. The Luftwaffe was wary, but barely had the Lancasters entered French airspace when Bf 109s swarmed in for the kill. The eight rearward-firing guns—each machine had a ventral turret at this stage—were insufficient to save them. KM-H : L7536, T : L7548, V : L7565 and P : R5506 of 44 Squadron were shot down. This left only two of 44 Squadron, one being KM-B : R5508 flown by the leader, Sqn Ldr John Dering Nettleton. On they pressed across France almost to the Swiss border, where they followed the River Lech which led them to the factory. It was clearly visible, as now, amongst a collection of tall chimneys. Flak around the city was intense and KM-A : R5510 crashed, on fire after its bomb run. Nettleton bombed, now 44's only survivor. 97 Squadron followed him in. Their leader, Sqn Ldr Sherwood, flying OF-K : L7573, was hit after his run in and crashed in flames. OF-P : R5513 was burning as it bombed. Another of 97 Squadron was shot down, leaving only five to return in darkness.

When they landed, their story was clearly one of great courage. For his devotion to duty, and to mark that of the others, the leader, John Nettleton, was awarded the Victoria Cross. He was killed later in the war but his

124   BOMBING COLOURS

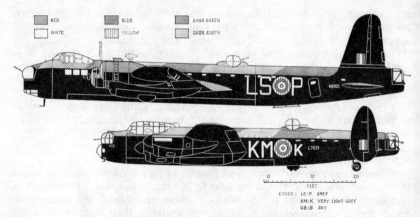

Figure 18; (*Top*) *Stirling I R9303 joined XV Sqn in February 1942 and became LS-P. She was one of the early machines with the more up-to-date dorsal turret. In April she was transferred to 214 Sqn, later serving with 101 Conversion Flt, 218 Conversion Flt, 1657 Conversion Unit and 1665 Conversion Unit. She survived until January 1945. (Above) The drawing here of the Lancaster is to the same scale as that of the Stirling, clearly showing what a large aeroplane the latter was, and may emphasise what excitement its emergence in 1940 brought. Lancaster L7533 joined 44 Sqn at the start of 1942, and is depicted as recorded in mid-February 1942. Her fuselage roundel is, as is the Stirling's, of 49-inch diameter. The letters KM are believed to have been 3 feet 6 inches high and the individual letter about 2 feet 6 inches. L7533 was lost on the night of May 8/9 1942.*

Lancaster of the Augsburg raid soldiered on and was operational even in 1944 when it was at Mildenhall as LS-C of XV Squadron. It survived the war and was broken up in 1947, a most regrettable act.

The cost of such operations was clearly prohibitive and so night raids followed against west Germany, Hamburg, Cologne, and culminated in a very successful set of attacks on Rostock.

Between April and October 1942 the Whitleys of 77 Squadron were detached to Coastal Command and repainted in a grey-green-white finish with grey code letters like Z9462 : KN-Y, Z9309 : KN-Y, and Z6978 : KN-P which sank *U-705* on September 3. No 10 OTU later had a similar detachment of aircraft, like AD703 : E and BD274 : D similarly coloured.

For much of May 1942 the weather was bad, limiting operations. To be really effective raids needed to swamp the defences which were becoming increasingly strong and well organised. This would require much larger forces than the 200 or so bombers usually operated. On May 18, Harris suggested in a letter to Portal, then Chief of Air Staff, a raid by 1,000 bombers. He estimated the Command could raise about 700 machines. Two days later his idea reached the Groups. Coastal Command, on learning of the scheme, offered 250 aircraft—Wellingtons, Whitleys, Hampdens, Hudsons and even the two Beaufort squadrons. At such an idea the Admiralty reared up in horror, and it was promptly vetoed. Training Command offered Wellingtons and Army Co-operation Command its Blenheims. Whilst these hurriedly planned schemes advanced, Bomber Command astonished itself, for in the two OTU Groups, Nos 91 and 92, it found it could raise over 350 Wellingtons, Whitleys and Hampdens. Finding crews for them might be a problem since some would have to be trainees whose losses might prove high. Choice of target had yet to be made. It was narrowed down to Hamburg or Cologne, the final choice being dependent on the weather. Virtually the whole of Bomber Command was to be thrown into one tremendous onslaught.

Once the plan was basically approved, the scheme gathered astonishing momentum, so much so that within a week the Operation Order was issued, and Operation *Millenium* was on.

Essentially the plan was simple. Wellingtons of 1 Group with Stirlings and Wellingtons of 3 Group fitted with *Gee* and carrying incendiaries would make a 15-minute opening attack starting fires for the main force to bomb on. The raid would be ended 1¾ hours later as Nos 4 and 5 Groups brought in their Halifaxes, Manchesters and Lancasters.

All was set for May 27 when the weather, ever fickle, prevented the executive order being given. It came soon after noon on May 30. For days the aircraft had been ready, air tests done and crews kept within the airfield confines. Rumour in the neighbouring villages was rife; something big was obviously afoot. Even before the raid rumours had circulated that Cologne was to be heavily bombed.

The dusk of Double Summertime was shattered over eastern England by an almost sudden outburst of din the like of which had never been heard before. It was the noise of some 3,000 engines needed to take the force of 1,046 bombers supported by intruders into action. As the sun set on that clear, calm evening one could see the bombers circling around their bases, gaining height and then forming into one of those mumbling bomber streams that characterised those days. Gradually it died away to the east as the cavalcade moved high across the streets in which many were watching one of the greatest events of the war unfold.

At 0038 on May 31 the first bombs fell on Cologne. By the end of the raid, 898 aircraft had claimed to unleash 540 tons of HE and 915 tons of incendiaries, loads relatively light by later standards, upon the lovely old city of Cologne. Conflagrations abounded as succeeding waves dropped their loads on the spreading fires. Mercifully, that beautiful Gothic structure, the cathedral, escaped destruction; in the city the scene must have resembled a mammoth version of the London fire raid of December 1940.

The operation cost the Command only 40 aircraft but another 85 were seriously damaged by flak, 12 more by fighters. A surprising aspect was that losses were higher among the front-line squadrons than in the training units, the reason never being fully explained.

Before the heavies were home, excitement was high at Horsham St Faith. After months of training and operational trials Mosquitoes of 105 Squadron were ready to play their part, to dash across the stricken city photographing the results of the raid. When GB-D : W4072, still in Dark Green-Dark Earth-Sky finish with black spinners and grey codes, reached her target it was so covered in smoke that photography was impossible. W4064, W4065 : N and W4071 : L also tried in vain. They merely aimed their 500 pounders into the smoke to create a new annoyance which was, years later, to pay handsome dividends: the Mosquito raider roaming the Reich at will and almost immune to interception. Before the day ended, Sqn Ldr Channer took GB-M : W4069 low across the countryside to burning Cologne. Here indeed was something the planners had not countenanced, the low-level strike form of Mosquito attack. It was highly successful right from the start.

While the huge force of bombers assembled for the first 'thousand bomber raid' was still poised for action, the Commander-in-Chief decided upon another strike. This time the target was Essen. Twenty fire-lighter crews of 3 Group, flying Wellingtons, were to open the onslaught. These were to be followed by selected crews from other Groups raining incendiaries on the

Krupp works. A total of 956 aircraft was despatched, including intruders, but only 767 attacked. The weather had deteriorated by the time the main force arrived and there was spill-over on to neighbouring towns. The hoped-for concentration on the main target was not achieved. Thirty-one aircraft were lost and 99 damaged. Such momentum could not be maintained, but a new powerful weapon had been blooded and the bomber offensive would never be the same as it was before the night of the Cologne raid.

Apart from Mosquitoes and intruders, the night bombers wore Dark Earth, Dark Green and matt black camouflage, the latter now usually ending as a straight line along the fuselage sides. It was during May 1942 that Dull Red codes generally made their appearance on bomber aircraft but the change-over took many weeks to accomplish. Nevertheless, there must have been quite a large number of aircraft wearing them and taking part in the large raids. Red was a far better colour for camouflage than the shades of grey used. For some months now 2 Group Blenheims, such as T2396 : WV-F of 18 Squadron recorded in March 1942, had been wearing red codes and serials. By April some of the medium and heavy bombers had Dull Red serials once more. One I well remember was a Wellington IC coded BU-L in grey and carrying the quite impossible serial 'DF9332'—and there is no doubt it was that! Another was Lancaster KM-C : R5556 at Duxford on May 5 for fighter interception trials. This had smaller codes than usual, a feature of 44's Lancasters for many months.

During April 1942, I recorded the markings of many bombers most of which still wore grey serials, and almost all were wearing grey identity letters. On April 7 Wellington III AA-D : X3667, the machine featured in the Airfix kit, was on one of Feltwell's southern dispersals. She had the very short life of two months and was missing from operations on April 22 1942. An oddity seen on April 12 was a Hampden with red-white-blue roundels beneath her wing tips so many months after these were generally removed. April 9 brought Wellington III SR-B : X3650 with grey codes and serials in the usual positioning. Three days later, Stirling AG-K flew over showing small grey unit codes more associated with the Stirlings of 7 Squadron. To confound the usual rule at this time were the Wellingtons of 40 Squadron at Alconbury, such as BL-A : X3598, for upon the squadron's aircraft the unit codes were positioned *forward* of the roundels on the port fuselage sides.

For me, May 14 was a memorable day since, as Lancaster OL-K came into my view, it was the first such aircraft I saw with new red codes and serials. Two days later Stirling BU-O had them, but these were still unusual as yet. Within these three days they were the only examples thus painted that I observed within a wide range of nearly 100 noted. What can best be said is that Dull Red codes were in use from early May 1942 and that within the next two months this colour replaced the grey of such long standing.

Before the Cologne raid there were still other markings and other points of interest to record. May 15 brought my first logging of a Halifax with any fairing at the base of its dorsal turret, a feature of TL-N : WJ046. On May 18 I noted that a passing Blenheim V had a grey-green-grey finish with red codes. May 22 brought Stirling LS-Y with grey codes and serial, along with two red-coded Wellingtons, SR-M : X3648 and OP-H. Two days later, DX-B and AA-R appeared with red codes, whereas Stirling OJ-H had grey. On the morning of the Cologne raid few bombers were flying but I did note Whitley V MH-G with red codes, and two Stirlings from 1651 CU, A : N6049 and P : N6099, both with grey codes and serials.

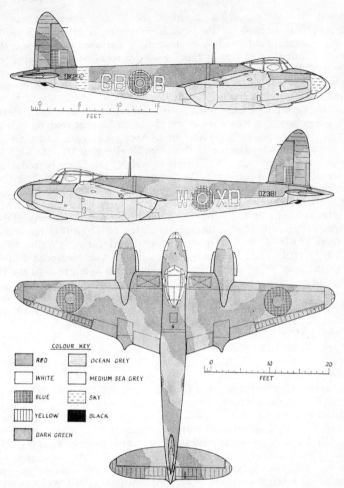

COLOUR KEY

▨ RED		▨ OCEAN GREY	
□ WHITE		▨ MEDIUM SEA GREY	
▨ BLUE		▨ SKY	
▨ YELLOW		■ BLACK	
▨ DARK GREEN			

Figure 19: (*Top*) *Mosquito IV Series II DK292 with Sky band, spinners and codes, and yellow wing leading edges. DK292 was with 105 Sqn from June to October 1942 and later served with 1655 MTU 13 OTU and in October 1944 joined 192 Sqn. She failed to return from an operation in the Munich area on November 27 1944. (Above) Mosquito XD-W : DZ381 of 139 Sqn. She joined the squadron on November 30 1942 and collided (near Kassel) with XD-R : DZ602 on the famous Jena raid of May 27 1943. It was her 13th operational flight.*

A point of detail concerns the Stirlings in use at this time. About February 1942, first deliveries were made of Stirling Is fitted with Lancaster-like FN50 dorsal turrets. My first close viewing of one came on April 7 at Lakenheath. It was OJ-H : N6081. Such aircraft were still few, for most had the old FN7 'Botha' turret like OJ-E : N6103, logged the same day alongside OJ-H. I saw many more Stirlings but it was April 20 before I spotted the next one with an FN50 turret, LS-P : R9303. Another in use at this time was R9304 'U' of 1651 CU, that unit's first example and one which had been in service with XV Squadron as LS-U since February. At the time of the 'thousand raid', aircraft thus modified were still quite rare, and Stirlings with the FN7 turret were used until the end of the war.

Another point of detail concerning markings that appeared at this time was the addition of a small number '2' aft of the aircraft individual letter indicating a second aircraft on the squadron wearing that letter. This was needed when some squadrons had their strength increased to include a third or 'C' Flight. I first noted one of these small numbers on May 2 applied to Wellington IC HS-B^2 of 109 Squadron. This was later commonly referred to as 'B squared'. It was still a rare item at this period and preceded the small bar painted over some individual letters later.

Inevitably the model maker must surely wish to include in his collection one of the bombers that took part in the 'thousand bomber raid' on Cologne. Aircraft in the list following are known to have taken part, and their code colours are as I observed them at that time. Wellington III KO-K : X3540 (red codes, unit letters aft), Wellington II PH-N : Z8652 (grey codes, unit letters aft of triangular windows), Wellington IV QT-B : Z1396 (red codes, unit letters aft of triangular window); Stirlings OJ-H : N6081 (red codes, FN50 turret), LS-D : W7524 (grey codes, FN7 turret); Lancasters KM-L : L7537 (grey codes), OL-O : R5625 (red codes, no ventral turret), EM-Q : R5628 (grey codes, no ventral turret); Halifaxes TL-D : R9444 (grey codes, dorsal turret), MP-B : W1016 (grey codes, dorsal turret); Wellington IC OP-R : R1252 (red codes, no triangular windows), and Hampden XG-K2 : AT195 (with '2' the same size as the unit coding, grey codes reading the same on either side). Other aircraft which took part in the operation included 9 Squadron: X3372, X3594 and X3686; 57 Squadron: X3221, DV816 and X3285; 61 Squadron R5691 and R5561; 78 Squadron: DG221, W1013 and W7670; 97 Squadron: R5502 : M, R5612 : R, R5607 : X and R5571 : A; 300 Squadron: Z1320 : K, Z1322 : D, Z1215 : E and Z1465 : S; 305 Squadron: W5447 : H, W5453 : E and W5420 : D; 405 Squadron: R9363 : U; 408 Squadron: AT870, AT227, AT154 and AD980; and 419 Squadron: X3308, Z1572 and X3723.

It was impossible to maintain these large forces intact very long for the Thousand Plan raids, desirable though they were seen to be. A build-up was again decided upon for the last week of June when, partly to placate the Admiralty, the naval target of Bremen was chosen. It was impossible for a variety of reasons to raise the entire force within Bomber Command, and assistance was therefore given by Coastal Command. As the target was a naval one, the Lords of the Admiralty could reasonably condone the operation and raised no objection this time to its contributing 102 Wellingtons and Hudsons. Over 60 intruders, including Bostons, supported the raid by 904 aircraft, which included some Blenheims, 198 Whitleys and Wellingtons of 91 Group and 106 Hampdens, Whitleys and Wellingtons of 92 Group.

Again the quiet evening air over eastern England was shattered by the roar then the mumble of nearly 1,000 aircraft. Leading this attack on June 25/26 were 50 Stirlings and 50 Halifaxes making a ten-minute raid. Then came Gee-fitted Wellingtons of Nos 1 and 3 Groups, 124 machines in all. Finally, there was the main force, including the Coastal Command element and crews of the OTUs. Six aiming points were listed, spread across the city, Stirlings fire-raising in its centre and Halifaxes in the docks and south-east part of the town. Hudsons, with hastily applied black under surfaces, took along 100 lb anti-submarine bombs, their numbers including AE643 : W and V9090 : A of 224 Squadron. The proportion of Lancasters on the raid had increased and they carried a mixed load of HE and incendiaries in equal proportions. All seemed to be well at take-off time, but unexpectedly the weather changed and by the start of the attack there was a 10/10 layer of strato-cumulus over the target. Many of the leading aircraft had to bomb by *Gee*. Nevertheless, an element of luck was present and damage to the large Focke-Wulf factory was particularly serious. Forty-four aircraft were lost and 65 damaged. Among the aircraft which took part, all wearing red codes, were MP-O: W1161, a Halifax II; OL-C: R5623, a Lancaster; and Wellington IIIs SR-P: Z1715 and SR-H: BJ590.

H

Chapter 15

Japan enters the war

LONG BEFORE THE WAR, thought was directed to the defence of Singapore, the naval base from which Britain ruled the eastern seas. The Lords of the Admiralty maintained that any attack upon the base would be from ships of the Japanese Navy, and that it would be a frontal assault. To counter this an assortment of guns was installed pointing seawards, among them 15-inch naval guns. To support their plans the Admiralty requested reconnaissance flying-boats and later some torpedo bombers.

To the Air Staff an entirely different direction of attack seemed possible—landings in Malaya and backdoor entry to the island. This notion was largely dismissed by the principal occupants of Singapore. But once the possibility of a northern attack was accepted, a start was made at building a string of airfields throughout the Malay Peninsula. This was difficult because of the vegetation, terrain, shortage of labour, and weather hardly conducive to the effort required, not to mention a general lack of belief in the need for the work.

During August 1939, two squadrons of Blenheims left Britain for Singapore. They were No 34 Squadron from Watton and No 62 from Cranfield. Among the Blenheim Is which 34 took were L1349, L1394, L1395 and L8366. No 62's aircraft included L1131, L1133, L1134 and L1259. These aircraft, in Dark Green-Dark Earth-Night finish, with Type B roundels, wore their respective code letters, but on arrival at Tengah the codes were changed, 34's to EG and 62's to PT. In India before the war, Blenheims were flying with Type A fuselage roundels and it is believed these were worn by the two Singapore-based squadrons. Also available at Singapore were Nos 36 and 100 Squadrons flying antiquated Vildebeest torpedo bombers. Both squadrons, like those in Coastal Command, were scheduled to re-equip with Beauforts. The intention was to increase squadron strength in about 1940 and, if there was any emergency, aircraft could be quickly flown to reinforce the Far East units, via the many staging posts Britain held in the eastern world. The dangerous parallel between this plan and that which currently exists is plain to see particularly with the change in the world pattern. When the need for re-inforcement arose the war in the Middle East was commandeering all the available reinforcement aircraft. The Royal Navy, in whose hands the defence of Singapore largely rested, was likewise fully engaged elsewhere to the limit of its strength and regrettably some British politicians never seem to learn from the most bitter experiences.

By 1941 it was only too apparent that the Royal Air Force would need to take the lion's share in defending Britain's Far East territory. Its weakness there was extremely alarming, and so every means needed to be used to ensure the Japanese were not drawn into the war. A risk existed that the Japanese would invade Siam, then stage an assault through Malaya. When this seemed likely, contingency plans for a British incursion into Siam, and the bombing of any airfields the Japanese might then seize, were brought to a state of readiness. Their enaction would have precipitated war with Japan, and so the British stayed their hand.

By December 1941, all aircraft in Singapore and Malaya were outdated. Amazingly there was no combined headquarters to control defensive operations for the 13 new operational airfields. This was to be a very serious omission.

Early that month, Hudsons of the RAAF spotted large convoys of Japanese ships off Siam. The signs were ominous, but it was policy not to provoke the Japanese in any way. Then came Pearl Harbour, and on December 8 1941, Japanese bombers raided Singapore.

The RAF bomber force in Malaya presently comprised about 35 Blenheims. These were mainly the Mk IVs of 34 Squadron still at Tengah, and Mk Is of 62 Squadron at Alor Star, whence they had moved in February. No 62 had about a dozen Blenheim Is. These were supplemented by a small detachment from 60 Squadron, Rangoon, on armament training at the Kuantan practice camp. The rôle of the two operational squadrons and the RAAF Hudsons was an anti-shipping one. Some crews for the squadrons had partly trained at a makeshift OTU established at Kluang, and equipped with Wirraways, ex-21 Squadron, RAAF, and some Blenheims loaned by 34 Squadron. It immediately disbanded when the Japanese attacked. All the units were very badly off for spares, so much so that they were permitted to fly each aircraft for only a maximum of five hours per month, so there was little flying.

Such fighter support as might be available gave cause for alarm, for the aircraft would be Buffaloes in squadrons only half ready for action. They faced a modern Japanese naval force whose equipment included the Mitsubishi Zero which, owing to confusion in high places, they knew little about. Possible assistance might come from 22 Marylands and nine Buffaloes that the Dutch had in the East Indies.

Hudsons and Catalinas watched enemy shipping on December 6 and 7 and on the latter day one of 205's Catalinas was shot down. As Singapore was being bombed, a Japanese Army force was landing at Kota Bharu on the east coast of Malaya and this was attacked by Nos 34 and 60 Squadrons, also RAAF Hudsons, while 11 Blenheims of 62 Squadron bombed Putani. Also on December 8 the Japanese, who had planned their skilful campaign with care, attacked RAF airfields heavily, destroying Blenheims of 34 Squadron at Tengah including V5381, V5465, V5633 and Z5799. Next day the Japanese reached Kota airfield and 34 Squadron attacked the invaders. A more important operation was quickly planned, against enemy airfields further north, in particular Singora in Siam. Crews from 34, 60 and 62 Squadrons were assembled at Butterworth where, not long before, Japanese bombers had bombed 62 Squadron as it was landing and reduced its strength to two serviceable Blenheim Is. Just as the big raid was about to be launched, Japanese bombers struck again.

Only one crew proceeded on the operation, possibly in Blenheim IV V5499, captained by Flt Lt A. S. K. Scarf. He reached Singora, in itself a gallant deed. But soon he was attacked by fighters, and mortally wounded. Nevertheless he brought his Blenheim back to Alor Star where he made a forced landing before he died. Record keeping at this time was chaotic and most of the official records for the campaign were lost. Much later, when news of his courage and example was known, Scarf was posthumously awarded the Victoria Cross. It was the first given for service in South East Asia.

The Blenheims at this time still had Dark Green-Dark Earth camouflage with Night under surfaces. Type A1 roundels were worn on the fuselage sides and Type B above the mainplanes. Fin stripes were carried and some aircraft (eg, L6667: PT-U of 62 Squadron) still had rudder serials. This latter point would apply only to pre-war built Blenheims. No under-wing serials were carried.

On December 10, Singora was raided again by six crews, three each from 34 and 60 Squadrons, three aircraft being lost. No 34 Squadron also made coastal reconnaissance flights from Kuantan, and enemy bombers again bombed RAF bases, forcing 62's two aircraft to flee from Butterworth to Taiping. Then all the Blenheims of 34 and 62 that could be made airworthy flew to Singapore for complete overhaul. On December 12, 34 Squadron yet again raided Singora, but few of the eight crews managed to get there owing to poor weather.

It was then decided to hold the decimated Blenheim force at readiness for attacks on further landings on the coast. An urgent call came on December 23, when 34 Squadron was despatched to attack a convoy which appeared to be heading for Sumatra. The crews of 60 Squadron were sent back to Rangoon for possible operations over Burma, their aircraft swelling the meagre strength of 62 Squadron.

On Christmas Eve the strength of 34 Squadron was about ten aircraft, and 62 had seven, all based at Tengah. Urgent pleas for reinforcement had fallen on neither deaf ears nor unwilling hands, but there were hardly any spare Blenheims available and the only possibility was really to transfer some squadrons. A dozen Blenheims were nevertheless despatched, seven of which reached 34 Squadron on Christmas Day.

Fear now was that the enemy would also land on the west coast. For the first few days of January the Blenheims patrolled the area and, on January 2, 3 and 4 1942, attacked Port Swettenham. Such was the confusion now in the Army that useful supplies were being left behind in the hasty enforced retreat, and one of the sad tasks of the Blenheim squadrons was the destruction of sorely needed supplies and equipment.

In an attempt to operate with reduced losses, some night raids against enemy airfields were attempted in which the Catalinas of 205 Squadron joined. On the 15th, three Blenheims operated against barges in the Liuggi River, under an escort of Buffaloes, which could have hardly given the crews much sense of comfort. By now the Dutch Marylands had come into action, six of them joining nine Blenheims in an attack on barges in the Muar River on the 16th. Next day, Japanese bombers heavily raided Tengah and six Blenheims were badly damaged. No 62 Squadron was now completely decimated and it was decided to re-establish the unit and equip it with spare Hudson IIIs currently arriving in lieu of Blenheims.

All the time the Japanese Army was successfully conducting its Malayan campaign and advancing towards Singapore. Plans for its evacuation had to be enacted hastily amid scenes of chaos. Aircrew were a precious commodity and were ordered aboard the troopships, whereas lots were drawn amongst the others to see who should go and who be left to the cruelty of the Japanese. One member of 34 Squadron related to me the story of how those tremendously gallant women in the Salvation Army tended the wounded and brought tea and comfort to the men who were to be left behind. As the last ship was about to sail these brave souls refused to board her, so a group of aircrew rushed ashore and dragged the screaming women to safety by their hair.

No 225 Group was formed on January 16 to continue bomber operations from Sumatra. Major reinforcements from the Middle East began to arrive on January 23, too late to save Malaya and too small in any case to stem the assault. Principally involved were Nos 84 and 211 Squadrons, whose ground crews were still coming by sea. Sixteen Blenheims of 84 Squadron moved into Palembang and 18 (including Z9573 and V5999) of 211 Squadron arrived between January 23 and February 14. The remnants of Nos 34, 62 and the RAAF Hudson squadrons were sited on a 'secret' airfield cut in the jungle near Palembang, 34 Squadron bringing its six Blenheim IVs on January 26 and leaving the Buffaloes and Hurricanes to fight it out over Malaya. Fewer than 50 aircraft reached Sumatra.

All of the Blenheims were now in a deplorable state and the reinforcement aircraft were in a bad way after their long flights. The Blenheim force was used for convoy escort and attacks on Malayan airfields, although the journey to the latter was very long and difficult. Between January 30 and February 5 they managed 31 sorties. It was a worthy effort considering that on the 31st 34 Squadron had only six Mk IVs; 62 had acquired five Mk Is and 10 Hudson IIIs; 84 had 10 Mk IVs; and 211 had four Mk IVs, none of which were in anything but fair condition. By February 14 there were 35 Blenheims left and most were unserviceable. No 27 Squadron, which had served as a Blenheim night-fighter unit that was virtually wiped out early in the campaign, had somehow contrived to exist again and on the 14th its Blenheims, along with those of Nos 62, 84 and 211 Squadrons, attacked a convoy heading for Sumatra. They, with 84 and 211 Squadrons, repeated their attacks on the 15th and repelled the convoy by their persistence only to be beaten ultimately when the Japanese landed paratroops.

With only six Blenheims left between them, the squadrons were ordered to Java on the 18th. Next day, five Blenheims attacked shipping at Palembang, repeating the operation on the 20th and 21st. Then Japanese bombers struck at their new base, Semplak. Nevertheless, they managed to get three aircraft away on the 23rd, the crews of which even claimed to sink a Japanese submarine !

On March 1, 84 Squadron was wiped out when the enemy army arrived at their base, Kalidjati, although a gallant band of survivors managed to escape and sail a small boat to Australia which they miraculously reached 44 days later. A grim end came to the Blenheim squadrons, which were simply wiped out. All along it had been the old story—too little equipment and too few men.

The fall of Burma

The Japanese invasion of Burma had a two-fold purpose. A successful campaign would cut the supply route to China, and open the way for an invasion of India and a thrust to join the Axis powers in the Middle East. In retrospect this would seem to have been almost impossible, for the supply lines would have required logistic support that the Japanese could surely never have afforded. However, the loss of India would have been a tremendous blow to the Allies.

Japan's campaign against Burma opened with a ferocious attack on Rangoon on December 23 1941. The only RAF units available for defence

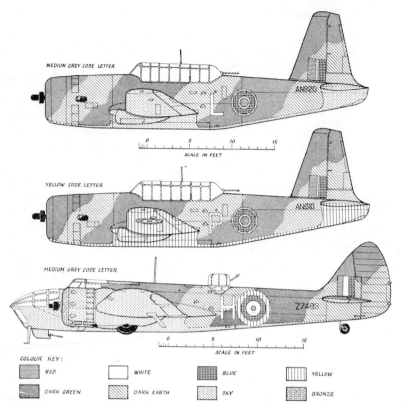

MEDIUM GREY CODE LETTER

AN920

SCALE IN FEET

YELLOW CODE LETTER

AN610

MEDIUM GREY CODE LETTER

Z7483

SCALE IN FEET

COLOUR KEY:

RED   WHITE   BLUE   YELLOW

DARK GREEN   DARK EARTH   SKY   BRONZE

Figure 20: (*Top to bottom*) *Vengeance I AN920 : L of 82 Sqn based on a photograph taken in March 1943. Vengeance II AN610 recorded at Feltwell on August 19 1943, when with the Bombing Development Unit. Note the old type under-wing roundel, in use long after it had been officially discarded. AN838-AP137 were Vengeance Is, and EZ800-999 were Vultee Vengeance IAs, Northrop-built and delivered under Lend-Lease. AF745-944 and AN538-837 were Mk IIs, Vultee-built and delivered against British contract. The Mk I had the Wright GR-2600-A5B5 engine and probably the Mk IA had the 2600-19 engine. The Blenheim IV is Z7483 of 60 Sqn in use in Burma at the beginning of 1942, and is based upon a photograph.*

were Buffaloes of 67 Squadron which had arrived at Rangoon from Malaya in October, and the Blenheim I and IV bombers of No 60 Squadron which also served as a communications and light transport unit. Reinforcements to stem the invasion were needed urgently. This came in the form of Blenheim IVs of 113 Squadron, followed a few weeks later by No 45's Blenheims. Both units now occupied Magwe Airport. No 113 Squadron reached Rangoon on January 7. Next day it despatched its Blenheims, including AD-B : V5627, C : Z9820, D : Z7592, M : Z7916, F : Z7623, G : Z7969 and J : Z9674, and two from 60 Squadron, including MU-K : Z7630; the target was Bangkok airport. All the aircraft wore Dark Green-Dark Earth-Sky camouflage; usual in this area where the later production Blenheims were in use.

The Japanese advanced slowly into Burma and 45 Squadron mounted a raid on Mingaladon which brought a rapid reprisal. Some 230 bombers raided Magwe—and only six Blenheims were left. By March 1942 the bomber force was all but wiped out. In any case, the small bomber force could not hope to delay the invaders in a country where jungle gave cover, and mountains made flying hazardous. Added to this there was a massive drift of Burmese refugees northwards.

No 11 Squadron had moved to Colombo, Ceylon, in March 1942 and stayed until January 1943, placed there in case the enemy attempted a landing, or positioned a naval force to attack Trincomalee. It was not long before the anticipated attacks developed and 11 Squadron's Blenheims went into action against shipping, losing five aircraft.

The conquest of Burma and the digestion of Malaya and other gains soon occupied the enemy's resources. Then came the summer rains, halting operations. For the Japanese it was a time of consolidation and preparation for an invasion of India. For the British the respite was a relief, allowing reinforcement aircraft into the theatre of operation to support any army offensives. The Far East was, of course, an essentially American area of operations and one decision was to use, where possible, American-built aircraft in RAF squadrons. The flow of American aircraft built up, but still the quality of many left much to be desired, especially as there was a spares problem too.

The Consolidated Liberator had found no niche in RAF bomber operations over northern Europe, but its long range was utilised by Coastal Command. This aspect was a great attraction and could clearly be put to good use in the Far East where distances are so vast. Therefore, a quantity of Liberator IIs, some with, and some without, dorsal turrets, were routed to India via the Middle East in March 1942. They arrived at a time when there was a desperate need for heavy bombers and so were held in Egypt and Palestine whilst the situation in the Far East sorted itself out. Part of 159 Squadron arrived in India to await them in May 1942, moving to Salbani in September and to Digri in October, where it stayed until March 1944. The first few Liberators arrived in India in July 1942, including AL537 in Dark Green-Dark Earth-Night camouflage. Medium Grey individual letters are said to have been carried and, by August, AL531, AL540, AL517, AL582, AL603 and AL579 are believed to have been with the squadron. The arrival of the Liberators posed a problem, for few spares were available for these relatively sophisticated aircraft, and this prevented operations until near the end of the year, by which time AL520, AL526 and AL531 were in use.

In 1940 the Royal Air Force was somewhat reluctantly attracted to the idea of a fast dive-bomber, for the success of the Stuka as an army support weapon had been much in evidence. There was a clamour for a dive-bomber from some excited politicians in Parliament; as if one could be pulled out of a hat. The Hawker Henley might have, indeed should have, been available, but it was too late to do anything about it. Specifications were issued to the industry in Britain and de Havilland, among others, hastily prepared plans. These were discarded in favour of a British specification placed with the Vultee company in America for the design of a dive-bomber, which became the Vengeance, first flown in July 1941. It was mid-1942 before the aeroplane began to be delivered to the British, by which time the considerable number on contract provided some embarrassment. The Vengeance was not fast enough for employment over Europe where its rôle would be of little value now. It was poorly armed, and came on to the scene when effective fighter-bombers were being evolved amidst vastly changing close-support ideas. The dive-bomber, many considered, was a sitting target to ground defences. In the Middle East, close support squadrons were successfully operating Bostons and Baltimores and there was no need for the Vengeance. An unkind notion later existed to replace the Blenheim in Bomber Command with the Vengeance, and AN888 and AN889 arrived for evaluation at Boscombe Down in July 1942. Mercifully, the latter-day Fairey Battle was not foisted on to the home-based squadrons; instead it was to pass to India and the Burma front where, it was reckoned, it could be operated with less risk than over Europe. The Vengeance virtually slid into SEAC supplies building up in 1942 and 1943, the initial commitment being two squadrons, Nos 82 and 84. AN609 later found its way to Farnborough for prolonged work and AN610 was brought to the Bomber Development Unit at Feltwell for further evaluation, which was completed at Newmarket in October 1943. My recollection of this aircraft is chiefly of the Harvard-like sound she made, her angular form being quite unlike any other aeroplane around at the time. AN610 was finished Dark Green-Dark Earth-Yellow. Like quite a few prototype and experimental aircraft she had a yellow letter 'P' on the fuselage without the yellow circle prescribed for prototypes.

The first Vengeance squadron in the Far East was No 82 which began equipping at Drigh Road. AN956 : U was with the squadron in June and other early aircraft included AN845, '852, '923 and '946. By mid-1943, Mks I, IA and II were in service. No 84 Squadron received Vengeances at Quetta; No 110 Squadron began getting them at Quetta in October; and No 45 received its first two Vengeances on December 11. The first operation with the new type was flown on December 17 with 'UX' coded Vengeances of No 82 Squadron, an anti-submarine patrol over the Bay of Bengal. No more operations were flown for many months, and No 110 Squadron commenced operations from Madhaigang on March 19 1943. Its aircraft at the time included N : AN927, G : AN916, P : AN917, S : AN895 and Y : AN929 which may have worn squadron letters too. Their finish was Dark Green-Dark Earth-Sky with Medium Grey letters.

To form the nucleus of a night-bomber force a few Wellington ICs reached Ansansol, India, in April 1942 in the hands of 215 Squadron, wearing the usual temperate scheme camouflage and with grey individual letters. Their subsequent bases were Pandaveswar between April and August, Madras until October, and Chaklala up to March 1943. No 215 was joined by 99 Squadron also with ICs which arrived at Pandaveswar in September 1942 and moved the following month to Digri.

Failure to develop a Blenheim replacement gave Bomber Command a major headache. The Bristol Buckingham might have fulfilled this niche but its requirement specification had been issued too late. The Mosquito, in its then current form, was not a replacement and was in very short supply. When the Blenheim's useful life ended in late 1941 there was nothing to take its place apart from the Boston, also in short supply. Bristol, however, had developed the Blenheim V, commonly called Bisley, designed as a close-support bomber, but it was only a small advance over the Mk IV. It was more to keep important production lines intact at Rootes than because the Air Force wanted it, that Mk V production proceeded at a rapid pace in 1942. In mid-1942 the Mk VD began to equip some home-based squadrons destined for North-West Africa. Since the Vengeance appeared to have tactical limitations, and because Blenheim spares were easily available, several Mk Vs were sent to India, replacing Mk IVs in Nos 11, 34 and 113 Squadrons in autumn 1942. No 113 Squadron, for example, received its first VD, BA578, on October 18 1942. It became evident that the fighter-bomber had more to offer than the Blenheim V which was ultimately replaced by the Hurricane. For operations in 1943 the Blenheim VD, Vengeance, Wellington IC and Liberator II were the aircraft that made up the bomber force.

With the increase in RAF strength in India and new aircraft types slotted into the squadrons, the Army Commander, General Wavell, felt that he could launch an offensive into Burma by December 1942.

Wavell had a choice of three fronts: the Arakan, Arakan-Imphal and the route to Mandalay. He chose to act with caution, and to attack Akyab and hold it as a forward base. Going was tough, with the RAF attacking villages, troops and transports ahead of the advancing army in a campaign that lasted until May 1943. By then all the new types had seen some action and the bomber force numbered 11 squadrons as follows:

Sqn No	Equipment	Example	Base	Notes
11	Blenheim IV/VD	Z7803	Feni, India	
34	Blenheim IV/VD	BA287	Madras	Mk V first received 12.42
45	Vengeance II	AN656: H-OB	Ansansol	Vengeance received 12.42, replaced Blenheim IV
60	Blenheim IV	Z9591	Dohazari	Replaced 8.43 by Hurricane
82	Vengeance I/IA	AN957: Y-UX EZ855	Ansansol	Left UK early 1942
84	Vengeance I	AN845	Ratmalana, Ceylon	Received 12.42, no operations until 16.2.44
99	Wellington IC	DV875	Chaklala	Began operations 11.42. No unit code
110	Vengeance I	AN927:N	Madhaiganj	Left UK 3.42
113	Blenheim VD	BA916	Chandina	Coded AD
159	Liberator II	AL603	Digri, India	
215	Wellington IC	HF900:T	Jessore	Began operations 24.4.42

Chapter 16

The offensive develops

FROM MARCH 1942 the bomber offensive had gathered momentum as never before. By night, there were the 'thousand bomber raids'. By day, Bostons with massive fighter cover flew *Circus* operations over France, tempting the Luftwaffe to battle. Between March and June 30, 700 sorties were flown by Nos 88, 107 and 226 Squadrons under the protection of about 22,000 Spitfire sorties. The response was disappointing, costing the RAF about 300 fighters and the Luftwaffe a little less than 100.

Boston IIIs were coloured Dark Green and Dark Earth with Sky under surfaces. In May 1942, Dull Red codes were introduced on the Bostons. There was another change too, the application of Type C1 fuselage roundels and revised fin flashes. Type A1 roundels with equal-width bands of colour in bright shades were suitable when close combat was common. Now it was decided to widen the red and blue areas of the roundels and reduce the white in the fin stripes. It might appear logical that such a major change for identity purposes would rapidly be adopted, but this was certainly not so. These roundels were seen on some aircraft in May, became common by mid-June, but were still replacing the old style on operational aircraft even in July. Two variants laid down for bombers were a medium size with red-yellow diameters ranging 12-16-32-36 inches and large size diameters 18-24-48-54 inches. Twin-engined aircraft had tail flashes 24 by 24 inches, band widths being 11-2-11 inches, in theory, anyway, because the Bostons often featured fin flashes 27 inches high. On heavies the fin flashes measured 24 by 36 inches, stripe widths being 17-2-17 inches, and this applied to Manchesters and some of the OTU Whitleys. Dull Red codes introduced at roughly the same time were referred to in Chapter 14.

By July, bombers were operational in two schemes—Night: Dark Green and Dark Earth with smooth Night finish, and Day: Dark Green and Dark Earth with Sky under surfaces, with Dull Red codes and serials, although here again some Bostons were different, retaining black serials for many months. Code letters were usually about 4 feet high on the heavies varying in style and precise location, 24 inches high on Mosquitoes and 30 inches high on Bostons. A few Bostons were painted black overall for intruder operations on the Bremen 1,000 bomber raid, some of 226 Squadron's being seen with red codes and serials.

Always the odd man out was the Mosquito. Even before it was operational it had been decided to replace Dark Earth camouflage by Ocean Grey, and to paint the undersides in Medium Sea Grey. This took time to implement and well into summer Mosquitoes were still to be seen in the old scheme, but these were probably rarely used operationally because it had been decided to rely upon camouflage as a ruse. Bomber Mosquitoes were unarmed, and there was constant fear that enemy fighter pilots, knowing this, would be more likely to press their attacks—assuming they could catch the raiders. Sky spinners and tail bands making the bombers look like fighters were therefore introduced, and some Mosquitoes even had yellow wing leading edges. These features were only retained until July 1942. They were a nuisance on low-level operations, making the aircraft too easily visible. There is no doubt that some Mosquitoes wore a dark shade of grey—probably Dark Sea Grey—instead of Ocean Grey. When in July the order was given to paint the spinners Ocean Grey it could easily be seen that the two greys used were quite different. One of the Ocean Grey-Dark Green-Medium Grey Mosquitoes with Sky spinners and tail band was GB-M : W4069, thus recorded on June 26. There were, of course, various combinations of the approved markings to be seen, but the most unusually marked Mosquito that I saw, one of the early BIV series 1 aircraft, was painted Dark Green and Dark Grey with Sky under surfaces and very exceptionally had Type C roundels under its wing tips. This I recorded on October 14.

The first 'Mosquito spectacular' was a raid on Flensburg on July 2, six Mosquitoes making a low-level attack. A week later another attack on Flensburg was made as a diversion to 40 Lancasters from Nos 83, 97, 106 and 207 Squadrons making a dusk raid on Danzig. Two Mosquitoes used with Sky adornments were GB-C : W4070 and GB-O : DK297. Mosquitoes making daylight cloud cover attacks on Germany carried on until October, when the rôle changed. No 105 Squadron tried to attack Berlin on September 19 but bad weather ruined the raid. On September 25, with GB-G : DK296 leading, a low-level raid was mounted on the Gestapo HQ in Oslo. With the daylight getting shorter it was decided to mount dusk and dawn attacks. Exhaust stacks of the aircraft used on such operations were now shrouded, very unpopular for it brought varying troubles.

At the end of May 1942, a new shape had joined Bomber Command, the dumpy Lockheed Ventura, the first of which reached Britain in April. No 21 Squadron equipped with Venturas and received its first North American Mitchell in July, too. Two new squadrons, No 487 formed in August and 464 formed in September, both at Feltwell, worked up on Venturas. These were finished in Dark Green-Dark Earth-Sky initially, and indeed for much of their service, although there was a brief period in September when some of 21's aircraft had black under surfaces, since the Ventura's initial employment was expected to be as an intruder. Red codes and serials were usual, as on EG-O : AJ216, unit letters forward of the roundels. Others similarly marked were YH-O : AJ452, YH-S : AE852, SB-F : AJ174, SB-C : AE732 and EG-B : AE684. The first coded specimen I recorded, in July 1942, wore the unit letters TU in red forward of her roundels. No 21 Squadron commenced operations on November 3, but it was on the Philips raid of December 6 when the Venturas entered the operational scene in force.

In August 1942, the Pathfinder Force, No 8 Group, formed. This was done in the face of disapproval from the C-in-C, who was against establishing a force of elite crews gathered from all the squadrons of Bomber Command. The Air Staff pointed out that the results achieved so far with *Gee* were not good enough, and that something had to be done to improve accuracy. The PFF would lead operations and study methods to achieve accuracy. The nucleus of 8 Group comprised 7 Squadron (Stirling), 35 Squadron (Halifax II), 83 Squadron (Lancaster I) and 156 Squadron (Wellington III), equipped with *Gee*. Tasks of the crews were to find the target, illuminate the target area and then mark it with flares and incendiaries, continuing the latter until the attack was well under way. If the weather was cloudy they would mark the target area with coloured flares. An incendiary wave would then attack and finally the Main Force with HE and incendiaries.

There were serious snags. Flares would quickly drift, and they could dazzle other crews and illuminate the aircraft for enemy gunners. *Gee* was being jammed and incendiary markers were soon lost when the Main Force attacked. There was frequent drift in the bombing, and so there was no room for complacency. Fortunately, fears that the aircraft would be sitting targets on their final run seemed unfounded. Luck was out at the start, for when the first PFF-led raid took place against Flensburg on August 18/19 (when Stirling MG-E : BF335 and Halifax TL-M : W1160 took part) the weather was bad, the attack going completely astray. By the end of 1942, 26 attacks had been PFF-led with varying success, but six times they had failed to find the target.

A possible solution to some problems seemed to lay in a very high-flying aircraft using a special radio aid, *Oboe*, and the Wellington VI was available. As long ago as 1938, a high-flying variant of the Wellington had been proposed, to operate from 35,000 feet and even reach 40,000 feet, then an astonishing altitude. The crew were to be in the pressurised compartment built into the nose of the aircraft, which was to be powered by specially developed Bristol Hercules VIII engines. These were delayed and in June 1940, it had been decided to fit Hercules IIIs as an interim measure. The first high-altitude Wellington, R3298, designated Mk V, flew in the summer of 1940. Much of the development flying was done from Squires Gate. There were many problems to overcome, particularly concerning icing and the intense cold. A second aircraft, R3299, was fitted with Hercules VIIIs but they were unsuitable for operational work. Interest switched to installation of Merlin 60s, two being fitted in W5795 (the next aircraft), now completed as the first Mk VI and finished in prototype colours, and flown in 1941. It was impossible to have a gunner in the tail turret at the altitude at which the aircraft was to perform and so a remote control system for the turret and guns was worked out using periscopic sighting. Despite largely unsolved problems, and risks to the crew, production of the Mk VI came under way with W5797-5815, delivery of which began in October 1941. These and DR471-479 were designated Mk VIA, whereas the remainder with '/G' serial suffix were known as Mk VIG and fitted with *Gee*, as were DR480-504 and DR519-528. Delivery of these machines spanned from May 27 1942, until the end of March 1943. Nearly all the VIs spent their time in MUs until they were scrapped. They were probably delivered in the prescribed factory finish of Dark Green-Dark Earth with Deep Sky sides and under surfaces, although some certainly acquired grey and green upper surfaces in RAF hands. Two examples, W5801 and W5802, were delivered to 109 Squadron at Stradishall in March 1942. This was a radio counter measures trials squadron and the Wellington VI had possible use. W5802 passed to the RAE on May 17 but W5801, despite an assortment of snags, was retained at Stradishall until July. Both aircraft had at some time been repainted Deep Sky overall and had only Type B roundels. Another Mk VI that I saw on July 30, incidentally, had Sky under surfaces. Tended in particular by Rolls-Royce engineers, W5801 was modified for some reconnaissance rôle. It seems that she made at least two operational flights over Germany in daylight.

A possible use for the Mk VI seemed to be as a flare dropper equipped with the new navigation aid, *Oboe*. A 1941 invention, it comprised two ground stations in contact with a receiver in the aircraft. One, the 'mouse' station, emitted an oboe-like sound which the crew of the aircraft could hear in their headphones. Whilst they heard the note they knew they were flying on the correct course. The set in the aircraft returned a signal to the 'cat' station which in turn sent back a signal picked up on the run up to the target. When it abruptly ceased the bomb aimer released his load. The greatest handicap to the equipment was its limited range, and the higher the aircraft flew the greater this would be. Only one aircraft could be handled at a time on the run-up and it meant flying straight and level for about ten minutes, not a healthy form of entertainment. *Oboe* could only be available to a small number of aircraft on one raid. Thoughts initially turned to the Wellington VI but then a better proposition came into view, the Mosquito. Accordingly, DK300 arrived at Stradishall for fitting out on July 21 1942. Because 109 Squadron was now switching to target marking, the squadron moved to Wyton, the 8 Group centre, where more Mosquitoes arrived to receive *Oboe*. One was DK318. On August 21, like the others, it was in grey-green finish, and her Ocean Grey spinners contrasted strikingly with the other grey of the top decks. During October the under surfaces of the Mosquitoes were painted black and in November red codes were applied, HS appearing aft on both sides of the aircraft. DK333 became HS-F and DK318: HS-B. A further brief flirtation with the Wellington VI came in December 1942-January 1943 when DR481 and DR485 served with 109 Squadron, but they were clearly outclassed by the Mosquito, although their load-carrying capacity as backers-up looked useful. By then the Mosquitoes were in operation attacking from 26,000-28,000 feet, almost the height at which the Wellington was supposed to operate. On December 20, six Mosquitoes, including HS-C: DK321 and HS-D: DK331, both with long-range wing tanks, were despatched on a calibration raid on the power station at Lutterade, Holland, which proved remarkably successful. They soon embarked on a determined attempt to mark the Krupp works at Essen.

As the PFF returned from Flensburg on August 18/19 1942, another force was about to attack, for the Dieppe landing opened at 0510 hrs. Bomber Command had only a limited, but none the less spectacular, share in the raid. Bostons of 2 Group covered the first landing parties by dropping smoke bombs on the cliffs. During the day some extremely courageous flights were made by other Boston crews laying smoke from SCI gear, MQ-B: Z2281 being one aircraft used for this. Army co-operation Blenheims in similar finish to the Bostons were scheduled to lay smoke but their missions had to be abandoned. Bombing support given to the army was small, partly due to the confused situation.

An interesting feature at this time was the assortment of colours carried by Blenheim VDs used by 2 Group squadrons working up for their part in the forthcoming campaign in North-West Africa. One recorded on June 28 had Ocean Grey and Dark Green upper surfaces with black under surfaces and sides. Another without a dorsal turret—this was common—had a tall radio mast in its place and was finished in Dark Green-Dark Earth-Sky with 'U' in red forward of the roundels. Another coded PF-P in red was black overall, when seen on July 27; but most of them had Sky under surfaces. On November 12, I noted another similar machine in Dark Green-Dark Earth-Sky finish with red codes and very long flame damper exhausts, and at the same time another was seen with Azure under surfaces in place of Sky. On August 23 I noted Blenheim IV all black with DP-A in red and a very small red serial. Her fuselage roundels were Type B.

Although Dull Red was the colour specified for bomber codes, there were exceptions. At the time of change-over to red there were to be seen a number of Halifaxes with yellow codes, including EY-U, EY-W, EY-Y and ZA-U. Others, presumably of a training unit, were seen over Yorkshire with single identity letters aft of their roundels. These letters were extremely conspicuous, but their purpose remains unknown. A little later 102 Squadron aircraft flew for some time with grey DY lettering and red individual letters as on DY-U, DY-G and DY-M. Well into the later months of the year grey codes were still in evidence.

Lancaster EA-O had grey codes on November 29, and when 1651 Conversion Unit introduced 'QQ' codes to its Stirlings in February 1943, some aircraft had grey codes. For the most part, however, the bombers conformed to red, like Stirling MG-P : R9267 with a 'Botha-type' dorsal turret and MG-X : R9324 which had no dorsal turret. Some of 106 Squadron's Lancasters were also flying at this time without dorsal turrets, whereas Halifax DY-Z, seen August 20 with the customary 'Hudson-type' turret, had a fairing around the base similar to that on the Lancaster. Wellingtons in use at this time with red codes and C1 roundels, etc, included AA-N : BJ679 and AA-Z : BJ832. Other aircraft in standard markings included Wellington IV QT-S : Z1338, and BH-S : Z1465, Stirling I OJ-W : N6079 (with FN50 turret) and Lancasters OL-M : R5626 and OL-H : R5743. Halifaxes included MP-P : BB242 and TL-B : W1047. At first the Mitchells of 98 Squadron—from the start wearing Dark Green-Medium Grey—had their Dull Red codes flanking the fuselage roundel, like VO-T (VO forward on both sides) recorded thus on December 13 1942. FL203 had black serials mid placed; others had them low on the fuselage. Black was the colour of Mitchell serials until the end of hostilities.

By September the die had been cast for the future Allied bomber offensive. Units of the US 8th Air Force had begun to take up stations in Britain and the first small-scale operations had taken place over France. The Americans were to operate by day and Bomber Command heavies by night. Day bombers of the RAF would eventually switch to army support in a tactical air force still some time away. But Bomber Command possessed a sizeable Lancaster force and the belief died hard that somehow the Lancasters could battle their way through into Germany in daylight. Their range was attractive, too, and 61 Squadron had a brief involvement with the war at sea. It was detached to St Eval, Cornwall, on August 3 to search for enemy shipping off western France. There were two highlights. On August 19 a large tanker was spotted in Biscay and nine Lancasters set out to sink her, losing two of their number, R5661 and R5605. With the help of a Whitley of 502 Squadron, R5888 sank the German submarine U-751. But Bomber Command needed all its Lancasters and 61 was back at its base on August 22. When 83 Squadron was transferred to the Pathfinder Force in August the Lancaster force was maintained by transferring 57 Squadron and its Wellingtons to 5 Group and then re-equipping the squadron.

At the end of September, highly secret orders reached 5 Group stations. Their squadrons were to prepare for a low-level raid in force and, in a great gaggle, flew a low-level training mission around Britain on October 1. Then they awaited the day of the raid, ordered on October 17. Ninety-four Lancasters from nine squadrons, over half the entire Lancaster force, were despatched in the afternoon. Flying very low and led by Wg Cdr Slee in W4196, they headed out over south-west England, swept round the

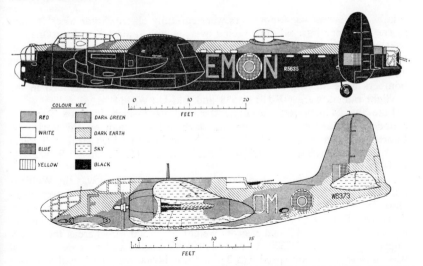

Figure 21: (*Top*) *Lancaster R5635 joined 207 Sqn on June 1 1942. It participated in the October raid on Le Creusot.*
In February 1943 it came on the strength of 1661 Con Unit and ended life as 3508M. Red codes EM-N and serials.
(*Above*) *Boston III W8373 of 107 Sqn in late 1942. She joined 107 Sqn early in 1942 and served until March 1943*
when she was transferred to North Africa and joined 114 San as 'A'. In the finish shown she participated in the
Eindhoven raid of December 6 1942. Red codes and black serials.

Brittany peninsular and turned into France at Ile d'Yeu. Then they flew a
dog-legged course to the great Schneider arms factory at Le Creusot which
81 aircraft claimed to attack with over 100 tons of HE and 40 tons of incendiaries. Five others of 61 Squadron bombed the transformer switching
station at Montchanin. Incredible, it seemed, when the force landed back in
darkness, that only W4774 of 61 Squadron was missing. There had been
hardly any fighter reaction nor much flak. Aircraft known to have participated
in the raid were: 9 Squadron: W4253, R5915, R5916, W4764, W4249, W4157,
W4248, W4265 and W4200; 44 Squadron: W4180 : D, W4199 : H, W4162 :
Y, R5666 : F, W4137 : L, R5740 : O, W4268 : Q, W4277 : S and W4259 : P;
49 Squadron: W4196, W4181, R5898, R5757, W4235, W4773, W4761,
W4306 and R5744; 50 Squadron: W4194, W4266, W4151, W4112, W4161,
W4135, W4117, R5726, R5691, R5702, R5733 and R5687; 57 Squadron:
W4201, W4190, W4317, W4257, W4189, R5865, W4165, W4775, W4250 and
W4251; 61 Squadron: W4774, R5560, W4301, W4326, W4629, W4769,
W4198 and five despatched to Montchanin; 97 Squadron: W4175 : U, R5552 :
P, W4255 : V, W4278 : T, R5497 : Z, R5569 : B, R5548 : A, R5538 : H and
R5490 : M; 106 Squadron: W4118, R5637, R5684, W4261, R5731, R5900
and three others; 207 Squadron: R5635 : N, R5908 : B, R5694 : F, R5745 :
T, L7547 : M, W4174 : V, W4191 : Q, R5693 : J, W4119 : J, R5783 : O,
W4164 : G, R5756 : D, W4134 : U and R5695 : C.
   On the afternoon of October 24, 88 Lancasters, escorted across the Chan-
nel, set out to attack Milan at dusk, a round trip of about 1,700 miles. They
had cloud cover over France and made their ways to the target individually.
Over Italy a few Fiat CR 42s and Macchi 202s were seen but they wisely
kept well away from the armada but for the odd brave soul. From Lake
Annécy, loose formations had been formed for crossing the Alps. Cloud was
down to 3,000 feet over Milan, so the bombing was from low level and quite

a large number of 4,000-pounders were carefully placed. Some aircraft went in very low, one intrepid crew racing over the city at a mere 50 feet. One can well imagine the panic the raid caused, and it was a very damaging attack, too. Only one Lancaster was shot down in Italy, two more falling to night fighters on the way home. As the Lancasters were touching down, more bombers were making a second wave night raid on Milan. Included in the daylight raiders were OF-H : R5538 and EM-U : W4134.

Like the Manchester, the Lancaster had its 54-inch fuselage Type C1 roundels set further forward on the starboard side than on the port side. Lancaster codes were usually 4 feet high and in 4-to 6-inch strokes. Typical aircraft of the period were OF-Z : R5497, OF-C : R5512, OF-F : R5572 and EM-R : R5852.

Autumn saw new bomber variants appearing. First, there was the Wellington X. A change in structure materials, coupled with higher power from Hercules VI or XVI engines, permitted increased load, although for operations over Europe from Britain the Wellington's bombing days were clearly numbered. The Mk IC had a gross weight of 28,500 lb, whereas the Mk X tipped the scales at 36,500 lb, no mean achievement as far as development was concerned. Its top speed was 255 mph at 14,500 feet and it had a service ceiling of 19,600 feet. It could carry a 4,500 lb load for 1,470 miles. It came along at a time when a Mk III replacement was needed and usefully equipped some new Canadian squadrons whilst they awaited four-engined aircraft. Main users of the Mk X were the OTUs, which employed them to the end of hostilities. X3374 was the prototype. The first production machine, DF609, was completed in July 1942 and used for trials at Boscombe and Filton. Subsequent Mk Xs were DF686 and '701 used by 22 OTU and '730 sent to the Middle East where many later served. Production came under way at Chester with HE147. The first to reach a squadron was HE149, delivered to No 466 Squadron. Other early recipients were 428 Squadron (eg, HE173), 429 Squadron (eg, HE160), and 431 Squadron (eg, HE203). A considerable number of Mk Xs were delivered in late 1942, although operations did not begin until early 1943. External differences between the Mk III and Mk X were almost nil. Early Mk IIIs with Hercules XI had the engine exhaust pipe on the port side of the cowling and the forward end of the air intake ended at the gill ring. Later Mk IIIs, also with Hercules XI, had the exhaust pipe on the starboard side but the air intake was extended, incorporating a filter, to the exhaust collector ring. Probably all Mk Xs had this, and many also had a propeller spinner fairing. One of the early Mk Xs was SE-G : HE198; another was DT-K : HE203 of No 192 radio counter measures squadron based at Feltwell. HE222 was QB-E by March 1943. Mk IIIs in use in late 1942-early 1943 included BK158 : EX-G, BK507 : EX-E and BK509 : EX-J.

As an insurance against loss of Merlin engine deliveries, two Lancasters (DT810 and DT812) were ordered to be fitted with Hercules engines. DT810 in standard prototype colours of Dark Green, Dark Earth with yellow under surfaces and 'P' prototype marking first flew on December 21 1941. Production was by Armstrong Whitworth at Coventry, the first example, DS601, being delivered September 1942, and used for A & AEE trials along with DS602. Squadron shake-down for these machines was with 61 Squadron, DS604 becoming QR-W, and others used included DS607-612. The first squadron to be fully equipped was No 115 based at East Wretham, equipment beginning at the end of 1942.

Early examples of the Mk II did not have the propeller spinner fairings

60 (Upper) Mosquito IV DK291 with Sky band and spinners, photographed on May 29 1942 at Hatfield. Finish is grey and green. Although it had a long career it flew very few operational sorties. It was initially delivered to 105 Sqn on June 21 1942 and was destroyed in a crash two weeks before the war ended. **61** (Lower) A fine study of Lancaster VN-N:R5689 of 50 Sqn in the summer of 1942. She was destroyed in an accident following an operation on September 19 1942. Note the well-worn appearance (Rolls-Royce).

62 *One of the early Lancaster IIs, DS604, with red codes and serials.*

63 *Boston IIIs of 107 Sqn in the autumn of 1942. OM-G is AL752. 'OM' is applied differently to the two aircraft* (D. Midex).

64 *(Left) Unusual night camouflage (black under surfaces) is worn by Boston III AL756, possibly applied for service during the Dieppe raid of August 1942. The aircraft was damaged beyond repair on September 24 1942.* (D. Midex).

65 *(Below) Mitchell II FL-191 in prototype markings with yellow under surfaces. Used for trials at Boscombe Down from October 1942 and destroyed in an accident on May 31 1943.*

66 *One of the early Wellingtons in the Middle East, T2818, 'T' of 148 Squadron, photographed at Luqa in January 1941* (Sqn Ldr G. N. B. Miller).

67 *Blenheim I L1479 was delivered to 8 Sqn in March 1939. This photograph shows her taxying out at Khormaksar in 1940. She was lost on operations on August 18 1940* (via G. Burn).

68 *A Blenheim I, possibly L6806 or L6807 of 211 Squadron, in Greece in 1941. It appears to be wearing two-tone fawn and blue 'desert' finish* (Imperial War Museum).

69 *(Right) Maryland AR713 joined 431 Flight at Upavon in October 1940 and proceeded to Malta in November. It is seen here, in a rare illustration, fitted with an Armstrong Whitworth manual dorsal turret, at Luqa soon after arrival* (Sqn Ldr G. N. B. Miller).

70 *(Below) Pre-war Type A1 roundels were still being worn by this Blenheim I of 8 Sqn, damaged by Italian bombs at Aden* (via G. Burn).

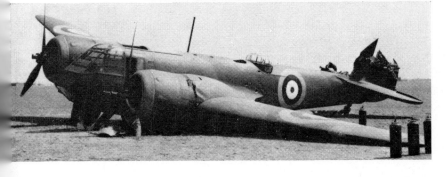

148

71 *A Blenheim IV, VE-X of 110 Sqn, during a detachment from 2 Group to Malta in 1941. In the foreground is rubble from persistent bombing* (Sqn Ldr G. N. B. Miller).

72 *Bombay N-SH of 216 Sqn photographed about June 1940. A yellow outline to the fuselage roundel has been applied; codes are grey, but no fin stripe has yet been added.*

73 *Not all the Liberator IIs had dorsal turrets. This is a photograph of 'P' of 108 Sqn which appears to be AL565. Under the wing tip can be seen faded or painted-out American insignia.*

74 *Vengeance EZ910, with quite large fuselage roundel which appears to retain a very narrow yellow outline. Traces of an underwing roundel are also visible. Camouflage tones well with the background.*

75 *Wellington II Z8515:B, possibly of 104 Sqn, seen in North Africa, 1942. Note the serrated edge to the night camouflage, red letter, and serial set above the tailplane. No 104 Sqn is believed to have carried the code 'EP' for some time in the Middle East. Note the absence of the side triangular window in the aircraft* (R Staton).

76 *Liberator B.VI KL372 has red codes 'EP' aft of the roundel and C on the fin. Its finish was green-grey* (Ron Clarke).

which gave a sleeker appearance to the later Mk IIs. Usually the IIs had a ventral FN64 turret or provision for one, which was useful against enemy night-fighters with upward firing guns. Many also had bulged bomb doors to accommodate the 8,000 lb bomb. The first successful sorties by Mk IIs, of 115 Squadron, were carried out on March 20 1943, when mines were laid off the French coast by KO-W : DS625, H : DS612, R : DS623 and T : DS622. The first Lancaster II bombing raid took place on March 22/23 when St Nazaire was the target. Machines used were A : DS614, H : DS612, L : DS624, N : DS615, R : DS623, U : DS621 and Y : DS613.

Another source of engine production for the Lancaster was the American Packard line. Their Merlin 28 was installed in R5849, but the true prototype Lancaster III was W4114, first flown in August 1942. Production examples began to appear in April 1943, with the batch W4983-5012. It was impossible to distinguish these aircraft externally, for even the serial numbers gave no sound clue. Some Mk Is were re-engined, and some aircraft even had a mixture of engines.

At the end of 1942 the production Halifax Mk II series 1A appeared with a neat curved transparent nose and provision in it for a Vickers K gun. It could have either Merlin XXs or XXIIs which, combined with streamlining, added about 20 mph to its top speed. In the dorsal position a 'Defiant-type' turret was fitted, also a feature of some Mk IIs with the 'solid Z-type' turretless noses. HR654, believed to be the first Mk II series 1A, was delivered to No 408 Squadron on December 21 1942. No 408 equipped first; then deliveries were made to Nos 102, 35, 10, 158, 51 and 405 Squadrons, although there was no steady stream of re-equipment. At the end of 1942 the Halifax V also appeared, in two versions, the Mk V series 1 (Special) and series 1A corresponding to earlier Mk II variants.

During the autumn, some re-orientation of bombing attacks came about. The invasion of North-West Africa was scheduled for November. To encourage the Axis to keep aircraft for Italian defence, attacks were ordered on Genoa, Milan and Turin. Mines were laid off Genoa and Spezia, and *Circuses* continued in an attempt to hold down Luftwaffe fighters. As the convoy for Operation *Torch*, the landing in North-West Africa, sailed on October 22/23 for Gibraltar, 100 Lancasters were bombing Genoa, the first night raid on Italy for a year. This very successful attack was followed by five more in three weeks. From November 18/19, seven attacks, each by about 200 bombers, were made on Turin.

It was during the third of this series, on November 28/29, that the Australian, Flt Sgt R. H. Middleton, was posthumously awarded the Victoria Cross. His Stirling, OJ-H : BF372, was hard put to cross the Alps and used up a lot of fuel. Middleton pressed home his attack from only 2,000 feet and on his third run his aircraft was hit. Jagged metal hit his right eye, tore his face and penetrated a leg and his chest. Others in the crew were also injured and Middleton determined to get them all home. The second pilot righted the aircraft at 800 feet and when Middleton regained consciousness he took over the controls, nursing the Stirling back to the English Channel despite more flak on the route. Five of the crew baled out, leaving two to stay with their captain, all to perish when the Stirling dived into the sea.

Circuses using Bostons continued to hold back fighters and damage the French rail network. Nos 105 and 139 Mosquito Squadrons carried on their brilliant low-level attacks, mainly against rail targets, spectacular raids being made on Liège and Hengelo and, on January 27, the Burmeister Wain factory

I

at Copenhagen, when aircraft taking part included XD-P : DK336, XD-Q : DZ416, GB-K : DZ413 and GB-O : DK338. Their highlight, though, without doubt, was the two-wave day raid on Berlin on January 30 by three aircraft (GB-K : DZ413, GB-F : DZ408 and GB-C : DZ372) of 105 Squadron in the morning and three others (GB-N : DK337, GB-H : DZ379 and GB-J : DZ367) in the afternoon, flown by crews of 139 Squadron.

Another spectacular raid of the winter came when 93 day bombers attacked the Philips works at Eindhoven on December 6. After some low-level practices over England, they were able to deliver their attacks in waves, Bostons leading and Venturas, making their first major operation, bringing up the rear. Aircraft taking part included Bostons RH-U : AL693 and MQ-L : AL285 and Venturas YH-B : AE892 and SB-Q : AE702.

In January 1943, No 1 Group was getting Lancasters, and 4 Group converting remaining Wellington squadrons to Halifaxes. By February, Bomber Command had a strength of 50 squadrons, 35 of them flying four-engined bombers. Many now had the much-improved Mk XIV bomb-sight. They could carry high capacity blast bombs, be guided by an *Oboe* force now dropping newly developed target indicators, and some aircraft had H2S radar. Each so fitted had what amounted to primitive TV gear which presented a radar picture on a cathode ray tube, showing a reasonable illustration of the terrain below, enabling large landmarks to be clearly seen on clear or cloudy nights. Halifaxes of 35 Squadron were the first with characteristic H2S 'bump' or cupola below the fuselage (no one then talked of radomes) and they could be seen fitted in several aircraft by mid-October. By the end of the year, H2S had been installed in 12 Halifaxes and Stirlings of 7 Squadron. Lancasters of 83 Squadron acquired them in January.

A much-refined offensive was getting under way by February. Hamburg was bombed on the 3rd; 198 aircraft were despatched to Turin on the 4/5th, when four Lancasters dropped 4,000 lb bombs on Spezia. To Milan on the 14th, 142 aircraft were sent and St Nazaire was attacked on the 28th with *Oboe* Mosquito HS-F : DK333 at the head of the force.

By March 1, Lancasters equipped Nos 12, 100, 101, 103 and 460 Squadrons of 1 Group and 5 Group had ten squadrons, too. Many of the Lancasters now had Merlin 22s. They were being operated with very mixed loads, including 4,000 lb HC bombs, 14 × 250 or 14 × 500 lb bombs or mixed loads including Small Bomb Containers carrying 8 × 30 lb or 90 × 4 lb incendiaries. On March 1/2, Berlin was the target for 5 Group; then Bomber Command prepared for the opening shot in the Battle of the Ruhr. Hidden in haze, the giant Krupp works at Essen had so far escaped much damage despite countless sorties despatched against it. Recently, *Oboe* Mosquitoes had tried their skill at marking it several times and all was set for a series of mighty blows. On March 5/6 the target for 450 aircraft was Essen, upon which, with eight *Oboe* Mosquitoes of 109 Squadron in the lead (including DZ356 : J), a devastating 38-minute attack was made, 500 tons of HE and 550 tons of incendiaries raining down upon the giant factory. The night offensive had turned on to its final run, and things would never be the same again.

Chapter 17

The 1943 offensive

BETWEEN MARCH 5/6 and June 28/29 1943, there were 26 major Bomber Command attacks on cities in the Ruhr, as well as attacks on other targets. The technique was superbly displayed upon Essen on March 5/6, when *Oboe*-equipped Mosquito IVs of 109 Squadron (DK331 : HS-D, DK318, DK333 : F, DZ436, DZ425, DZ433, DZ435 and DZ430), backed up by Lancasters of 83 Squadron (OL-B : ED313, F : ED312, C : R5622, K : R5671, T : ED601, M : R5626, O : ED372 and V : W4847), led the force making a great on-slaught on the huge Krupp works. The operation was repeated with varying success, first on the inland port and industrial centres of Duisburg, which suffered five times, also at Düsseldorf, where 693 aircraft were despatched on June 11/12, and then at Wuppertal on May 29/30, where the force included Stirling R9266 : MG-J. In all these raids colossal damage was sustained by the enemy.

Losses were never light, for the enemy night-fighter force was presented with a large number of relatively slow aircraft closely placed and flying in streams. On the Wuppertal raid alone, 33 bombers were lost, 21 to fighters; the result of 76 engagements. Sixty more bombers were damaged by flak.

A high proportion of the aircraft lost fell in Holland to the Nachtgeschwader operation from Venlo and Gilze Rijen. Quite a number came down in the Ijsselmeer. Recent drainage of the area has revealed to the expert investigators of the Royal Netherlands Air Force the resting place of many a bomber. Being in fresh water, metal does not corrode in the Ijsselmeer, but it requires meticulous research to identify the fragments retrieved. Two of 10 Squadron's Halifaxes came down there, for instance, DT732 on May 14 1943 and W1217, a veteran aircraft. Between March and the end of June 1943, 628 bombers failed to return from the Ruhr raids and 34,750 tons of bombs had been dropped.

Of all the operations of the period none was to grip the imagination more than that mounted on May 16/17 1943 against the Ruhr dams. The Mohne Dam controlled the flow of water from the Mohne Lake and the level of the River Ruhr, and thereby water to many power stations. If it were to be breached a massive flood of 130,000,000 tons of water would be released. It was a tempting, but difficult, target. The Eder Dam controlled the Weser, and the others served similar purposes. For maximum effect the lakes needed to be drained as the summer approached.

No 617 Squadron formed, to breach the dams with bouncing bombs, on March 20 1943 under Wing Commander Guy Penrose Gibson. Eventually 21 crews were trained for the highly secret task. They had to be proficient at very low flying, training by night or in simulated darkness and at tree top height. A Lancaster flying so low was a memorable sight. The only one I saw on its rounds was a standard aircraft, AJ-D (AJ ahead on the port side) so low over Godmanchester on the afternoon of April 24 that I was able to read the red serial as ED763. In all external respects it was a standard Lancaster.

Research went apace on the special weapon, Dr Barnes Wallis' bouncing bomb, which underwent initial trials dropped from a Wellington. Casings proved too weak and there was no mean panic to develop the weapon in time. Some of the trials were undertaken at Ashley Walk, the A & AEE range, where recently an end casing of a trial round was retrieved. Work also proceeded on the smaller weapon, intended to be used by a force of Mosquitoes of 618 Squadron who were to bounce their weapons into the *Tirpitz* in a Norwegian Fjord during a daylight raid. These attacks were to be undertaken almost simultaneously to prevent the enemy taking appropriate counter measures. Development of the 'naval weapon' had to be delayed and only the dams raid took place.

There were five possible dams to breach during the operation carried out by Lancasters shorn of their dorsal turrets. A large V-strut was fitted to each side of their cutaway bomb bays. Spinning mechanisms were installed which, by means of a chain drive, spun the cylindrical bomb placed between the two arms; when this was spinning the arms sprang apart to release the bomb. Each weapon was found to be of differing weight, and various compensatory balances were needed on the weapons, which weighed around 10,000-11,000 lb.

Three waves of Lancasters were to make the attack, the first going for the Mohne Dam, then the Eder and, if they had any bombs left, the Sorpe. Five aircraft forming the second wave were to breach the Sorpe Dam, and the third wave was to form a mobile reserve. Nineteen Lancasters were despatched on the raid. Four of the Sorpe force failed to make the target, and only Flt-Lt McCarthy's bomb, dropped from ED923/G : AJ-T, hit the dam.

The great event of the night, however, was the assault on the Mohne Dam. Five Lancasters attacked it with varying success and, as the sixth began to line up, the dam gave way. The three remaining Lancasters in the force then set off for the Eder Dam, which was breached after Flt-Lt Shannon in ED929/G : AJ-L and Plt Off Knight in ED912/G : AJ-N positioned their bombs accurately. Of the 19 which set out, eight Lancasters were lost, and two more had aborted. For his courage during the operation Wg Cdr Guy Gibson, flying ED932/G : AJ-G, was awarded the Victoria Cross, and 33 other personnel were decorated. The losses to 617 Squadron were very heavy, as had been expected, but it was decided to keep it intact as a force for special operations where precision bombing was required. To the end of the war it was maintained in this capacity.

By the end of June, bomb damage in the Ruhr was considerable. In an attempt to prevent this continuing the enemy constantly improved his night-fighter forces, equipment and techniques. Because of this Bomber Command decided to switch the target areas. Short nights did not permit very deep penetrations, although one raid was directed by 5 Group on the Zeppelin radar works at Friedrichshafen, after which the small force flew on to North Africa. But such operations were not really viable owing to servicing problems. Instead, a devastating assault on Hamburg was planned. Four raids upon this city proved to be the most destructive carried out by Bomber Command. Hamburg was the second largest German city. Within its confines were 3,000 industrial targets and some 5,000 others, mainly connected with commerce and shipping, not to mention the large Blohm und Voss shipbuilding yards. Nearly half the U-boats had been built at Hamburg and one might argue that the civilian population was largely geared up to the war effort, virtually para-military. Hamburg was an easy target to find, its shape distinctive on H2S radar, now coming into use. This was used for the first time during a Berlin raid on March 1/2 1943, when one of the participants was Wg Cdr Mahaddie, flying Stirling MG-C : R9257, one of the first to be fitted with the familiar H2S 'bump' on her belly. To throw the Hamburg defences into confusion it was decided to use, for the first time, short metallic strips, code name *Window,* which would confuse enemy radar. This it did very effectively, and of the 791 aircraft despatched on July 24/25 (which included Stirlings AA-E : BF518, MG-X : EF364 and WP-G : EF441) 741 attacked and only 12 were lost. Seventy-four aircraft were carrying H2S. On July 27/28, when LS-J : EH893 was participating, 2,417 tons of bombs rained down and the first fearful firestorms rampaged through the city. Two more raids followed. Of the 3,095 aircraft despatched, 2,630 claimed to attack and 87 were lost. Half the houses in Hamburg were destroyed and one third of the population perished. Germany, responsible for the destruction of Warsaw, Coventry, Rotterdam and many other towns and cities, was being repaid in kind.

On August 17/18 571 out of 600 bombers despatched delivered a very effective raid on the rocket and pilotless aircraft research station at Peenemunde on the Baltic Coast. Known to have been in the force were Stirlings MG-M : JA932, LS-F : EH929, JN-P : EH949 and WP-A : EH944; Halifaxes KN-K : JB839, NP-S : JD260, NP-G : JD300, NP-V : HR942, WL-K : EB258, HR856 of 405 Squadron and JD151 of 78 Squadron; and Lancaster IIs KO-G : DS667, KO-D : DS720, and KO-H : DS630. Enemy fighters were very active, aided by bright moonlight, flares, searchlights and the observer corps. Despite the use of *Window* 40 bombers were lost and 32 seriously damaged.

On August 23/24 the target was Berlin, the 'Big City', which suffered three attacks in ten days but cost the Command 125 aircraft. By now it was clear that the Stirling and Halifax were suffering very badly at the hands of the defenders. With Lancaster production going well it was decided in September to restrict Stirlings and Halifaxes to more shallow penetrations, and after October the Stirlings flew very few major operations, although they contributed much to the mine-laying campaign. Two types of mines were being dropped—1,000 lb and 1,800 lb— at the rate of about 1,100 per month. These needed to be laid from around 600-800 feet which meant these were quite hazardous operations. Some 13,776 mines were dropped in 1943.

During a raid on Düsseldorf on November 3/4 a new radar aid came into use, GH, which was virtually *Oboe* in reverse. Four squadrons of Lancaster IIs had the gear and 38 machines were despatched on this raid, although it functioned in only 15 aircraft. These aircraft had provision for carrying 8,000 lb bombs and about half the load fell within half a mile of the aiming point. Lancaster IIs KO-B : DS827, KO-Q : DS766 and KO-Y : DS734 were among those that raided Berlin on November 22.

By now night raids were mighty undertakings as hundreds of bombers swarmed across the sea, and whose return brought very considerable problems, especially when the weather turned bad. Feint attacks were being mounted and the Main Force was often cunningly routed to disguise its eventual target. Mosquitoes flew ahead dropping *Window* and sometimes they operated independently, misleading the enemy then bombing widely separated targets, bringing confusion to the defenders. Other Mosquito IIs of the newly introduced 100 Group were beginning limited bomber support by engaging night-fighters. How different it all was from a year earlier.

In June 1943 another major change had come in the Command. For the present it gave up entirely any idea of conducting daylight operations. On June 1 the day raiders—Bostons, Venturas and Mitchells—were transferred to Fighter Command, to form part of the new Tactical Air Force supporting the invasion. Throughout the summer they continued attacks in daylight on fringe targets, with massive fighter cover in very elaborate operations, the largest of which was in support of a feint invasion of the Pas de Calais in September. From November, by which time they were part of 2nd TAF, the day bombers were thrown into the vital campaign against the flying bomb sites then mushrooming in France. This continued until May 1944.

The aircraft

The principal night bombers of 1943 were the Lancaster I and III; Halifax Mk II series 1, 1a and Mk V; Stirling I and III; and Wellington X. Basically all wore the same camouflage colours—Dark Green, Dark Earth and Night which (usually) terminated in a straight line, high on the aircraft's side, although on some Halifaxes termination was still in a wavy line. Codes were Dull Red, like serials, but within these bounds there were various points of detail concerning modifications and markings.

Halifax IIs with the turretless 'Z' Type nose entered service in late 1942, but it was about March 1943 before they were plentiful. One of the early ones was NP-U, which had a red-white-yellow gazelle-like animal painted on its nose, another was NP-G : BB209. Perhaps this is a useful time to point out that the individual nose decorations on RAF bombers were by no means common. Indeed quite often a visit to any airfield of those days revealed few aircraft so decorated. Frequently though, sorties were recorded on aircraft by small painted bombs in varying colours—usually red, white or yellow, but it is wrong to think that almost all the bombers carried adornments. Lancaster OL-V : R5484 was quite typical and when seen on March 13 was bare of individual trimmings.

Since the start of the war the finish known as Night, colloquially as matt black, had undergone several changes from rough to very rough and then smooth. Often a mixture of finishes was in evidence. When the Stirlings went to the large Sebro works for overhaul after accidents or battle damage they emerged, in late 1942 and through 1943, in a very matt finish. This was also seen on some aircraft in squadron service, and particularly on those of XV Squadron based at Bourn where the Sebro machines were test flown. LS-M : EF345 and BK699 : LS-E had this very flat finish, also BU-Q : BK600 (BU aft on starboard side) and OJ-N : BK601 (OJ forward of roundels both sides). All of these aircraft had FN 50 turrets.

The number of windows in Stirling fuselages varied irrespective of mark number. BU-Q and OJ-N each had three in the starboard rear side of the

Figure 22: (*Opposite page*) *The Halifaxes portrayed here were in use at Middleton St George in the winter of 1943-44, except for SE-A then based at Croft. The other aircraft are illustrated in the state in which they were seen setting off for mining operations from Middleton on April 18-19 1944, and depict clearly the diverse state of the aircraft then on the Halifax squadrons. (Top to bottom) HR925 : VR-D is a Mk II Srs 1a with the usual 54-inch outside diameter fuselage roundels, fin flashes 2 feet × 3 feet, and 4-foot red codes. JD212 is VR-X and NA-V is JN969. The latter and NA-B : JP191 have a small fairing at the turret base, and differing shape fins. SE-A, the Mk V, is LL175. The last one is LW325 : H-VR. No upper turrets were fitted to any of 419 Sqn aircraft (VR code), and 431(SE) and 434(WL) did not then have H2S radomes. On their early Halifax IIIs they had a belly gun position. Squadrons which arranged their codes like 419 Sqn were 415(6U), 424(QB), 427(ZL), 429(AL) and 433(BM). Those with unit codes ahead on the port side and aft on the starboard included 420(PT), 425(KW), 431(SE), 432(QO) and 434(WL).*

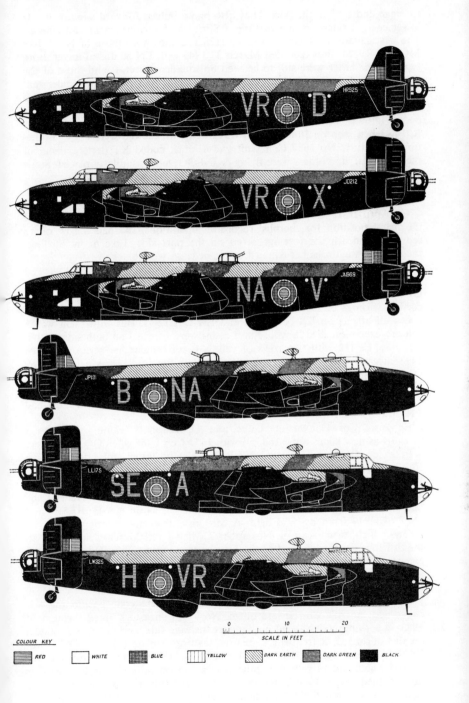

COLOUR KEY

RED   WHITE   BLUE   YELLOW   DARK EARTH   DARK GREEN   BLACK

fuselage and four in the port. They also had a bulged forward window in the lower cockpit sides, again a feature of Stirlings of various marks and vintage. The first squadron Stirlings to carry H2S radomes were those of No 7, like MG-M : R9261, thus recorded March 27 1943 with FN 50 dorsal turret. Both types of the latter were still to be seen on squadron aircraft and those of the principal Stirling Conversion Unit, No 1651. This unit's markings underwent two rapid changes in the spring of 1943. First, individual letters were repeated on some aircraft, such as 'RR'. Then in May the unit began to exhibit unit codes, initially BS applied ahead of the roundels on both sides. BS-U was R9147 when seen on June 13, and was fitted with the old-style FN 7 'Botha' turret. By July, No 1657 Con Unit had aircraft coded XT (letters ahead of the roundels), and others were flying coded OG, letters similarly placed. Some of the XT-coded machines acquired small codes after the manner of 7 Squadron. The latter's codes, incidentally, varied in size but were much smaller than usual.

On April 16 1943 I noted OJ-F : EF336 landing at Lakenheath. Instead of the usual position for 'bombs' recording operations, she had a row of 12 red ones beneath the fuselage serial on the port side. Like many Stirlings then in the squadrons her exhaust collector rings were black.

By August 1943 the Stirlings of 622 Squadron (formed August 10) were in evidence. Coded GI they had unit codes aft on both sides of their aircraft, GI-C : EF461 being noted on August 19 at Mildenhall. The same day I recorded Stirlings of 199 Squadron at Lakenheath and these too had squadron codes all aft, as on EX-N : EF450 and EX-U : EE941. But with them was a solitary exception, EX-C, whose unit codes were forward on both sides! OJ-F was now EF412 with two rows of yellow bombs under her serial. Some of 149's aircraft had various length aerials below the fuselage as evidenced by OJ-M. EF481 : BU-J, seen the same day, had BU aft on her starboard side. XY-V was similarly marked, and 90 Squadron also opted for codes fully aft, as on WP-D : EF431 recorded October 30 1943. All of these Stirlings had FN 50 dorsal turrets.

Expansion of Conversion Units and Operational Training Units was obvious as new codes appeared. So with 1651 Con Unit when QQ codes were seen as on QQ-E : EF386, and YZ-P : N3721, the latter still fitted with an FN 7 turret. Another new Stirling squadron was No 196 which moved into Witchford, for operations, on July 19 1943, and whose aircraft with unit codes ahead of both side roundels was typified by ZO-D : EH961. Nearby the Stirlings of 75 Squadron had unit codings all aft, as on AA-E : BF518, and JN-P : EH949 from its 'C' Flight. A Stirling with a nose motif was YZ-T : EF389 which, when seen on November 27, had a red Mercury figure. Of all the Stirlings I recorded in 1943 the most unusual was surely that seen on the evening of July 24 in the usual British camouflage, but with USAAF 'star and bar' markings on the fuselage side. She wore only a white star with white bars flanking it, and seems to have escaped full identification.

As with the Stirlings so with other bombers where code positioning was concerned; no rule can be laid down. No 97's Lancasters opted throughout 1943-44 for unit codes ahead on the port fuselage side, and aft of the roundel on the starboard, a frequent Lancaster feature seen on OF-R : ED875, Mk IIs QR-L and KO-B : DS691, GT-E : EE178, OL-V : ED876 and OL-M : W4905 which had 14 yellow 'bombs' painted on her nose alongside a luscious nude named 'Sugar Plum'. All these were noted July 17. Expansion of some squadrons to three flight level had already brought along the 'squared' individual letter and a bar painted above the individual letter. Mid-1943 witnessed a second unit coding, such as XU for 'C' Flight, 7 Squadron. In this instance it was short-lived, but during the time these letters were in use they were applied small as on the 'MG' aircraft, like Lancaster MG-Z : JA585. Some squadrons kept two unit codes to the end of the war; others featured 'barred' individual letters.

From a modelling point of view where the Lancaster is concerned one needs to discover which window arrangement was appropriate, the small slit windows being seen well into 1944. No serial block from which these windows were deleted seems ever to have come to light but up to the JB range they were usual, although one sometimes did see earlier aircraft on which they were overpainted, or from which they had even been deleted. They were a feature of ED911 : OF-E, for instance, and ED932 flown by Wg Cdr Guy Gibson on the dams raid. Another feature that always occasioned interest was the fitting of, or provision for, a ventral turret. A handful of early Lancasters had them and some of the later ones had provision for them. OF-W, noted on August 15, had such a turret. At that time H2S radomes on the under fuselage were still relatively rare on Lancasters. The Pathfinders seem to have had them first and GT-M was fitted thus at this time, also OF-A : JA923 which had the full array of side windows. EE129 : MG-Y was another.

Since there were so few, you were lucky to catch sight of one of 617's specially modified machines, but I spotted AJ-N (AJ aft on the starboard side) on August 31. She retained her special bomb gear and did not have a dorsal turret. Shortly after this, 617 Squadron was recoded KC; these letters were worn by EE150 : Z and EE130 : M in time for the famous raid on the Dortmund Ems Canal on September 15.

Normal Lancasters in use at this time were ED999 : EA-A, EE187 : DX-Y and JA703 : KM-A. More interesting were some then flying without nose turrets. A surprising sight over Peterborough on August 23 was ZN-V (ZN aft of the roundels on both sides) which was fitted with a nose like the Lancastrian of later years, also ventral and dorsal turrets. September 26 brought another thus modified but uncoded.

My October Lancaster recording included OF-H with ventral turret installed and on the 30th I had a close view of another oddity. I had seen on September 13 a Lancaster at Newmarket with Dark Green and a very dark shade of grey camouflage. I was sceptical of what I had seen at first but on the 27th and 30th I had a close look at the aircraft and was able to confirm the colouring. With 'E' aft in Dull Red, she was ED952. Three of her companions had now acquired similar paintwork.

Introduction of the Lancaster II has previously been mentioned. To about May 1943 those in service seem to have had electric propellers with the small spinner. Then there appeared Mk IIs with hydraulically operated propellers with large streamlined spinners. KO-B (KO forward on port side, aft on starboard) had these features, like JI-H : DS813 and JI-K : DS824 in use late November with codes placed as on 115's aircraft. These latter two had bulged bomb doors to permit carriage of 8,000 lb bombs, full side windows as on JI-L : DS736 and FN 64 belly turrets. The latter, for which provision was usual, were not always fitted. Other Mk IIs in use at the end of the year included DS827 : A⁴—D (these unusual markings signifying Squadron's 'C' Flight and being recorded at Witchford in December) and DS761 : KO-W. Other Lancasters in use at this time included OL-M : JA705, with highly

polished spinners and engine cowlings and another variant of 'Sugar Plum'
on her nose, and LM394 : VN-R (codes forward on port side aft on starboard).

From the modelling angle the main point to watch about a 1943 Halifax
would be the nose/dorsal turret/fin combination. Mk IIs with Z noses were
common by the spring. TL-P : W7881 was one of these which had no dorsal
turret (codes on port forward, starboard aft positions). TL-L : W7823 was a
Mk II in use in March with the old 'Hudson-type' turret and the original
nose. TL-R : W7874 was a Mk II with Z nose, with no dorsal turret but
fitted with H2S radome when recorded April 20. Medium Grey codes had
still not entirely vanished for TL-L mentioned above had them, also
Lancaster EM-W (EM ahead on port side, aft on starboard) which hove
into view on April 2 1943.

Mk II series 1a aircraft with shapely perspex noses were around in some
numbers by the summer, such as TL-A : HR865 with four-gun dorsal turret
and H2S radome. On June 5 LQ-Z (LQ forward on both sides) was seen to
have combing at her dorsal turret base similar to that on the Lancaster. One
with very large codes was EZ-V. There were often variations in the code
positions on any one squadron, for LQ-X on July 7 had LQ aft on the starboard side.

By the autumn of 1943 some Halifaxes on the squadrons were fitted with
the new rectangular fins. On November 1, 35 Squadron's rectangular-finned
IIias with radomes and four-gun turrets included TL-O : HX160 and TL-J :
HR817.

My first logging of a Halifax III was on July 24 1943. It was R9534, the
prototype shortly before fitted with new Hercules VIs, and was flying from
Radlett. Her propellers were of the electric type, and the outer engine nacelles
had been lengthened to about 3 feet aft of the trailing edge. She had no dorsal
turret, and had 2 radio masts after the manner of many Mk Is. Under surfaces
were yellow, upon which were painted Type C roundels. Aft of the fuselage
roundels was a yellow 'P' without any circle, and she had a 'Z' type nose.
The first production Mk III flew in about August 1943 and the second
(HX227) on August 27. During October the latter was tested at 63,000 lb
all-up. HX232 was the first taken on squadron charge, by No 35 on October
4, becoming TL-H but it was 466 Squadron which fully equipped first and
433 also had some of the early examples. HX239 was HD-G in November.

Throughout 1943 Handley Page carried out various experiments with
Halifaxes. L9515 featured streamlined air intakes, bulbous nosed ailerons and
was the first to fly, albeit a mock up, with rounded wing tips during tests in
May and June. During the latter month she had wing slats installed and her
tail turret was removed and faired over. Much work was undertaken on
DG281 which in February was flying with 'square' fins and rudders and an
FN 64 ventral turret. More bombers than is commonly supposed had ventral
turrets, fitted to discourage belly attacks by Bf 110s and Ju 88s. In October,
for instance, DG281 was flying with twin ventral .50 inch guns. The main
trouble was that such mountings occupied the space usually needed for H2S
gear, but later Halifaxes were operated with a small bulge beneath the rear
fuselage over the gun mounting in lieu of H2S. Early in the year V9985
tested enlarged bomb doors, but this modification was apparently never introduced on squadron aircraft. Retractable tailwheels were an attractive idea
on all the heavies, but they brought considerable troubles. R9534 was testing
one in February 1943 and EB208 in July. Both V9885 and EB208 also tested

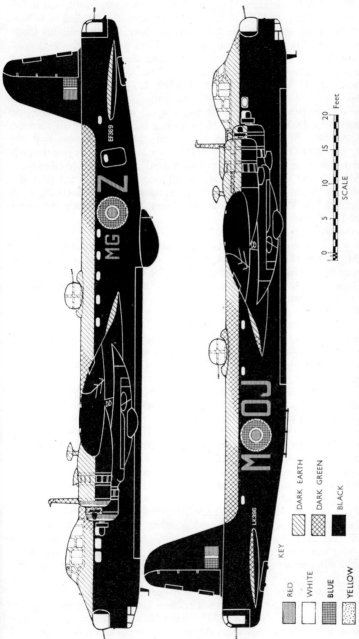

KEY

RED

WHITE

BLUE

YELLOW

DARK EARTH

DARK GREEN

BLACK

0   5   10   15   20   Feet

SCALE

Figure 23: (Top) Stirling I EF369, used by No 7 Sqn between April and July 1943, had the small MG coding (positioned ahead of the fuselage roundels on port and starboard sides) and was fitted with an H2S radome. (Above) Stirling III LK396 as recorded at Lakenheath on August 27 1944. She began squadron service with No 622 but soon went to No 75 Sqn who passed her to No 218 Sqn in April 1944. Here she served as HA-M. In the middle of August 1944 LK396 joined 149 Sqn. Flown by Flg Off J. J. McKee, she was the last Stirling to complete a bombing sortie in Bomber Command, participating in the early morning attack on Le Havre on September 8 1944.

anti-shimmy tailwheels. HR845, another experimental machine, had a mock-up of the Bristol B.12 turret in May. She later featured in an attempt to improve range, with forward belly tanks also experimentally installed in W7650.

Most of the Wellingtons in use belonged to Operational Training Units, which had mainly Mk IIIs. In front-line service for much of the year however was the Mk X. One of the squadrons using these was No 192, which flew radio counter-measure operations from Feltwell, and whose equipment in August included DT-S : HE498, DT-X : LN349, DT-E : LN556 and DT-F : HE857. Most of the Xs had hydraulic propellers, whereas Mk IIIs, like X3372 noted April 9 with F in red aft and a small white F on the nose, had electric propellers. JS-X : BK449 of 16 OTU had its unit coding all forward. whereas OP-A : R1370, a Wellington with a very large astrodome, had unit codes fully aft. AM-O : DV921 of 14 OTU, seen June 1943, wore extremely thick lettering, no side windows and had twin fixed aerials like a Wellington I. ZB-O, a Mk III, had ZB aft on the starboard side, forward on the port, like another Mk III of July 1943, HS-G of 109 Squadron, also Mk III PL-U. A grey and green Mk VI with Sky under surfaces was noted with red codes, possibly of 109 Squadron.

Very occasionally one saw aircraft with 'impossible serials'. One of these I remember well was Wellington III UA131 with a red 'L' forward, seen with 1483 Flight, Newmarket, on August 30 1943. She was one of a group there with a target towing hook immediately aft of the tailwheel.

Earlier types of bombers were still in evidence, but Hampdens were getting rare. The most interesting trio of these I saw on April 9. Their upper camouflage still extended only to the base of the fuselage and they were even wearing 1941-style roundels! Whitley Vs had found a new rôle as tugs for Horsa gliders, particularly at Brize Norton whose aircraft, like EB332 : 45, BD628 : 12 and LA774 : 33, had a light blue identity number ahead of the roundel and on the nose. Whitleys in use in 1943 included BD537 : XH-A (XH aft on starboard side, forward on port) seen March 1943, also BD627 : SG-Q and N1419 : ZV-M of 19 OTU noted in November. Barely coming into the true bomber category was MH-D long since with 51 Squadron but which still languished in its coastal slate grey and green with white sides and under surfaces, and red codes and serials. Z9487 : GO-H was in the markings of 42 OTU and Z6722, with a red P outlined white, came from 3(C) OTU but was in bomber colours. K9026 which had been with 19 OTU still had camouflage extending down its fuselage sides, and had its original tail turret. A Mk V coded RK-U had unit codes forward on both sides, and the glider tugs of 295 Squadron merely carried an individual letter aft, like B-BD415, seen towing off Horsa DP152 in September. XE-K : K9010 (XE forward) in standard 1943 colours was seen on September 8 and another interesting specimen was Z6472 with HG over-painted ahead of its roundels and at one time with 24 OTU. Its wing under surfaces were Sky; its under belly was black and it had experimental wing de-icing boots. A low-flying Whitley target-tug seen over Morecambe Bay on September 5 was coded KG-E. She came from 3 OTU where Z9219 : KG-Q and Z9298 : KG-A had been in residence.

It was still possible to come across a Blenheim I, the most interesting group which I recorded hailing from 17 OTU. They were in residence at Steeple Morden, still in Dark Green-Dark Earth-Sky finish with red codes. Aft of the coding they wore white identity letters, JG-S being 18, this number unfortunately blotting out the serial. Others seen that year included WJ-A with red codes and Mk IV LW-Y of a Signals Wing. For good measure there was sometimes to be seen a Harrow of 271 Squadron ambling on its way, moving fighter squadron personnel or on similar 'passenger' duty. Some had azure blue under surfaces; others had yellow like K6964 and '6970 which moved 21 Squadron from Methwold in August 1943. Both had red BJ coding and were of the 'Sparrow' type.

When day bombers were transferred to Fighter Command on June 1 the Mosquitoes passed to the Pathfinder force. Some acquired black under surfaces but it seems unlikely that any of the IXs had this in 1943. In March some of the Mk IVs had black under sides but later that year this was a usual feature. Codes were red and a machine with black under surfaces was DT-T : DZ375 (DT forward on both sides) which had only whip aerials like HS-K : DZ425 (HS aft). An unusual companion aircraft on April 21 was HS-A which was black overall. Although it had been decided to delete the feature a year before, one of 139's Mosquitoes still had Sky spinners in July 1943, and even when they were on night operations some of 139's Mk IVs retained Sky codes, like XD-M : DZ521 (XD forward on port side, aft on starboard when seen on December 4) with 12 yellow bombs painted on her nose and black serials. The same day AZ-A (codes as on DZ521) serial DK313 had red codes and black serial on her grey and green finish.

The remaining bombers were the Ventura, Boston and Mitchell. Until their withdrawal the Venturas were camouflaged Dark Green-Dark Earth-Sky with red codes and usually red serials like YH-H : AE730.

During the first few weeks of March 1943, most of 2 Group was involved in Exercise *Spartan*. Some of the Venturas had their port under surfaces painted over with black distemper, although the amount of the aircraft coloured black varied from machine to machine. AE692 : YH-K merely had black bomb doors, but along the side of her nose she had shark's teeth painted. Many of the Venturas had a red individual letter painted on the perspex nose, outlined yellow in the case of the J on SB-J : AE854 noted April 16 1943. An example used by 487 Squadron was EG-T : AE713.

Boston IIIs were uncommon by 1943, for the Mk IIIA was in use and many of these wore a Dark Green-Medium Grey finish with red codes and black serials, like BZ371 : OM-S and AL280 : OM-O, in use August 1943.

Finally, there were the Mitchells. Although the first examples arrived mid-1942 it was January 1943 before the type went into action, and then disastrously. There were teething troubles and the aeroplane was unsuitable for low-level operations. The Mitchells did a lot of flying before getting into their stride in the spring of 1943, when examples in use included FL197 : EV-G and FR141 : NO-B in Grey-Green finish with red codes and black serials, individual letters being painted on the nose and unit codes ahead of the roundels, as on the Bostons.

Chapter 18

Prelude to Overlord

THE OPENING WEEKS of 1944 found Bomber Command in the thick of the Battle of Berlin, which had commenced on November 18/19 1943. By March 24/25 1944, 16 major raids had been carried out on the 'Big City' for the shattering loss of 492 aircraft. What this means in aircraft alone is apparent when you consider that, placed wing tip-to-wing tip, the lost bombers would stretch for 9½ miles. During the heaviest raid on the city, carried out on February 15/16, over 800 aircraft dropped 2,642 tons of bombs for the loss of 42 aircraft. By now the Halifax III was fully operational, a state reached in February. Restrictions placed upon the Halifax did not apply to this refined variant.

Losses at this period were frightful, and they reached a climax on March 30/31 when, of 795 aircraft despatched to Nuremburg, 710 claimed to bomb the target and 94 were lost, including HX241, a Halifax III of 78 Squadron, LW429 of 425 Squadron, and LW500 of 640 Squadron.

The final stage of area attacks on industrial cities came on April 24/25, when Munich was the target. Varying marking techniques were in use and on this night the vital part was undertaken by Wg Cdr Leonard Cheshire who, in Mosquito NS993, flew very low to place his spot fires accurately. His aircraft was hit many times, as it had been during his four tours of operations. For continuous courage and example he was awarded a well-deserved Victoria Cross.

In the reckoning, almost 75,000 sorties had been flown by the Command since March 1943. A staggering total of 2,824 aircraft were missing on operations; about 9,000 men had been killed. Up to 1,000 aircraft could now be despatched on one night, as a result of which about 70% of the buildings housing the German aircraft and its ancillary equipment industry had been destroyed or damaged. Ironically, this destruction whipped the enemy to fever pitch. With zeal he set to and repaired a considerable amount of the damage, dispersed his industry and was able to step up production. But what he could never do was wrest the offensive from Bomber Command and the courageous USAAF, whose efforts by day did so much to assist the Allied cause even if their bombs were small and their total effort about half that of the British.

This combined offensive drew from the Occupied Countries men and equipment that could ill be spared with the invasion coming. Never again was the Luftwaffe able to mount an effective offensive. Its energy was sapped by the overwhelming demand for defence and its morale suffered badly despite the number of enemy bombers it destroyed.

A change of plan was evident in March 1944 when Bomber Command's targets lay closer to hand. It had been switched to destroying the enemy rail network in France and adjacent areas as part of Operation *Overlord*. On

March 6/7, 263 bombers opened this highly effective campaign by raiding Trappes. With *Oboe*, and other radar and radio aids, target marking was usually very accurate and civilian casualties were low.

Eight more raids on rail centres were staged in March. These attacks continued almost to D-Day, a repeat attack on Trappes concluding the phase, with the enemy sustaining damage to 33 rail centres. As a result, the rail network was almost useless.

Over the period November to June, the day bomber offensive took a very different turn. Throughout the summer of 1943 reports came in of the construction of small concrete sites in many parts of northern France. There was uncertainty about their purpose; was it for launching long-range rockets, for the siting of heavy guns, or could it be that pilotless aircraft would be flown from these bases? Eventually opinion favoured the latter. On November 5, No 2 Group and the US 9th Army Air Force opened a sustained campaign against them which continued whenever the weather was suitable, interrupted the *Overlord* plans, and ended only at D-Day. At first, three Boston IIIA and four Mitchell squadrons were used, also Bomphoons and B-26s, with massive fighter support. In December, by which time sufficient were available, Mosquito VIs of 2 Group began making hazardous low-level attacks, which proved to be the most productive of all against the tiny, heavily defended targets. Before the end of the period, Bostons and Mitchells were neutralising selected airfields, assisting attacks on rail targets and occasionally trying to destroy bridges, notoriously difficult targets. It was during this period that the gradual ascendancy of the fighter-bomber in attacks on tactical targets was so obvious, with Spitfires dive-bombing bridges and rail installations and Typhoons forsaking their 'Bomphoon' mantle for the carriage of rocket projectiles. The dividing line between fighter and light bomber was now slender indeed.

By night, too, the fighter-bomber Mosquitoes were active. Since December 1943 they had shown a new face to the enemy, operating as night-fighters and intruders, making attacks on night-fighter airfields and accompanying the bomber streams under the aegis of the new 100 Group. Their aircraft usually had black under surfaces, whereas those of 2 Group retained their 'day' camouflage which was mostly the same as that applied to Mosquito night-fighters anyway. Some had Sky spinners, some dark grey in their upper camouflage, although it is wrong to assume that all the intruders had this.

And so the prelude to the greatest seaborne assault in history, the Normandy landing, was over. The operations plan for *Overlord* was massive. It listed ten heavy gun batteries on the Normandy coast, a part of Hitler's West Wall, which were to come under a tremendous bombardment from much of Bomber Command, with *Oboe*-equipped Mosquitoes of Nos 105 and 109 Squadrons marking. Bombs from 1,136 Halifaxes and Lancasters, including PH-Y : LL909, PH-U : ND627, JI-H : DS813, A2-K : LL670, MG-A : JA911 and MG-P : ND912, crashed down around the gun emplacements. They did not destroy them, but they stunned the gunners, which was equally effective. At dawn the US 8th AAF continued the treatment.

Meanwhile off Dover, 16 Lancasters of 617 Squadron (LM482 : W flown by Grp Capt Cheshire, LM492 : Q, ME561 : R, ME557 : S, ME560 : H, DV383 : A, DV402 : P, ME559 : Y, ME554 : F, LM485 : N, ME562 : Z, EE131 : L, DV393 : T, DV246 : U, DV403 : G and ME555 : C) co-operated with ships and balloons, dropping *Window* in a highly successful diversion operation, leading the enemy to think a large force was approaching the Pas de Calais.

Stirling IIIs of 218 Squadron (HA-A : EF133, F : EF207, G : LJ632, I : LK401, K : LJ472 and N : LJ522) flew a similar feint off Boulogne, whilst others of 149 Squadron (OJ-A : EF140, C : LK389 missing, G : EJ109, L : LK388, M : LJ621 missing, R : EF161 and T : EF193) joined Halifaxes of 138 and 161 (SD) Squadrons dropping dummy paratroopers near Yvetot. Just before the troops landed Bostons wearing fuselage and wing white and black 'AEAF stripes' trailed smoke across the landing craft to screen them, the aircraft including RH-C : BZ383, RH-F : BZ377, RH-S : BZ357, OA-N : BZ270, OA-T : BZ376 and OA-P : BZ338. No 2 Group had made night-long intrusions against tactical targets around Caen. These latter operations continued for many nights. *Gee*-equipped Mosquitoes marked trains, tanks and motor transport for attack by Bostons and Mitchells, the latter including NO-A : FR191, NO-G : FR202, NO-C : FR151 and NO-D : FR164 of 320 Squadron, all again wearing the full array of AEAF markings.

A spectacular attack on the Saumur tunnel on June 8 by Lancasters LM492 Q, LM485 : N, DV246 : U, DV391 : O, DV385 : A, DV403 : G, DV393 : T, EE131 : L, DV380 : X, DV402 : P, ME560 : H, ME559 : Y, ME557 : S, ME562 : Z, ME555 : C, ME561 : R, ME554 : F and JB139 : V of 617 Squadron, coded KC, was the first occasion that 12,000 lb 'Tallboy' earthquake bombs were used.

Bomber Command now resumed attacks on Germany, but held itself ready to support the armies if required. British and Canadian forces were held west of Caen and the heavies were then called in, first to smash the enemy at Villers Bocage on June 30. Squadrons of Lancasters of 3 Group, including WP-E : EE178, WP-F : LM588, WP-U : LM618, WP-V : LM164, JI-N : DS814, JI-Q : LL666, A2-G : LL716 and JI-C : LM206; Halifaxes of 4 Group; and Lancasters and Mosquitoes of 8 Group, including HS-M : MM241, HS-L : MM112, HS-D : ML939 and HS-P : ML898, delivered a blistering attack, but it was insufficient to cut a path for the land forces. On July 7, 457 bombers hammered at the German divisions north of Caen, and the Allies were able to enter the city. On July 18, nearly 2,000 Allied bombers delivered a mighty blow on a suburb of Caen. This offensive, Operation *Goodwood*, allowed a further advance but brought heavy civilian casualties; and still the Germans did not give way. Four more heavy day raids took place before the end of July and two in August before a hole was effectively punched in the enemy lines.

By this time it was clear that the Halifaxes and Lancasters must turn towards a new menace, the flying-bomb offensive. Many sites destroyed had been rebuilt or re-positioned and from June 15 the V-1s were roaring across the Channel and little could be done to halt them. Taking out the sites was an almost impossible task. Instead, the heavies were directed against supply depots and large sites like that at Watten. These day raids, with huge fighter support, continued until early September. By then the Allied armies had overrun much of France and by capturing the V weapon launching areas they brought the menace largely to a close.

Along the French coast the Channel ports held, their garrisons fighting with commendable courage in the face of some murderous onslaughts by wave upon wave of Halifaxes and Lancasters. First Le Havre, then Boulogne and Calais were shattered. Dunkirk was left alone, useful as a practice target for 2 Group. In any case, its inhabitants could be besieged into submission; and it had no shelter for E-boats.

Bomber Command's support for the armies was almost completed, but it

77, 78 and **79** *Liberator squadrons in the Far East in 1944-45
used distinguishing rudder markings, as displayed by these Liberator
B.VIs: EW284 of No 215 Sqn with
white horizontal bars on a black
rudder; EW287 of No 355 Sqn with
a rudder of black and white vertical
stripes; and KH284 with a white
diagonal cross on a black rudder.
Photographs were taken after the
aircraft had been withdrawn from
service and were awaiting disposal in India* (G. A. Cull, via
Bruce Robertson).

80 *Wellington X OP-L: LN???
of No 11 OTU. Usual finish with
red codes and serial above tailplane and no side windows. Possibly
it is LN299* (I. E. Young).

81 *Mosquito B.XVI, MM183:
P3-A of 692 Sqn. Initially delivered
to 128 Sqn on September 16 1944,
it went to 692 Sqn on September 25,
was involved in a flying accident on
February 1 1945, and passed to
de Havilland for repairs but was
instead struck off charge on March
23 1945* (Imperial War Museum).

82 *Three Lancasters of 90 Sqn,
the leader bearing the two yellow
bars denoting it was G-H equipped.
Note the anti-gas cross by the
turret on each machine. Photo was
taken in 1945.*

83 *Lancaster RA530:DX-Y of 57 Sqn has red codes outlined yellow in the customary 5 Group manner. Her fins are red with a black vertical stripe.*

84 *Lancaster LS-N:PA170 taxies out at Mildenhall in the autumn of 1944, seen from below the wing of a sister machine.*

85 *A later photograph of LS-N: PA170, after it was shot down on December 4 1944 (Archief Documentatiegroep Breda 1940-45).*

86 *Lancaster LM170:2K-X was delivered to 1668 Con Unit in October 1944. She flew as 2K-D and later as shown. She crashed on April 13 1945 and her front-line service was with 44 Sqn from June 1944 as KM-E (C. J. Peacock).*

87 *Lancaster II 'N', reputedly of 432 Sqn, on a typical airfield dispersal. She has a large nose motif but it is barely visible on the original (J. A. Banks via W. H. Lynn).*

88 *Halifax III 'N Nan' of 43 Sqn awaits her crew from the crew bus, the 'liberty bus' of the war years (J. A. Banks, via W. H. Lynn).*

89 *Baltimore V FW332 with an attractive nose motif and legend 'Redwing', plus ops tally (Imperial War Museum).*

90 *Halifax II Srs 1 (Special) with the Type Z nose. Note the exhaust stains and weathered upper surface paintwork. She carries a nose painting and bomb symbols denoting four sorties. BB324 of 10 Sqn joined that unit in April 1943. She was lost on June 22/23 and may have come down in the North Sea (Real Photographs).*

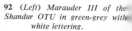

91 (*Above*) *Liberator VIII KP136, featured in the drawing on page 188, has the SNAKE inscription and typifies the finish of Liberators in SEAC service. Roundel centres and fin flash sections are probably pale blue but could possibly be white.*

92 (*Left*) *Marauder III of the Shandur OTU in green-grey with white lettering.*

93 *This photograph of a Baltimore—probably a Mk IIIA or IV —shows the usual camouflage pattern of Dark Earth and Middle Stone. The effectiveness of the camouflage in breaking up the outline of the aircraft is apparent here. Note the worn and patched finish* (Imperial War Museum).

94 *A view of AD661, the prototype Blenheim V (HA), with Dark Green-Dark Earth-Sky finish.*

played a major part in the capture of Walcheren dominating the mouth of the Scheldt. On October 3, 247 Lancasters, including OJ-A : PB488, OJ-C : PB509, OJ-E : LM697, HA-A : PD277, HA-O : PD279, HA-R : ME842, JI-A : PB142, JI-L : NF968, A2-H : NG142, PH-H : NF117, PH-Q : ME788, PH-J : PD289, WP-C : LM157 and WP-K : HK610, led by Mosquitoes, including GB-R : ML995 and MM134, attacked the main dyke. The sea poured in, more raids followed and the enemy was driven from the island or drowned.

1944 colour

Basically there was no change in the camouflage colouring of the heavy bombers in 1944. They retained their Dark Green-Dark Earth-Night finish, the texture of which was quite smooth. Codes and serials were Dull Red. Exceptions in the case of aircraft on night operations were Mosquitoes, which wore Dark Green and Ocean Grey camouflage with Medium Sea Grey under surfaces. Their codes were red and serials black.

The most important bomber was certainly the Avro Lancaster, typified on January 4 1944 by OF-W : JB299 and OF-T : JB659 of 97 Squadron. Both had H2S radomes. From Oakington, No 7 Squadron was busy marking for some of the Berlin raids. Its aircraft still had small 'MG' coding, A : JB682 being seen on January 1 a few hours before it was lost on a Berlin raid. Others in use that night included JA911 : MG-N, JB414 : MG-Y and JB224 : MG-W, all fitted with H2S radomes.

Occasionally, a Lancaster would be seen bearing some minor modification. One such I recorded at Warboys on February 21 was GT-L : ND454 (GT forward on the port side, aft on the starboard). She had a small plastic blister immediately aft of the bomb aimer's window to permit a view aft. Like late production Lancs, she had the customary enlarged bomb aimer's dome, but an aeroplane that did not was LS-C : R5508, now fitted with an H2S radome. Squadron codes were in the customary fore and aft positions. On the only occasion when I saw her, at Mildenhall on April 5 1944, she was on a dispersal roughly where the large concrete apron now ends and at its north-east corner. With her was LS-L : LL889, the first Lancaster I saw with a small part of the rear of the H2S radome unpainted. Dispersed at the east end of Mildenhall was 622 Squadron, whose LL885 : GI-J (codes as usual fore and aft) also had part of her radome unpainted. Sitting alongside was GI-Q : LL793, the first Lancaster noted with paddle bladed propellers. She was one of the many Lancasters which had a small *Window* chute under the port side of the nose. Some Wellington IIIs and Xs, incidentally, had this modification.

So often today's illustrations of RAF bombers in books and pamphlets show individualistic nose emblems, but even in 1944 there were a large number of aircraft without any such embellishments. Sometimes squadrons painted aircraft individual letters on the side of the nose in red, in Flight colours or yellow. Raids were often denoted by painted bombs, with other shapes for mining or special operations. An exception was ND340 : GT-J, upon whose nose, on the port side, an artist had painted Jane (of *Daily Mirror* fame) tearing up a swastika.

When the squadrons had a third or 'C' Flight added they sought means of indicating which aircraft belonged to it. By 1943 many of the most acceptable code combinations had been allocated, the US 8th and 9th AAFs having

J

letters within the British system. During 1943, letters 'I' and 'C', and numbers
up to '9' were introduced into the code system, since the number of units in
existence was so large. This led to Stirlings of 623 Squadron being coded IC
and Lancasters of 582 Squadron wearing 60, 625 Squadron using CF (eg,
CF-A : ND992 and CF-P : NN748), 170 Squadron using TC (eg, TC-J : RF199
and TC-C : LM732), and 150 Squadron IQ (eg, IQ-U : NN742 and IQ-V :
PB781). One of the squadrons that was awarded a second coding was No
514, flying Lancaster IIs from Waterbeach, whose 'C' Flight wore A2 on its
aircraft. They included LL678 : A2-L, LL697 : A2-B and LL698 : A2-J, the
latter being lost on the Nuremburg raid of March 30/31 1944.

Division by Flights was important operationally on all RAF squadrons.
One Flight could be stood down, or given a particular task, etc. So Flight
markings were variously useful. During March 1944 they appear to have been
extended to the spinner tips of a number of Lancasters. On OF-R on March
23 they were white. Two days later, OF-G : ND500 had red tips, but all were
soon removed.

A more unusual sight visible on April 12 at Bourn was that each Lancaster
had a metal fairing in place of the nose turret. One thus modified Lancaster
was OF-N : ND346. At the same time all of 7 Squadron's aircraft, also part
of 8 Group, were similarly modified, like MG-R : JB653.

A typical Lancaster II of the period was JI-U : LL731. When I looked her
over on May 21 she had provision for a ventral .50 inch gun but later was
flying with the usual two-gun ventral turret which Mk IIs all had provision
for, and frequently carried in the case of 3 Group aircraft. Under her nose,
which had the earlier small bomb aimer's dome, was the now customary
Window chute. Above the mainplane she had black lines indicating safe
walking areas. Her bomb bay had accommodation for six incendiary containers and one 8,000 lb bomb, and her bomb bay doors were bulged, again
as usual on the Mk II. Beneath the rear turret she had a *Monica* radar aerial
to assist in gun laying. No H2S radomes were fitted to the Lancaster IIs.

One of the great nights of the period under review was June 5/6, when
Lancasters operating against the guns of Normandy included MG-A : JA911
marking Longues, and SR-O : LL833 and A2-F : DS786 which, with A2-L :
LL678, aimed at Ouistreham. The day raiders against Villers Bocage on June
30 included Lancasters JI-C : LM206 and A2-E : LL677.

The first six months of 1944 saw an extensive re-equipment programme.
Four squadrons, Nos 75, 149, 214 and 218, flying Stirlings, were to equip
within the year. Halifax IIIs joined Nos 10 (from March 1944; ZA-M :
HX323), 51 (from January; MH-V : HX330), 76 (from May; MP-O : LK780),
78 (from January; EY-V : LK847), 102 (May; KN-A : MZ325), 420 (January; PT-E : LV953), 424 (January: QB-O : LW119), 425 (January; KW-J :
LW390), 427 (February; ZL-L : HX279, lost March 19 1944), 429 (March;
AL-L : HX352), 431 (April; SE-S : LK828), 434 (May; WL-K : LW173, lost
June 13 1944) and 640 (January; C8-Z : LW434, lost June 3 1944). Code
positions for some Halifaxes in 1944 included (1) those with unit codes ahead
of the roundels: 415(6U), 419(VR), 424(QB), 427(ZL), 428(NA), 429(AL)
and 433(BM); and (2) those with unit codes ahead on the port side, aft on the
starboard: 420(PT), 425(KW), 431(SE), 432(QO) and 434(WL). Some of the
early Mk IIIs soon had under turrets for .50 inch guns fitted, especially on Nos
431 and 434 Squadrons which had previously fitted them on their IIs and Vs.

There were many Halifax Mk IIs and Vs flying in 1944, mainly in Conversion Units like OO-F : DK149 of No 1663. A Mk II series 1a of January

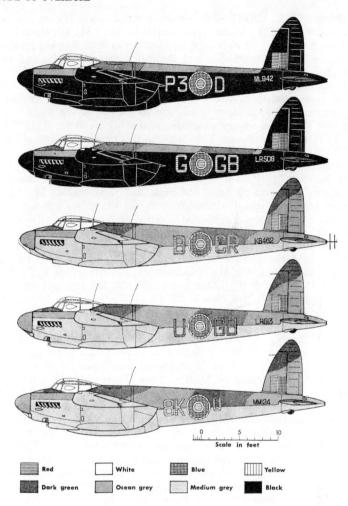

Red | White | Blue | Yellow
Dark green | Ocean grey | Medium grey | Black

Figure 24: (*Top to bottom*) *Mosquito bombers of 8 Group, 1944-45. The basic colour of these aircraft was Dark Green and Ocean Grey with either black or Medium Sea Grey under surfaces. Codes were Dull Red normally, and their size varied between units from 2 feet to about 2 feet 6 inches high usually, although 571 Squadron had individual letters smaller than usual. Serials were black, and red on the black aircraft.*

ML942 was initially delivered to 1409 Met Flight on January 29 1944, went to 139 Sqn on February 4 1944 and to 692 Sqn on March 13 1944 in whose markings it is seen. It passed to 571 Squadron on April 19 1944 and was written off on January 6 1945. It was a Mk XVI.

LR508 is depicted as an Oboe-equipped aircraft of 105 Sqn and wears the markings portrayed on March 25 1944. All its nose windows had been overpainted. It served with 109 Sqn from June 19 1943, became GB-F in July and, after a battle accident in January 1944, was recoded GB-G. It joined 109 Sqn on December 6 1944 and was burnt out during an accident on operations on April 24/25 1945. It was a Mk IX.

KB462 was a Mk XXV which arrived at 13 MU Henlow for operational gear on October 17 1944, joined 142 Sqn on November 14 1944 and on December 17 1944 passed to 162 Sqn at Bourn where it became CR-B. It was recorded in the markings shown in March 1945. Note the white outline to the codes and the tail warning radar. It joined 142 Sqn on April 30 1945 and 627 Sqn on August 14 1945. After the war it was also used by 109 Sqn and was finally struck off charge on October 22 1947.

LR513, a Mk IX, served first with 109 Sqn and joined 105 in the autumn of 1944, became GB-U (dark blue codes). It was recorded thus in October. On November 6 1944 it returned to 109 Sqn with whom it served until September 19 1945. Nose and nose windows were overpainted.

MM124 was a typical Mk XVI used by 571 Sqn from May 25 1944 until written off on January 2 1945.

1 1944 was TL-L : HR847 with rectangular tail, small fairing around the
dorsal turret and H2S radome. HX239 : HD-G was a Mk III which I looked
over on a '60-footer' on February 20. Unit codes were forward on the port
side, aft on the starboard. She had the usual rectangular fins and rudders
which all the production Mk IIIs had, and small fairings around her dorsal
turret. An unusual Mk II series 1a coded BL-H used for trials at Wittering
had her nose perspex painted over. Early 1944 Halifax IIIs with elliptical
wing tips came into squadron hands, but to the end of the war many were
flying with the earlier square wing tips. Such a Mk III in use April 1944 was
HX337 : W of 466 Squadron. Two in use at this time with elliptical tips were
LW633 : O of 425 Squadron and LW460 : J of 640 Squadron.

In August 1944, the Halifax IIIs of 76 Squadron included MP-$\overline{H}$: LW627,
MP-Q : MZ691, MP-P : NA570 and MP-D : NA571, all with square wing
tips, 'square' fins and rudders, and none had radomes. MP-D and MP-C
both had ventral turrets. The aircraft of the leader, MP-G had just acquired
white fins and rudders as squadron identity. It is said that at this time 51
Squadron's leader had the fins and rudders of his aircraft painted in pink
and white squares.

During 1944 the number of Mosquitoes in Bomber Command steadily
increased. Most famous of the squadrons was No 105 which, by March, was
using Mk IVs like GB-B : DZ429 and J : DZ548, Mk IXs without deepened
bomb bays like GB-B : LR500 and GB-C : LR503, and a few XVIs including
GB-J : ML964, the latter wearing Ocean Grey-Dark Green-Medium Grey
finish.

Many of the IVs and IXs had Night under surfaces and red serials. Whereas the later marks had their GB coding aft on both sides of the aircraft, some
of the IVs had GB ahead on the starboard side. Examples of the IXs with
half black finish recorded on March 25 are GB-W : ML920, GB-L : ML916
with three rows of yellow bombs on the port side of her nose, GB-E : ML913
and GB-G : LR508. All had two whip aerials above the fuselage.

A month previously at Graveley, 692 Squadron using Mk IVs and XVIs
could be seen to wear 'P3' ahead on the port side, aft on the starboard. A
'black' Mk IV was P3-B : DZ647 and one in 'day' colours was P3-B : ML969
which had a black serial. An unusual machine was ML966 in 'day' colours
with a black rectangle along the fuselage carrying the roundels and 'P3-O'.

The first Mk XVI operation was carried out by ML938 : GB-D. 105 was a
three Flight squadron which had barred letters on 'C' Flight machines like
ML987 : GB-$\overline{C}$ (day colours) and ML983 : GB-$\overline{F}$. The latter, with ML986 :
GB-G, ML916 : GB-P and ML914 : GB-N, was responsible for part of the
marking of the Caen area during Operation *Goodwood* on July 18. No 109
Squadron at Little Staughton also operated a mixture of 'day' and 'night'
Mosquitoes for marking purposes. HS-B : ML907 having black under surfaces
like HS-R : LR511, and HS-C : ML989 having 'day' colours. On the night of
June 5/6, No 105 Squadron despatched a marker force including GB-G :
LR508, H : LR504, J : ML923, F : LR507 and E : ML919.

Marker Mosquitoes were also operated by 5 Group. For the raid on
Mailly-le-Camp of May 3, NS993 : N and ML976 : N of 617 Squadron in
'day' colours, with DZ525 : AZ-S and DZ521 : AZ-M of 627 Squadron (also
in day colours), were part of the marker force.

Stirlings in 1944 use were largely in training units of which more anon.
They carried out a lot of mining and gave support to partisan forces. An
operational unit flying them almost to the end of the war was No 199 Squad-

ron based at Lakenheath. In April 1944 it was carrying its unit letters ahead of the roundels, like 149 Squadron. EX-P : LK397 and EX-A : LK385 (with a wasp motif on her nose and 24 yellow bombs recording sorties) were both in use on April 5. OJ-O was then LK394. By this time Stirlings were rarely seen to retract their twin tailwheels. To give the aircraft added protection from belly attacks, aircraft of 149 and 218 Squadrons had .50 inch guns in retractable mountings.

A new bomber introduced at the start of 1944 was the B-17F Fortress II. First to have them was No 214 Squadron which moved to Sculthorpe on January 17 to commence training in a radio counter-measures rôle in 100 Group. Its aircraft had Dark Green-Dark Earth-Night finish with red codes and serials. 'BU' was painted ahead of the fuselage roundels and the individual letter painted aft, repeated on the fin aft of the fin flash and again in Dull Red. Extra aerials were fitted but no guns in the central or waist positions, and sometimes the ball turret was unarmed or replaced by more electronic gear. A large H2S radome was placed beneath the chin. Operations commenced on April 20/21 1944 when a raid was mounted by four aircraft (SR388 : H, SR386 : N, SR377 : M and SR382 : B) on the La Chapelle marshalling yards. During May sorties continued, mainly over Occupied Territory, and in June extended to Germany. For the Kiel operation of July 23/24 the squadron despatched BU-D : SR378, H : SR388, O : SR379, M : SR377, S : SR380, and F : SR383, and some of its newly acquired Fortress IIIs BU-A : HB767, C : HB780, T : HB763, G : HB774 and B : HB765. Others used at different times included A : HB780, C : KJ111, L: HB779 and S : HB795 called *Joie des anges*.

The final operations by Wellingtons of Bomber Command came on March 3/4 1944, when 300 Squadron laid mines off Lorient. But this was far from the end of the Wellington in a bomber rôle, since nearly all of the OTUs and some Gunnery Schools were equipped with Mk IIIs or Xs to the end of the war, albeit in training Groups. Their markings sometimes varied from the norm, as for example on a Mk III noted on January 29 merely with a white 'O' ahead of its roundels. A Mk IC seen flying on February 20 had 'V' in similar position and in white.

There were quite a number of trials and experimental Wellingtons in use now. One was LN151 (red serials) with HP-O in white (HP ahead on the port side, aft on starboard) serving the Gunnery Research Unit. If you were lucky you caught a glimpse of one the Wellington jet test beds, one of which I saw in Dark Green-Dark Earth-Yellow finish on July 21 leaving a trail of black smoke and bearing Type C roundels under its wings.

Occasionally it was possible to glimpse a Whitley. Many were now in the hands of the airborne forces, some at OTUs but mainly rested in MUs. One noted in March 1944 was N1475 : ZV-X; another seen April 4 was EB302 with B aft on the starboard side and XR overpainted. There were several at Henlow, for para-dropping trials, where Z9485 sat forlorn and tail-less on April 19. Her top camouflage still extended to the base of the fuselage.

The light bombers were very active within the period. Boston IIIAs and Mitchell IIs in their Dark Green-Medium Grey finish with red codes included Boston RH-F : BZ377 and Mitchell VO-B : FV928. Usually the codes were positioned ahead of the fuselage roundels, with the individual letter on the nose. To make the codes more easily evident on some Mitchells the unit letters were painted aft, as on VO-N : FW205. Its serial in black (as usual) was painted at the base of the fuselage. Basically a Mk II, it had a tail position like a Mk III and a large side window in the rear fuselage sides below the turret position, and was thus seen on June 11 without the then customary black and white wing and fuselage AEAF stripes, as carried on Boston RH-A : BZ210 and VO-F : FW253, a Mitchell II. In the case of 320 Squadron a yellow triangle, outlined black and painted on the nose, proclaimed their Free Dutch association, as on NO-R : FR182 and NO-F : FR189, both with AEAF stripes.

The most unusual of the light bombers I saw at the time was a Boston IV noted on January 4. It wore dark grey upper surfaces and Sky under surfaces. The Mk IV mainly belonged to a later period.

In addition, there were the miscellaneous bombers like the Blenheims, now largely collected at No 12(P) AFU, Grantham (eg, L1139 : 115 and BA102 : 106 where they carried individual numbers between '1' and '115'). There they wore trainer colours and white letters/numbers. Mk IVs of Nos 526 (eg, T2005) and 527 (eg, T2336) Squadrons had red codes and retained their early war Sky under surfaces, and a number of all-black Mk Vs were still around flying from OTUs.

The Bristol Buckingham was at last leaving the Filton lines. These bombers wore an unusual scheme of Dark Green-Dark Earth-Azure undersides. The first one I noted was in June 1944 and soon after I recorded KV321 fully armed and wearing this unusual colouring, more applicable to a transport aircraft, in which rôle later Buckinghams were produced.

Behind the lines

Always the key to an effective force is its training programme. In this aspect the Royal Air Force has always excelled. During the war the pattern of pilot instruction was Initial Training Wing—Elementary Flying Training School—advanced training—Operational Training Unit—Operational Conversion Unit and sometimes, where bomber pilots were concerned, a spell with a specialised training unit for type conversion. Once on the squadron, initiation into current practices followed. Then the first sorties were flown, usually against easy targets. These flights were known as 'freshmen'.

Units previous to OTUs were strictly non-bomber outfits. The OTUs equipped with bomber types were introduced in April 1940 and mushroomed tremendously. They varied in strength but usually comprised two or three squadrons each of about 20 aircraft, generally Wellingtons. In addition, they often had a further unit of Ansons for navigational training, some Oxfords for bombing training, and many boasted a further flight of target-towing and fighter aircraft for fighter affiliation duties.

Bombers in these units wore standard bomber colours with current code colours, although sometimes the latter varied from the norm in colour and presentation. In early 1944, No 10 OTU was still operating some Whitley Vs from Stanton Harcourt, including BD237 : RK-M and Z6952 : ZG-R. An Anson with that unit's navigation training flight was AX297 : UY-J and it wore training colours and red codes. In the early part of the war such Ansons had black under surfaces and grey codes. Later in 1944, No 10 OTU equipped with Wellingtons, including RK-W : NC715, RK-U : NC714 and ZG-C : NC480. All had their unit codes placed aft. No 19 OTU was another ex-Whitley unit that swopped to using Wellingtons which in 1944 included UO-D : NC740 and UO-I : LP804. Examples of aircraft of other OTUs of this vintage, all with unit codes aft, are JM-S : HE488 and JM-L : LP752 of

20 OTU, WJ-X : BK212 and JG-A : NA795 of 17 OTU, LN546 : DD-S and HF623 : LT-C of 22 OTU, and FB-Z : LN290 and TY-M : HE411 of 24 OTU.

To the end of the war No 13 OTU trained crews for 2 Group, latterly using Boston IIIAs, Mitchells and Mosquitoes, with Ansons for navigation training. Two Bostons used were BZ346 : XJ-P and BZ397 : XJ-O. They had green/grey finish with red codes, unit letters ahead of the roundels and the individual letter on the nose. Mitchells included FV999 : FV-A, FW114 : FV-D and KQ-A : FW119. Two of the Ansons were AW974 : SL-B and DG839 : SL-D, both with red codes, unit letters aft. Fighters posted to OTUs also retained their usual camouflage colouring, like Hurricanes UH-F : LF743 and UH-P : LF717 of 21 OTU. Two Martinets of that unit were UH-U : HP375 and UH-X : JN301, which wore the usual target-towing colours. They had Sky codes, like the Hurricanes.

Allied to these aircraft were those of each Group Towing Flight. Formed early in the war, these units equipped progressively with Battles, Lysanders, Defiants and Martinets and were later re-designated, No 1 Group Towing Flight (or Target Towing Flight) becoming No 1481 Flight, 2 Group Flight becoming No 1482, etc. Some expanded to include aircraft of types used operationally to give advanced gunnery and bombing training. Thus, Whitley N1436 joined 1481 Flight, like T4176. Later still, some smaller Flights were formed specifically to give bomber defence training for air gunners. These units equipped with Hurricanes and Spitfires, one of the latter, BM134, going to 1688 Flight. An unusual feature of some of their aircraft was that the cannon were removed leaving the barrel fairings *in situ*.

On April 7 1942, a special marking had been ordered to be applied to operational types in some of the affiliation flights. They were instructed to carry an 18-inch wide Sky band around the rear fuselage immediately ahead of the tail unit. It was to apply to the Wellington IA and Whitley V of 1481 Flight and its four Lysander target tugs, the five Wellingtons and the six Defiants of 1484 Flight, and the two Hampdens, four Wellingtons and three Whitleys of 1485 Flight. Possibly they were worn and certainly one Wellington was flying with these markings late in the war.

After leaving OTUs, crews were posted to one of 19 Conversion Units (later called Heavy Conversion Units). These were part of Bomber Command and sometimes flew on operations. Into these were gathered the Conversion Flights which many squadrons were operating in 1942. Some squadrons identified conversion flight aircraft with a barred individual letter. The first Conversion Unit was No 1651 formed at Waterbeach in January 1942 to supply Stirling crews. In 1944 it was at West Wickham where an aircraft in use was BS-P : R9193, thus recorded on April 14. The second unit was No 1652 formed to train Halifax crews. One of its later aircraft was GV-K : MZ637, a Halifax III with rounded wing tips. It was some time before Lancasters could be spared for any Conversion Unit, and Manchester crews were trained at 25 OTU Finningley. In April 1942, No 1653 CU formed to train more Stirling crews, its 1944 aircraft including AK-F : EF309, which had small unit letters ahead of the roundels and an H2S radome. No 1654 Conversion Unit began to form at Swinderby on May 19 1942, with eight Manchesters and eight Lancasters, the first supplying 5 Group crews.

No 1655 Training Unit was somewhat different. It was established as the Mosquito Training Unit to produce crews for Nos 105 and 139 Squadrons. It converted them by way of the Oxford and Blenheim V, the former used for navigational and bombing training and including AB644 : G1 and

T1053 : N1. Three of its Mosquitoes operating from Wyton in the summer of 1944 were KB153: H, DZ436: R and DZ632. Unit codes were not carried.

No 1656 CU was the first to form in 1 Group and it arose from Nos 103 and 460 Conversion Flights. It flew some Manchesters, like L7437: BL-Y, but later concentrated on Halifaxes, then Lancasters, such as NN814: EK-O.

Expansion of the Conversion Units continued until the end of 1943 and later they were concentrated in 7 Group. In November 1944, Stirlings were phased out, since 3 Group was then Lancaster-equipped and sufficient crews were available already for the airborne forces. Some of the last Stirlings in use, with 1657 HCU, were LK613 : XT-W, LK608 : XT-X, LK434: XT-Y and LK608 : XT-Z, all in use in November 1944. Most of the HCUs had a flight of Oxfords for navigational and bombing training as well as blind approach training. Indeed, some of their Oxfords retained the four yellow triangles associated with aircraft in the latter rôle. Some BAT Flights had earlier used Wellingtons, as well as Whitleys, like N1477 used by No 2 BAT Flight in 1941.

Late 1943, special units known as Lancaster Finishing Schools were formed converting crews to Lancasters who had previously done conversion to four-engined aircraft on Stirlings and Halifaxes. Each Lancaster Group operated an LFS, 3 Group forming theirs at Feltwell in December 1943. One of its aircraft was A5-F : ND623/G, codes in the usual positions.

One other training unit deserves mention, the Navigation Training Unit at Warboys. It formed at Gransden on April 10 1943, and moved to Upwood and the Warboys satellite in June. Its aircraft came mainly from 8 Group units and by June Mosquitoes were in use, although mainly it used Halifax II srs 1 and Lancasters, coded QF. Lancaster QF-T was EE371 in April 1944; QF-L was JB384 and QF-M : JB183; these aircraft equipping 'B' Flight. Some of them, like ED842, were modified for dual control.

The survey here is not intended as an exhaustive one where the training element of Bomber Command is concerned. There were many Flights, for instance No 1429 which trained crews for the Czech Squadron, No 311. But the brunt of training rested on the OTUs and the Conversion Units.

Chapter 19

Finale in the Middle East

THROUGHOUT OCTOBER 1942, softening up of enemy forces in the Western Desert continued, without revealing details of the coming offensive. Meanwhile, the Eighth Army gathered strength to push routes through the enemy minefields, thus allowing armour to advance and engage enemy formations to the rear of these minefields.

At 2150 hours on October 23 1,000 guns engaged selected targets in the enemy positions, ten minutes later switching to a creeping barrage followed by infantry. Overhead 60 Wellingtons of Nos 37, 40, 70, 104, 108 and 148 Squadrons laid their bombs by the light of flares dropped by Albacores of 821 Squadron, FAA, on to dazed enemy positions.

By first light on the following morning the infantry had overcome many centres of resistance and the sappers had cleared some paths through the minefields which were now choked with advancing tanks and guns.

At full daylight the standard bombing force went into action. Usually this comprised 18 Baltimores or Bostons, with elements of the USAAF B-25 force, led by six Kittyhawks with bombs and six without, 12 more Kittyhawks providing top cover to the rear of the bombing formation. During October 24 alone, Nos 3 and 232 Wings, with B-25s of 82 Squadron, managed 254 sorties, the Baltimores of 55 Squadron, including AH144 : C, AG846 : P and AG914 : W, unloading 250 lb bombs. Standard colouring for these aircraft was Dark Earth-Mid Stone-Azure Blue with red code letters. Repeatedly the day bombers, including SAAF Bostons, hammered the enemy and at nightfall the Wellingtons and Albacores took over.

Allied tanks swept forward on the night of the 24/25th and next day light bombers made seven attacks on concentrating enemy armour. After blow and counter blow, there appeared to be stalemate. To a greater extent than elsewhere the Desert War was one of supply and attrition, and off the coast Wellingtons, Beauforts and Baltimores saw to it that no tanker could bring fuel to Rommel. Then a gap was punched in the Italian sector and anti-tank guns holding the Allied forces were mercilessly assaulted. By mid-day on November 3 enemy transport was streaming west along the coast road to Fuka; against these vehicles the day bombers, then the Wellingtons, went into action, although acting against scattered targets did not suit the Baltimore formations so well. Once the anti-tank screen was swept away all seemed set for a resounding victory. On November 6, a mighty deluge descended upon the desert, transforming it into a sea of mud. Allied armour ground to a halt and Rommel's forces escaped to re-group. The battle of El Alamein was over. The enemy had nonetheless lost the initiative, although progress was slow and it was not until January 23 1943, that the Eighth Army entered Tripoli.

Meanwhile, a new offensive of a very different nature had been launched.

Invasion of the European mainland was clearly impossible in 1942, the necessary forces not being available. It was decided in July 1942 that it would be preferable to ensure victory in North Africa, then mount an attack on the soft underbelly of Hitler's Europe. Accordingly, it was decided to support the desert fighting with an invasion of French North Africa. It was hoped that the French would be reasonably co-operative.

On October 22, the first troop convoy sailed from the Clyde, and a great build-up of fighter aircraft to support the invasion was started at Gibraltar. Ground crews for a tactical bombing force operating Blenheim Vs then sailed on the *Arundel Castle*, whilst in Britain Nos 13, 18, 114 and 614 Squadrons flying Blenheim Vs (known also as Blenheim VDs and Bisleys) prepared for overseas. These were short-range aircraft, and it was planned to operate them as close support bombers from captured bases.

In its original form the Blenheim V had a four-gun ground attack nose. AD657, the prototype, flew on February 24 1941. When I first saw it on May 15 at Duxford it had a most unusual finish, a dark shade of grey and greyish-green upper surfaces with dark grey under surfaces. It ended its days in a flying accident at the Gunnery Research Unit in July 1942.

Before it had flown, its specification was revised to include a 'high-altitude' rôle. A new interchangeable nose section was designed with offset bombing station and a trough which served as a navigation post, and this mounted twin guns for rear defence. AD661, the second prototype, was the first 'high-altitude' machine which initially had a Dark Green-Dark Earth-Sky finish. After trials it served as a trainer at 12 (Pilot) Advanced Flying Unit, where it crashed in November 1944.

Production deliveries of aircraft powered by Mercury XVs began in September 1941, and a month later deliveries were made to Egypt and India, but operations were some way off. Delivery of 'BA' serialled aircraft began in January 1942, and many of these went to home-based units like Nos 51, 54, 60 and 132 OTUs and the large Blenheim training school, 12 (P) AFU, where the first pre-production aircraft, DJ702, was used. The second, DJ707, flew at the Rootes works on research schemes and became 3289M in July 1942. As mentioned in Chapter 14, Blenheim Vs could be seen over Britain in 1942 sporting a variety of finishes. Those destined for North Africa, however, acquired Dark Earth-Mid Stone-Azure Blue finish at MUs or at the factory and on squadrons. They had black serials and Dull Red code letters. Unit codes seem never to have been applied.

By early November the assault landing force was in the Mediterranean and on the 8th landings were made at Algiers. Airfields at Maison Blanche and Blida were quickly seized and the French were soon placated. Oran fell after some fighting, and on the west coast an American force seized Casablanca. German reaction was fast and effective, reinforcements quickly entering Tunisia. The Allies took some large strides, capturing Bone on the 12th. By November 28 they were 16 miles from Tunis, but major snags had occurred. Forward troops now lacked good air cover, airfields being few and mud plentiful. The Luftwaffe, operating from established bases in Tunisia and Sicily, waged a very effective campaign and its skill spelt disaster for the Blenheim V squadrons. The best-known of these was surely No 18, whose 18 aircraft left Portreath for Blida on November 11 1942. Only 11 completed the journey successfully, including BA803 : A, BA780 : B, BA794 : C and BA 828 : H. The squadron straightaway went into action bombing El Aoina airfield, and made raids against Bizerta and Sidi Ahmed. Such flights were long, difficult and risky by day, so on the 30th they moved east to Canrobert where the Blenheim squadrons soon formed 326 Wing. One of these was 114 Squadron which arrived in Africa on November 14 and made its first sorties, by night, on November 16/17, using BA754 and BA727. BA751 : Z was in use in December.

The change to night operations was forced upon the Blenheims because they were suffering heavy losses, none of which was more serious than that of December 4. Using its own aircraft, and some borrowed from 13 and 614 Squadrons, No 18 Squadron attacked the landing ground at Chouigui that day, then landed to refuel at Souk-el-Arba, for Canrobert was 180 miles from Tunis. Led by Wg Cdr H. G. Malcolm in BA875 : W, ten took off again (BA734 : Y of 614 Squadron, BA796 : D of 13 Squadron, BA820 : Q and BA800 : D of 614 Squadron, BA769 : H, BA795 : N and BA862 : Y of 13 Squadron, and BA869 : N of 614 Squadron). With them was BA825 : J of 614 Squadron which crashed after take-off. The Blenheims ran in at 1,000 feet and immediately a swarm of Bf 109s dived upon them. Unescorted they jettisoned their bombs and had to flee, but five were soon a smoking mess. Eventually, like BA820 : Q and BA796 : D of 13 Squadron and BA800 : D of 614 Squadron, they were all shot down. As a mark of tribute to the courage of all who took part, the formation leader was awarded a bravely won Victoria Cross and gave his name to the RAF's Malcolm Clubs.

There was considerable borrowing of aircraft at Canrobert and on December 27, No 18 Squadron was operating again, making night raids by moonlight, particularly on the roads to Sfax and Tunis. The inadequacy of the Blenheim hastened its replacement by the Boston III, although this aircraft was in short supply and not until 2 Group gave up its Mk IIIs as the supply of IIIAs permitted did the situation improve. By then it was April. Some American Bostons were acquired and, like 233223 : H and 233206 : U, retained their US fin serials and American camouflage, which consisted of a tan shade and neutral grey. The colours worn by all the aircraft in the theatre weathered considerably and fast, soon bearing little resemblance to original hues.

There were so few Bostons that the Tactical Bombing Force (326 Wing) reverted for a time to Blenheims, making advanced moves with them to Oulmene and Souk-el-Khamis (alias 'King's Cross').

It was the end of March when the Bostons became available in large numbers and on April 21 Nos 18 and 114 Squadrons flew their first fighter-escorted raid on troops near Medjex-el-Bab. These aircraft, which had been tropicalised in Britain, wore Dark Earth-Middle Stone-Azure finish with red letters and black serials. They included AL747 : F, AL494 : P, AL296 : D, AL738 : G, AL775 : C, AL497 : S, AL492 : M and 233229 : A of 18 Squadron, and AL676 : L and W8329 : P of 114 Squadron.

The bomber force in North-West Africa was strengthened in December by the arrival of Nos 142 and 150 Wellington Squadrons at Blida. No 142 brought DF693, DF551 : E and HF670, unit codes QT. No 150's machines included HF671 : JN-M and HZ191 : JN-J. These aircraft had Dark Earth camouflage with Dark Green replaced by Middle Stone. Their Night shades and under surfaces were retained, also red codes and serials. They bombed targets at Bizerta and used their range to reach Sicily and Sardinia. Soon their targets were overlapping those of 205 Group in Egypt, whose operations became rather limited as the battle moved away from Egypt and the need to capture intact ports and airfields increased. Its Wellingtons currently included

LF-P : HE132 of 37 Squadron. The day bomber force also met similar limitations. On February 18 the entire air force in the Middle East became part of the Mediterranean Air Command.

There were some Wellington IIs in use at this time and they included W5555 : D and Z8331 : U of 148 Squadron. Another type in the Dark Earth-Mid Stone-Black finish was the Halifax II. Nos 10 and 76 Squadrons had detachments in Egypt in 1942 which on September 7 were put together to form 462 Squadron. Its aircraft, believed to have only individual letters, included W1156 : Y, in use December 1942, and W7848 : Y, in use February 1943.

A tough fight had been put up by the Germans on both fronts; indeed they mounted a hefty counter-attack on the Americans at Faid on February 14. Meanwhile, the Eighth Army was hammering the Mareth line with the heavies making night raids on its rear. After one last throw, Rommel retreated and on March 20/21, Montgomery's forces made an all-out attack supported by the Desert Air Force. Gradually the distance between the two fronts dwindled until the final capitulation on May 13. The great desert fight had been won, and from it the most useful lessons in the use of air power for the support of ground forces.

As soon as the desert war was over, eyes turned to an obvious stepping stone, Sicily. First the island of Pantelleria was invaded, the bomber force giving support. The invasion of Sicily was then set for July 10. At this time the Tactical Bombing Force, still using aircraft in desert camouflage, comprised Nos 55 and 223 Baltimore Squadrons, 18 and 114 Boston III/IIIA Squadrons and three SAAF squadrons. Both 13 and 614 Squadrons were now with the Coastal Air Force. For night operations there were nine Wellington squadrons, Nos 37, 40, 70, 104, 142, 150, 420, 424 and 425, the last three having arrived from Britain during May. Wellington Xs of 142 Squadron now in use included HF795 : A, HE593 : G and HE679 : Z and in 424 Squadron A : HE513, E : HZ371 and N : HE540. Examples of 425 Squadron's Mk Xs were KW-A : HE930 and KW-Q : HE592. All wore Dark Earth-Middle Stone camouflage with red codes and serials with black sides and under surfaces.

Baltimore squadrons, supplied with crews from 72 and 75 OTUs (the latter's aircraft including AH111, '154 and '169), were now using Mks III, IIIA and IV. The IIIAs began to arrive in the theatre during November 1942 and the Mk IV, which featured a two-gun Martin dorsal turret, from March 1943. Between August and December 1943, Mk Vs arrived and with further armament modifications. Serial batches and associated American variant/serial number tie-ups for the Lend-Lease Baltimores were as follows :

Mark	US variant	British serials	US serials
IIIA	A-30-MA	FA100-380	41-27682-27962
IV	A-30A-1-MA	FA381-490	41-27963-28081
	A-30A-5-MA	FA491-674	41-28082-28256
V	A-30A-5-MA	FW281-880	43-8438-9037

The Mk Vs comprised the following sub-types, RAF serials running consecutively against the USAAF serials :

	A-30A-10-MA	43-8438-8562
	A-30A-15-MA	8563-8662
	A-30A-20-MA	8663-8762
	A-30A-25-MA	8763-8862
	A-30A-30-MA	8863-9037

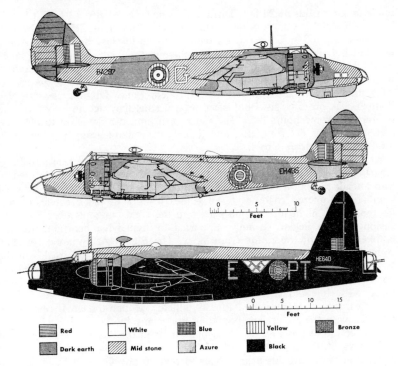

Red   White   Blue   Yellow   Bronze

Dark earth   Mid stone   Azure   Black

Figure 25: (*Top to bottom*) *Blenheim Vs were put to a variety of uses in the Middle East. BA297 was used at Fayid in 1942 for training purposes, and was an early series Blenheim V. EH495 represents the late production Mk V and was seen in late 1943 at Foggia in the state depicted. Bomber squadron aircraft had a dorsal turret but many Blenheim Vs in Britain and overseas flew with them removed. EH495 also features the small blister on the nose transparency which many production aircraft had. Blenheim Vs served as general reconnaissance aircraft in the Middle East as well as bombers. Wellington X HE640 wears the Middle East two-tone camouflage, but otherwise has the trim of a home-based bomber. She belonged to 420 Sqn.*

Early July night attacks were delivered against ports such as Naples and Bari, and the rail network that could be used to bring supplies to Sicily. An intensive series of day and night raids then followed on Sicilian airfields from which German fighters operated. On the night of July 9/10, 83 Wellington Xs of 205 Group delivered various diversion attacks and Bostons bombed and dropped dummy paratroops to divert enemy attention, while a large airborne invasion of Sicily was mounted. Next day the tactical bomber force went into action and throughout July and August, as the Army fought bravely and tenaciously, Baltimores and Bostons waged an intense campaign. During July, 205 Group's Wellingtons attacked Sicilian airfields by night and also frequently hit at communications and rail targets in Italy, preventing supplies from being brought forward. Army progress was rather slow but it finally led to an onslaught on Messina. Around this area many Germans sailed for the mainland. Throughout this phase fighter-bombers played a very large part, supplanting much of the possible effort mediums might have been called upon to deliver.

To dissuade the Axis powers from denuding north Italy of its defences, and help persuade the wavering Italians to accept surrender rather than have their country destroyed by the Allies, Bomber Command was called in. It made massive raids on Milan, Turin and Genoa. On August 12/13, Flt Sgt A. L. Aaron, DFM, was piloting Stirling EF452 : HA-O of 218 Squadron. It was shot up, and suffered serious damage to its fuselage and wings. Aaron endured horrific wounds and soon his place at the controls had to be taken by the bomb aimer. Aaron gave him instructions which enabled the aircraft to be flown. Realising they could never make the journey home across the Alps, they bravely headed for, and reached, Bone. Landing the crippled bomber was no easy task, but after several runs they accomplished it, and Aaron died some hours later. He had shown immense devotion to his crew and tremendous determination and joined that valiant group posthumously awarded the Victoria Cross.

As soon as Sicily was vanquished, the Allies prepared to stride into Italy. Apart from a direct assault across the Straits of Messina, it was decided to leap ahead, placing a landing force ashore at Salerno. Before this occurred bombers hammered roads and rail routes leading to the beachhead area. Bostons made night interdiction sorties to the area. On September 2 the invasion of Italy began, strongly supported by fighter-bombers and the day bomber force now operating from Sicily. The Eighth Army landed in Italy with an important initial object, seizure intact of a group of airfields in the Foggia area, which fell into Allied hands late in September. This enabled the bombers to move in and allowed 205 Group to bring forward its night raiding force. Now it could strike at southern Germany, Austria and the Balkan countries, not to mention the Ploesti oilfields. Round-the-clock raids were possible, with the Americans pounding the enemy by day.

A diversion at this time involved operations in the Aegean. Halifaxes and Liberators of 178 Squadron with Halifax IIs of 462 Squadron carried out night attacks on airfields near Athens to prevent any German build-up, and they bombed the Aegean islands. Kos was invaded on September 30, but the invaders were insufficient in strength to hold it and the entire venture had to be abandoned.

Resistance to the Allies around Salerno was very strong, but, nevertheless, they entered Naples on October 1, a city which the RAF had heavily bombed by day and night. At the end of October, Baltimores and Bostons of 18, 55, 114 and 223 Squadrons moved into the Foggia complex forming 232 Wing. Apart from close Army support the squadrons flew day and night tactical sorties along the east coast of Italy, some of their aircraft having black under surfaces.

Soon the entire Allied force faced an awful winter. Arid land was transformed into a sea of mud by winter rain which almost prevented flying and seriously delayed the Army until spring 1944. So slow was the advance that it was decided to leap ahead again, with a landing made at Anzio on January 21 1944. Reaction was extremely strong and the Army found it impossible to break out for some time even with massive air support.

Operations by 232 Wing and South African Air Force squadrons were closely allied to those of the Americans. Indeed, there was some loaning of aircraft to the RAF which meant, for instance, that 18 Squadron operated some A-20Gs wearing USAAF fin serials and RAF roundels. By this time the RAF Boston squadrons were using aircraft in the same Dark Green-Medium Grey finish common to those in Britain from whence some of the 29 Mk IIIAs supplied had come. They also flew a few Bostons in Olive Drab-Gray American colours.

Baltimores during that winter were still frequently seen in desert camouflage. One was FA289 of 223 Squadron used from September 1943 to May 1944. Its red letter 'S' outlined white was painted aft of the fuselage roundel on both sides of the aircraft. Others similarly marked included FA436 : B of 223 Squadron (replaced by FA 382); FA389 : Z shot down over Italy in September; FA394 : R frequently flown by 223 Squadron's CO and later used by 39 Squadron, SAAF; FA424 : H written off after a raid on Naples; FA475 : D of 55 Squadron later D of 223 Squadron shot up over Venafro and written off; and FA479 : X of 223 Squadron destroyed by a direct hit over Mighanico on December 8 1943. All of these aircraft wore the Dark Earth-Mid Stone-Azure Blue finish.

When the better weather came, the armies moved forward, and Rome fell on June 4. All of the bombers were intensively employed but the immense value of the fighter-bombers was so unquestionable that the most famous Baltimore squadron, No 223, was disbanded on August 12, its place being taken by 454 Squadron, whose aircraft included FW818 : Q.

The first of 111 Boston IVs (A-20Js), with revised noses and dorsal turrets, joined the squadrons in July 1944 wearing Dark Green-Medium Grey finish with red individual letters on the nose. BZ548 : J and BZ529 : K were both with 13 Squadron in January 1945. BZ502 : T and BZ511 : M served with 18 Squadron. Before the end of 1944, the Boston V (A-20K) was in service, all the aircraft of this final mark being sent to the Mediterranean area. BZ588 became 'S' of 55 Squadron, BZ603 : D of 18 Squadron and two Mk Vs of 13 Squadron in use in January 1945 were BZ621 : M and BZ641 : V. Squadrons operated mixed marks of aircraft. By the start of 1945, Bostons were making raids close to Allied lines under instructions from mobile radar control posts.

The arrival of the heavies at Foggia had been immediately put to good use, particularly effectively in a mine-laying campaign in the River Danube. In April 1944, 205 Group could call upon six Wellington X squadrons and three heavy bomber squadrons to attack Budapest, Ploesti and Belgrade, and make sustained raids on the rail networks of Hungary and Rumania to give some aid to the Russians. On April 8/9 three Liberators dropped flares for 19 Wellingtons making the first Danube mining operation near Belgrade. There were 18 such forays, during which 1,382 mines were laid, effectively halting river traffic and preventing it from transporting supplies which the railways could no longer take. The final operation of the series came on October 4/5 when four Liberators lit the river area for 18 Wellington mine layers. In October 1944 Nos 142 and 150 Squadrons flying Wellingtons disbanded, both to re-form in Britain. In the case of 142 Squadron, its Wellingtons in use at Regina in July 1944 had included MF120 : Q, LP189 : H, LN961 : T and LN864 : W. Two months later, LP548 : H, HE964 : Y and MF632 : W were in use.

The Wehrmacht consolidated itself across Italy on what became known as the Gothic Line. It was breached on August 25/26, whilst Halifaxes, Wellingtons and Liberators hammered at the railway installations at Ravenna, and Bostons and Baltimores attacked rail and road transport and routes immediately behind the front. Similar operations followed by night and day, Halifaxes of 614 Squadron (whose crews wore the Pathfinder badge) taking on the task of finding and marking the targets at night.

Since 1942, Liberators had been flying in 205 Group. They were particularly useful for operations in conjunction with partisan forces by virtue of their range. To mid-1943, Liberator IIs had been used, and indeed these were operating in the autumn of that year with 178 Squadron. Some examples of its aircraft and their uses include the following: AL525 carrying the customary 6,000 lb load bombed Larissa and Heraklion in support of the 1943 venture into the Aegean, on September 27 and October 29 respectively; AL536 bombed Athens on September 26, and AL552, which after the war was civilianised as G-AHZR and later SX-DAB, raided Maritza on November 15 1943; and AL555 : O bombed Catania airfield on June 12 1943, during the softening up of Sicily and five nights later attacked Comiso. It would be interesting to hear from any aircrew who flew in the Liberator II force in the Middle East, for the records of their use seem sparse and muddled.

Replacement of the Mk II by Mk IIIs in 178 Squadron seems to have been erratic, but by March 1944 Liberator IIIs were in use like BZ892 : E, BZ928 : B, BZ932 : Y, BZ947 : N and BZ946 : Z.

The Wellington X and Halifax II were ageing types by 1944. In June of that year 148 Squadron was flying Halifaxes which included JP177, JP220, JP286, BB318 and BB421. The chosen replacement type was the Liberator VI/VIII which entered 205 Group in September 1944. First 37 and 614 Squadrons had them, and then 148 (which by May 1945 was operating BVIs including KL616 : P, KL531 : T, KL569 : X and KL545 : Z). They joined 40 and 70 Squadrons in January and 104 Squadron in February. The Liberators apparently wore squadron codes applied in red with unit letters aft of the fuselage roundels. BL-S : KL501 served 40 Squadron which first operated with Liberators on March 18/19 1945. KH285 : H was used by 37 Squadron and EP-U : KL373 of 104 Squadron had its individual letter repeated on the bases of the fins in white.

December saw the equipment of No 39 Squadron with Marauder IIIs. Since the summer of 1942, the Marauder had been in RAF hands, No 14 Squadron flying them almost exclusively on maritime operations and using Mk Is and IAs. South African squadrons also had them, but not until the end of 1944 did the RAF equip bomber squadrons with the maligned aeroplane. By now the B-26 Marauder was quite a success, many of its 'widow-making' qualities having been removed.

Both B-26Fs and B-26Gs with Dark Green-Medium Grey finish were supplied to 39 Squadron under the same designation, Mk III.

In September 1943, first deliveries of the Marauder II had been made. They wore the serials FB400-522 and ranging through the B-26C-MO series from the 'dash 33' to the B-26C-45-MO, the first of which was FB493 (42-107497). Later the Mk IIs were B-26C-48-MO aircraft. Nearly all of them went to SAAF units.

Mark III delivery began in April 1944 with HD402 being diverted to Boscombe Down for trials. The first of the mark were B-26Fs of the following series :

British serials	US variant	US serials
HD402-501	B-26F-2-MA	42-96329-96428
HD502-601	B-26F-6-MA	42-96429-96528

These were followed by B-26Gs, also known as Marauder IIIs, ranging as follows :

British serials	US variant	US serials
HD602-676	B-26G-11-MA	43-34415-34464
HD677-751	B-26G-21-MA	44-67990-68009

Marauder deliveries were completed in March 1945.

Gun packages were soon removed from the forward fuselage on 39's aircraft, as were the flexible mounted 0.5 inch nose guns. Operations by boxes of 4, 6, 12, and sometimes 18 aircraft were flown at heights of up to 17,000 feet on raids of up to six hours duration and 1,400 miles range. No 39 Squadron operated as part of the Balkan Air Force from Campomarino, by the sea at Termoli, Southern Italy. Rôle of the squadron was tactical support to the partisan forces of General Mihailovitch and Marshal Tito.

The squadron considered the aircraft to have a top speed of 270-280 knots TAS, to cruise at 210-220 knots TAS and stipulated a landing speed of 120 knots. They looked upon the Marauders as reliable, comfortable and roomy machines, a little sluggish on the controls but considered generally free of vices. Take-offs and landings were, however, protracted on the Summerfield track from which they operated in Italy. Mostly the squadron flew B-26Fs, the B-26Gs being received shortly before the war ended. With HD serial prefixes they included B-'606, F-'607, K-'610, O-'644, P-'647, R-'625, S-'636 and T-'665. Three of the late B-26Fs were HD570 : W, HD558 : X and HD531 : Z.

Some Marauder IIs served at the OTU. This version had short span wings and was slightly faster than the III. Some of these aircraft had two 0.5 inch tail guns, some just one. At the close of 1944 four B-26 squadrons were operating with the SAAF and another, No 25, was part of the Balkan Air Force.

The former four, used on raids over Italy, could be identified by the following markings : No 12 Squadron white nose and fin letters, No 21 Squadron yellow nose letters only, No 24 Squadron white nose letters only, and No 30 Squadron yellow letters outlined white on the noses and tails.

One unusual squadron operating bombers in the Middle East was No 162 which flew radar calibration and trials flights from Gambut. In January 1944 its equipment included Wellington IC BB500 and Baltimores AG936 and AH110. Baltimore AG853 : P and Wellington III HF733 : L were being used in April and four months later the squadron had some Wellington Xs (which it called Mk XA) including LN960.

Another squadron worthy of special mention is No 614. It had re-formed on March 3 1944, upon the re-numbering of 462 Squadron and used Halifaxes such as JP227, JP289, JN892 and JN978, as previously mentioned, in a Pathfinder rôle. In September 1944 it began to receive Liberators, operations with which commenced in October. Mostly they were Mk VIs, but some VIIIs were operated, externally distinguishable by the manner of the retraction of the nosewheel doors. KG837 was one of the VIs. In January 1945, first deliveries of Mosquitoes were made, one flight equipping from February 1945. The only Mosquito operations flown by the squadron were, however, by a Mk IX, LR442. It is believed the squadron had some Mk XVIs and possibly some Mk XXVs, considerable numbers of the Canadian-built aircraft being delivered to the Middle East too late to take part in hostilities.

On May 2 1945, the enemy forces in Italy capitulated. The Allies had won the war in the Middle East after a long, tiring and costly haul, with the balance of power tipping to and fro like the successes of the opposing armies. Link up between the European Axis powers and Japan, and the seizure of the oilfields, were proven to be as impossible as they were impracticable, but there were times when tremendous disaster was close at hand. Oil supplies were soon relatively safe, but perhaps the greatest contribution to ultimate victory came in the 1942 offensive from Alamein. This operation was superbly planned and for once the British forces could mount their version of a *blitzkreig*. They showed the enemy how combined land and air forces should operate—and they applied their learning to the Normandy campaign.

K

Chapter 20

Victory in the East

WAVELL'S 1943 ARAKAN CAMPAIGN had limited success, yet until it took place there was only limited air activity. Although the Army made a satisfying advance, and Akyab was reached, it could not maintain its position. Vengeances and Blenheims, usually wearing Dark Green-Dark Earth-Sky camouflage (although some of the Blenheim Vs had Middle East colours still), gave good support, but it was rather too soon after the disaster of recent months for such an extensive venture. The Royal Air Force also gave active support to General Wingate's first Chindit strike behind the Japanese lines in Burma, but it was principally transport aircraft that were involved.

The thrust into Arakan ended as the monsoon broke in June 1943, a period of intensive army support being brought to an end. Currently the bomber element of the Air Force in India included seven squadrons out of a total of 53, and changes were afoot. Nos 11 and 60 Squadrons were still flying Blenheim IVs, 60 Squadron machines including Z7343, Z7691, Z7706, Z9591 and Z9828, and three squadrons had unpopular Blenheim Vs, machines which had outlived their usefulness. What was needed was very close tactical support for the Army, a rôle in which the Blenheim was unsatisfactory. Therefore, large deliveries of Hurricanes were made to the Theatre at this time. Between August and October, during the rainy season, they replaced Blenheims in Nos 11, 34, 42, 60 and 113 Squadrons, final Blenheim operations being flown in August 1943.

Although the Vengeance had given surprisingly good account of itself as a dive-bomber during the Arakan thrust it was only safe when air superiority was assured. Desirable as it was, no immediate replacement type was to hand. A Command decision was made, and the Air Ministry agreed, to see whether the Mosquito was suitable for this area. Although the Mosquito had at birth been designed to be suitable for tropical service, doubts were held about its wooden construction, and its adhesives. How would the high humidity affect the aircraft? Inevitably it seemed the Mosquito might be eaten by lesser breeds of insect!

Four Mosquito IIs were shipped to India in May 1943, and picketed out to assess the effect of weather and other influences. To those in the Theatre the temptation to use them offensively was too great to resist—they soon reached Nos 681 PR and 27 fighter Squadrons. The requirement was really for the Mosquito FB VI, but this was only just entering service and was in great demand in the Mediterranean area, and especially in north-west Europe. For the time being the Vengeance must soldier on.

For night bombing operations the first advance was the arrival of the Wellington B.X with which Nos 99 and 215 Squadrons equipped in 1943. The first Mk Xs are believed to have reached India in July 1943. These wore the same Dark-Green-Dark Earth-Night camouflage common to home-based machines, red letters and serials and South-East Asia roundels.

Expansion of the long-range bomber force began in August 1943, with the formation of No 355 Liberator III Squadron at Salbani on August 18. At this time Mk IIIs also formed the backbone of No 159 Squadron.

A major alteration to the entire RAF organisation in India came in November 1943, with the formation of SEAC (South-East Asia Command), the British and American Air Forces coming under one Command. With the arrival of Vice-Admiral Lord Louis Mountbatten as Supreme Commander of SEAC, the whole area was revitalised. The combined air force was re-organised into three large groups, as a Tactical Air Force, Strategic Air Force and Troop Carrier Command. These had four principal tasks: (1) To destroy the Japanese air force in Burma, (2) The defence of India, (3) Give support to the 14th Army and (4) Support General Wingate's jungle offensive.

By December 1943, 49 RAF squadrons were operational and an additional 12 were working up. Airfields, almost non-existent in 1942, had been carved out of seemingly impossible places and, even more important, a large number of Advanced Landing Grounds from which operations would be undertaken had been built.

Despite appalling weather Wellingtons and Liberator IIIs were attacking communications and supply dumps in Burma, leaving the Vengeances to operate around forward positions. There was no visible front line, for the troops faced each other in jungle areas where there were few distinctive features, the lines passing haphazardly across rivers, clearings, swamps and high ground, all of which made it difficult for the air forces mounting operations overhead.

At the end of 1943 a four-pronged thrust into Burma began. Again the Vengeance squadrons gave close tactical support leaving Wellingtons to attack by night, airfields, ports, roads and rail communications, the latter being most important to the enemy. A quarter of the longer range bombing operations were directed against railways, especially around Rangoon and on the Burma-Siam route, which cost so many British lives during its construction. Aircraft used by No 99 Squadron during these raids included HE957 : A, HE958 : B and HZ948 : K. A typical Mk X was HZ950 which wore the usual camouflage and roundels and had Z ahead of the roundels in red and serials placed above the tailplane.

Using their very long range capability, Liberators could hit the rail installations as far away as Bangkok and Moulmein, but for the crews these long flights were exceedingly tough going because of the length of time spent in the air.

At the beginning of 1944 the Liberator force was further expanded, and re-vitalised by the introduction of the Liberator B.Mk VI. On January 15 1944, No 356 Squadron, first to equip with Mk VIs, was formed at Salbani. Mk VI aircraft wore two similar schemes. Many were initially delivered in American camouflage of khaki green with grey under surfaces, which some machines retained until their demise. Indeed, some of the ex-SEAC Mk IIIs, which were used after the war by Transport Command squadrons based in Britain, still had American paint-work. Others are known to have been repainted with British paints, Dark Green and Medium Sea Grey. Official directives indicate that there was even some mixing of the schemes, presumably because of the close association between the Americans and the British in SEAC.

Most long range Liberator operations were by day, but over Burma night

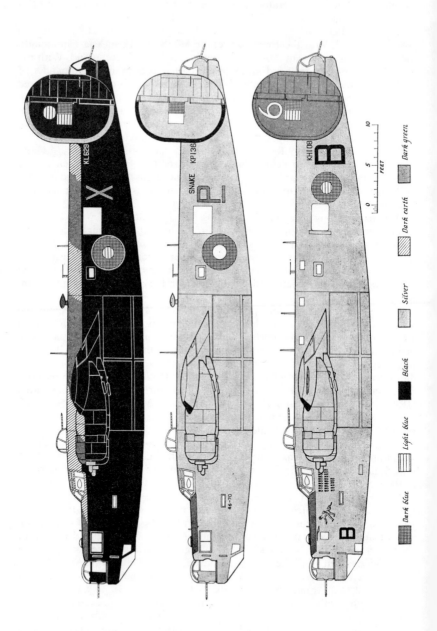

raids were mounted, for which reason some Liberators had black under surfaces and sides in north European manner and wore red codes and serials. No definite ruling appears to have been adhered to with respect to the placing of the individual letters, but usually they appear to have been forward of the roundel. Normally the ball turret was removed from RAF Liberators as on KL629 (X aft) of 99 Squadron, a machine with black under surfaces. To hasten delivery the word SNAKE was applied aft of the serials on some Liberators passing through the Middle East to the Far East, but this seems to have been applied infrequently.

An interesting point is that for a limited period Liberator squadrons appear to have worn squadron code letters. EV902 of 355 Squadron is known to have worn the letters EG-S in September 1944, at which time EV910 was EG-F. When, and for how long, the aircraft were coded seems to have gone unrecorded. Perhaps readers who served in India can shed some light upon this.

A counter attack in the Arakan peninsula was made by the Japanese in February 1944. Their objective was to punch a path through the British Army in very difficult terrain and enter the gateway to India. But the Army held its position, and looked to the Vengeances of 82, 84 and 110 Squadrons, and Hurricanes, for close support. In use at this time were Vengeances AN932 : Q, AN959 : K, AP105 : U, EZ811 : G and FP686 : R, all Mk Is of 110 Squadron which was also using Mk IAs EZ862 : Y and EZ901 : P. Among those in use with 82 Squadron were AN615, AN701, AN737, EZ867 and EZ985.

In March the Japanese mounted a second phase to their offensive. There were weeks of fierce fighting before the enemy was routed. Fighters and light bombers maintained close support throughout the battles of Kohima and Imphal, by the end of which the monsoon season had broken again. The British Army, nevertheless, continued towards Mandalay and Rangoon, the weather becoming steadily worse, eventually forcing them to halt until the monsoon season was over.

By September Liberator VIs were serving with Nos 99, 159, 215, 355 and 356 Squadrons although not all of these were operational. No 99 Squadron, for instance, began using them when flying air-sea rescue patrols and made its first Liberator bombing raid on November 20. All except two of its operations are believed to have been in daylight. Targets for the Liberators in Burma became progressively fewer and a pattern of employment evolved that took them on some quite fantastic operations. Basically they had four tasks : the cutting at long range of the supply routes to Burma, the destruction of supply and fuel depots in Burma and the adjacent territories, the halting of shipping coming into Rangoon, and on a number of occasions giving close support to British troops.

Figure 26: *(Opposite page) (Top)Liberator B VI KL629 : X of 99 Sqn wears a style of camouflage scheme carried by some Far East Liberators. More usual was natural finish and Dark Green-Medium Grey, or Olive Drab-Neutral Gray and combinations of these colours. KL629 has Dark Green and Dark Earth upper camouflage. Her letter and numbers are red, and the fuselage roundel appears to have a very fine yellow outline. (Centre) KP136 is in natural finish, the aircraft letter and bar being grey. Her roundel centre and fin flash have white areas or very pale blue. The anti-dazzle panel is Dark Olive Green. (Bottom) KH108, also in natural finish, is more unusual. She has additional aerials and three high set windows. 'B' was 4 feet high in black on the rear fuselage and the figure '6' was crudely applied in white chalk on the olive green fin when the details of the aircraft were recorded in October 1944. There was a black 'B' on the nose 2 feet high and 26 mission symbols were painted on. Also, a khaki-coloured Japanese soldier being prodded by a black pitchfork had been applied. On the tail of each bomb painting was added a 'rising sun'. Fin flashes on this aircraft were only on the outer faces of the fins, which was unusual. It seems reasonable to assume that the aircraft had originally been Olive Drab and Neutral Gray in finish. Another interesting feature is the under-wing roundel. I would like to hear from any readers who served on the Liberator squadrons and who may be able to tell me more about their individual markings.*

Between Bangkok and Moulmein lay some 5,000 miles of rail track involving the use of over 700 bridges, many built by British prisoners of war. These bridges were vital to the rail network and repeatedly hit in Liberator day raids. Being mainly of wood they were quickly repaired, the track likewise ; labour for the Japanese was cheap—and expendable. Often the targets involved trips of over 1,000 miles and the load was about 3,000 lb. Careful fuel consumption tests were made and later the bomb load was pushed as high as 8,000 lb. Moulmein could be reached, Bangkok (a 2,200-mile trip), the Kra Isthmus—and even the Malay Peninsula, a journey of some 2,800 miles. To do this was the equivalent of bombers based in Britain making raids on North Africa from home bases. By early 1945 such lengthy trips were quite frequent for the Liberator crews, whilst 160 Squadron, also operating Liberators, concentrated on maritime duties. A number of close support operations with the Army were also undertaken, but the targets were tiny and the raids difficult to mount. In the later stages of the campaign some use was made of primitive radio-controlled bombs to strike bridges and small targets. For target photographs the Liberators were dependent upon deep reconnaissance sorties by Mosquitoes of 684 Squadron.

A little-known squadron formed on November 8 1944 was No 358, which operated Wellington Xs and Liberator VIs. It flew a few bomber sorties, then transferred to special duties and supply dropping. Its Wellingtons carried the squadron code TA and included TA-L : LN613 and TA-C : HF134. What seems to have been unique to this squadron were several Wellingtons, each fitted with a dorsal gun position. Some of the Liberators, like others in use in this area late in the war, had natural metal finish with black individual letters only and black serials, KG977 being 'L'.

By the start of 1945 Liberators of the bomber squadrons were wearing squadron identity markings on the tails of their aircraft. No 99's machines wore a white disc on a black fin; No 215's had black rudders bearing two white horizontal stripes; No 355's aircraft had white rudders with three vertical black stripes; and No 356's wore black rudders with white X's.

Mosquito fighter-bombers served briefly for operational service with 27 Squadron from the end of 1943 into 1944, but were soon withdrawn. On February 29 1944, LR250 arrived on 45 Squadron as its first aircraft, conversion being assisted using Bisleys, with the Vengeances leaving in March. A Conversion Unit, No 1672, had formed at Yelahanka to supply crews. No 82 Squadron began conversion on July 4 at Kolar, although it was late 1944 before the Mosquitoes wearing Dark Green and Sea Grey Medium camouflage were ready for operations. Trouble really hit the Mosquito force on October 20 1944, when a machine on a practice bomb run suffered major structural failure which caused all Mosquitoes to be grounded, the result of heat and moisture in the tropical climate. No 45 Squadron resumed operations in November and 82 Squadron began intruder sorties on December 19. Nos 84 and 110 Squadrons converted in 1945. Operations were concentrated over Burma, intruder flights often being made to targets of opportunity, with 47 Squadron joining the fray particularly at the end of the war.

During 1945 the re-conquest of Burma was undertaken on three fronts until Rangoon was captured and Burma fell. Plans were then made for the invasion of Malaya. Before this could come about, the first atomic bomb was detonated over Hiroshima and the mass destruction there, and later at Nagasaki, led Japan to sue for peace. The war in the East was hard for all concerned, and relatively little photographic material has survived from that zone, so perhaps this is an apt moment to appeal to any who still have pictures from their days in the East to bring them forward for the many with historical interest in this theatre of the war.

After the war ended one task awaited the Liberators, the supply of food and medical supplies to those wretched souls who had been so callously treated by the indifferent Japanese. Like the large Dakota force, the Liberators were then engaged upon repatriation of POWs, assisted by many British-based Liberators, and ex-Coastal Command aircraft, quickly modified into transports for the Far East run.

Bomber squadrons in the Far East, 1943-45

Squadron	Equipment	Example	Notes
No 11	Blenheim IV	Z9654	Equipped with Hurricanes in 8.43
No 34	Blenheim V	BA616	Re-equipped with Hurricanes, first received 8.43
No 42	Blenheim	AZ997: S	Re-equipped with Hurricanes, first received 18.10.43
No 45	Vengeance IA, II	AN656: H	Began operations 8.43. Mosquito
	Mosquito VI	HP881	re-equipment began 2.44. Aircraft used included HR291, HP941, LR306 and LR307
No 47	Mosquito VI		Received 2.45; possibly coded KU
No 60	Blenheim IV	V5587	In use 3.43. Re-equipped with Hurricanes 8.43
No 82	Vengeance I, IA, II, III	FB975: B (III)	Mosquito conversion began 7.44. FB975 in use 5.44
	Mosquito VI	HR557: M	In use 5.45
No 84	Vengeance I, IA, II, III	FD105: U	Mosquito introduced 11.44; soon withdrawn. Vengeance served 12.42 to 1.45
	Mosquito VI	RF698: C	Re-introduced 2.45
	Blenheim V	EH354	Used during conversion
	Mosquito VI	HR526: PY-B	In use at the end of the war; silver finish, black codes
No 99	Wellington X	HZ720: G	In use 2.44
	Liberator VI	KG976: L	In use 12.44
No 110	Vengeance I, IA, II, III, IV	FP686: R	In use 12.43
	Mosquito VI	HR620: P	Re-equipped 11.44; example given in use 4.45
No 113	Blenheim V	AZ942	Last Blenheim operation 15.8.43; Hurricane received 9.43
No 159	Liberator II, III, VI, VIII	EV966 (VI) KN812 (VIII)	Mk VIII externally identifiable by outward opening nosewheel doors
No 215	Wellington X	HE957: V	
	Liberator VI	EW284: Q	Grey-green finish
	Liberator VIII	KH372: H	'Silver' finish
No 355	Liberator III	BZ955: F	Mk III used 10.43 - 4.44
	Liberator VI	EW245: D	Mk VI in use 3.44 - 9.45
	Liberator VIII	KN774: Q	'Natural' finish. Others used included KP136: P
No 356	Liberator VI	KL611: W	Used 1.44 - 11.45; example with green/black finish
		KH119: S	Green/grey finish
No 358	Wellington X	HF134: TA-C	Wellingtons coded,
	Liberator GR.VI	KG866: M	Liberators uncoded. 'M' had 'natural' finish

Other units in the Theatre using bombers included No 1 AGS equipped with Liberators such as A:EV909, H:EV975, J:EW259 and C:KG889.

Chapter 21

The battle is won

DURING SEPTEMBER 1944, Bomber Command was removed from the control of the Supreme Allied Commander and put under the Chief of Air Staff for a new strategic campaign directed principally against oil and petroleum targets, ball-bearing works and motor vehicle factories, although the Command would still be available to attack tactical targets if required.

Casualties remained heavy but by October 1944 they were falling, since there was less enemy territory to cross before Germany was reached. *Gee* and G-H stations were soon positioned nearer targets and operations became more and more complex and much larger. Added to this, 100 Group was really coming into its own, making feint attacks, upsetting enemy radar gear, engaging night-fighters and generally confusing the enemy interception forces.

September witnessed the withdrawal of the Stirling from bombing operations in Bomber Command. Since July 17 1944, and under strong fighter cover, a few daylight raids had been flown. It was during the course of one of these, against Le Havre, by LK401 : G, LJ632 : P, LJ481 : U and LK396 : M, that the final bombing took place, these aircraft being of 149 Squadron. Stirlings of 218 Squadron made their last operation on August 2, again in daylight. Contrary to what has appeared in print these were far from the last bombing raids by RAF Stirlings. In January and February 1945, Stirling IVs of 38 Group were committed repeatedly to night bombing of Rhineland towns in aid of the Allied ground forces. The final offensive Bomber Command Stirling sorties were flown by EX-H : LJ516 and EX-G : LJ542 on March 10/11 1945, when they took part in radio counter measure operations from North Creake.

By October most of 3 Group Lancasters had G-H fitted, this Group making day raids using about 200 Lancasters. A G-H leader, whose aircraft wore two 18-inch horizontal yellow bars on both sides of its fins, headed boxes of two or three others not so equipped. About 80 G-H aircraft could be handled per operation, the range of the equipment being about 250 miles.

Allied commanders were eager to take Walcheren, since it overlooked the entrance to the Maas and, on October 3, 247/259* Lancasters were despatched to breach the sea wall at Westkapelle, allowing sea water to flood part of the island. On the 7th, dykes at Flushing were attacked, and again on the 11th. Then a wider breach was caused at Westkapelle to allow assault craft to pass through, followed by further tactical attacks made on Flushing's guns.

A massive onslaught was delivered on Duisburg on October 14 by 1,007/ 1,063 aircraft, of which 15 were lost. The following night 988/1,005 repeated the dose and six more were lost. To protect the force, another 141 aircraft

* Numbers printed thus indicate number of aircraft attacking and number of aircraft despatched respectively.

flew diversions, and 233 sorties were delivered against Brunswick. A training feint was launched against Hamburg, which was bombed by Mosquitoes, who also flew a feint to Mannheim. The Duisburg raid was in two waves, the second of which went in as the Brunswick force withdrew.

Daylight raids were effective, although smoke and dust were handicaps to visual bombing. At night, crews aimed at Target Indicators which, if correctly placed by the Pathfinding Force, brought more accurate bombing on many occasions than by day. On October 25, for instance, when the new campaign opened, 199 Halifaxes, led by 12 Mosquitoes and 32 Lancasters of 8 Group, bombed the Meerbeck synthetic oil plant at Hamburg without loss. Another 771 aircraft attacked Essen.

Maritime targets were not overlooked and, on October 4, 6 Group raided the U-boat pens at Bergen. This attack was repeated by 244 Lancasters of 5 Group on October 28/29, an operation seriously impaired by poor visibility. On October 5, 5 Group sent 221 aircraft to Wilhelmshaven, each Lancaster taking 10 × 1,000 lb HEs and a few incendiaries, a break with normal practice since the Group was currently taking 80% incendiaries on operations. Twelve squadrons of 5 Group using 237 aircraft operated against Bremen on October 6/7 with two aircraft of each squadron carrying HEs and the rest complete loads of 4 lb incendiaries. Nuremburg, Dortmund, Stuttgart and Cologne were also bombed in October during which, on the 24/25th, 955/1,055 aircraft bombed Krupps at Essen, losing eight of their number.

Without doubt the most spectacular performers in the Command were now 9 and 617 Squadrons. On October 7, 14 of 617 Squadron (including KC-D: EE146, M : ED923, F : ME554, T : DV393, W : LM492, X : DV482, N : LM 485, O : DV391, A : LM489, V : PB416, Q : LM482, S : PB415 and K : ME 562), half forming a high level force at 5,000/8,000 feet, with the remainder at 500/800 feet, breached the Kembs barrage, thereby preventing the Germans controlling flood water to halt the Allied advance. Three squadrons of Mustangs covered them. On the 15th, 18 Lancasters of 9 Squadron (including WS-O : LM715, Y : LM220, P : NF929, C : LM548, L : LL845, E : NF937, M : LM448, X : ME809, W : PD198 and F : PD213), six with half-hour delay Tallboys, the rest with 11-second delay Tallboys, tried for the Sorpe Dam which 617 had been after in May 1943. It was tough, however, and even these earthquake bombs failed to breach it.

It was still desirable to knock out the battleship *Tirpitz*, now sheltering in Norway. Nos 9 and 617 Squadrons had tried for her in Alten Fjord on September 15 when operating from a Russian airfield, Yagodnik, but a smoke screen over the ship resulted in only one bomb from 27 Lancasters hitting her. She moved to Haak Island, Tromsö, coming within range of Lancasters based at Lossiemouth and Kinloss. Merlin 24s were fitted to these bombers giving 18 lb plus boost for take-off and allowing take-off weight to increase and range to be extended by the installation of a Wellington long-range tank and a Mosquito drop tank. The fuel load, 2,406 gallons, permitted a 2,252 mile track.

Luck was out on this operation; four aircraft did not bomb owing to cloud at the vital moment. NF920 of 617 Squadron was hit by flak and force landed. Some of the others returned with quite a lot of fuel despite the length of their sorties.

On November 11, the 9 and 617 Squadron force again flew to Scottish bases, 36 Tallboy Lancasters, with the Film Unit machine, a meteorological reconnaissance Mosquito and transport aircraft. Modifications to the Lancasters, including the loss of their dorsal turrets, permitted an all-up weight of 70,000 lb, including 2,400 gallons of fuel. The force took off for the third attempt at 03.00 hours on the 12th, and this time 29 attacked, 18 of 617 Squadron and 11 of 9 Squadron, the latter squadron despatching WS-M : LM448, P : ND929, E : ND937, B : NG220, C : NG232, S : NG249, R : NG 252, G : PA172, A : PB368, V : PB696, W : PD198 and NN722. One of the first bombs hit the *Tirpitz*, then two more, resulting in her turning turtle.

Meanwhile, the grand offensive against Germany was in full swing. On November 2/3, 946/992 aircraft bombed Düsseldorf and 16 were lost. Losses were generally lower now, and on the 16th when 1,188 Lancasters and Halifaxes attacked Julich, Duren and Heinsburg, only four failed to return. The heavy raids on oil targets continued unabated, G-H being useful on cloudy days. By the end of November the Command had despatched 15,008 sorties. Mine-laying continued, too, 1 Group topping the bill with 270 mines laid in November.

Between the start of October and the end of December, only five out of 20 attacks on the Ruhr had been delivered at night, yet it was not until December that sizeable formations of enemy fighters tried to interfere. Massive Spitfire and Mustang escorts were provided for these daylight *Ramrods*. Only when escorts were absent did the enemy have any success. But flak was still heavy and dangerous, and on October 6, when 126 Halifaxes of 4 Group, led by eight Mosquitoes and 23 Lancasters of 8 Group, bombed the Sterkrade oil plant, 70% of the Halifaxes were hit by flak, although only three were brought down. Some idea of the strength of the fighter cover may be seen from that afforded Lancasters bombing Wanne Eickel on November 9, when Nos 19, 41, 122, 124, 126, 129 and 234 Squadrons (nearly all Mustangs) gave cover.

There were 19 day operations in December. Five were against oil plants and four on the Urft Dam to prevent the enemy controlling possible flood water. On the 3rd, 200 Lancasters of 1 Group set out for the dam but cloud prevented an attack. Next day, 30 crews of 8 Group attacked it, 129/205 on the 8th when visibility was bad, and 180/239 bombed it on the 11th. But the results were poor and it was decided to capture it instead.

On 23 nights in December the Command operated, putting over 1,300 aircraft up on two nights. From 15,333 sorties, 135 aircraft were missing. One of these was Lancaster PB371 piloted by Sqn Ldr R. A. M. Palmer. His machine was attacked by fighters but he continued and marked the rail installations at Cologne despite having two engines on fire after fighter attack. For his example he was awarded the Victoria Cross. By this time some of the effort had been diverted to communications targets to damage von Rundstedt's counter attack. The oil offensive was not forgotten, however, and on December 6 a record force (291 Lancasters of 1 Group, 123 of 3 Group and 71 of 8 Group with 12 marking Mosquitoes) bombed the Mersburg plant. On the 29/30th, 1 and 6 Groups combined to attack the plant at Gelsenkirchen.

Despite its mighty power, Bomber Command still delivered attacks which went astray. On December 13/14, 61 aircraft of 54 Base (5 Group-Base 4) were sent to attack shipping in Oslo Fjord, in particular the cruiser *Koln*, active from different berths. Mosquitoes selected the target then a visual attack developed—by the end of which it became apparent that the effort had been wasted on a merchant ship ! *Koln* was two miles west, a few aircraft having attacked her and missed.

A deeper penetration was to Gdynia on the 18/19th, a base for the remnants of the German fleet. Some 227 aircraft attacked, but the target was out of Mosquito range so Lancasters had to mark the target instead. The Master Bomber, however, gave the wrong wind vector so the target was missed, although a 'Schleisen' class ship was left down by the stern. A third attempt to get the *Koln* was made on December 31 by 28 Lancasters of 5 Group. Twelve were from 617 Squadron and carried Tallboys set to explode in 100 feet of water. During the raid the ship moved, but so mighty was the explosion of one Tallboy that she was swung round 90 degrees and stopped. Special operations by 617 Squadron against E-boat pens were flown on the 15th and 29th, then on the 31st 627 Mosquito Squadron made a low-level attack on the Gestapo HQ in Oslo in 2 Group style. Such operations required skill that few crews possessed and only two aircraft bombed the building. All were hit by flak but came home safely.

There were 10 day raids in January and the Main Force was out 21 times at night making some very effective raids on oil installations. Mosquitoes operated on 16 nights. One special attack was carried out by 5 Group on the Dortmund Ems canal at Ladbergen. During this, Lancaster PD377 : WS-U was badly maimed. Flt Sgt G. Thompson of 9 Squadron faced the flames in the aircraft to save the two gunners, but died of wounds later. He was awarded the Victoria Cross posthumously.

In February there were 17 day raids and 23 at night. The month opened when 292 Halifaxes of 4 Group and 6 Group with 40 Lancasters and eight Mosquitoes of 8 Group bombed Mainz. Oil products were now scarce in Germany, for the 1944 offensive had played havoc with supplies. The most notorious operation of the month was the Dresden raid of February 13/14. Here was a target hitherto neglected, to quote the official directions, a 'main centre of communications in the southern half of the Eastern Front'. It was a centre of government, a transport centre where photographs had shown many vehicles and rail trucks, and a justifiable military target. What, perhaps, it did not justify, was such a mighty hammering as it received from the RAF and the Americans. Its decimation began when Lancasters (including PH-A : NN800, PH-M : PB750, PH-W : PD207, OJ-J : NG224, OJ-K : NF973, OJ-B : PP506, MG-B : PB490, MG-C : PB622 and MG-F : PB487) bombed the already blazing city, aided by Mosquitoes of 627 Squadron (AZ-W : DZ631, Q : DZ650, Y : KB406, J : KB345, G : DZ611, H : DZ606, P : KB416 and F : DZ599), and Dresden was left a burning mess for the Americans to stir in the morning. Next night a very similar target, Chemnitz, was given the same treatment by 671 aircraft (including PB849 : PH-S, ME323 : PH-P and OJ-T : ME352).

Captain Swales of 582 Squadron was the Master Bomber for the Pforzheim raid of February 23/24. An enemy fighter shot up his Lancaster PB538, but Swales continued his dangerous task. Eventually he ordered his crew to bale out. He was killed when the aircraft crashed, and was posthumously awarded the Victoria Cross.

The tempo of operations was now quite tremendous, attacks taking place on 24 days and 29 nights in March. One of the heaviest raids came on the 11th when over 1,000 bombers made the 15th massed raid on Essen, delivering 4,680 tons. When Main Force could not operate there was always the Light Night Striking Force of Mosquitoes of 8 Group—a group within a Group, which readily operated when others were grounded. Their contribution was out of all proportion to their size and loads, and for such a little aeroplane to fly at will over Germany, then to deliver a 4,000-pounder whenever it chose, was an outstanding and significant achievement.

Small yet vital communications targets always proved difficult to wipe out and there were still many intact rail routes leading to the western front. On some of these were large bridges and viaducts, notably at Arnsberg and Bielefeld. In February, it was decided that the destruction of 18 bridges or viaducts would isolate the Ruhr. The heavies were called in, especially 9 and 617 Squadrons. During February, they attacked E-boat pens at Poortshaven (from where midget submarines were harassing Antwerp) and the pens at Ijmuiden. On February 22, 17 Lancasters of 9 Squadron demolished part of the Altenbeken rail viaduct, whilst 617 Squadron went for a similar structure at Bielefeld. One bomb burst beneath a span but it still stood. The first real success came on March 14 when Sqn Ldr C. C. Calder took PD112 : YZ-S to Bielefeld. From her fell the first 22,000 lb DP Grand Slam bomb. The bridge was shaken to its foundations and much of it collapsed. More Grand Slams were dropped on the 15th and 19th as the build-up for the Rhine crossing took place. On the 19th, 617 Squadron took 13 × 12,000 lb HC and 3 × 22,000 lb DP bombs to wreck the Arnsberg viaduct. On the 23rd, aircraft (including PD119 : J and PD114 : B), with 5 × 22,000 and 12 × 12,000 pounders, were taken to destroy Nieunenburg bridge, but one Grand Slam and three other bombs were sufficient.

On April 6, area attacks on German cities were discontinued. Operations would now be directed against oil, maritime, transport and tactical targets. On April 7/8, the last important oil plant-cum-thermal power station at Molbis was attacked. Mosquitoes marked for 186 Lancasters of 5 Group and considerable damage was caused.

Special operations by 9 and 617 Squadrons continued. On April 9, 17 aircraft of 617 Squadron, supported by 40 Lancasters of 53 Base, attacked U-boat pens at Hamburg. For once enemy fighters were up in force, among them a number of Me 262s. A running battle developed and four Me 262s were claimed by the gunners of 617 Squadron. On the 16th came the highlight of April when Lancasters of 617 Squadron (PD113 : YZ-T, PD134 : Y PB415 : O, PD119 : J, PD116 : A, NG494 : KC-B, PD128 : N, PD128 : KC-U PD115 : K, PB997 : E, PD133 : P, PD132 : X, PB996 : C, PD139 : L, PD130 H, PD127 : F, PB998 : D, PD114 : B, PD371 : KC-W, and PD118 : M), carrying Tallboys, attacked the *Lützow* in Swinemunde. Another aircraft, NG 228 : KC-V, was shot down on the run in and, although bombs just missed the ship, these hefty weapons were sufficient to cause her stern to sink.

At the beginning of April, intelligence sources suggested that the enemy was retreating into Lower Bavaria and Bohemia, where he might hold out for quite a considerable time, until forced to capitulate. On April 4, 244 aircraft of 5 Group attempted to kill Nazi and military personnel from Berlin who were in Nordhausen. *Oboe* Mosquitoes of 8 Group marked, and 55 Base bombed the barracks. The whole town was devastated. Another terrific onslaught followed, this time against the island of Heligoland. Some 943 Lancasters, Halifaxes and Mosquitoes—of which three were lost—took part.

Had the British public been asked to name one target in Germany that should be destroyed they would surely have cried 'Hitler !'. The thought must often have crossed the minds of those in high places. More to prove to the Nazis the futility of continuing the fight than to kill their already crippled leader, Bomber Command directed one of its last operations against Berchtesgaden (Hitler's hideout in Bavaria), where British Prime Minister Neville Chamberlain signed the infamous Munich Agreement in 1938. On April 25, 318

Lancasters took off with, as their target, Hitler's 'Eagle's Nest' high above Berchtesgaden and his more often used residence, Berghof. It was not a particularly successful operation, despite the delight with which it was undertaken. Nos 9 and 617 Squadrons led the Main Force to attack Wachenfels with 12,000 lb HCs. It was a tiny target, which 9 Squadron over-ran. Although six of 617 Squadron bombed, there were no hits on the eyrie. Within 617's contribution were PB998 : D, PD127 : F, PD134 : Y, PD135 : W, NG340 : U, PD150 : U and PD114 : B. The Lancaster B1 (Special) aircraft were coded YZ, the others KC.

The great bombing offensive was all but over. The much-vaunted 5 Group flew its last operations on April 25, when 55 Base and 49 Squadron had despatched 123 aircraft to Berchtesgaden, dropping 287 tons. At night, 5 Group had 119 aircraft operating against the oil refinery at Tonsberg, while 72 mines were laid by 14 aircraft. These operations were the last by Main Force, and ended the mining campaign which brought far better results than had been expected.

The final offensive action by Bomber Command was taken, significantly, by Mosquitoes attacking airfields and making a 124-strong raid on Kiel, supported by 100 Group Mosquitoes, Liberators, Halifaxes and Fortresses. The participants included, from 128 Squadron D : PF428, L : PF410, C : PF461, F : RV297, V : RV354, W : MM192, Z : PF458, S : PF432, X : MM204, G : PF462, H : PF440, K : RV302, T : PF449, R : RV345, U : PF457 and Y : PF413; and from 163 Squadron G : KB624, Q : KB539, R : KB555, S : KB623, T : KB464, U : KB411, X : KB427 and Y : KB541. The RCM force included Halifaxes RG373 : EX-T, NA164 : O, ON345 : L and NR244 : V of 199 Squadron. The high-speed unarmed bomber concept had been amply proven, and the Canberra (then already under consideration) was to carry on de Havilland's revolutionary concept.

Although the war was almost over, an urgent problem had arisen. In retaliation for the non-co-operation of Dutch railway workers, the Germans had caused a large slice of land to be flooded. The net result was drowning or starvation for many people. It therefore fell to Bomber Command to attempt some relief. Quick dropping trials were held in 115 Squadron at Witchford, as a result of which it was decided to deliver packages of food and essential supplies to the Dutch people. This, Operation *Manna*, was a task in which all who participated would never forget. The sight of hundreds of huge bombers roaring low over Britain and Holland would last a lifetime. Used as we had been since September 1939 to seeing the bombers slowly climb on circling their bases, it was indeed tremendously thrilling to stand in the flat lands of Eastern England and witness an armada, the like of which was soon to vanish, and see it at deck level. To those starving people it meant life from a force that had been built to kill. And kill it had; for the contribution to victory made by Bomber Command was surely one of the biggest factors in the Allied triumph.

Markings in 1944-45

Alteration to types of aircraft involved in the closing months of the bomber offensive against Germany consisted of modifications and detail changes where markings were concerned.

By now the ascendancy of the Lancaster I and III was unquestioned. 1, 3 and 5 Groups were fully equipped, and 6 Group to varying degrees, although

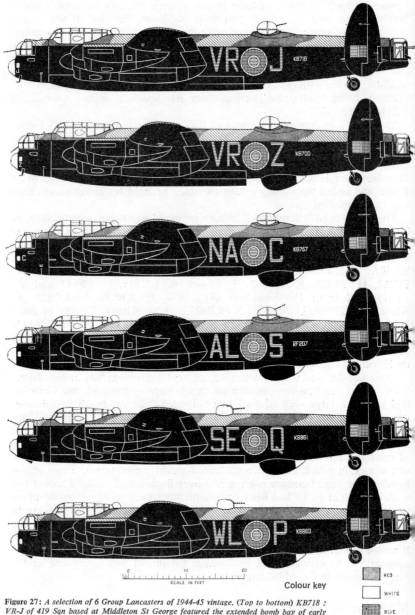

Colour key

	RED
	WHITE
	BLUE
	YELLOW
	DARK EAR...
	DARK GRE...
	BLACK

Figure 27: *A selection of 6 Group Lancasters of 1944-45 vintage. (Top to bottom) KB718 : VR-J of 419 Sqn based at Middleton St George featured the extended bomb bay of early Mk Xs. KB700 : VR-Z 'Ruhr Express' as recorded at Middleton. Previously coded LQ-Q, it became VR-Z and then had its bomb bay extension cut away to allow the fitting of an H2S radome. Two 'standard' Lancasters of 6 Group: KB757 : NA-C has the usual bomb bay doors and 'C' on her nose in Dull Red. She belonged to 428 Sqn at Middleton. RF207 : AL-S of 429 Sqn was based at Leeming. Both of the lower aircraft featured a Martin turret (fitted to some of the later Canadian-built aircraft) fitted further forward as on the Mk VII. SE-Q : KB861 belonged to 431 Sqn, Croft, and WL-P : KB863 to 434 Sqn, also based at Croft.*

this formation was never fully Lancaster-equipped until almost the end of the war.

What 1 Group never exhibited by way of interesting markings, apart from its special nose disc marking, it did make up for to some extent in other ways during the last few weeks of the war. By this time a number of Lancasters had modified turret arrangements. Some of them had Rice-Rose rear turrets fitted with two .50 inch guns, as on AS-C in May. But a more striking combination was the fitting of a Frazer Nash turret moved forward and sited as the Martin turret on the Mk VII. Lancasters in the batches NX548-589 and NX603-610 had this feature. Machines from the production run, both in use in May 1945, included AR-O and SR-U : NX575. In the case of NX572 : SR-S, NX577 : TC-K and IL-I : NG402, two-gun Rice-Rose tail turrets were fitted at this time, and some Lancasters had AGLT radar in place by now.

All of these Lancasters had standard red codes in the usual fore/aft positions, and all had H2S, which by now graced most operational Lancasters. Typical examples of these, recorded at the start of May 1945, were HA-R : SW269, HA-W : PD279, IL-A : PB756, IL-B : ME803, IL-E : PB757 'Easy Does It', PH-O : RE122 and PH-V : RA585. Others with the usual style and colour codings at this time and which had the standard turrets were IO-E, IQ-D, OL-A, BQ-G, GA-V, HW-B, PM-B, TC-W, P4 : C, TO-M (which was flying with a fairing replacing its nose turret), LF-M, AP-R, AR-M, QR-L, 60-M, 60-Z, HC-A, CF-P and UL-D. Some of these code letters still remain to be assigned to squadrons.

Most of the aforesaid Lancasters wore standard markings, but this was not true of some in 5 Group. About August 1944 a few of their aircraft appeared with special tail markings. The intention was for these selected machines to act as 'flight leaders' within the daylight gaggles of Lancasters, and certainly the number which received tail markings was limited. When I recorded these I noted that only occasionally would a machine be seen with these markings, and was only able to tie down ZN-A of 106 Squadron (with a red horizontal bar across her fins) and KM-S : PB380, with a large red 'X' across the entire outer tail surfaces, in September 1944. ZN-A was probably JB663. DX-Y : RA530 of 57 Squadron had red on both sides of each fin with a narrow vertical black stripe, whereas the others quoted had colours on only outer faces, as late as February-March 1945. On April 9, I spotted an uncoded Lancaster with similar markings on her tail. No 467 Squadron had at least one aircraft, PO-O : LM583, with white outer fins with probably a black + at the top, this in August 1944. One aircraft of 619 Squadron had red fins with a black chordwise band slightly higher at the leading edge than at the trailing edge. It used to be tempting to surmise that the style of these markings was connected with the Base (or clutch of stations) within whose care they were held, but this seems unlikely. In October 1944, when these colourings were in vogue, 5 Group Bases and associated squadrons were No 53: 9, 50, 61, 463 and 467; No 54: 83, 97, 106 and 617; No 55: 44, 57, 207, 630 and 619; and No 56; 49, 277 and 189. Illustrations of known Lancaster tail markings may be seen on the front end paper of this book. It would be interesting to hear from any readers who flew these special aircraft or who logged any.

Another feature that appeared late August 1944 on 5 Group Lancasters was the narrow yellow outlining to codes which was a feature of some, but never all the Lancasters, in 5 Group squadrons. Two examples were NE165 : OL-Y (October 1944) and OL-J (May 1945). Although I logged many 1 Group Lancasters in the closing months of the war, the only one of that Group that I saw with yellow-outlined codes was AS-N; interesting because, unlike most Lancasters, she had her unit letters ahead of the roundels on both sides of the fuselage. Some 5 Group Lancasters had their unit codes painted in red above the port tailplane (to be read from the leading edge) with the individual letter above the starboard tailplane, but again this feature does not appear to have been anything like usual. Another item sometimes boldly applied was the aircraft's individual letter positioned on the outer surfaces of the fins in red outlined yellow. Aircraft in Nos 9, 50, 61, 49 and 463 Squadrons are known to have had this identity, featured by VN-E : PB821 of 50 Squadron. But in the field of markings all things seem possible—KC-A : LM489 of 617 Squadron in February 1945 merely had red codes!

A very low-flying Lancaster thundered over my home on March 15 1945, then circled. She was unusual since her upper camouflage extended to the base of the fuselage, in which the bomb bay was deeply cut away. She was uncoded but it was not long before another, equally strange, came into view, YZ-C : PB996. This wore the usual Lancaster camouflage with red codes and, like the former, had her nose and dorsal turrets removed. Night bomber markings did not last long on these Special Mk I aircraft and in April I saw several with red YZ coding outlined yellow and with their under surfaces Medium Grey. Serials remained red on the camouflage now extending down to the 60 degree tangent. One was YZ-L : PD117, lost on March 21 1945. PB996 : YZ-D was similarly marked. Tallboy droppers retained their black undersides when serving in 617 Squadron, the camouflage carried by NG339 : KC-G and NG494 : KC-B which participated in the raid on Dreys in March 1945.

Lancasters of 3 Group carried only one distinctive marking. This consisted of two horizontal yellow stripes (occasionally they were white), sometimes painted on all four faces of the vertical tail surfaces, sometimes on the outer faces only. These markings came into use late October 1944, my first of many loggings being of A2-G of 514 Squadron. I spent a day with 514 on October 4 1944, when the squadron was preparing for a night raid on Saarbrucken. One of the participants was JI-B : LM274, which wore one distinctive feature, red spinners in her Flight colouring. A2-E : NG118 in impeccable state had blue spinners, whereas JI-Z : PB423/G had traces of previously being 'S', such a feature often being visible on wartime bombers. I only found one machine on the squadron with a nose painting, JI-D : LM827, with a lamp post at the foot of which was a busy dog alongside the legend 'DIRTY DOG'. On October 28 I recorded LS-E of XV Squadron with four red squares set low on her outer fin and rudder surfaces, and no fin flash. Two later 514 Lancasters with yellow tail bands denoting G-H equipped aircraft were JI-Q : ME422/G and JI-A : LM285 noted on March 25 1945 at Waterbeach. A week later, JI-E had them, also A4-L and LS-E.

Canadian-built Lancaster Xs began to arrive in Britain in September 1943, the first, LQ-Q : KB700 'Ruhr Express', making a sortie on November 22, before passing to 419 Squadron and becoming VR-Z. Mark Xs went to 6 Group, which was partly Halifax-equipped to the end of hostilities. Lancaster introduction was as follows: 405 Squadron (LQ) first used Mk III for pathfinder rôle on August 2 1943; 408 Squadron (EQ) Mk X received, May 1945; 419 Squadron (VR) first Lancaster operation (using Mk X), April 27/28 1944, when KB706 : VR-A and KB728 : VR-V took part; 420 Squadron (PT) equipped in April 1945, flew no operations; 424 Squadron (QB) Mk I received in January 1945, first operation—eight Lancasters to Ludwigshaven on February 1 1945; 425 Squadron (KW) Mk X received, May 1945; 427

201

95 *Lancaster KM-D of 44 Sqn, wearing white codes and under-wing serials at Exeter in the summer of 1946* (M. W. Payne).

96 *Lancaster B.1(FE) KO-J: PA412 of 115 Sqn, wearing white and black finish, intended for Far East operation. Black codes, Type C1 roundels above the wings and white spinners.*

97 *PD119, a Lancaster B.1 (Special) used at RAE for post-war weapon and load dropping trials. Silver with yellow T. band, and black and yellow stripes on under surfaces* (Eric Watts).

98 *RE414 'Mercury II', a Lincoln used by the Empire Radio School at Debden for research and demonstration work, and photographed in January 1948. Type D roundels on natural finish with black lettering* (via Keith Braybrooke).

99 *Washington WF445:KO-J of 115 Sqn in natural finish with black codes. The squadron leader's pennant appears on the nose* (Ministry of Defence).

100 *Lincoln RF406:SR-A of 101 Sqn in 1947 during detachment overseas. Dark Green and Dark Earth finish with white codes and red serials* (R. Davies).

101 *Lincoln WS-C of 9 Sqn fitted with H2S Mk IV. Grey upper surfaces.*

102 *SX975 boldly applied to a grey and black Lincoln of 148 Sqn whose white spinners identify the unit* (Eric Watts).

103 *(Left) Lincoln RF443. 'F' of the Armament Wing, Technical Training Command, at Debden in autumn 1951. Type D roundels and grey-black finish. Later codes TDE-F and S-F* (Keith Braybrooke).

104 *(Below) Full post-war markings on a Lincoln of 50 Sqn. Grey black finish with Type D roundels and white codes* (Bruce Robertson).

105 *Brigand B.1 VS816 of 8 Sqn carried a letter 'A' aft in white, and a white 'A' and the squadron badge on her nose.*

106 *Brigand RH776, 'K' of 84 Sqn, in grey-black finish, delivers a hefty punch with rockets during Operation* Firedog *in 1951* (Ministry of Defence).

107 *(Right) A Mosquito B.35 CX-W:TA695 of 14 Sqn at Luqa on March 14 1949. Dark Green-Dark Sea Grey-Medium Grey finish with yellow codes outlined black. Squadron badge on white disc on fin* (P. Clifton).

108 *(Below) Mosquito B.35 TH989 in grey-black finish with red fuselage serial. Used for guided weapon research at Hatfield in 1952.*

109 *A line-up of Canberras at Salmesbury in early 1951, including WD929, WD930 and VN828, all in Grey-black finish. This finish is also worn by Lincoln SR-B which has wartime style of roundels (BAC).*

Squadron (ZL) Mk I/II received in March 1945, first operation on March 11;
428 Squadron (NA) Mk X received in May/June 1944, first operation on
June 14/15 when aircraft used included KB705 : F and KB742 : M; 429
Squadron (AL) Mk I/III received in March 1945, first operation on March 31
1945 against Hamburg; 431 Squadron (SE) received Mk X in October 1944,
first operation on November 1, aircraft included KB741 : SE-Y; 433
Squadron (BM) Mk I received in January 1945, first operation on February
1; and 434 Squadron (WL) received Mk X in December 1944, first operation
on December 24, aircraft included P : KB863. 6 Group's final bombing operation was on April 25 1945, with Wangerooge as the target, aircraft participating including VR-M : KB999, VR-V : KB728, NA-R : KB882 and NA-Z :
KB739.

On February 17 1945, at Farnborough, I had a look at ND673 : F2-V, a
Lancaster VI, its engines installed as 'power eggs'. These were annular
cowled Merlins designed for easy maintenance and removal. Otherwise she
was a normal Lancaster as regards marking, with F2 in the fore/aft style.
Paddle-bladed airscrews were fitted, and she lacked a dorsal turret. In the
well-known picture of her by John Rawlings she appears to have striping on
the tail, but this was not a special operational marking. An interesting feature
was her radar. Over the tail turret she had a long arm with tail warning radar
as well as bow and arrow aerials pointing at about 45 degrees from the base
of the extreme rear fuselage. She had served on 635 Squadron at Downham
Market from August to November 1944, where JB675 : U, ND418 : Q and
JB713 : Z (missing August 18/19 1944) also flew trials. The Mk VIs were no
real advance over earlier marks, but they paved the way for the engine installation on the Lincoln.

No mention of the Lancaster would be complete without some reference
to outstanding examples. Over 20 managed 100-plus sorties, remarkable when
one considers the usual loss and damage rate. They included QR-N : ED860
of 61 Squadron which had completed her 130th trip by October 30 1944, by
which time it had flown 1,032 hours; QR-M : EE176 flew her 120th trip on
December 3 1944, and had 971 hours to her credit; VN-G : ED585 completed
her 127th sortie by August 29 1944, having flown 1,052 hours; and JB138 :
QR-J flew 113 sorties and LL843 : QR-R her 118th by May 8 1945.

The principal version of the Halifax in use in the closing months of the war
was the Mk III, many of which had square wing tips. They equipped 4 Group,
which introduced tail identity squadron colours about August 1944. Many of
these have been illustrated elsewhere and typical machines in August 1944
were MP-G and MP-T, both IIIs of 76 Squadron with white outer faces to
their fins and rudders from which fin stripes were deleted.

Limited use was made in 1944 of the Halifax B VII; then came the Mk
VI initially used by 102 Squadron from February 1945. By then a fair pro-
portion of 4 Group's Halifaxes, apart from wearing elaborate tail markings,
had yellow outlines to their codes, as on H7 : N-NP763 and later Mk VI
RG510 : DY-K. The VIs all seem to have had radomes, as carried by EY-E :
RG652 and MP-K : RG496.

Examples of Halifaxes with extended rounded wing tips include KN-G :
MZ359 (with H2S), QO-A : NP755 (H2S), PN446 : DT-V (H2S) and PN367 :
AL-J in use March 1945. Aircraft were mixed on the squadrons, 78 Squadron
at one time including EY-B : MZ764 (H2S, rounded tips), EY-D : LL602
(ventral guns, square tips), EY-Q : LW236 (square tips, no H2S) and EY-X :
NR113 (rounded tips, H2S).

L

Halifaxes of 100 Group carried varying assortments of aerials. Z5 : S (Z5 forward on the port side, aft on starboard) had two tall masts above the fuselage, and one below the nose, ahead of which was a short one. Another of the squadron's aircraft had five short masts on the belly ahead of the H2S radome and two aft between which was a long one. In contrast to these were the remaining Mk IIs in training units, one of which I noted, a Mk II Series 1, on October 7, wearing the red letters GG-V (GG aft on the starboard side) with a small white '4' in the squared position by the V. She came from 1667 HCU Sandtoft.

In January 1945, the Mosquito Light Night Striking Force consisted of ten squadrons. Apart from a few Mk IXs and XVIs in 105, 109 and 692 Squadrons, with black under surfaces, these aircraft wore Ocean Grey-Dark Green-Medium Grey finish with red codes and black serials. Code positions varied, 571 Squadron favouring unit letters forward on both sides of the aircraft. Many of the 8 Group Mosquitoes were Canadian-built Mk XXs and XXVs, variously equipping seven squadrons. KB225 was XD-P of 139 Squadron, which also used KB217 : XD-H. KB439 was 4H-G and KB397 : 4H-P of 142 Squadron. No confirmation has come of the unit coding of 163 Squadron, Wyton, so perhaps a reader can fill this long-standing blank. Three of its Mosquitoes were KB505 : A, KB510 : B and KB474 : C. One unit displaying original trim was 571 Squadron, whose aircraft in 1945 had their spinners painted in Flight colours. MM124 : 8K-U had yellow spinners whilst 8K-L : ML941 had black under surfaces.

The most interesting Mosquitoes were to be seen at Little Staughton and Bourn. Both housed three Flight squadrons which painted bars over the individual letters of their C Flight aircraft, HS-Ō being LR498. Among the interesting Mosquitoes of 105 Squadron at Bourn on December 16 1944 was PF407 wearing a grey-green-black finish with red serials and blue codes. Narrow white rings surrounded the fuselage directly forward and aft of the roundel to denote her an *Oboe* leader for day operations. Her nose transparencies were over-painted. GB-F : LR507 was another black machine with blue codes, like LR513 : GB-E, both of which had painted nose transparencies. RV303 : GB-J, seen a few days later, wore the usual 'day' camouflage but had white codes. A most unusual one in use at the end of 1944 was LR504 : GB-H which had night finish, and during 1944 displayed varying arrangements of AEAF stripes reduced to under belly white bands by December 1944. Very few aircraft in Bomber Command had them other than 100 Group Mosquito fighters.

Over-painted noses were also a feature of 162 Squadron's H2S-equipped aircraft. In December 1944 these were KB191 : CR-L, KB214 : CR-M and KB184 : CR-R.

Quite rare because there were so few of them were the Fortress IIs and IIIs of 214 and 223 Squadrons and Liberator IVs of 223 Squadron, 100 Group. These were finished in Dark Green-Dark Earth-Night, usually with red codes. One of the Liberators I saw was 6G : L. Her ball turret had been removed and she had a tall radio mast amidships, and a shorter one a little way forward, and was from 223 Squadron. This unit carried its squadron codes aft. Other IVs used were: 6G-N : TS532 and TS528 : 6G-R. Crews for 223 Squadron were trained by No 1699 Flight, whose Liberators included TS538 : B.

Fortresses generally had a Dark Green-Dark Earth-Night finish with red codes and serials, but there were some exceptions. On January 14 1945, I noted that Fortress III BU-B : KJ110 (unit codes forward), with chin H2S radome and a tall radio mast amidships, was a very matt black overall. This was somewhat unusual for the Night finish had long since taken on a much smoother, slightly shiny finish generally. On March 23, I recorded another Fortress in the standard camouflage scheme but with a white letter B aft of the fuselage roundels. She had an array of radar aerials flanking the rear guns and the usual tall radio mast. Next day I noted 4Z-X (unit code forward) applied in yellow on a camouflaged Fortress and a few days later another with yellow codes, 4Z : K. Fortress crews were also trained by 1699 Flight, whose aircraft included HB793 and HB818. Those of 223 Squadron included 6G-B : KJ121, 6G-Z : KL836, 6G-H : KJ118 and 6G-M : FA741.

What made wartime spotting so exciting was that the scene, wrapped as it was in secrecy, offered so many surprises. Squatting by 'E' Hangar at Farnborough on September 30 1944 was the prototype Mosquito PR XVI, a Mk IV bomber converted. This, DZ540, was finished Ocean Grey and Dark Green with yellow under-surfaces extending half way up the fuselage. The yellow prototype marking was partly outlined Dark Green. A few moments later the prototype Windsor NK136 in Dark Green-Dark Earth-Yellow finish passed over quite low from Wisley. Next I noted a Vengeance FD218 in grey-green-grey camouflage. With her was another, black overall and with a red serial. A few weeks later I found a Ventura, AJ181, where that Mosquito had stood, with a red 'B' aft outlined black, and nearby an RAF Marauder in green-grey finish, FB482.

Chapter 22

Bombers during the aftermath

ALTHOUGH THE WAR in Europe ended in May 1945, the cruel fighting in the Far East was far from over. Requirements for bomber operations in that theatre were very different from those of Europe. The Air Staff foresaw this in 1942 when Specification B.14/43 was drawn up for a 70,000 lb very long range bomber able to operate at heights up to 35,000 feet, and powered by four two-stage Merlin engines.

Roy Chadwick's team at Avro prepared two long-range versions of the Lancaster, Mks IV and V. Eventually they re-designed their schemes, and the Lincoln was born in September 1943.

It was similar in layout to the Lancaster, but the Lincoln's high aspect ratio wing spanned 120 feet. Its fuselage was longer, and it was faster. Remotely controlled turrets were in vogue at the time and accordingly the nose was completely redesigned to include a remotely controlled 2 × .50 inch gun turret and an excellent new angular viewpoint, the gunner/bomb aimer's station. A Bristol B.17 dorsal turret mounting two 20 mm cannon was decided upon. The AGLT-controlled rear turret mounted 2 × .50 inch guns.

PW925, the prototype finished in Dark Green and Dark Earth with yellow under surfaces and full yellow 'P' marking, flew on June 9 1944. Boscombe Down trials revealed general handling superior to that of the Lancaster, a maximum speed of 300 mph TAS and service ceiling of 28,000 feet. The 'Ideal Nose' impaired the pilot's view, but was nevertheless proceeded with. PW925 later had a Martin dorsal turret with 2 × .50 inch guns but this made movement in the fuselage difficult. The second prototype, PW929, flew on November 9 1944, and wore similar markings (like PW932, which did not fly until November 6 1945).

Provision for a Redwing belly gun mounting had been made on PW925; but fitting of this or the planned FN 88 meant that no H2S radome could be installed and the latter was essential gear. With an all-up weight of 75,000 lb the Lincoln carried a 12,000-lb load for a 857-mile range—1,235 lb for 6,000 miles. Tallboys and 12,000-lb bombs could be carried by simply changing the bomb doors but, because of the extensive modifications required, it was decided that only the existing fleet of 30 or so 'Grand Slam' Lancasters would carry the 22,000-lb bomb.

One way of extending range was the fitting of a saddle tank, but the large tank would impair performance considerably. If such a 1,000-gallon tank had been fitted to the Lincoln, range would have extended to 1,070 miles when carrying a 14,000-lb load, but the decrease in speed and increased vulnerability caused the programme to lapse. In-flight refuelling was considered, but since development was considered to be lengthy this, too, was abandoned. The Lincoln at an all-up weight of 75,000 lb went ahead.

Meanwhile preparations for a Lancaster force to operate in the Far East proceeded. Late 1944 it was decided to prepare a tropical version of the Lancaster with a saddle tank providing the necessary range for a bomber force based in India or Burma. Two trial machines were tested, HK541 and SW244, but handling was poor. At the same time LM730 was set aside for in-flight refuelling tests at A & AEE, but it was decided to operate the force from Pacific islands to cut the need for special range-promoting features. All along, the Air Staff wanted the Lincoln for the Far East 'Tiger Force', but the makers stressed that this would completely wreck the Lancaster production lines. The B.17 turret was in trouble too, so Lancaster production continued at a very high rate. A specially modified Lancaster, PD328 'Aries', set off on long-distance touring that took it to the new possible theatre of operations. Others went to the Far East for operational trials.

Eventually it was decided Tiger Force would operate from one island, a ten-squadron formation with six squadrons of long-range fighters—probably Mosquito XIXs—giving fighter support during the projected night bombing missions. On February 24 Tiger Force formed and instructions were also given that Lancaster Is and VIIs, from the AWA and Austin lines respectively, would be completed to FE standard. NX611 was the first Mk VII(FE) to be built and was delivered on April 16 1945. Under surfaces on the FE Lancasters remained in matt black finish but fuselage sides above the 60 degree tangent were smooth white with a slight gloss evident. Above the wings such aircraft had Type C roundels and their serials on the fuselage sides were black. Delivery of the B.Mk 1 (FE) from AWA began in June. Initially the aircraft entered MU storage to await formation of the squadrons for the Far East; then were flown to Short & Harland at Belfast for full conversion and painting.

Once commenced, the in-flight refuelling trials were continued and, by August 1945, Lancaster ND834 was in use at BDU Feltwell as a tanker aircraft with a reel of rubber piping carried immediately aft of her bomb bay. NE147/G served as receiver, having equipment fitted beneath the rear turret. These aircraft in the usual paint scheme operated alongside the BDU's normal Lancasters like H : ND991, R : ND793 and W : ND674, all of which carried a single letter aft in red. Halifaxes F : MZ784 and S : LW376 were similarly marked and with them was EX-K : NA278 (EX aft on the port side, forward on starboard). Already the Lincoln was in use, evidenced by RE240 with 'L' aft, recorded at Feltwell on July 18 1945.

The first production Lincoln delivered to the RAF, RE230, left Avro on February 26, with the RF series following from AWA and RA from Metropolitan Vickers. Some 45 Lincolns had been delivered by VE-Day. By that time RE251 had been passed to the RAF, also RF334; RF339-341 were being erected and about 50 were complete. RE227, the first machine, was delivered to A & AEE in April 1945, and RE228 to A & AEE and Rolls-Royce in March 1945. RE229 went to TFU Defford on March 20 and RE230 was used by Rolls-Royce and Boscombe Down. RE240 was passed to BDU on May 21 1945, the first to enter other than a research or maintenance unit. All of these aircraft had Dark Earth-Dark Green-Black matt finish with red serials, Type B wing roundels and Type C1 fuselage roundels. The long span wings called for a more elaborate camouflage pattern than the Lancaster had.

All early machines were Mk Is with Merlin 85s which were then giving quite a lot of trouble, so much so that nearly all the Mk Is RE227-257, RE 258-268, RE281-288, RF333-334 and RA628-655 spent their entire lives in MUs. They initially had twin .50 inch guns in their Martin dorsal turrets and FN121 4 × .303 inch gun tail turrets. RE289, the prototype Mk II (Merlin 68), was delivered July 6 1945 and featured a 20 mm cannon dorsal turret and had H2S Mk IIIG fitted. Already other Mk IIs were in Service hands, for the first of the RF series production aircraft had left the AWA works before VE-Day, and RE230 was converted into a Mk II in March 1945.

Engines in the Mk II were also proving troublesome and many modifications were required before the Lincoln II was suitable for squadron use. A few Mk Is were modified into Mk IIs.

In August 1945, a Mk II with fully modified engines was despatched to Khartoum for tropical trials, and on August 3 the order was given for six fully modified Mk IIs, all in the black/white FE scheme to be delivered to squadrons. Three went to 57 Squadron, East Kirkby, RF385 arriving on August 23, and RF386 and RF387 on the 27th. RF389, RF383 and RF388 went to No 75 Squadron at Spilsby. Whether 75's aircraft acquired squadron markings is unknown, but RF385 became DX-G and RF387 became DX-F, their code letters being black.

On September 12 authority was given for an experimental Lincoln II, RF393, with Merlin 85s to commence AGLT trials at BDU. The saddle tank Lincoln Mk III had been cancelled, but already Coastal Command was interested in the aircraft's range capability. On September 20 a Mk I (Merlin 85) was loaned to ASWDU for trials.

Meanwhile both squadrons were busily trying their new aircraft, although no gun firing from the B.17 turrets was possible, and the Boulton Paul 'D' turrets had no recoil reducers fitted. No heating was installed—and the nose, for all its splendid view, was a draughty post. The aircraft supplied had an all-up weight increased to 82,000 lb but their range/bomb load now worked out about the same as for the Lancaster. Indeed, even at 75,000 lb, load/range characteristics compared unfavourably with the Lancaster at 68,000 lb, but the general wind-down of the Service may have had an effect upon capabilities. In any case it had already been decided to equip post-war Bomber Command with the Lincoln, initial trials of which continued until December 31, with 44 Squadron taking over 75's commitment when the latter disbanded on October 15 1945.

Tiger Force was not needed now. It had been decided that its Lancasters would have a 400-gallon belly tank but no dorsal turrets. Before this modification was incorporated the war had ended, and Tiger Force disbanded on October 31 1945. This left an increasing pool of tropicalised Lancasters in white-black finish. Nos 9 and 617 Squadrons equipped with the modified aircraft and proceeded to Salbani for policing duties in January 1946, their Lancasters having Type C upper wing roundels and Type C1 fuselage roundels. Codes, in the usual positions, were black like the serials. The first public display of a 'Far East' Lancaster came on September 29 at the ATA White Waltham show, when NX638 from the Elmdon plant was displayed. It portrayed another feature that had, by now, become common on Lancasters, and indeed all RAF aircraft—it had under-wing serials.

Late July the first Lancasters to wear these were reported, but it was some weeks before they were common and indeed many wartime aircraft were withdrawn from the squadrons before these were applied. HK733 had them by August 3, and 9J : T could be seen wearing them on August 9, but these were exceptional at the time. Another feature that appeared in July was the wearing of white squadron codes. Again it was many weeks before this was at all common. On July 21 LS-G with G-H tail bars had white codes, also LS-J and LS-L, but none of these had under-wing serials.

Already Lancasters were flying experimentally with a very large radome to accommodate H2S Mk IV with which Lincoln squadrons largely re-armed many months later. The first Lancaster I noted with this feature was AF-N (yellow codes) seen on May 21 1945. Many RAF aircraft had for some months worn Type C upper-wing roundels, but yet again this applied to only a portion of the bomber force so far. Even in 1947 it was relatively unusual On May 23 1945 I had my last sighting of an intact Hampden (coded U-VK) at RAE, close to Fairey Battle K7698 with circled 'P' prototype marking aft of the Type C1 roundels, and in Dark Green-Dark Earth-yellow camouflage. Keeping her company were two Lincoln Is, distinctive with their three-bladed propellers.

The months immediately following the war were of the utmost interest to any observer of the military scene. New types of aircraft shed their security wraps. Many a wartime aircraft seemed somehow to emerge from obscurity, and interesting modifications appeared to abound. Mosquito IV DZ615 (JS-K in red) could be seen with ejector exhausts and an extra window beneath her nose. Mosquito XVI AZ-B (AZ forward on port side, aft on starboard) had acquired a silver outline to her red codes, whereas Mk XXV AZ-Q: KB490 had red codes outlined yellow repeated above her tailplane (AZ on the port side) in like colours in the usual 5 Group style. There were many Wellington Xs flying from OTUs, like A-ED with nose turrets removed and a fairing in place. On a bombed site in Oxford Street, Halifax NP-F : LV907 was on show with red codes and serials, yellow fin diagonal markings, 128 bombs on her nose (53 of them denoting day raids) and red-white spinners.

Mosquito B.35s were coming off the production lines usually in Ocean Grey-Dark Green-Medium Sea Grey finish, although TA704 somehow managed to acquire dark blue spinners. On July 22 I saw the first all-silver machine (for Far East service) TA648, closely followed by TA687, TA689 and TA690, all with Type B upper-wing roundels.

The wind-down in squadron strength, though, was rapid. Nevertheless, one might still see a Lancaster III with deepened bomb doors like UM-C, oddities like Mosquito 35 TH993 without deepened bomb bay, and the remains of Stirlings long gone into obscurity like EH951 : TV-B noted on August 16. Next day a Lancaster AA-A with NN704 on her under surfaces was noted. In the Gloucester area on August 23 the sight of Whitley BD369 entirely Dark Earth on top and black beneath was another oddity, whilst overhead Whitley 'A895' passed, obviously partly painted. Trailing behind was a Dark Earth-Dark Green-Black Wellington XIV with PF962 on her under surfaces. Sixty Buckinghams on the field at Filton that day all had under-wing serials, like KV410 and KV424, and all were half converted into transports, but retained their unusual Dark Green-Dark Earth-Azure finish.

By the end of August Lancasters with under-wing serials and white codes were more common, like JI-M : PB820 and JI-A : LM544. The siting of under-wing serials varied, like the style of letters and digits. One had PD under the outer starboard wing, 30 between the engines, and nothing more. In the more relaxed peacetime conditions there was a period when flight colours seemed to gain prominence. GT-H : PB991, a Lancaster at Wyton on September 1 with AGLT, had red spinners; other aircraft had blue. OL-D : ND529 with AGLT had red codes outlined yellow but no under-wing serials.

Halifax bombers were mostly withdrawn into storage depots as soon as the war ended, 4 Group rapidly changing to a transport rôle.

At Hendon on September 15, the date of the first Battle of Britain open day, Lancaster ND591 : OL-A (OL aft on the starboard side, forward on the port) portrayed red codes outlined yellow, repeated above and below her tailplane. The letters read OL-A when viewed from above looking forward and OL-A when viewed underneath from ahead. Her tail turret mounted two .50 inch guns. On her nose a bathing beauty languished alongside about 80 bomb signs.

Another of the stations open was Upwood where the 'solid nosed' Mosquitoes of 139 Squadron were on show, including XD-W : PF519, XD-U : PF526, and M5-D : PF428 of 128 Sqn (M5 ahead port, aft starboard), codes white and serials black, in day bomber finish. With them were PR.XVIs of 1409 Met Flight, like AE-B : NS736 and AE-F : NS734 with red codes. 8K-U : PF500 and M5-A : PF525 took part in the flying. Only 1409's Mosquitoes had under-wing serials. These latter were evident on Lancaster GT-X : PB926. In place of a front turret, Wellington ED-K : LP716 (no under-wing serials) had a wooden framework over which there was a fabric fairing. Few records of this first Battle of Britain Day seem to have survived; it would be fascinating to be able to compile a full report of this event—surely the most interesting ever.

On September 17 3 Group Lancasters flew a bombing exercise. In the gaggle were KO-E : PA310, KM-U : NN709 and one of the interim Mk VIIs, LS-V : NX559, all with white codes and under-wing serials. One of these treks appeared over the White Waltham Show of September 29 when UM-R could be seen to have 'PA' under her outer mainplanes and '990' squeezed between the engine nacelles. FM142 landed, her turret placed forward as on the Mk VII. OF-Q with yellow outline to her codes was then ME533.

In various parts of the country huge dumps of aircraft were accumulating, all for destruction. On October 14, for instance, 54 MU's sub-site presented all sorts of excitement. There was the poor old Desoutter HM507—I quickly removed as much as I could of her serial before the flames consumed her ! Stirling EE899 : JF-B of 1654 CU was rubbing remains with two Herefords (L6060 : R ahead of roundels and L6058 : U). Both had yellow individual letters, black serials and yellow 'M' numbers, 3032M and 3033M respectively. They still wore their tall 1940 fin stripes and Type A1 roundels. An unusual item was Stirling R9277 coded M-AI.

The Farnborough Show of October-November 1945 was a memorable event in a memorable period. Lincoln II RE325 was there in white-black finish and Windsor DW512 in green-brown-yellow prototype colours. The well-known Lancaster VI F2-V now sported a dorsal turret and two 10-foot tall whip aerials amidships. Halifax III DH-N : LK661 (DH aft on the starboard side) lay in pieces, but JD376 with white under-wing serials showed a Lancaster-style fairing around the root of her dorsal turret.

At Mildenhall in December, Lincoln trials were proceeding now that 44 Squadron had taken over 75's commitment, despite the poor serviceability of the aircraft. One was KM-O : RF390 in 'Far East' finish. Painting of the Lancasters in post-war finish was still far from complete, KM-A : PD228 being still with red codes and no under-wing serials. KM-C : PB818 had red codes and fuselage serials and white under-wing serials. LS-O with white under-wing serials and white codes had the usual red fuselage serials and large bomb doors to accommodate a 12,000-lb bomb. Well-known LS-J :

LL806 was resplendent in the latest colour scheme, and mingling with these were a few Lancaster B.1 (Special) aircraft which had been handed over by 617 Squadron which now flew Lancaster VII(FE). One was LS-R (LS ahead in white on both sides of the fuselage). Her paint scheme was Dark Earth and Dark Green with Medium Grey under sides, although the latter, on close inspection, looked to be more silver than grey. She had no H2S radome but instead racks for the carriage of four flares or small bombs. Paddle-blade air-screws were fitted, and there were two .50 inch guns in the tail turret, but no nose turret. Another almost identical machine was LS-S : PD127. On a model of one of these 'Grand Slam' machines it would add to the realism if a silvery wash be painted over the grey under surfaces, for the colour even on close inspection had a strange 'washed-out' appearance.

Late 1945 the Lancaster B.1(FE) began to filter into Lancaster squadrons of 3 Group, initially going to 35 Squadron. TL-Q : PA414 was one of its early aircraft at Graveley and soon 115 (eg, KO-H : PA383), 149 (eg, OJ-W : TW906), 207 (eg, EM-B : TW910) and 7 Squadrons (eg, MG-D : TW659) had them. These were to remain their equipment until they received Lincolns. Their standard markings on the black-white finish with its slight gloss were Type C wing roundels, Type C1 fuselage roundels, black codes and serials and white 54-inch under-wing serials. Normal fin stripes were also carried. Overseas, Mk VIIs equipped Nos 40 (eg, NX729 : BL-F and NX690 : BL-W) and 214 Squadrons (eg, NX731 : EP-Q), whilst in India, Nos 9 (eg, NX673 : WS-L and NX756 : WS-C) and 617 Squadrons (eg, NX744 : KC-J and NX783 : KC-G) flew B.Mk VII (FE) Lancasters.

Build up of the Lincoln force progressed slowly. On October 10 1945, it had been decided that half of a fully equipped squadron—ultimately No 15 —would have provisioning for Tallboy, and that deepened doors would there-fore be fitted. This squadron would in any case retain an element of Grand Slam Lancasters, principally for trials against German E-boat pens in 1946. A further 2½ squadrons would hold in their stores doors to accommodate the larger bombs which would also permit the carriage of spare engines for over-seas use. On November 26 all the Lincoln Is in service hands were ordered to have fully modified Merlin 85 engines installed to fit them for possible training purposes. All Lincoln IIs in store would be modified to RAF standard by contractors, but as yet only a few modified Merlin 68s were available. Following this the Lincolns needed to go to English Electric for fitment of the latest radio and radar gear. Consequently, although many Lincolns had been built, they had all to be modified considerably before squadrons could accept them. In the event the Lincoln Is languished in MUs, almost all of them until declared obsolete in February 1949.

Bomber Command requested replacement for its Lincolns in the trials squadrons in order that trials could continue and be undertaken by aircraft whose all-up weight was 82,000 lb. Three would be AWA-built aircraft, RF405, '406, '407 for 44 Squadron, the first of which was delivered on Feb-ruary 27 1946. The others (RE379, '380 and '377), which Avro built, joined 57 Squadron in March 1946.

On April 2 1946, Bomber Command agreed that it was prepared to accept the Lincoln II in squadron service. The first machines probably entered service with 101 Squadron in June 1946, when 97 Squadron also began con-version. RE302 joined 97 Squadron and RE305 was one of 101's first aircraft. During July, 9 Squadron received Lincolns, among them WS-A : RF462 received July 15 1946, which remained on strength (latterly as WS-X) until

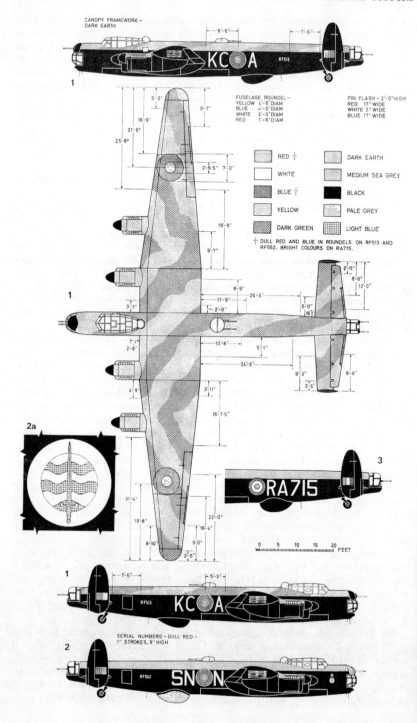

CANOPY FRAMEWORK –
DARK EARTH

8'-6"   7'-6"

KC·A   RF513

1

5'-2"

9'-7"

16'-9"

21'-6"

25'-8"

2'-9·5"   7'-0"

FUSELAGE ROUNDEL –
YELLOW 4'-6" DIAM
BLUE   4'-0" DIAM
WHITE   2'-0" DIAM
RED   1'-6" DIAM

FIN FLASH – 2'-0" HIGH
RED   17" WIDE
WHITE 2" WIDE
BLUE 17" WIDE

RED ✝

WHITE

BLUE ✝

YELLOW

DARK GREEN

DARK EARTH

MEDIUM SEA GREY

BLACK

PALE GREY

LIGHT BLUE

✝ DULL RED AND BLUE IN ROUNDELS ON RF513 AND
RF562. BRIGHT COLOURS ON RA715.

19'-9"

9'-7"

2'-11"

8'-6"

12'-0"

8'-9"   26'-3"

1

11'-9"

3'-1"   2'-0"

5'-0"

16'1

2'-8"

10'-8"

5'-1"

24'-3"

9'-3"   9'-6"

2'-6"

4'-9"

3'-11"

16'-7·5"

2a

3

⊙RA715

31'-4"

22'-0"

19'-8"

16'-4"

8'-10"   9'-0"

2'-5"

0   5   10   15   20
⊢⊢⊢⊢⊢⊢⊢⊢⊢⊢⊢⊢   FEET

1

7'-6"   5'-3"

RF513

KC·A

SERIAL NUMBERS – DULL RED –
1" STROKES, 8" HIGH

2

RF562

SN·N   N

June 1949. The large number of Lincolns immediately available made possible rapid delivery to squadrons which switched quite quickly from Lancasters.

Although very few Lincolns were ever based in overseas units, squadrons rotated to the Middle East on Exercise *Sunray*. To render them suitable for possible service in tropical conditions, many of the aircraft were modified to Mk II(FE) standard, those from the AWA production, for instance, including RF329-331, '37, '39, '45, '57, '59, '61-67, '69-70, '83-84, '86-87, '90, '92, '94-98, '400-402, '404-413, '17-19, '21-24, '26-27, '40-41, '43, '45, '47, '49-51, '58, '62-64, '66-67, '69-85, '98-99, 500-07 and '10-15. Conversion to FE standard of the RA-serialled aircraft was undertaken by Short and Harland; the RE series were modified at Langar and RF's at the AWA factories. About one third of the Lincolns in squadrons or other active flying units had the white-black finish typified by RF395 : DF-E (DF aft on both sides of the fuselage in black) in use in September 1946 at CBE Marham. RE360, in tropical finish, was demonstrated at the 1946 SBAC Show.

A pointer to future development was at this time evident on DF-C : RE238, a Dark Green-Dark Earth-Black machine with white codes and Dull Red fuselage serial, at CBE. In place of the usual radome she had the very large dome required for the carriage of H2S Mk IV.

Long-term storage of many Lincolns had led to some corrosion problems which it was decided during December 1946 should be rectified before further issues. Turret modifications too were incomplete, and at this time Lincolns were being re-engined with Merlin 68As. RA677 was set aside for corrosion investigation. New designations were promulgated in February 1947, these being for the Lincoln B.2/3G with H2S 3G, the B.2/4A with H2S 4A and the Mk 4A fitted with G-H Mk II radar. Further corrosion investigation was ordered early in 1947 when RE380, which had served with 57 Squadron from April 27 1946 to December 1946 when it passed to 50 Squadron, RF359 with only MU storage to its credit, and RF383, originally delivered August 18 1945 and used by 101 Squadron from July 8 1946 to January 15 1947, were brought in for special analysis. Bomber Command hoped to have 1 Group squadrons equipped with H2S IVA aircraft (at one time designated Mk IIa) and 3 Group squadrons with H2S IIIG aircraft by June 1947, but this programme was repeatedly delayed until June 1949 when the modified aircraft began to enter service with 9 Squadron.

Not all of the aircraft modified to FE standard retained their white-black finish by the time they were ready for issue to squadrons. DF-O : RF339 of CBE, for example, had the usual green-brown-black finish with red serials on the fuselage and white codes, like DF-C : RE238, QR-G : RF358 (QR aft on starboard side, forward on port) and KM-G : RF445, all in use in June 1947. A white-black machine at this time was DF-P : RF498 'CRUSADER' of CBE.

Lancasters equipped 3 Group squadrons until early 1950, most of them in white-black colouring, but there were the inevitable exceptions like NN782 : EM-E of 49 Squadron wearing Dark Green-Dark Earth-Black finish and in use July 1946, and Lancaster B.1 (Special) PD121 was now in similar colouring. OJ-V : PA401 (OJ ahead on port side, aft on starboard) had no H2S radome when recorded March 23 1946. More usual were OJ-W : TW906, PA482 : MG-D and EM-D : PA442 with the normal H2S radomes, which usually had the aft third of the dome unpainted. Some Lancasters were exhibiting trainer markings by mid-1946, among them RE219 in the usual night bomber finish with large yellow rectangles aft of the fuselage roundels and carrying black unit identity. Another oddity was Lancaster LL795 : TV-Q (white codes, usual position) which still had a ventral turret when it was earmarked for *Amber*, the night flying training aid. Another trainer of 1946 vintage in normal bomber colours was Lancaster A3-G : ME315. Some of the bombers now had Type C upper-wing roundels, but this was still unusual, as evidenced by Lincoln RE250 in September 1946 which had Type B wing roundels and red fuselage serials, like RF402.

Not all of the bombers in Flying Training Command units had any yellow trim yet, as for example Wellington III BK395 : FJ-SQ (FJ ahead on the port side, aft of roundel on starboard). In October 1946 Wellingtons of the OTU at Silverstone, like JG-G : LP847, JG-N : LR138 and JG-D : PG393, had standard night bomber colouring and white codes positioned as usual on Wellingtons. In 1947 Lancasters similarly painted were still in use, like NF-J : NX571.

On April 16 1946, interim post-war paint schemes were promulgated for RAF aircraft. In the case of bombers the upper surfaces and spinners were to become Dark Sea Grey and lower surfaces matt black, the latter covering fuselage sides, fins and rudders. Under-wing serials were ordered to be 48 inches high on four-engined aircraft and 36 inches high on twins. No evidence has come to light that these colours were worn in 1946, the first reporting of machines in this finish being of Mosquitoes DF-V : PF446 and DF-Z : PF556 in April 1947. Codes and serials were white, fuselage roundels Type C1 and wing roundels Type B. CBE's Lincolns, though, retained the Dark Green-Dark Earth-Black finish like DF-O : RE307 and DF-C : RE238 with red fuselage serials and white codes. An exception was DF-L : RF339 which had Sky codes. Another was the famous EXCALIBUR RF484 : DF-A in high-speed aluminium finish with black codes outlined white; spinners were black. CRUSADER, black and white DF-P : RF498, had matt Dark Green anti-dazzle panels on the inner sides of her engine nacelles and ahead of the pilot. Lancasters presently in the green and brown finish, included RA722 : DF-E, with yellow H2S Mk IVA radome, and WB-G : PB986. There were still quite a number of white-black Lincolns flying, but QR-G : RF358, seen on June 16 1947, represented the usually camouflaged type as did KM-G : RF445.

Two squadrons continued to fly Mosquito B.16s. Their finish was still Dark Green-Ocean Grey-Medium Sea Grey with white codes (squadron letters aft) as on HS-C : PF565 and XD-C : PF511. No 109 Squadron's aircraft had yellow spinners; No 139's were red.

A vast number of wartime RAF aircraft were struck off charge on June 21 1947, up to which time many of those memorable aircraft languished in MUs. One of the remnants was Lancaster II prototype DT810, whose fuselage lay for many years at the entrance to Gransden Lodge. Her ventral turret was still *in situ* on her yellow under surfaces and she had Dark Green-Dark Earth finish with the 'P' in a circle marking aft of the roundel. Her fuselage serial was Dull Red, not black as has been depicted elsewhere.

Nothing can be safely assumed in the field of aircraft markings. Anomalies seem always there, as with Lincoln II SR-A : RE372 noted on June 23, exceptional since she had her SR coding aft of the roundels on both sides of the fuselage. A Halifax, with a yellow band encircling her fuselage upon which the roundels were applied, had TC-AD flanking the roundels, and RG976 in the usual style and positions. Meanwhile, Debden's Halifax Mk VI MERCURY was in silver finish and had a tail cone replacing the rear turret, Type C wing roundels and serials RG815 in black.

On May 15 1947, post-war aircraft finishes were ordered to be introduced, although it was still to be many months before they were the norm. Bombers would now have Medium Sea Grey upper surfaces, some aircraft having a matt finish at first, some glossy before glossy finish became general. Under surfaces, too, were to be glossy black. On May 16 1947 new roundels and fin flashes were ordered to be applied, the roundels known as Type D. These were easily recognisable by their blue and white bands being of equal width and the red centre disc having a diameter the equal of the width of the other bands in the roundels. Bright Red and Bright Blue shades were also specified, but again it was many months before these were to be seen, and some aircraft retained wartime shades in Type D roundels. One of the first machines to wear the new bright Type D was the prestigious Lincoln MERCURY II of the ERS Debden which had them on its silver finish, these also appearing on the under surfaces of this aircraft. Lincoln B.II (FE) aircraft were still to be seen in their white-black finish, like DF-E. The Lancasters at Stradishall retained their 1946 Far East finish, examples in use in September 1947 including QN-W : TW883, EM-D : TW869, TL-F : TW880, WP-Y : TW881 and KO-K : PA441. Mosquitoes, also, were grey-green and Mosquito B.35s TA706 and TA650 were currently fitted with small radomes under their rear fuselages. Lincolns, too, still usually had the 1946 finish, like NF-V : RF395, KM-G : RF445 and LS-D : RF532, also Lancaster NG494 : KM-A.

Among the bombers were the inevitable trials machines, like Lancaster B.1 (FE) V7-U : TW887 with dorsal turret removed and a fairing replacing the nose turret.

Even at the end of 1947 the grey-black finish was still very rare, but Lincoln II OL-G : RF516 (OL ahead on the port side, aft on the starboard) had it by late December. Under surfaces were glossy black, upper surfaces matt grey, codes and wing serials white and fuselage serial red. Spinners were grey, and the machine had Type B upper-wing roundels and Type C1 fuselage roundels. All-silver CRUSADER DF-P : RF498 had Type D roundels by January 1947 and a white H2S radome.

In Germany, Mosquito XVIs equipped No 14 Squadron, a typical example of its equipment being PF612, noted on January 20 1948 wearing Dark Green-Ocean Grey-Medium Sea Grey finish. Above her wings she had Type C roundels with Type C1 on the fuselage. Her spinners were yellow like her code letters CX-G (CX aft), outlined black. On a large white disc on the fin was the unit's badge. CX-F : PF616 was similarly painted.

A few Lincolns were flying with XV Squadron at this time with enlarged bomb doors to allow the carrying of 12,000 lb bombs. LS-A : RF370 (green-brown-black finish with white codes) was one of these. In March 1948, typical Lincolns were QR-P : RF358 and HW-B : RF472 in green-brown-black finish, whilst DX-M : RF468 and QR-R : RF482 had the grey-black scheme, yet none had the new roundels.

With aircraft strength low on many squadrons—usually about eight machines, but variable—3 Group devised an interesting system for the aircraft individual letters at each station. In 1947-48 each 3 Group station housed four squadrons and the alphabet letters, excluding 'I', were allotted in groups to the squadron. At Upwood A-G, S and Z were used by 7 Squadron; H-N were used by 49 Squadron; O-U by 148 Squadron and N and W-Z by 214 Squadron, the letters roughly being allotted by the digital value of the squadron numbers. Stradishall had A-G for 207 Squadron, E and H-M for 115 Squadron, N-R for 35 Squadron, and S-Y for 149 Squadron, with a few additional aircraft falling outside the main allocations. At Wyton the system was for A-H on XV Squadron's Lincolns, with G-M for 44 Squadron, N-S for 90 Squadron and T-Z for 138 Squadron. No 1 Group stations had a similar system for its three squadron units. At Waddington A-G, N, U and V were allotted to 50 Squadron; H-M, W and X to 57 Squadron; and O-T, Y and Z to 61 Squadron, although again there were some slight variations later and it is believed 57 Squadron was re-coded QT for a time in 1949.

At Binbrook the early letters were allocated to 101 Squadron and repeated on 9 Squadron, whereas 12 Squadron had the middle section of the alphabet and 617 Squadron the latter, with some overlaps. At Hemswell the system was different, only the early letters being used by 83, 97 and 100 Squadrons. Mosquitoes, too, used only the early alphabet letters. By October 1950, Upwood's Lincolns were carrying individual letters A-H for 7 Squadron, J-Q for 49/102 Squadron, S-Z for 148, with 214 Squadron having double individual letters AW-HW. Whilst at Binbrook 9 Squadron had A-H and J; 12 Squadron F and J-P; 101 Squadron A-G, O and J; and 617 Squadron Q and U-Z.

Lincolns were now being refurbished at Baginton, and as they left the works they did so in grey-black finish like RF459. On August 22 1948 the Lincolns at Waddington included RF513 : VN-B and RF358 : QR-P in grey-black finish.

Some of the training units still had Lancaster VIIs in 1949, like NX721 : FGG-A in 'FE' finish, and there were still some Lancaster B.1(FE) about, like TL-T : PA440. One uncoded machine seen on March 18 had Type D fuselage roundels, like a grey-black Lincoln DX-M : RF405 in use in March 1949.

Mosquito B.16s served the two target marking squadrons of Bomber Command well into 1948, and were based at Hemswell. The units identified their aircraft by painting the spinners yellow for 109's machines and red for 139's. The all-yellow Mk III trainer, VA928, used by the Station Flight had blue spinners. During 1948 Mosquito B.35s gradually replaced the Mk 16s, although some of the latter were in use almost to the end of the year. Crews for the squadrons were supplied by No 16 OTU (later re-named 231 OCU) whose aircraft were painted like those in front-line squadrons and coded GA and JS (eg, GA-W : PF510). In Germany, Mosquito B.16s were used by Nos 14, 69, 98 and 180 Squadrons until mid-1948, by which time a number of Mk 35s had replaced them.

There were three paint schemes for the B.35s, firstly the Dark Green-Ocean Grey-Medium Sea Grey finish with sky codes, secondly high-speed silver with black codes and serials (eg, TK620 : XD-L with Type D roundels), and thirdly Medium Sea Grey with black under surfaces, fins and rudders and fuselage sides. Spinners were usually distinctively coloured. Notes on the Mosquitoes and their squadrons appear in Appendix 4.

Item No 18 in the 1949 SBAC Show's flying display was destined to change the entire British bomber scene. It was the English Electric A.1, the B.3/45 Canberra prototype in a glossy greyish-blue overall finish with white fuselage and wing serials (VN799). Type D roundels were worn and full prototype markings appeared aft of them. Its performance was truly startling, for it rolled and looped like a fighter. The bomber scene would soon be quite transformed; the jets would take over, but not for two more years. The unveiling of the Canberra heralded a new, highly professional air force. It would become far removed from all that had gone before.

Chapter 23

Bombers of the 1950s

AT THE START of the 1950s the home-based bomber force comprised squadrons of Avro Lincolns and de Havilland Mosquito 35s. Re-equipment with the Lincoln Mk II/IVAs was continuing, as it had been decided in March 1949 to equip 9 and 12 Squadrons at Binbrook first during the middle of that year, then the four Mildenhall squadrons (35, 115, 149 and 207), followed by Upwood's contingent (7, 49, 148, 412), 101 and 617 Squadrons. Following this would be Nos 50, 57 and 61 Squadrons at Waddington, then the Wyton squadrons, the latter receiving them by mid-1950. A later decision altered this scheme. After long controversy Bomber Command was to take up the suggestion many times mooted that, because its range, strength and general capability was limited, and because of the increasing intransigence of the Russians, it must acquire more long-range bombers. Under the Mutual Defence Aid Programme, Bomber Command was initially to acquire 70 examples of the Boeing B-29 Superfortress which, in RAF hands, was known as the Washington B.I.

The first Washington, a B-29A-35-BN 44-61599, touched down at Marham in March 1950. Like the remainder it arrived in natural finish. Type D roundels were applied on the fuselage and above the wings, and soon the serial WF434 was added. The first seven aircraft were WF434-440, a mixture of B-29As, and were all posted to the newly formed Washington Conversion Unit at Marham and coded (in numerical order) FB-K to Q, black unit codes being painted aft of the roundels and the individual letter on the fin. WF442, which became KO-J, was no newcomer to Britain since, as B-29-26-MO 42-65274, she had been brought to Lakenheath by the 96 Bomb Squadron of No 2 Bomb Group, USAF, in August 1948. She had seen war service in the Pacific and traces of bombs denoting 12 sorties, some over Japan, were then evident, as were repairs to flak holes. Traces, too, were visible of a 'G' in a triangle tail marking and a number '31' aft. On her nose was the name *Bad Penny*. WF443, ex B-29A-50-BN 44-61883, had also been to Britain before as part of 301 Bomb Group whose identity had been 'V' in a triangle on the fin. WF444, ex 42-94052, had come to Britain as well with the 301st, and WF503 had previously been 44-62231 *Forever Ambling* of the 2nd Bomb Group.

The first Washington squadron was No 115 which began to equip at Marham in June 1950, initially receiving WF444 : KO-C, WF445 : KO-F, WF446 : KO-B, WF447 : KO-G, WF448 : KO-A and later WF495 : KO-N. Next to re-arm with Washingtons was No 149, eg, OJ-S : WF490, and 90 Squadron re-formed at Marham in October 1950, its aircraft including WF500 : WP-C. Soon XV Squadron at Coningsby was equipping, including WF499 : LS-B on its inventory, and then 44 Squadron re-formed at the start of 1951 with KM-coded aircraft like WF508 and WF509. No 57 Squadron

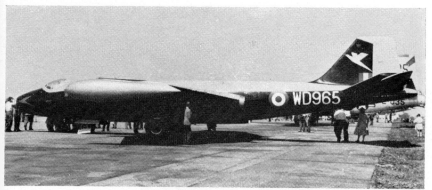

110 (*Above*) *A Canberra B.2 of 10 Sqn with the Honington pheasant motif on her fin. Silver tip tanks and red speedbird on nose.*

111 (*Right*) *Canberra B.2 WD995 in August 1952 in grey-slate grey-PRU Blue finish with white serials and the red lightning flash of 617 Sqn.*

112 (*Right*) *An all-silver Canberra B.2 WH920 of 57 Sqn carries the Cottesmore Station motif on her fin* (Eric Watts).

113 (*Below*) *Canberra B.2 WJ728 of 231 OCU, photographed in April 1971. Light Aircraft Grey overall with red dayglo trim and unit motif on nose and tail.*

114 *A Canberra B.6 of 9 Sqn, photographed in August 1960. Blue-grey fin with white disc and squadron motif. Blue nose flash.*

115 *A Canberra B.6 of 139 Sqn with red tail flash outlined white and grey fin panel. Photograph was taken in May 1958.*

116 *At first Canberras of the Middle East squadrons were finished in High Speed Silver, like WH652. This machine is shown in the blue and white striping of 32 Sqn (Ministry of Defence).*

117 *Canberra WJ981, camouflaged Dark Green and Dark Sea Grey with silver under surfaces and white serial. Operated in the Far East by 45 Sqn.*

118 *Canberra B.2 WK164, wearing one of many unusual finishes applied to such aircraft. This one was white overall with pale roundels, pale red cheat line and anti-dazzle panel. Aircraft was serving at A & AEE at the time (Ministry of Defence).*

119 *High Speed Silver was the original finish for the Vulcan B.1, as on XA890 here performing at Farnborough in 1955.*

120 *Vulcan B.1 XH481 with 101 Sqn badge on her fin. Bright roundel shades are shown in this photograph taken in June 1957.*

121 *Vulcan B.2 XM601 has pale anti-flash roundels and pale blue fin serial, with a pale grey-green variation of 9 Squadron's tail motif. Photographed at Coningsby in 1964.*

122 *Overspray of camouflage gives an unusual effect on Vulcan B.2 XH559 in service with the Waddington Wing in September 1965.*

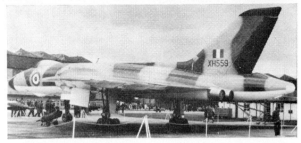

123 *XL443, a Blue Steel-equipped Vulcan B.2A which was based at Scampton in June 1969. She is finished in low-level camouflage markings and the upper paintwork wraps around the wing leading edges and intakes.*

124 *A fine study of a Vulcan B.2A of 617 Sqn whose 'pink' unit motif, based upon the squadron badge, appears on the fin. Pale national identity markings are worn, and a Blue Steel missile nestles in the bomb bay* (Hawker Siddeley).

125 *By way of contrast, Vulcan B.2 XM649 scurries! ow over the Fenland in 1970-style camouflage with only one Type D roundel above the mainplane. Blue and red identity markings now characterise the Vulcans, and Light Aircraft Grey under surfaces are becoming standard* (Hawker Siddeley).

equipped in the spring of 1951 (example, WF550) and 207 a few weeks later, its aircraft including WF566 and WF567. Conversion complete, the WCU was re-formed on September 1 1951 as 35 Squadron whose aircraft retained the FB coding for a short time. Whilst equipment with Washingtons had been taking place a major change in markings had manifested itself.

It will be recalled that in the autumn of 1949 finishes for the Lincolns embraced a mixture of Dark Earth-Dark Green-Black with white codes, as on OJ-X : RF570, and the Medium Grey-Black finish with white codes and red serials, as borne by OJ-V : RA709 and KO-J : RE361, both fitted with H2S IVA. These markings were retained during 1950, an interesting variation being yellow fins and rudders carried in June for exercise purposes by Lincolns, including EA-P : RF336.

A notable event which took place at that time was the 1950 Royal Air Force Display, the only post-war successor to the Hendon Shows. Included in the static parks were Lincoln B.2/IVA SN-N : RF562 and SN-L : RF350 of 230 OCU, Scampton, in grey-black finish with white codes, red fuselage serials and the unit's crest on the nose; Mosquito B.35 TH983 in high-speed silver finish with Type D roundels; and Lancaster B.7s NX673 and NX773, unusual in their grey-black finish with red fuselage serials and Type D roundels. Among the aircraft seen on the airfield were Fortress III HB778 in silver finish, and an all-silver Lancaster with yellow 'T. bands'. Event No 25, one of the highlights, was an impressive fly-past by Dakotas, Sunderlands, Hastings and 27 B-29s of the 301st BG, followed by a sky-full of 61 Lincolns flying some 2,000 feet above the other formations. Among them was a sight possibly unique in Britain, an all-silver Australian Lincoln B.30 A73-46 with Type D roundels, including those below the wing tips. The RAF Lincolns could be seen to wear the usual mixture of paint schemes and roundels.

Summer passed, by which time a majority of Lincolns were in grey-black finish, like LS-F : RF530 with Type D roundels and blue spinners which the squadron had now adopted. SR-D : SX981 participated during the Battle of Britain Day displays, as did AU-S : RE361, also fitted with the large H2S Mk IVA radome.

Another highlight of the last RAF Display was the simulated raid on the Amiens Prison by all-silver Mosquito B.35s. First came 14 Squadron (CX aft), including A : TH999, B : RS704, S : TA694 and Z : RS708. These were followed by a lone Mosquito 35, VP178, with 'RC' aft in light blue outlined black, representing the photographic machine on the actual raid. Then came the second wave, from 98 Squadron, including VO-Z : TJ120, VO-X : RS710 and VO-A : TJ133.

By the beginning of 1951 there had been little change in bomber markings, typified at the time by Lincoln QN-HW : RF349 (grey-black) noted thus on March 9 1951. Three days before, the Russians had shot down Lincoln RF 345 of CGS just after it had entered the Berlin air corridor. WD149, the final production Lincoln II (Merlin 68A), was delivered from Armstrong Whitworth on April 5 1951.

Washington WF432 was still wearing its FB coding, and on March 15 1951, WF493 : OJ-W was seen without serials or roundels on its under surfaces, whereas the same day WF491, also of 149 Squadron, was wearing under-wing serials and roundels, but was now uncoded. A few days later one of the Washingtons was noted with black under surfaces and no wing serials or unit letters. During April 1951, more bombers were to be seen shorn of unit codes

M

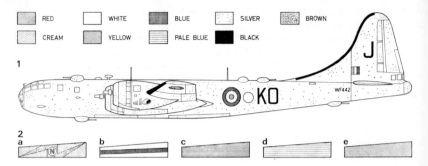

Figure 29: 1. *Washington WF442 of 115 Sqn, as recorded in July 1950.* 2. *Nosewheel door colours depicted are as follows: a) 35 Sqn; b) 44 Sqn; c) 57 Sqn; d) 115 Sqn; e) Washington Conversion Unit, Marham.*

and it was soon obvious that these, a feature since 1938, were being over-painted, as on Lincolns RF411 and SX937, and Washington WF509 which retained under-wing serials. Removal of revealing unit letters took place rapidly.

In July 1951, a new feature appeared. Lincolns began to wear coloured spinners which took the place of squadron letters as a unit identity feature. At first it might be considered that, whilst bombers were hiding their identity, fighters with increasingly colourful markings were gaily proclaiming theirs. At the same time, it can be seen that the use of coloured spinners to identify squadrons was in keeping with the new style. Colours were adopted by most squadrons, including No 7 (blue), No 49 (white), No 97 (red), No 100 (green), No 148 (red), No 214 (yellow) and No 617 (red). Colours were duplicated since the squadrons were based at different airfields. An unusual choice was blue and white, worn on the spinners of 199 Squadron's Lincolns, like RA648 and RA657.

As colours appeared on the Lincolns, so the Washington squadrons came into line. Without large spinners to decorate, the RAF followed the American practice of decorating B-29 fins tips and/or nosewheel doors. WW343 had a yellow fin tip and nosewheel door, identifying her as belonging to 35 Squadron. WF505, previously LS-D, acquired a blue nosewheel door. Some of 115 Squadron's aircraft had Sky nosewheel doors; 44's had white doors with a horizontal blue stripe; whilst 90 Squadron opted for red doors, and some of the unit's aircraft had red fin tips.

Enter the jets

Four prototypes of the English Electric B.3/45 Canberra, VN799, VN813, VN828 and VN850 were ordered on January 4 1946. VN799 first flew on May 13 1949. Originally, a radar bomb sight was stipulated for the aircraft, but this was delayed. Accordingly, a third crew member was now needed, but production of the first few aircraft proceeded with two crew stations. These aircraft were designated B.Mk 1. VN831 was powered by Rolls-Royce Nenes as an insurance against troubles with the Avon, but Avons were fitted in VN828, which was first flown on November 22 1949, and VN850 which was flown on December 20 1949.

The first B.5/47 Canberra Mk 2, VX165, with transparent nose and Avon 101s, flew on April 23 1950. Another machine, VX185, was built as the only

B.22/48 Canberra 5 (Avon 109) target marker with special radar.

On May 24 1951, Canberra B.2 WD936 arrived at Binbrook for 101 Squadron. Production examples, the first of which WD929 was flown on October 8 1950, appeared in Medium Sea Grey with Black under surfaces schemed in August 1948, paint work being glossy. The intention was that eight prototypes, VN799, VN813, VN828, VN850, VX165, VX169, VX177 and VX185, should wear this scheme. Of these, VN799 appeared in the special blue-grey finish and VX169 and VX177 were never flown. The others appeared in the scheme also worn by production aircraft WD929-966 and WD980-986. Two replacement machines WP514-515 also wore it. The completed prototypes were all intended to carry a 3-foot yellow ring out-lining the prototype yellow P marking, and like production aircraft they had 84-inch outer diameter Type D roundels above the mainplane and 4-foot under-wing white serials. Those on the fuselage were the standard 8-inch size, and in white.

Summer 1951 witnessed 101 Squadron gradually equipping with the new brilliant performer. WD934 arrived at Binbrook to serve as special transport for the AOC 1 Group flown by 101 Squadron, but most of the early aircraft were set aside for experimental work of a wide variety. WD929 and '930, for instance, were used by TRE. WD931 in RAE hands was one of the first to have wing tip cameras. WD932 and '940 were passed to the Americans, and WD939 became A84-307. WD 941, '944, '946 and '948-950 were among those which equipped 101 Squadron in 1951.

It was unfortunate that the Canberra entered service at a time when bomber markings had been toned down. The non-availability of more aircraft in the first batch, because so many were earmarked for trials work, meant that it was January 1952 before 617 Squadron began to equip, its aircraft then including WD949, WD945 and WD982. No distinguishing markings had yet been adopted, and so it was decided to paint a lightning flash on the noses of aircraft in the Binbrook squadrons. In the case of 101 Squadron they were black and white and 617 Squadron chose red. The third Canberra squadron, No 12, began to receive B.2s in April 1952. One of its first machines was WP515 in grey-black finish.

The next alteration to markings became evident in March 1952, when bombers first appeared with enlarged fuselage serials. On the Lincolns they were white and usually 42 inches high, although some were 4 feet high, the same height as the outer diameter of the fuselage side roundels. Mosquitoes had them and a few Washingtons, although these usually had large fin serials with WF above the digits, as on WF562 of 57 Squadron flying in August 1952 with a blue nosewheel door. Usually 57 Squadron's aircraft featured blue and white striped nosewheel doors. Fin serials on the Washingtons were applied some weeks after the Lincolns adopted enlarged serials.

When the Lincolns first appeared wearing enlarged fuselage serials evident confusion in the positioning could be seen. SX appeared ahead of the roundel and 977 aft on the port side, when the machine was noted on April 7 1952. RE397, seen four days later, had the serial in the intended position, aft of the roundels. It featured a white H2S radome. These enlarged numbers linked with spinner colours—RF539 had red spinners and RE295 green at this time—proved a much more easily identifiable feature for both air and ground crews. Some Lincolns continued to have an individual letter on the nose, however, and it was common to see them at this time with the squadron badges on their noses.

When WD987 touched down at Binbrook on April 16 1952, it was seen resplendent in 'Mod 312', the second scheme devised for the Canberra. The new scheme laid down on August 18 1951 consisted of upper surface camouflage of Medium Sea Grey and Light Slate Grey with PRU Blue under surfaces which extended up the fuselage sides to a point which, when the aircraft was exactly side on, ended 19½ inches below the top line of the fuselage. This brought the Blue level with the base of the tailplane. Fuselage Type D roundels were, as before, 3 feet in diameter. The fin stripe was 24 inches square. Above the wings Type D roundels of outer diameter 84 inches were still applied, centred 128 inches from the wing tip, and the outer diameters of the inner rings were 28 and 56 inches. Four-foot high white under-wing serials were applied, each digit/letter being spaced 6 inches apart.

External finish on early Canberras applied to all except the plywood covering of the fin which was finished in a variety of light greys. After the aircraft had been cleaned the primer coat was applied, followed by stopping of rivet holes, etc. Two more coats of primer and filling were then sprayed on to the aircraft. Then the machine received its first final coat, the chosen shades being three parts colour to one part thinners, after which the paintwork was rubbed down. It was again painted in final colours; then only the PRU Blue surfaces were rubbed down again, following which a third coat of PRU Blue was applied. Finally, external markings and instructions were applied to meet Specification DTD 722. All the final paints were Dockers High Gloss.

WD987-999 and WE111-122 all left the factory in this fashion and certainly to WE120 these aircraft initially wore 8-inch fuselage serials. WE114-122 inclusive entered service with No 231 OCU, Bassingbourn, the unit which was to provide operational conversion for some 6,000 Canberra crews, when it began to receive Canberra B.2s in February 1952. From their introduction these aircraft all had enlarged fuselage serials, 2 feet high and white. At this time 231 OCU had some Meteor T.7s, silver with yellow 'T. bands' and large serials, like WH127. Canberras WF886-892 and WF908-918 were delivered in the grey-slate grey-blue scheme and WF907, '908 and '916 were delivered to 9 Squadron in May 1952 serving at first with 8-inch fuselage serials. WP514, which joined 9 Squadron in July, retained the original grey-black finish. Some of 9 Squadron's aircraft had a black lightning flash on the nose.

The first of 65 Handley Page-built Canberras, WJ564, flew in December 1952 and, like the later ones from the parent firm, had the sea grey-slate grey-blue scheme with an 8-inch serial. About the first 20 seem to have worn this pattern. A. V. Roe built 75 Canberra B.2s; WJ971, the first, made its maiden flight on November 25 1952, in grey-slate grey-blue, but very few in this production run wore this colouring.

Canberra Mod 626 was dated January 13 1953. Its issue required Canberra bombers to be finished overall in High Speed Silver finish with glossy black serials. Roundels and fin stripes remained in the same size and colours, this scheme being introduced on production aircraft in January 1953, and following on from the medium grey-slate grey-blue scheme on the production lines. Some B.2s were finished retrospectively in silver during refurbishing, etc, and very few of the WH6.. series appeared in camouflage. High Speed Silver finish remained in vogue on Bomber Command Canberras until the type was replaced.

Overseas there had been a trace of a return to the pre-war pattern of equipment. The Empire steadily contracted, and guerilla forces and insurrection could best be contained by fighter-bombers supported by, if necessary, detachments of Lincolns, later Canberras, of the home-based forces.

The last piston-engined bomber type based entirely overseas was the Bristol Brigand. The first production Brigands were completed as torpedo bombers and there seems a likely possibility that more than the 11 Brigand TF.1s often mentioned were actually completed. It is sometimes stated that these served with Nos 36 and 42 Squadrons, but there is no truth in this. They underwent various modification programmes and a number swapped their Ocean Grey-Sky finish for Ocean Grey and matt White. Torpedo fighters were outmoded by operational requirements which lapsed whilst Brigand production came underway. Accordingly, most Brigands were completed as tactical bombers for tropical service, were finished in glossy Medium Sea Grey and Black, and fitted with external bomb and rocket racks. RH797 was the prototype conversion to B.Mk 1, and it is possible that all the preceding aircraft began life as TF.1s. The number of aircraft available soon considerably exceeded requirements and some never passed beyond maintenance units. Many Brigand bombers were converted to Mk 4 or 5 radar trainers for home service, but three squadrons of Brigand B.1s were formed.

Firstly, 84 Squadron at Habbaniya equipped at the start of 1949. A detachment of 45 Squadron crews trained on the Brigand Met 3 in Britain in late 1948. In January 1949, they formed No 45(Met) Squadron at Manston. Their six aircraft, VS817, '820, '821, '822, '823 and '824, flew to Negombo, Ceylon, where the unit became 1301 Met Flt in February 1949. Two other squadrons, No 8 at Khormaksar and No 45 at Kuala Lumpur, equipped with Brigand bombers at the end of 1949, but some of their aircraft had deteriorated a lot in storage.

Aircraft of 8 Squadron had white individual letters aft of the roundel repeated on the tip of the nose, also in white. The squadron badge was applied to both sides of the nose. No 8's aircraft included RH822 : D, RH827 : F, VS854 : G and RH812 : D. In 1952 the upper surfaces and fuselage sides of some aircraft were painted white, as on RH830 : C. Not all of their machines had their colouring changed. In December 1952, the squadron re-equipped with Vampires.

No 84 Squadron left Habbaniya for Tengah in March 1950 to participate in the anti-terrorist Operation *Firedog*. Its aircraft were quite distinctive, for they wore either a black club or red heart on a white square painted below the fin stripe. A : VS868, D : VS836 and G : VS854, for instance, wore the black club with a variant of their squadron badge on a white disc on the sides of the nose. H : RH831 had a red heart motif. Aircraft used by the squadron included A : RH817, A : VS816, C : RH810, E : RH815, G : RH811 and H : VS831.

No 45 Squadron left Kuala Lumpur on December 5 1949. At Tengah, its new base, it gave up its beloved Beaufighter for the Brigand. The newcomer was not happily received, for it could do little that the Beaufighter could not, and was less manoeuvrable. No 45's aircraft carried the letters OB in white immediately aft of the fuselage roundels and individual letters further aft. Its Brigands included VS838, VS855, VS857 and VS864. They were employed in Operation *Firedog* until February 8 1952, when the last Brigand sorties were flown by the squadron.

During 1953 there were few changes in bomber markings. Lincolns in squadron service wore the grey-black finish, but one obvious change was the removal of dorsal turrets begun in 1952. By the end of 1953 a Lincoln with

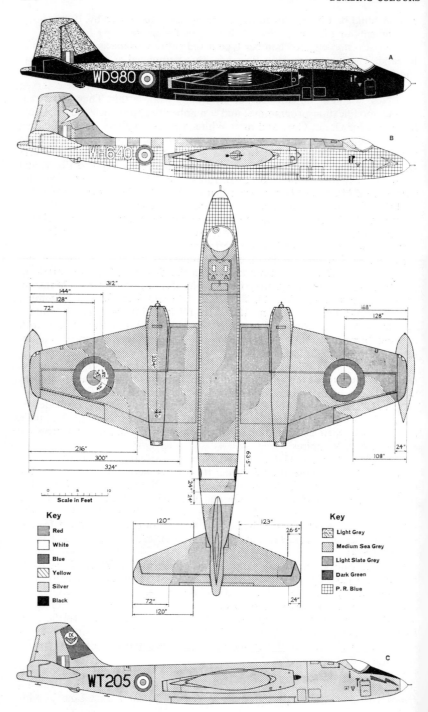

A

WD980

B

WH640

144"
128"
72"
312"

168"
128"

216"
300"
324"

24"
108"

63·5"

24"
24"

0   5   10
Scale in Feet

Key

	Red
	White
	Blue
	Yellow
	Silver
	Black

120"
123"
26·5"

Key

	Light Grey
	Medium Sea Grey
	Light Slate Grey
	Dark Green
	P. R. Blue

72"
120"
24"

C

WT205

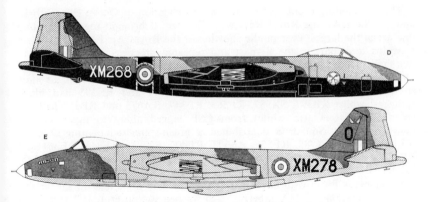

Figure 30: *(Opposite page and above) the English Electric Canberra.*

A. *WD980 exhibits a variation of the originally specified Medium Grey-Black finish for Canberras in that she has a partially grey fin. Otherwise her markings are normal for an early machine. She served with XV Sqn after flying with No 617. She was also used by 57 Sqn, and the Bomber Command Holding Unit in whose markings she is depicted here.*

B. *This profile and the plan view show a machine in Medium Grey-Slate Grey-PRU Blue finish with white serials. The plan view is based upon the English Electric drawings for this scheme and includes the measurements as laid down. These, of course, were not slavishly followed but gave a detailed indication of the paint scheme. WH640 is shown in 10 Sqn markings and 'Suez stripes'. These comprised three white bands and two black, the latter left off the profile in order to show the camouflage pattern more clearly, and omitted from the plan view for the same reason. The nose retains the red 'Scampton speedbird' and the white Honington pheasant is outlined black. Silver tip tanks carry 10 Squadron's red wings and black arrow.*

C. *Canberra B.6 in all-silver finish with matt black anti-dazzle panel. The nose flash and fin panel are shown here in Roundel Blue, but for some period of its service with 9 Sqn the aircraft wore both a grey-green fin panel. WT205 appeared on the nosewheel door in black 4-inch digits. 'IX' on the fin disc was red.*

D. *XM268 of 16 Sqn, a B.Mk 8 in Black-Dark Green-Dark Sea Grey glossy finish. No belly gun pack. Some Mk 8s had their black areas ended at the 60-degree tangent, like WT362 of 14 Sqn.*

E. *Canberra B(I)8 XM278 exhibits the later camouflage scheme for this mark and is shown in the markings of 14 Sqn with which she served in 1968. During her career the aircraft wore both a rounded style of 'O' in black on her fin and one of squarish style. Some B.8s like XM276 of 3 Sqn had the silver under surfaces terminated almost half-way up the fuselage. This machine also had a white serial on the fuselage. No serial appeared on the nosewheel door on XM278, and indeed this was unusual on the Mk 8s. Silver or black belly gun packs were fitted to these aircraft.*

dorsal armament was an unusual sight. By summer 1953, many Lincolns were flying with Medium Grey spinners, although the Upwood Wing retained squadron colouring longer than the others. RE295 was seen in August 1952 without a dorsal turret and wearing 7 Squadron's badge on both sides of her nose. She, however, had grey spinners like RF554 and RA674 of similar vintage. At the same time RE291, with dorsal turret and grey spinners, had an 8-inch Bright Red fuselage serial.

A group of three interesting Lincolns flying at this time comprised RF339:S-D, RF443:S-F and RE416:S-G of the Armament Division, Technical Training Command. These machines, which came into use in the autumn of 1950, wore TDE codes in 1951 and switched to the 'S' unit letter in autumn 1952. Fully armed, they were finished in the standard grey-black style and had white letters and small red fuselage serials. By April 1953, RF339 had acquired yellow training bands around the wings between the engine nacelles and around the rear fuselage, a feature of some other Lincolns in training units. Another oddity was the so-called 'Lincolnian' with nose and tail contours similar to those of the Lancastrian. RF561, Dark Green-Dark Earth-Black, had modifications of this nature and was in use by the Bomb Ballistics Unit at Martlesham in April 1953.

The outstanding event of 1953 was the Coronation of Queen Elizabeth II, and for the RAF the Royal Review at Odiham. It brought together around one arena the largest ever public showing of the Royal Air Force. Forty-five Lincolns took part in the fly-past and repeated practices were required to marshall such a large fly-past. Eighteen of the Lincolns came from Upwood. On July 8, for instance, RE360, SX975, SX958, RE322 and RE299 had yellow spinners; SX988, RE301, SX982, RE345, RE348 and RE295 had black spinners; whilst RE397, SX987, RF565, RE347, RA673 and RE357 had red spinners. SS716 : C (in white) from CSE tagged along to make up the number. No 61 Squadron contributed a green-spinnered contingent comprising RA681, SX985, RF555, RE323, RE407, SX978, RF348, RE361 and RE320, whilst another formation with grey spinners consisted of WD148, SX989, SX944, SX979, RA714, SX933, RF349, RE359 and SX937. All wore the grey-black finish with large fuselage serials, and none had dorsal turrets.

Two formations of 24 Canberras each formed station groups. Those from Binbrook, including WD948, WD956, WD950, etc, mainly had the grey-black finish, whereas the Hemswell Wing was flying grey-green-blue aircraft and a few in the new silver scheme. A few of the Washingtons in the fly-past practices had black under surfaces, like WF509 noted on July 7 with white wing serials.

Parked on Odiham were several Lincolns, including RA665 of 57 Squadron, SX926 of 61 Squadron, RE311 : 48 of 116 Squadron with red spinners, RE411 of 100 Squadron, RF448 of 230 OCU, and RE309 which carried a yellow training band aft on the fuselage with 'D' in white on the sides of the nose. She had a Bright Red 8-inch fuselage serial. Lincolns, presently wearing identity letters or numbers on the rear fuselage, or 'T.bands', had red serials at this time.

Four Washingtons on show were all squadron aircraft. WF572 had a cream nosewheel door with a brown flash and the letter N on a disc. WF545 of 90 Squadron had a red and white nosewheel door, and WF565 of 207 Squadron exhibited no squadron colours. All of these aircraft had fin serials as well as black 8-inch fuselage serials.

All of the Canberra B.2s shown statically had grey-slate grey-blue finish and 8-inch serials in white. They comprised WH639 and WH673 of the Flying College; WH856 of 10 Squadron; WJ568, the fourth of 76 Short-built machines and from Coningsby; and WJ973, an Avro-built aircraft. Some of 50 Squadron's Canberras could be seen in the fly-past, recognisable by their orange nose flashes.

Apart from the formation or re-equipment of more squadrons with Canberras, 1954 witnessed no basic marking changes. Silver Canberras began to predominate, like WH877 with a 2-foot black fuselage serial aft but no unit markings. She was on the strength of 231 OCU. This unit shunned any special identity almost to the end of its stay at Bassingbourn. Lincolns decreased in number, but an example of 1954 vintage is RE323 which had white spinners.

Washingtons were almost a memory now, for the 'last one' (WF438) officially passed through Prestwick on its return to the USA on March 16 1954. This official statement was not strictly accurate for, although the Washington had been phased out of Bomber Command service by now, a handful of the Washingtons continued to serve for trials purposes at Watton for some years. Indeed, on the day that the 'last' Washington left Marham, six more were lurking in the shade ! But the middle of 1954 saw the Washingtons gone from Bomber Command.

Sufficient Canberras were now available for many squadrons to be equipped, and they adopted individual markings within a station motif. At Binbrook the lightning flash was retained. No 617 Squadron had now adopted blue, 12 Squadron what it called 'gold', and 101 Squadron retained its black and white flash. No 10 Squadron for a time wore a white shield with a red cross and yellow Fleur de Lys on its aircraft's fins (Waddington's Lincoln Arms station badge still carried on its Vulcans). No 10 moved to Honington where, by 1956, an interesting tail insignia was adopted. There were persistent rumours of an albino game bird—reported both as a pheasant and a partridge—living near the airfield. Many attempts were made to catch it and the interest aroused was such that when a station motif was needed Honington adopted a bird in flight, which was painted white on the fins of its Canberras and outlined in the respective squadron colour. The squadrons there brought with them a nose device something like a speedbird, the colour of which indicated the squadron. No 10's colour was red, No 18's blue. The latter squadron had a red-winged horse painted on its tip tanks where No 10 placed its red bow and black arrow.

Marham's aircraft in the mid-1950s settled for coloured tip tanks, 115's being, for instance, black and 35's blue. The latter squadron added a black and yellow flying horse's head to the tails of its aircraft in February 1956, and by the time the squadron was at Upwood this device was also carried on the tip tanks. No 90 Squadron applied a yellow hind to the tails of its Canberras in February 1956.

On the tip tanks of its Canberras, 61 Squadron painted a red Lincoln Imp, again retained during its stay at Upwood and in a refined style. Hemswell's two squadrons had an acute-angled triangle as station symbol, 109 Squadron's being yellow and 139's red usually outlined white. The Wittering Wing went in for yellow and blue fin checks in 1955, a green disc distinguishing 100 Squadron and a red disc No 40.

At Binbrook in 1956 101's aircraft acquired a CI design around a red rampant lion. No 9 Squadron's machines, now wearing a blue nose lightning flash, added on the tail a grey-green bat based upon the squadron badge. 'IX' surmounted this, usually in yellow. Further details of Canberra markings appear in Appendix 6.

Canberra development was still proceeding. The Mk 8 intruder prototype VX 185 first flew on July 23 1954 and the first production machine WT326 flew on June 8 the following year. Production machines wore a Dark Green-Dark Grey-Black finish with 2-foot white fuselage serials.

The first Canberra B.6 WJ754, in silver finish with 2-foot fuselage serial, first flew on January 26 1954. The first batch, WJ754-784, equipped Nos 9, 12 and 101 Squadrons and the special trials squadron, No 76 during 1955. The B.6, of which 88 were built by English Electric and 30 by Shorts, had more powerful engines (Avon 109s), integral wing tanks and extended range. No 9 Squadron again applied the bat emblem on its aircraft and 12 Squadron painted a red running fox on the tails of its Mk 6s.

Canberra stations in 1955-56 held aircraft in the full assortment of finishes. No 231 OCU at Bassingbourn on April 4 1955 had Canberras in all the basic schemes. WJ581 was slate grey-medium grey-blue; WD938 was in the original grey-black colouring and WH862 was silver. All had enlarged fuselage serials. The T.Mk 4s on the station had all-silver finish with yellow fuselage and wing bands and featured 8-inch fuselage serials.

July 1955 saw the Golden Jubilee of the RAE. One of the exhibits at its display was the Short Sperrin VX161, a stand-by aircraft in case the V-bombers did not reach expectations. All silver, it had black serials and was surrounded by various possible dark green weapon loads. Lancaster RT690 with nose probe was still in her white-black finish. On the field was a red Lincoln, WD125. Drone Lincolns were at this time under development. Indeed, on February 1 1956, RF393 made the first Lincoln U.5 test flight under remote control. RE366, also converted, was not flown, and the proposed ten conversion sets were cancelled before the aircraft could be converted at Langar. Two Lincoln tankers, for in-flight refuelling of Meteors of 245 Squadron, had seen service by now, SX993 being modified for the task in 1951 and RE293 in 1952.

Also at the 1955 Jubilee Show was the Marham Canberra Wing whose four squadrons made a fly-past. All the aircraft were silver, and all had enlarged fuselage serials. They included WJ648 and WK106 of 207 Squadron (red tanks), WK104 and WH870 of 90 Squadron (white tanks), WJ719 and WH909 of 35 Squadron (blue tanks), with WJ753 (black tanks) and WK110 (green tanks) of 115 Squadron.

Now flying was the silver prototype Canberra B(I)6 WT307. It first flew on March 31 1955 and silver examples were delivered to 213 Squadron in 1956.

During 1955 and 1956, the period of the introduction of the V-bombers, markings of the Canberras remained basically unaltered. All of the B.6s were delivered in High Speed Silver finish, their roundels and serials unchanged in size. Many of the B.2s continued to serve, and indeed served to their withdrawal, in the grey-slate grey-blue scheme, and some of these were involved in the highly controversial operations in the Middle East in November 1956.

In the autumn of 1956 a number of Canberra squadrons were detached from Britain to Cyprus and Malta to stand by for any possible operations that might arise from the tense situation around the Suez Canal. In November the British contribution to the attack on Egypt was mounted with the Canberra force much to the fore. The intention was that the British force should identify itself with black and yellow stripes painted around wings and fuselages. Distemper supplies were short and many of the aircraft had to be decorated with black and white stripes and these were mainly applied to Canberras. A typical machine was B.6 WH967 of 12 Squadron. On its silver finish it wore 24-inch bands—three yellow and two black—encircling the wings but not painted over the serials. The inner band coincided with the innermost point of the under-wing serial and the outer band with the outer lining of the second figure of the number. The fuselage bands commenced level with the forward side of the fuselage roundel white band, and the two rear bands completely encircled the fuselage. WH959, also of 12 Squadron, and with a red fox on the fin, had striping in almost identical positions but her bands were black and white which showed up far less. The colloquially called 'Suez stripes' were retained on many aircraft for some months after the operation—and by then the V-bombers were increasingly taking their places. Slowly the Canberra force began to wind down.

Chapter 24

The V–Bombers: Valiant, Victor and Vulcan in the 1950s

ONCE THE JET ENGINE was a viable proposition manufacturers and Ministries were quick to appreciate possibilities. Despite early unreliability of the engines and their lack of power it was obvious that they would be the prime movers in the future. Wartime need to maintain high-production rates precluded a switch to new basic types, as was the case with the Lincoln. Behind-the-scenes schemes for jet bombers were nevertheless being formulated. The first successful British jet bomber, the Canberra, has already been mentioned. Its main failing was a lack of range, and its size precluded much carriage of sophisticated radio and radar gear—essential in warfare for the 1950s and beyond.

In 1945-46 a new requirement was formulated, for long-range very high performance 4-jet bombers, and crystallised in Specification B.35/46 issued on January 1 1947. Companies which had provided Britain with her wartime bombers took up the challenge. To achieve the required speed/range/load carrying qualities, and at the same time operate at very high altitudes, necessitated some radical schemes. Avro eventually opted for a delta planform at a time when the handling qualities of deltas were little known, apart from work carried out in Germany. Equally radical was the giant Armstrong Whitworth flying-wing bomber which was not proceeded with. Handley Page chose the unique crescent wing to confer good handling characteristics over a wide speed range.

Bludgeon or Rapier? The wartime bomber force had certainly been the former. Now that one bomb could produce devastation the equal of a 1,000-bomber raid surely the policy must be for the rapier. A rapid, accurate thrust by a handful of aircraft might, in a fleeting moment, decide the outcome of any conflict. So the die was cast ; for a small number of superb performers modelled on the Mosquito concept which officialdom had avidly pushed aside. Like the Mosquito these would depend for safety upon speed and height. They would be unarmed, although suggestions were mooted that they might carry missiles for self defence. Both at the time of conception and introduction the V-bombers were unequalled anywhere in the world.

Results of German research on swept wings came to hand. In their requirement the Air Staff expressed a need for aircraft incorporating some 35 degrees of wing sweepback.

There lurked that old fear that the bombers might not meet the stringent demands, and in what now appears to have been a questionable mood the Air Staff laid down an outline for less radical aircraft. Specification B.14/46 led to the Short Sperrin of which only two prototypes were built. Vickers had tendered for the high-performance bomber, but their tender did not appear to offer the range required. It was less radical than the other designs too, and a special Specification B.9/48 was drawn up around the Vickers proposals.

Two prototypes of this, WB210 and 215, were ordered in February 1949. In shining natural finish with black serials the first of these flew on May 18 1951, but was destroyed in a flying accident on January 12 the following year. The second machine flew on April 11 1952.

Handley Page's ideas were crystallised in the HP 80. Originally the company opted for a flying-wing design with fins at the tips but with a tailplane on a slender rear fuselage. By the time plans for prototypes had materialised they were for a more conventional aircraft with shapely fuselage and swept fin and rudder. To prove the basic points of the design, scaled down wings and tail unit were fitted to a modified Supermarine 510 fuselage. This black aircraft with white serial, the HP 88, made its first flight on June 21 1951, but crashed soon after.

Two prototypes of the HP 80, WB771 and WB775, were ordered in February 1949, and 25 examples of the aircraft in June 1952. Both prototypes emerged in silver finish, the first flying on December 24 1952.

Work at Avro on their contender made faster progress. Originally a swept wing and slender fuselage leading to the swept tail unit were decided upon. The effect of wing sweep suggested a shorter fuselage, so the fins were then placed at the wing tips. Finally a delta planform was decided upon and submitted in May 1947 as the Avro 698. It was accepted for development by the Ministry of Supply in November 1947. During 1948 engine positioning was altered, circular air intakes to the grouped engines being changed to rectangular intakes in the wing roots. Equally radical was the decision to have a central fin, useful if ever a tailplane needed to be fitted.

Just as Handley Page decided to test its ideas on a reduced scale Avro did the same. Aerodynamic qualities of the huge wing needed to be fully explored and centre of gravity problems, etc, grappled with. In 1948 it was decided to build a single-engined small delta, the Type 707, for low-speed research, and a twin-engined aircraft to explore the high-speed qualities of the design. Eventually only the single-engined experimental aircraft was proceeded with and emerged as VX784 in natural finish with a yellow 'P' marking on its nose. It was a fairly primitive machine utilising a Meteor canopy and nosewheel and Athena main wheel units. It first flew on September 4 1949 at Boscombe Down and appeared as a static star attraction at the 1949 SBAC Show. The machine was destroyed soon after owing to a stall induced by airbrake failure.

A second Avro 707, almost complete, became the Avro 707B, after modifications resulting from the earlier accident. This machine, VX790, was finished in blue and again had the yellow prototype marking on its nose.

The third machine to fly was the orange Avro 707A, WZ736, intended for high-speed research. Wing section had been changed, since that of the Avro 698 bomber to follow had also been altered. The third prototype incorporated flying controls similar to those proposed for the bomber.

Work had meanwhile proceeded apace on the full-scale Avro 698. The prototype, VX770, was finished in high gloss white to a scheme finalised on August 5 1952. Above the mainplanes VX770 had 7-foot diameter Type D roundels. Beneath the wing tips and on the sides of the nose the roundels were 4 feet 6 inches in diameter, and included the customary Blue (Bright) and Red (Bright). The under-wing roundel was set 21 feet from outside the engine bay. The bomb bay, undercarriage bays and engine bays were finished in Aluminium DTD 260B and the fuselage tail cap, made of Ondzote, was Sky Grey. Black under-wing serials were 4 feet high and composed of characters 2 feet 6 inches wide. Above the swept fin stripe the black serial was 8 inches high.

VX770 first flew powered by RA3 Avons on August 30 1952. After 32 hours of flying the giant delta was re-engined with Sapphires and commenced flying again in July 1953, when bomber development of the aircraft really started.

The second prototype, VX777, with Olympus 100 engines, and in a finish similar to that of the first, flew on September 3 1953. After a heavy landing at RAE on July 27 1954, Olympus 101 engines were installed. High-speed flight trials of VX770 in 1955 showed that when higher-powered Olympus engines were fitted the performance would be near the high Mach number buffet threshold, and it was decided to increase the wing chord by 20% over the outer 20% of the wing span. This resulted in a kinked leading edge, a mock-up of which was tested on WD280, the Avro 707A. The new leading edge was fitted to VX777 in the summer of 1955, by which time the machine had undergone various aerodynamic trials. The first production all-silver Vulcan 1, XA889, had flown in February 1955, with wing planform identical to that of the first prototype, and by this time the B.3/48 Vickers-Armstrongs Valiant had entered service.

An order for 25 Valiant B.1s had been placed with Vickers in April 1951. These were delivered between December 1954 and July 1955, embracing B.1 Type 674 WP199-203 ; B.1 Type 706 WP204, W206-216, 218, 220 and 222 ; and B(PR)1 Type 710 WP205, 217, 219, 221 and 223. Additionally, a prototype of the B.2 WJ954 was ordered. Its rôle was to be that of a low-level pathfinder. Distinctive it was in its all-black finish with white serials on the fuselage and below the wings, and pods protruding from the trailing edge into which the undercarriage retracted. The B.2 existed in prototype form only.

Gaydon was the first station to receive Valiants. It was the home of 232 OCU, formed to train crews for the Valiants which were to establish the new V-force. No 138, the first Valiant squadron, re-formed at Gaydon on January 1 1955, and received its first Valiant, WP206, on February 8. Most Valiants initially had high-speed silver overall finish with 5-foot diameter Type D fuselage roundels and 7-foot diameter roundels above their wing tips. Black 4-foot serials were applied beneath the wings. The forward part of the nose radome was matt black, while the aft part appeared a medium greyish-green shade.

In July 1955, the squadron moved to Wittering, its operational base, and at the 1955 SBAC Show a selection of Valiants drawn from the squadron and 232 OCU flew over, headed by the second prototype WB215 with WP211, 213, 216, 217, 220, 221 and 223, and four from the second batch WZ363, WZ361, WZ364, and 366. On Battle of Britain Day that year WP204 operated from Boscombe Down and WP221 from Gaydon.

The second batch of 24 aircraft was delivered from August 1955 to March 1956, comprising WZ361-375 and 377 as B.Mk 1s (Type 706); WZ376, 378-379, 381, 383-384 as B(PR) 1s; and WZ380 and 382 as B(PR)K. 1s, fitting them for reconnaissance and tanker rôles. The third batch delivered from March to July 1956 comprised WZ389-399 as B(PR)K. 1s and WZ400-405 B(K) 1s. Finally came the XD series, XD812-830 and XD857-875 which were delivered from March 1956 to August 1957.

Nine bomber squadrons equipped with Valiants between February 1955 and the end of 1957, the order of equipment being 138, 7, 214, 49, 207, 148, 90, 18 and 199 Squadrons, the latter two equipping long after the others.

Aircraft of 138 Squadron in their silver finish and black serials generally did not wear any squadron markings for a long time, except for the squadron badge on the noses of some machines. No 232 OCU, too, had no special distinguishing features, and all had black under-wing serials. This was also true of 214 Squadron in the summer of 1956 when its aircraft included WP211, WZ377 and WZ379.

Victor production had meanwhile come underway. The first prototype, WB771, acquired grey wings and tail unit with a matt black fuselage and red cheat line for the 1953 SBAC Show. During a test flight on July 14 1954, it crashed at Cranfield owing to a weakness in the tail unit. The second machine, WB775, first flew on September 11 1954. At the 1956 SBAC Show it appeared in a Cerulean Blue overall finish. By then the first production Victor, in silver finish with Type D roundels on the fuselage and above the wings, was flying, XA917 making its first flight on February 1 1956. By July 1956 XA921 was flying in a glossy white anti-flash overall finish with roundels sited as on XA917, the aircraft being the first in the scheme that was to be worn by service aircraft. She retained black fuselage serials and under-wing serials.

No 543 PR Squadron equipped with Valiant B(PR)K. 1s, eg, WZ394 and WZ396, in the summer of 1956, distinctive with their FR nozzles and again wearing all-silver finish but no unit markings. An interesting exception to the usual trim was evident on WZ380, and later WZ391, both of which had red outer wing panels and fixed tail surfaces with the fin above the tailplane being red. But these, although similar in appearance to Valiant bombers, were reconnaissance aircraft.

On October 11 1956, Valiant WZ366, in silver finish, dropped the first British atomic bomb, at Maralinga, Australia. At about the same time Valiants of Nos 138, 148, 207 and 214 Squadrons, including WP211, WZ377, WZ393, WZ404, WZ405 and XD813, and yet to wear squadron markings other than badges, flew to Luqa in Malta, to be ready to participate in any operations against Egypt. On October 31 Valiants went into action against Egyptian targets in the first V-bomber operations. None of the machines are known to have had 'Suez stripes'.

At the end of 1956 the first all-white Valiants appeared on the squadrons retaining black wing and fuselage serials, but it was many months before they were anything but rare.

The first production Vulcan, XA889, flew in February 1955 and, at the 1955 SBAC Show, XA890 appeared in all-silver finish as laid down in August 1952. Roundel sizes remained the same as on the prototypes, also wing serial size, but no under-wing roundels were carried on production V-bombers. On their fins production Vulcans had 18-inch high serials, the letters/digits being $11\frac{1}{4}$ inches wide in $2\frac{1}{4}$-inch strokes with $2\frac{1}{4}$-inch gaps. Early production aircraft had straight wing leading edges, but in October 1955 the second prototype flew with a kinked wing leading edge and the first production aircraft was grounded for similar modifications, flight trials commencing in February 1956. Following A & AEE trials, the initial CA release for the Vulcan B.Mk 1 came on May 29 1956, and the aircraft entered RAF service in August 1956. Training began at No 230 OCU Waddington, early aircraft in use being XA895, '896, '898 and '900.

Figure 31: (Opposite page) 1. Valiant WP215 in white finish with black serials and Bright roundels. Motif of 18 Sqn carried on the fin. The plan view is of the same aircraft. 2. Valiant XD863 with black serials, Bright roundels and 90 Sqn fin pennant. 3. Valiant XD827 with anti-flash pale roundels and pale blue serial. The fin crest is of 49 Sqn, illustrated on the front end paper in enlarged form.

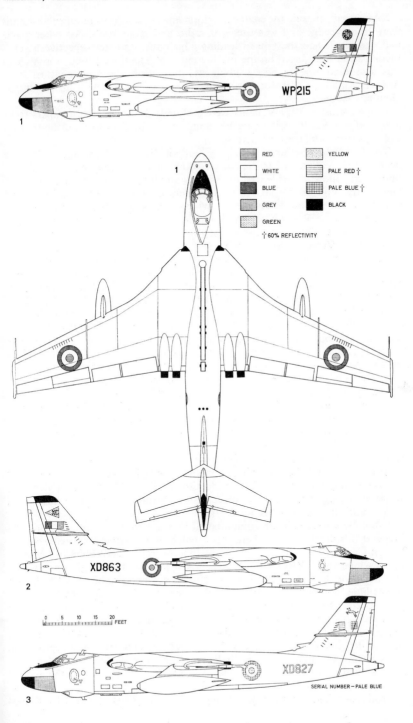

1

1

RED
WHITE
BLUE
GREY
GREEN

YELLOW
PALE RED †
PALE BLUE †
BLACK

† 60% REFLECTIVITY

WP215

XD863

2

0   5   10   15   20
                    FEET

XD827

SERIAL NUMBER – PALE BLUE

3

XA889 was set aside for engine development work. XA890 retained a straight wing leading edge and was used for radio and radar trials. All other production aircraft had the kinked leading edge either as a retrospective fit or a modification introduced on the production line. The third production Vulcan was also used for engine development, the fourth for armament trials at A & AEE and the fifth for development work connected with higher output Olympus engines.

In the spring of 1957 Valiants were still devoid of unit identity apart from nose badges. WZ395, with nose FR point, was typical in her dull finish with 214 Squadron's badge on her nose.

The first V-bomber units to display individualistic markings appear to have been (1) the Valiants of 90 Squadron which wore a green pennant with XC upon it in yellow, as evidenced by XD862, an all-white aircraft, in April 1957 and (2) the Vulcans of No 230 OCU which had on their fins the shield and red cross with yellow Fleur de Lys which had periodically been carried by aircraft based at Waddington. Vulcan XA895, a silver machine with underwing serials, was wearing this marking in April 1957, the shield being white. By this time Vulcan XA900 was flying.

All the time now white was slowly overtaking silver as the finish of the Valiants. In May, for instance, newer aircraft in service had this finish, like XD864 which displayed a new V-bomber marking on her fin, the dark blue disc with seven mullets of Ursa Major denoting her as from No 7 Squadron. At the same time WP207 and WZ378, also serving at Honington, had no distinguishing features on their silver finish. Marham continued to house Valiants without special squadron identity, dreary looking machines like XD815. This latter aircraft had a list of her crew members in black on the port side of the nose entry door, headed by 'Wg Cdr Wright, DFC', whose rank pennant appeared on both sides of the nose. XD826, silver Valiant with 7 Squadron's new fin disc, appeared at the 1957 open day at Wethersfield. Another 7 Squadron white Valiant was XD864 in use July 1957, with fin disc and Squadron Leader's nose pennant. She had black fuselage and wing serials, and a matt dark green anti-dazzle panel which some Valiants had at this time. WZ397 of 214 Squadron in silver scheme now carried the squadron's badge on the port side of her nose.

At the 1957 SBAC Show, where a memorable sight was the massed fly-past by contrailing bombers, the last production Valiant XD875 was on view, all-white with long range tanks in place (a new feature at this time) and a thin yellow line surrounding her fin flash.

V-bombers were still far outnumbered by Canberras, a point well brought home at this display where there was a batch of experimental machines. The Gyron Canberra, a very rich shade of blue overall, had WF909 in white on her fuselage and GYRON JUNIOR CANBERRA in red dayglo on her nose and a Gyron DJG.1 in her port nacelle. The Nene Canberra VN813, also bright blue, now sported a 2-foot fuselage serial and, like WF909, had a thin white outline to her roundels. The all-silver Olympus Canberra WH713 with an 8-inch fuselage serial, an ex-XV Squadron machine with black nacelles, had as company the Scorpion Canberra WK163, silver with red titling on her nose and a red scorpion painted thereon. The V-bombers were represented by VX770, now flying with Rolls-Royce Conways; XA889, still silver and with kinked leading edge; and the all-white Victor 1 XA918, the second production aircraft.

Production Vulcans were now flying in all-white finish, typified by XA904

126 (Above) All-white Victor B.1
XA938 with 10 Sqn's tail marking
in red, and Bright roundels.
Photographed at Cottesmore in
April 1958.

127 (Right) All-white Victor B.1A
XH667 with anti-flash roundels and
pale 57 Squadron motif on fin.
Photographed in September 1961.

128 Victor tanker XH587 camouflaged, although the upper surface
colours do not wrap around the
wing leading edge. Dark lines
below the wings are to aid the pilot
of the re-fuelling machine. '57'
appears on the fin in red outlined
white.

129 A 1968 shot of a Victor B.2R
XM717 in camouflage finish, carrying Blue Steel and wearing the
yellow Wittering lion on her fin. Her
paintwork dated from August 1967
and she was carrying Blue Steel
round number 129.

242

130 *Valiant WP220 of 138 Sqn in silver finish shortly after the introduction of the Valiant in 1955 (Ministry of Defence).*

131 *Valiant XD863 in all-white finish and black serials, with 90 Sqn's fin pennant and Bright roundels. Photographed in August 1960.*

132 *A later shot of XD863, now in the tanker rôle. Pale roundels and blue serial contrast with the dark green squadron flash.*

133 *Valiants XD857 and WZ393 in camouflage, photographed in April 1964, soon after the introduction of the new finish. Both belong to 214 Sqn, part of the tanker force then based at Marham.*

134 *A camouflaged Valiant flying over Coltishall in September 1964. Note that the camouflage wraps around the wing and tail leading edges.*

and also XA907 of 83 Squadron. The latter with two white Valiants, XD818 and XD868, appeared on September 5 at the Show. XD818 of 49 Squadron was particularly interesting. Completely white, her radome having been over-painted like a few other Valiants, she had dropped Britain's first hydrogen bomb on May 15 1957. There were still many silver Valiants about though, for example XD820 of 148 Squadron. With her at the 1957 Upwood Battle of Britain display was Lincoln B.2 with H2S IVA WD143 in grey-black scheme with red spinners; her home unit was the Bomber Command Bombing School at Lindholme. Upwood was a Canberra station and T.Mk 4 WT479 of the Station Flight was on show, silver with yellow 'T. bands', and wearing Upwood's red lion badge on a white shield, the latter outlined black. She had the customary 8-inch serial usually worn by T.4s and a 6-inch serial in black on her nosewheel door. Vulcan 1 XA905, all-white with kinked wing leading edge, and 83 Squadron's badge on either side of the nose, also appeared at the display.

A silver Valiant of 207 Squadron, in use in October 1957, was XD812. She had the squadron badge on the starboard side of her nose. Radome colours varied from aircraft to aircraft and behind the specially finished black portion the rear panelling on '812 had a purplish hue. WP219 of 199 Squadron at this time had a red fin disc with white waves, quite different from that which the unit generally displayed.

Throughout 1956 and 1957 Victor production slowly built up. From June 1956 Victors left the lines in all-white finish with black fuselage and under-wing serials, XA921 being the first machine to leave the line in the new trim. The delay in introducing the Victor was due to updating of radar and radio gear until, in November 1957, XA931 was delivered to 232 OCU, Gaydon, which had split into two parts, half to train Valiant crews and the other to train crews for the Victor. In April 1958, No 10 Squadron, the first to fly Victors, formed and was based at Cottesmore. All its Victor B.Mk 1s were delivered in glossy white anti-nuclear flash finish, and were soon carrying a Bright Red winged arrow device painted on their fins. They also had squadron badges on both sides of their noses. Black aircraft serial numbers were later painted on both nosewheel doors.

Valiants were still to be seen wearing either of the two schemes, silver machines including XD817 and XD828 of 7 Squadron bearing tail motifs, like XD867 and XD870 of 90 Squadron whose green pennant was usual now on the squadron's aircraft. Some of the earlier Valiants were now in white finish, like WP213 and WZ372 of 199 Squadron serving with WZ365 in silver. White just about predominated now.

Two V-bombers of August 1958 were Vulcan 1 XH481 of 101 Squadron and Valiant XD817. The former, completed in March 1958, was white with ample red instructions on the forward fuselage, and red ejector seat warnings on the nosewheel door. XH481 had her squadron badge on the port side of her fin and the Lincoln Arms badge on the starboard side. Dielectric areas on the fin root and fuselage spine were olive green as usual, and the fin tip was black like the nose radome. No 101 Squadron, the second to equip with Vulcans, had re-formed at Waddington in October 1957. Valiant XD817 had the customary black radome with grey area aft. Her only squadron identity was the badge of 148 Squadron on the port side of the nose. None of Marham's squadrons had any squadron motifs on their aircraft yet.

No XV Squadron, the second to equip with Victor 1s, re-formed at Cottesmore in September 1958.

N

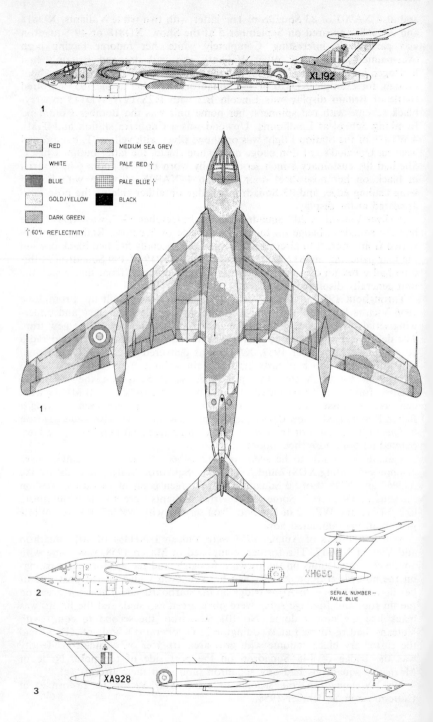

Behind-the-scenes development was proceeding apace on the Mk 2 versions of the Vulcan and Victor, with interim Mk IA variants being planned carrying modified radar and ECM gear, etc. Test flights of the Vulcan 1, production of which ended March 1959, had indicated that more modifications to the wing would be needed to take full advantage of increased power becoming available from the Olympus. In August 1955, schemes were submitted to the Ministry of Supply for a new planform to suit Vulcans fitted with Olympus B016 engines. Design work began at the end of 1955; a prototype order was placed in March 1956, and a production contract followed a few weeks later. Outer wings of increased span and chord were then fitted to VX777, which first flew on August 31 1957, still in a white finish. XH533, the first production Mk 2, flew in July 1958 in the usual white finish with black serials. It was powered by Olympus B016 engines, had the new outer wings, elevons in place of the elevators and ailerons of the Mk 1, enlarged air intakes, stronger undercarriage and modified electronic gear.

Some features of the new Victor were apparent at the 1958 SBAC Show where Mk 1 XA930 appeared with a new flight refuelling probe and large external wing tanks, the aircraft having flown in this configuration for the first time on August 27. The Victor 2 was a development along similar lines to that of the Vulcan 2—increased span coupled with more engine power from Rolls-Royce Co 11 engines. XH668, the first Victor B.2, flew on February 20 1959. With about twice the engine power of the B.1 the new version had not only increased cruising speed, it also had a much higher operating altitude.

The 1958 Battle of Britain Day displays exhibited plenty of the V-force. At Honington, Valiant WP213 in white finish was shown wearing the blue and white fin disc with two yellow swords of 199 Squadron. Vulcan 1 XH480 had 83 Squadron's badge on both sides of its nose and on the sides of the fin wore the Waddington shield. This varied in base colour on different aircraft and on this machine the shield was pale grey, outlined black, and carrying a red cross with a yellow Fleur de Lys. All the Valiants on the field had white finish, like WP223 and WZ393 of 90 Squadron. Making a public debut was a Valiant of 207 Squadron wearing recently applied fin motif, a red lion with yellow wings.

Vulcan XH499 of 617 Squadron—which had re-formed at Scampton in May 1968—settled only for the squadron badge on the sides of her nose. Valiant XD820, now white and of 148 Squadron, similarly had only squadron badges on the nose. V-bombers at this period usually had their squadron badge transfers on their noses—sometimes on both sides, sometimes on one, like the Canberras. No distinctive markings were carried by 148 Squadron over a very long period. All-silver Vulcan XA896 had a white-red Waddington shield on her fin and was flying with 230 OCU. Victor 1 XA929 appeared at the displays with the red tail motif of 10 Squadron.

V-bombers were now frequently making overseas flights, mainly for training purposes which at the same time allowed for some flag waving. Evidence of this aspect was carried by XD819 and XD859 in the autumn of 1958 for, just ahead of the crew door, they had Union Jacks 24 inches by 18 inches, applied because they participated in a US Strategic Air Command contest.

Figure 32: (Opposite page) 1. Victor XL192, wearing low-level camouflage markings and the yellow lion motif carried by the Wittering Wing, as recorded in July 1968. The plan view is of XL192. 2. Victor 1A XH650 in white finish with anti-flash roundels, etc. Fin motif of 55 Sqn. 3. Victor B.1 XA928 of 10 Sqn in white finish with Bright roundels and black serials. 1958 finish.

Late 1958 the next change in V-bomber markings manifested itself. Reconnaissance Valiants of 543 Squadron were the first squadron aircraft to feature it and its WZ382 was one of the first in Service hands to feature pale blue fuselage and wing serials with pale blue and pale red anti-nuclear flash colours in their roundels and fin flashes. Slowly, very slowly, these new shades replaced the Bright shades in vogue on bombers for 11 years. But the norm for many months stayed—white finish with black serials and squadron badge on the nose side(s), as on XD861. One of the first Valiant B.K. 1s with pale blue serials alongside the old Bright roundels was WZ391 which had acquired them by January 1959.

In April 1959, Victors of 10 and XV Squadrons were displayed during a visit to the V-force by the then Prime Minister, the Rt Hon Harold Macmillan. Aircraft of XV Squadron featured a black hind's head flanked by yellow wings aft of which XV appeared in a brownish-orange shadowed black. The squadron badge appeared on the sides of the nose and black serials were painted on all the nosewheel doors of Cottesmore's Victors at this time, a feature now common on Valiants. Victors in this scheme included XH591 and XH594 of XV Squadron, also XA928 and XA938 of 10 Squadron, all of which had the usual Bright Type D roundels and black serials.

A white Valiant in use in mid-1959 was XD813 which had black serials in the usual positions and on both nosewheel doors as well as 207's lion marking on her port fin side only.

Victor XH669 appeared at the 1959 SBAC Show in all-white finish with pale roundels and fin flashes. Completely absent were external serials, XH669 being stencilled only on the sides of the crew entry door. This represented the ultimate 'low' in V-bomber markings !

Each day at the 1959 Show V-bombers demonstrated Quick Reaction Alerts, and in all cases the aircraft wore Bright roundels and black serials, like Vulcans XH497, XH483, XH502 and XH501 of 617 Squadron with only nose badges to identify their owners. Another day it was Victors of XV Squadron that performed, revealing themselves as XH588, XH589, XH590, XH591 and XH592. On Battle of Britain Day the only exception to the standard colours was Valiant XD829 of 49 Squadron, Wittering, which had Bright roundels but pale fin flashes. There are, however, always anomalies in marking states, as was illustrated the same day by Victors XH614 and XH620 of 57 Squadron, which had no under-wing serials.

Thus at the end of the 1950s V-bomber markings were changing, but the two principal changes belonged to the 1960s.

Chapter 25

Power for peace

THE ANNOUNCEMENT of March 2 1960 that four V-bombers could be airborne in less than four minutes, following a warning of a Russian attack, showed that the V-Force had achieved a high state of operational readiness. In February 1958 it had been stated that Canberras of Bomber Command and 2nd TAF were being given nuclear capability. Then in August 1958 came the announcement that the first Thor intermediate range ballistic missile squadron, No 77, was forming at Feltwell. It received its first missile on September 19. By the start of the 1960s the bomber force thereby consisted of a three-prong power for peace backed by Canberra squadrons based overseas. The pattern for the 1960s was set in the deterrent policy.

Another 1958 statement had revealed the existence of a second series of V-bombers for which stand-off bombs were being developed. On December 17 1958 had come the announcement that a new Strike/Reconnaissance Canberra replacement, the TSR.2, was being proceeded with. To give the vital few minutes' warning of any attack a huge radar complex at Fylingdales in Yorkshire would open in 1963.

By March 1960 Thor deployment was complete. Many squadrons with famous number plates were now missile-equipped at airfields in East Anglia. From time to time the soul-less white missiles were raised into launching positions, but mercifully for all they were destined never to be fired, although one may guess that their alert states must have been high during the Cuba missile crisis.

To increase the effectiveness of the Vulcan force quantities of American Skybolt air-launched ballistic missiles were to be bought once the weapon was a going concern. On August 2 1960, it was announced that the order for the Victor 2 was being reduced. Aircraft armed with Blue Steel and Skybolt made for a more effective means of penetrating enemy airspace than a larger number of bombers with free-fall weapons. Long-range capability of the V-Force was often demonstrated at this time, with the aid of Valiant tankers refuelling the bombers. In October 1961 a detachment to the USA caused no mean stir, since the British high-performance machines proved themselves capable of easily pentrating American air space.

At the beginning of 1962 it was stated that Nord AS.30 air-to-surface missiles would equip Canberra squadrons to improve their capability until TSR.2 took its place. At the same time a large team of RAF technicians set off for the USA to form a trials unit to aid development of Skybolt for the Vulcan force. In Britain, Vulcan 2 XH537 was flown with mock-ups of the missiles for development purposes. By now the Vulcan held the premier place among the V-bombers.

In December 1962, and with dramatic suddenness, rumours that Skybolt development might be cancelled by the Americans were confirmed during the Nassau meeting between Harold Macmillan and President Kennedy. How much this was a political decision as opposed to a military one may never be known. Instead of Skybolt, Britain would build four nuclear submarines equipped to fire Polaris missiles, and the spearhead of the nuclear strike force would pass into the hands of the Royal Navy.

Now that the V-Force was fully equipped with Vulcans and a smaller contingent of Victors, it was decided to place the Valiant bomber squadrons at the disposal of NATO, and give them a tactical rôle.

A milestone as far as the RAF was concerned was the first flight of the TSR.2 on September 28 1964. Another, most disturbing, was the discovery of fatigue cracks in the Valiants. So serious were these that the entire Valiant force, not long after it had been placed in a low-level attack rôle, had to be grounded some years before its planned withdrawal. Nos 90 and 214 Squadrons' Valiants were at this time employed as in-flight refuelling tankers and their loss was very serious.

Already the general effectiveness of the V-bombers had been reduced by the rapid development of surface-to-air guided weapons which seemed likely to destroy considerable numbers of bombers operating at high levels. Consequently, it had been decided that, in addition to operating under the cover of highly sophisticated ECM equipment, Vulcans and Victors would operate at low levels retaining the use of stand-off Blue Steel bombs.

The loss of the tanker force was not off-set until mid-1965, when the first Victor tankers became available. Subsequently, they equipped the three Marham squadrons, Nos 55, 57 and 214. The tankers were particularly required for in-flight refuelling of fighter aircraft.

The heaviest peacetime blow ever to be wielded at the RAF came in the Budget Statement of April 6 1965. It was the cancellation of TSR.2 whose performance on trials had so far been exceptionally outstanding. To quell the justifiable alarm which this cancellation brought, the Labour Government decided to allow the RAF to have 50 F-111A swing-wing bombers. This decision it had to accept since it would be that or nothing.

On January 16 1968, the economy axe struck again, this time upon the F-111. It left the long-range future strike potential of the Royal Air Force as nil. As if to rub home the point Bomber Command itself was disbanded on April 30 1968, and this just as the RAF was celebrating its 50th Birthday.

Some months before the Polaris submarines began to take over the deterrent rôle in 1969, the Victor 2 squadrons were disbanded and Blue Steel was also withdrawn causing the Vulcan force to resort to free-fall weapons. The great days of a mighty force had ended, incredulously as the potential foe was increasing his military strength at a then (and still) terrifying rate.

Under the new arrangement the Command was cut to being merely 1 Group of the unfortunately named Strike Command. To a large extent Britain's safety was now in the hands of the Americans, a sad state of affairs for the nation that had pioneered nearly every major stride in aviation technology. Certainly the cost of weapons was becoming prodigious, but in retrospect it can be seen that it would have been wiser to select a few and to have developed them thoroughly. This was very true of TSR.2.

The moral of all history is that if a nation wants freedom then it must be prepared to fight to keep it. Defence is exceedingly expensive—but defeat is even more costly.

Such, then, has been the checkered course of the British bomber in recent years. What of the aircraft, and their markings?

The Vulcan

The Vulcan remains the mainstay of the long-range bomber force. The first Vulcan Mk 2 production machine flew in August 1958. The second Mk 2, also all white with black serials, was the first to have an enlarged tail cone containing ECM gear featured by subsequent Mk 2s and the Mk 1A. Vulcan 1 production ended in April 1959 with XH532. In May 1959, XA903 first flew with modifications to permit the carriage of Blue Steel in her belly and soon after the first Mk 1A, XA895. Other early aircraft modified to Mk 1A standard included XA904, 906, 909, 910 and XH475, 477, 478, 481, 482, 483, 497, 498, 500, 501, 502, 503, 505 and 506. These entered squadron service in 1961. A typical example of August 1960 was XH505, one of the first Vulcans with pale blue-pale red anti-flash markings and blue fin serial. XH483, another Mk 1A, was in use in September 1961 with 50 Squadron, and carried the Lincoln Arms tail motif in pale red and pale yellow colours.

No 83 Squadron became the first squadron to equip with the Mk 2, when XH558 in white finish with pale roundels, etc, left Avros for Waddington on July 1 1960. She soon acquired 83 Squadron's badge on her nose and the pale style of Lincoln Arms on her fin. No 83 Squadron passed its Mk 1s to 44 Squadron which re-formed in August 1960 and later flew Mk 1As. The second Mk 2 squadron was No 617, and upon its re-equipment it passed its Mk 1s to No 50 Squadron, re-formed at Waddington on August 1 1961. Meanwhile, No 27 Squadron had re-formed with Vulcan 2s at Scampton on April 1 1961.

During the summer of 1962 the first production Blue Steel stand-off bombs were delivered to 617 Squadron. Training went ahead, and in February 1963 the squadron was declared operational with Blue Steel, operational rounds being painted white. No 617 Squadron was followed first by 27 Squadron and then by 83 Squadron, making a three-squadron Wing of Blue Steel Vulcans based at Scampton.

At Coningsby Nos 9 (eg, XL356), 12 (eg, XH560) and 35 Squadron (eg, XH562) were re-formed as Vulcan 2 units in 1962, and all of their white aircraft featured pale anti-flash national identity and squadron markings.

The overall white ELR Cellulose DL 5628 finish with pale roundels and fin serials on the Vulcan 2 dated from May 6 1960, but it was many months before the entire Vulcan force had switched to pale markings which included Pale Orange instructions painted on the aircraft in a shade also with 60% reflectivity.

A typical Vulcan 1 of May 1960 was XA901 based at Waddington. She still had Bright roundels, and her Waddington station badge on the tail was grey with a red cross and gold Fleur de Lys. Fin and under-wing serials were black. The nose radome was finished in the special Goodyear 23.56S erosion-resistant coating system and appeared matt black in colour. All the undercarriage legs were in a cellulose glossy black finish, and the interior of engine bays and doors was white cellulose, whereas the steel jet efflux pipes were unpainted like the interiors of the undercarriage and bomb bay doors. Small external instruction notes were usually in 6 mm figures. The interior of the cabin was black, apart from the roof of the signaller's compartment which was grey.

During the early 1960s there was quite an assortment of markings to be seen on the Vulcans, mixtures of Bright and pale colours, etc. XJ824 in June 1961 had a dark green elephant painted on her fin, identifying her as

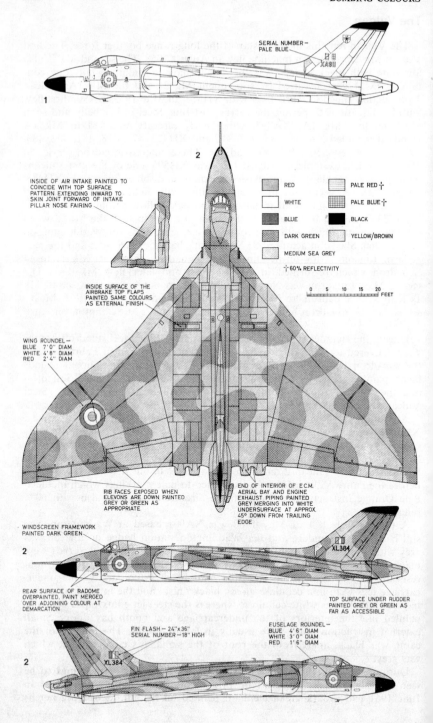

1

SERIAL NUMBER—
PALE BLUE

XA911

2

INSIDE OF AIR INTAKE PAINTED TO
COINCIDE WITH TOP SURFACE
PATTERN EXTENDING INWARD TO
SKIN JOINT FORWARD OF INTAKE
PILLAR NOSE FAIRING

RED		PALE RED ⊹
WHITE		PALE BLUE ⊹
BLUE		BLACK
DARK GREEN		YELLOW/BROWN
MEDIUM SEA GREY		

⊹—60% REFLECTIVITY

0   5   10   15   20
FEET

INSIDE SURFACE OF THE
AIRBRAKE TOP FLAPS
PAINTED SAME COLOURS
AS EXTERNAL FINISH

WING ROUNDEL—
BLUE 7'0" DIAM
WHITE 4'8" DIAM
RED   2'4" DIAM

RIB FACES EXPOSED WHEN
ELEVONS ARE DOWN PAINTED
GREY OR GREEN AS
APPROPRIATE

END OF INTERIOR OF E.C.M.
AERIAL BAY AND ENGINE
EXHAUST PIPING PAINTED
GREY MERGING INTO WHITE
UNDERSURFACE AT APPROX.
45° DOWN FROM TRAILING
EDGE

WINDSCREEN FRAMEWORK
PAINTED DARK GREEN

2

XL384

REAR SURFACE OF RADOME
OVERPAINTED. PAINT MERGED
OVER ADJOINING COLOUR AT
DEMARCATION

TOP SURFACE UNDER RUDDER
PAINTED GREY OR GREEN AS
FAR AS ACCESSIBLE

FIN FLASH— 24"x 36"
SERIAL NUMBER—18" HIGH

FUSELAGE ROUNDEL—
BLUE 4'6" DIAM
WHITE 3'0" DIAM
RED   1'6" DIAM

2

XL384

from 27 Squadron. Her roundels were pale and her fin serials pale blue, and no under-wing markings were carried. At the same time Victor XA935 of 232 OCU was still flying with Bright identity markings and black fuselage and wing serials. Vulcan 2 XJ780 of 83 Squadron, in use September 1961, had pale identity markings with blue fin serials only, yet the nose badge of 83 Squadron was in dark colours. Even in September 1962, Vulcan 1 XA896 of 230 OCU, now wearing a blue fin shield with a white rose, had Bright roundels and fin stripes with black serials.

XH562, a 35 Squadron Mk 2 recorded in June 1963, had pale identity markings and fin serials with pale yellow and pale grey winged horse's head insignia on both sides of her fin. By autumn 1963 pale roundels, etc, seem to have predominated as on XM574, a Vulcan 2 with a dark green elephant emblem of 27 Squadron on her fin. This machine was fitted to carry Blue Steel. A Waddington Mk 1A, XA906, with pale identity markings had a black outline shield with three blue Fleur de Lys emblems. Another Mk 1A, XH502, similarly marked had the normal style of Waddington station shield. A Mk 2A aircraft (the type equipped to carry Blue Steel) in use in 1963 was XL361, which carried three pale red lightning flashes on her fin denoting her allegiance to 617 Squadron. On the tail of XL426, resplendent in pale roundels, etc, was the Bright Red antler motif of 83 Squadron.

At the end of 1963 Victor 2 XL513 was busily scudding low across the countryside in company with a white Victor, both of which were being repeatedly photographed. The former was wearing what at the time seemed an amazingly complicated camouflage pattern of glossy Dark Green and Medium Sea Grey in NATO shades which looked strange on a British aircraft. An interesting feature was that she carried a Bright Red-White-Blue roundel above her port wing tip only, with Bright Type D fuselage roundels and Bright fin striping. Her fuselage serials were white. The change in markings was demanded by the decision to operate the V-Force at low level, and the upper camouflage was soon wrapped around the wing and tail leading edges to help hide the aircraft during head-on approach.

Similar camouflage was introduced on the Vulcan as Mod 2129 to Spec DTD 5580 standard and came into use about February 1964. One of the earliest machines repainted was Mk 2 XM647 which arrived at Coningsby in the new paint scheme in March 1964. An early camouflaged Mk 1A was XH478. At the time these aircraft joined their new stations, central servicing schemes were in being and so they did not acquire any squadron markings, although the Scampton aircraft had markings of the three squadrons forming their Wing applied to the nosewheel doors. The only serial carried was the customary 18-inch fin serial now applied in black.

Since 1964 there has, until recently, been very little change in Vulcan trim, although polyurethane finish has been applied to the aircraft since 1970. The Mk 1A was phased out in 1968 and camouflaged B.2s, like XL443(B.2A), XM572(Mk 2A), XM574, XM606, XM609, XM645 and XM649, have replaced the earlier versions. XM606 was carrying 44 Squadron's badge on her nosewheel door in May 1969, and in September of that year Mk 2A XL427 had the three red dayglo flashes signifying 617 Squadron applied to her fin. Some of the Vulcans were fitted with small matt black nose radomes in the

Figure 33: (*Opposite page*) 1. *Vulcan B.1A XA911 in white finish with pale anti-flash markings as recorded in September 1963 at Waddington.* 2. *Vulcan B.2, shown in the colours laid down in the Hawker Siddeley Drawing ZH903 of the Vulcan in camouflage markings. XL384 is depicted in this finish, which varied slightly from aircraft to aircraft* (Hawker Siddeley Ltd).

mid-1960s, like XM608 and XM609. In 1972 Vulcans at Waddington again started to carry the Lincoln Arms badge on their fins, as on XM653.

According to the manufacturers the latest paintwork for the Vulcan 2 is represented by Mod 2327, dated September 3 1971. By this, the Medium Sea Grey (B.S.381c/637) and the Dark Green (B.S.381c/641) are applied in matt polyurethane paint, and under surfaces are ordered to be B.S.381c/627 Light Aircraft Grey. Red and Blue roundels replace the Type D, and fin stripes are also Red and Blue. All of this Low Visibility paintwork now becomes matt, but very few aircraft had, at the time of writing, yet received the newly pre-scribed colours. An interesting feature of some Vulcans in the mid-1960s was the merging of the demarcation lines of the camouflage, but it seems to have applied to only a few aircraft. Deviations in patterning were set at plus or minus 1 inch from those laid down precisely, but in reality the camouflage patterns have varied more from aircraft to aircraft. It seems likely that more aircraft will carry squadron or unit markings, and XL320, an ex-Blue Steel machine, now of 230 OCU, was carrying that unit's white fin disc with blue waves and yellow sword on her fin in September 1972.

The Victor

From XH613 the Victors were delivered as B.Mk 1A which, like the Vulcan 1A differed from earlier aircraft mainly by having more sophisticated radar and ECM gear. The B.1A entered service with XV Squadron in mid-1960 and by September of that year examples were with No 57 Squadron (re-formed on January 1 1959) and included XH614 and XH619 with Bright roundels and black fuselage serials only and XH651 with pale roundels and blue fuselage serials. These aircraft carried a blue and red phoenix tail badge based on the squadron badge. XH593, used by 57 Squadron in 1962, had pale identity and squadron markings. No 55 Squadron, formed on September 1 1960, also used Mk 1As like XH650 with pale identity markings and a pale blue hand and spear emblem on her fin in July 1962. At this time a B.Mk 1A of XV Squadron with pale trim was XH651, and Mk 1 XA933 in like finish had a pale red 'A' on her fin—she was in the hands of 232 OCU.

Like the Vulcan 2, the Victor 2 had enlarged engine air intakes and in-creased wing span. Retractable intakes on the rear fuselage led to emergency power turbo-alternators, and a duct in the extended fin root led to a cooling system.

XH668, the first Mk 2, flew on February 20 1959 and was destroyed in an accident off South Wales on August 20 1959. The prototype exhibited a unique feature—it carried no national markings whatsoever, and had no external serials. The second machine had pale roundels and fin flashes only, but there was talk at the time of applying pale blue serials above the wings.

Production Mk 2s began to leave the line late in 1960, but not until Nov-ember 2 1961 was the first Victor 2 (XL188), all white and with pale identity markings and blue serials, placed in RAF hands. This joined a special Victor 2 Trials Unit set up at Cottesmore, part of 232 OCU.

On February 1 1962 No 139 Squadron re-formed to operate Victor 2s from Wittering, followed by 100 Squadron, formed on May 1. The aircraft al-located to the squadrons all wore an overall white finish with pale roundels and fin flashes, with pale serials only on their rear fuselages. XL232 in May 1962 bore only 139 Squadron's badge on her nose, but a few weeks later XL190 was seen with a fin motif. This consisted of a pale blue disc with a white moon, white axe head and a red axe handle. 'JAMAICA' was in pale blue beneath the disc, and the squadron retained such markings until its aircraft were camouflaged. No 100 Squadron settled for a pale blue or pale red fin disc with a white skull and bones painted upon it. XM717 had a red disc.

The final Victor 2, XM718, was delivered in May 1953. Subsequently, Handley Page modified many of the Victor 2s into B.2R with provision for Blue Steel and fitted with Kuchemann drag-reducing fairings on the wing trailing edges. These bulges housed *window* storage areas. Tail cones now sprouted an array of small blisters to help accommodate more sophisticated ECM apparatus. Delivery of Blue Steel aircraft began in September 1963, the first being XL164, XL162 and XM511.

In January 1964 XL513 arrived at Wittering in Dark Green-Medium Grey camouflage with anti-flash roundels but Bright fin flashes and white fuselage serials. Its display to the Press soon after was the first public indication that the V-Force had switched to a low-level rôle. When fitted with Blue Steel the Victor 2s were designated Mk 2BS, and further camouflaged examples at Wittering early in 1964 had black fuselage serials and Bright roundels sited one above the port wing tip and the others on the fuselage. The two squadrons pooled their aircraft before any squadron markings were applied, and as a station marking adopted a rampant yellow Stamford Lion on such aircraft as XL192, XL512 and XM717. These markings remained until the squadrons were disbanded in 1968.

Before the Valiants were grounded in 1965 flight refuelling trials with the Victor were under way, mainly to fit them for the refuelling of fighter aircraft. XA918 served as prototype, fitted with a pod and drogue beneath each outer wing. After Nos 10 and XV Squadrons disbanded in 1964 their aircraft were returned to the manufacturers, still in their overall white finish with pale roundels and markings, to be converted into tanker aircraft. Six of them were hastily modified to have two refuelling points, to take the place of the retired Valiants. Re-designated B(K)1A, the first, XH620, appeared in April 1965 in Dark Green and Medium Grey finish with white under surfaces and Bright roundels, as placed on other V-bombers. Fuselage serials were black. These tankers were delivered to No 55 Squadron at Marham in mid-1965. This squadron had been operating Victor 1As in the low-level bombing rôle. The unit quickly worked up and was operational in late 1965.

In November 1965, the first three-point tanker, Victor K.1 XA937, which unlike the earlier tankers had no bombing capability, was first flown. In February 1966 No 57 Squadron began to equip with three-point refuellers and further examples were also converted from remaining 1As as Victor K.1As. No 214 Squadron, which had used Valiant tankers, re-formed at Marham on October 1 1966 with Victor K.1s. Also an assortment of bomber and tanker Victors equipped the Tanker Training Flight whose aircraft became identified by red letters TTF outlined white painted on their fins, as on XH592, a B.1A in use September 1968.

Victor tankers of 55 Squadron have worn a blue arm and spear outlined white or painted on a white fin disc. No 57 Squadron first wore '57' in red outlined white and later had '57' in red on a white fin disc, as on XA926. Victor tankers of 214 Squadron have carried two red bird motifs joined around a red nightjar based on the squadron badge. Later a dayglo variant of this was adopted with white trim as on XA939. 232 OCU now carries its unit number in white on a red fin disc.

Above their wing tips some Victor tankers have an area painted yellow for easy identity. Beneath the wings black line-up markings have been worn, on either side of the refuelling pods. This and dayglo trim, along with matt black markings beneath the fuselage, are all to aid the receiving aircraft to line up accurately on the tanker.

The Valiant

The start of the 1960s witnessed the gradual application of pale national identity and squadron markings to the Valiant force. During 1960 they were uncommon, the norm being more represented by aircraft with Bright Type D roundels and dark squadron colours, like WZ405 with 207 Squadron's winged lion on her tail. After the change to pale roundels and blue serials quite a number of Valiants continued to fly with dark tail squadron markings, like XD863 of 90 Squadron whose blue serials were repeated on the nosewheel doors. Some of 138's aircraft also retained dark fin markings, like XD821 and XD875. Machines with pale squadron identity trim and pale national insignia included WP218 of 49 Squadron in use March 1962 and WP219 of 207 Squadron in use a year later. A white Valiant of 232 OCU with pale roundels was XD866 which was in use September 1964. Valiants of 148 Squadron seem not have worn any squadron markings, apart from the unit badge on the port side of the nose on aircraft with pale roundels, like WZ393 in use September 1963.

First to operate Valiant tankers was No 214 Squadron at Marham. Its white aircraft carried on their fins a red and later pale red twin bird motif around the nightjar of the same colour, pale in the case of XD816 with pale roundels, etc. Others similarly marked included XD860, XD858 and XD870, all in use in 1962. Usually 214's Valiants had their squadron badge on the port side of the nose. Generally, Valiants did not carry their blue serials on the nose-wheel doors. The drum refuelling gear was carried in the bomb bay of the tanker Valiants, as in XD870 which was first used wearing black serials and Bright roundels. Tanker trials were conducted with WZ376 and WZ390, the latter as receiver.

Early in 1964 the Valiant bomber force, like the other V-bombers, began to fly aircraft camouflaged Dark Green-Medium Sea Grey-White with Bright Type D roundels and tail flashes. No squadron markings were carried, as in the cases of WP221 in use at Marham in camouflage in March 1964 and usually flown by 207 Squadron, XD828 Marham-based in 1964 and XD821 of 232 OCU.

Canberras of the 1960s

Bomber Command gave up its last operational Canberra when 35 Squadron retired its B.2s on September 11 1961. Only No 231 OCU was left, operating a mixture of B.2s, PR.3s and T.4s. Mostly they were silver like WH914, WJ728 and T.Mk 4 conversion WJ677. The T.4s, when delivered initially, were all silver with yellow T. bands and they retained 8 inch serials for many years. An assortment of dayglo training bands was applied from 1958, and the positioning of dayglo trim varied considerably at any one time. In 1968 the Canberras of 231 OCU (apart from PR 3s) were painted Light Aircraft Grey overall and carried strips of red dayglo mostly 8 or 9 inches wide and applied to the sides of the nose and fuselage, to the fins and above and below the wing tips, as on B.2 WJ677 and T.4 WT480. Two-foot black serials were normally carried, also black under-wing serials in the standard size for Canberras. On their fins aircraft of the unit now displayed its cheetah badge, which some machines like WJ728 also wore on a smaller white shield on the starboard side of the nose. At various times aircraft of the unit displayed a white individual letter on the black anti-dazzle panel.

Overseas, the progression of Canberra finish was from silver to Dark Green and Dark Sea Grey upper surfaces with the lower surfaces remaining silver. Serial numbers, usually 2 feet high, were black on silver aircraft, like WJ362 of 45 Squadron whose blue camel with red wings was applied to a white fin disc. On camouflaged aircraft the 2-foot fuselage serials were applied in Glossy White, although there were the inevitable exceptions, such as Canberras with 8-inch serials, also white. Squadrons originally decorated tip tanks and fins with unit markings. Later these were also applied, by some units, to the flanks of the fuselage roundels. Again no overall pattern applied. Indeed, squadrons in Cyprus were sometimes to be seen with a variety of markings on their aircraft. These included adaptations of the Akrotiri station badge featuring a flamingo, and the style of this varied in shape as well as colour. Some of the individual unit markings are portrayed on the end papers of this book.

Two refined interdictor variants of the Canberra appeared in 1960, the B.15 and B.16, both of which were conversions from Canberra 6s previously used by the Coningsby squadrons or in the Middle East. The first of 30 B.15s began to appear in their new guise in the spring of 1960. They were finished in Dark Green-Dark Sea Grey-Silver with 2-foot white serials and black under-wing serials. Among the earliest machines were WH955, WH957, WH970 and WH984. The B.Mk 15 featured revised radio gear and an F.95 camera in the nose. In addition to its 6,000 lb internal bomb load it could carry a 1,000 lb bomb beneath each wing or a Microcell rocket pod, trials for which had been undertaken on B.Mk 8 WT333. The first B.16 wearing similar colouring appeared later in 1960, the initial conversion being WT302. It differed little from the B.6 and also served in Cyprus. Among the users of the B.15 was 32 Squadron, WH966 wearing the blue and white stripes of the squadron across its fin flanking a white disc bearing the squadron motif.

Canberra 8 intruders in Germany initially wore Dark Green-Dark Sea Grey-Black glossy camouflage with 2-foot white fuselage serials and squadron markings as described in Appendix 6. XM268 of 16 Squadron was typical in basic colouring, and had the unit's white nose disc with crossed keys and the black fuselage band linking the roundels and outlined by a 3-inch wide yellow band. The nose disc had an outside diameter of 2 feet, the white being surrounded by a 1-inch wide blue rim, when recorded in September 1959. A year later WT368 of 88 Squadron was noted as having a medium brown band placed as on 16 Squadron's machines, and she also had a yellow and black serpent motif on her fin.

In the mid-1960s a gradual change took place during which under surfaces on the B.(I)8s were repainted silver. On some aircraft, like XM276 of 3 Squadron which carried that unit's fin band and cockatrice motif, the silver covered the same areas as the black had previously. Others had the silver terminated at the 60-degree tangent, as on XM278 fitted with a black belly gun pack when seen in May 1968. This aircraft had a black 'O' on her fin with 14 Squadron's white and red disc and yellow wings painted above it. On the nose was the squadron's white and blue diamond marking inherited from its Hunter days. One of that unit's black under-surfaced aircraft, noted

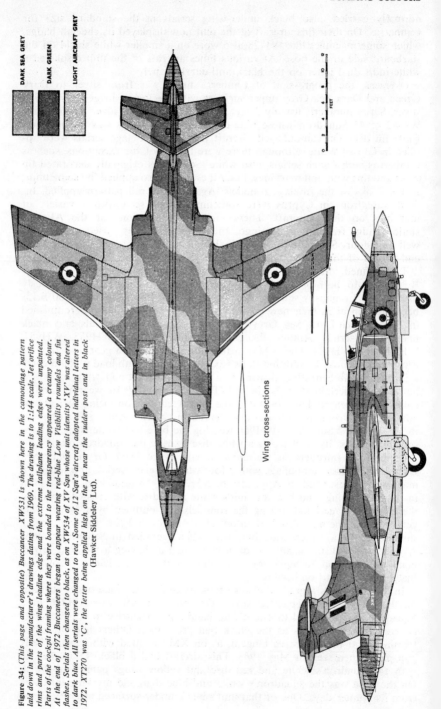

DARK SEA GREY

DARK GREEN

LIGHT AIRCRAFT GREY

FEET

Wing cross-sections

Figure 34: (This page and opposite) Buccaneer XW531 is shown here in the camouflage pattern laid down in the manufacturer's drawings dating from 1969. The drawing is to 1:144 scale. Jet orifice rims and parts of the wing leading edge and the extreme tailplane leading edge were unpainted. Parts of the cockpit framing where they were bonded to the transparency appeared a creamy colour. At the end of 1972 Buccaneers began to appear wearing red-blue Low Visibility roundels and fin flashes. Serials then changed to black, as on XW534 of XV Sqn whose unit identity 'XV' was altered to dark blue. All serials were changed to red. Some of 12 Sqn's aircraft adopted individual letters in 1972. XT270 was 'C', the letter being applied high on the fin near the rudder post and in black (Hawker Siddeley Ltd).

256

BOMBING COLOURS

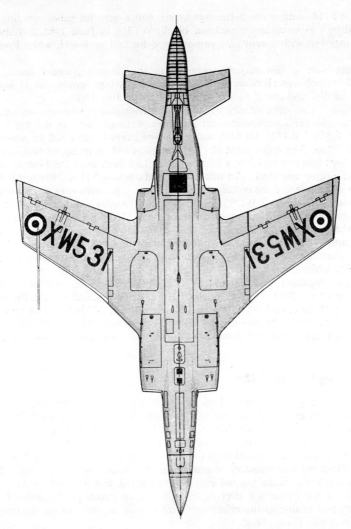

in May 1965 with only the squadron's tail marking above a white 'A', was
XM245.

White serials at first were worn on the silver under-surfaced aircraft, but
by 1968 many of the Canberras thus coloured had acquired black serials.
Before final withdrawal of the B.(I)8 in June 1972 some of the machines had
acquired Light Aircraft Grey under surfaces, as on XK952 in use May 1969
and then wearing the nose crossed keys insignia and yellow-black fuselage
band of 16 Squadron and a 2-foot black fuselage serial.

Canberra B(I)6 interdictors of 213 Squadron acquired Dark Green and
Dark Sea Grey camouflage on their silver finish in 1957, as on WT324 in use
November 1957 and then wearing an 8-inch serial which was general for
these aircraft. WT322, however, was one of the inevitable exceptions with a
2-foot white serial, and was flying in this state in February 1958. At the same

time WT314, with a small fuselage serial, had a grey fin panel carrying 213 Squadron's Hornet device outlined black. WT316 in June 1965 had similar markings but with a normally camouflaged fin and an 8-inch white fuselage serial.

There were a few major exceptions to the general intruder finish, like WT333 which was all silver with 2-foot black fuselage serials and 45 Squadron's fin disc and camel motif, when recorded in July 1960.

Unusual Canberra markings, highly individualistic schemes on aircraft generally in use for experimental purposes, were plentiful in the 1950s and 1960s. B.Mk 2 WJ725, for instance, was white overall with a red fin panel and red tailplane. The outer third of each wing was red on its upper surfaces and the 2-foot fuselage serial was black. WJ725 had been used for Folland light-weight ejector seat trials. An interesting B.Mk 6 was XH567, the top half of which was silver and the remainder glossy black. Tip tanks were dayglo orange in June 1961. B.Mk 2 WD953 with wing tip cameras exhibited a most odd appearance in 1961. She retained her original Medium Grey upper surfaces but where once she had been black she was now white. Her fin remained black and WD953 appeared in white on a black under-wing rectangle. XH568, white overall, had a red dayglo nose with a long probe extending from it. WH876, white overall, had an in-flight refuelling probe and other all-white machines included WH723 and WH727. WH669 'ARIES 4', an all-silver machine of the RAF Flying College, had red wing tips and a red tailplane at the start of 1960, and WH902 was similarly painted. WJ565 was an all-black Mk 2 fitted with a belly gun pack for trial purposes. WK135, all white, had a 2-foot black serial and a red nose during the time she was used for Fire-streak trials.

Preparing for the 1970s

It says much for Air Staff thinking during the late 1940s that the principal bombers they chose then should still be viable propositions in the 1970s. This is particularly true of the Vulcan, which looks like soldiering on well into this decade. Ideally, TSR.2 should have taken its place by now. Instead it was cancelled and, coupled with the loss of the F-111 order, added up to a blow from which recovery might never be made. With the Multi-Role Combat Aircraft some ground may be recaptured, but it seems unlikely that the Royal Air Force will ever again have a deep penetration bomber force. This in part is due to the effectiveness of missile defence, likely to continue to improve in years ahead.

One surprisingly effective outcome of the troubles of the 1960s was the decision to order a small number of Buccaneers for the RAF. For many years the Air Force considered askance the thought of adapting a naval aeroplane to its needs. In service the low-attack Buccaneer has been seen to be a particularly useful addition to the armoury, especially for any possible maritime operation. Now it also equips Nos XV and 16 Squadrons in Germany where it has an overland strike/attack/reconnaissance rôle. Its initial employment began in October 1969, when No 12 Squadron at Honington was equipped. This unit, which became operational in July 1970, flies Buccaneer 2s bearing a brown-white-black fox's head on a grey base on the sides of engine intakes, as on Mk 2A XV350. Basic finish of the Buccaneer is Dark Green-Dark Sea Grey-Light Aircraft Grey with Type D roundels sited above and below each wing tip and on the fuselage sides. White 8-inch fuselage

35 *Canberra B.(I)6 WT317 in Dark Green-Dark Sea Grey-black and wearing an early form of 213 Sqn's marking on her fin.*

36 *Canberra WT314, also of 213 Sqn, wears silver under surfaces and has a later style of 213 Sqn's fin marking, still yellow and black but with white wings.*

37 *Standard grey-green-black finish is visible on Canberra B.(I)8 WT366 of 59 Sqn, photographed in August 1960.*

38 *Canberra B.(I)8 XH208 in Dark Green-Dark Sea Grey-silver finish wears the green band 3 Sqn across her fin and the cockatrice device on a white disc.*

39 *Canberra B.(I)8 XM268 of 3 Sqn whose black and yellow fuselage band she carries. The squadron badge is on the nose. Photographed shortly before the final withdrawal of the Canberra from an operational bomber rôle in June 1972*

140 *A formation of Buccaneer S.2 bombers of XV Sqn, with white 'XV' on their fins as unit identity. Machines a* *XW541, XW530, XW540 and XW542, serials being white* (Ministry of Defence).

141 *The present style of low-visibility marking carried by Buccaneer XW534 of XV Sqn (XV in red on the fin). T* *finish is now matt, and national identity markings red and blue. Part of the radome has been over-painted* (Ministry Defence).

serials are worn, repeated in black beneath the wings in the manner illustrated by the diagram on page 257. In recent months there has been a slow introduction of Blue and Red roundels in all positions and red and blue fin stripes. These roundels are coupled with matt finish on the aircraft.

In retrospect

Looking back over the changes in the RAF's bomber force since the mid-1930s development at peak periods is surely amazing. The Wellington of 1932 origin was still operational in 1945—yet within six years the Valiant was flying. Only nine years parted the last lumbering Heyford from the first Canberra. The last Virginia was doing her rounds over Henlow at the same time as the Lancaster and Mosquito appeared. In a strong wind the 'Ginny' almost hovered, and one of my youthful memories was the momentary sight of a Virginia being blown backwards. What a contrast the Mosquito provided, sleek and so fast and agile. When the first V2 slammed into southern England one's immediate reaction was to feel that the day of the manned bomber was finished. This has not really proven to be the case. It is more likely that the surface-to-air guided weapon may have sealed its fate. Bombers of the past were generally large, multi-engined aeroplanes, yet some of today's bombers are overgrown fighters with a crew of two or even one, able to pack a devastating punch, as much as or even more than 500 Lancasters.

Two turning points stand out vividly from the last 30 years. One is the successful post-war introduction of the jet engine which was applied somewhat late to the bomber but most skilfully in the British designs of the 1940s. Undoubtedly, the other was the Mosquito concept that hurried ahead of official thinking, the marriage of high speed to the unarmed bomber. This combination led to the Canberra and also to the V-bombers.

Ironically the important thing about the bomber of today is that it should never roar into global action. It remains to be seen whether mankind is wise enough to control the bomber's horrific potential.

Development of military aircraft is now so costly that fewer and fewer types and examples are likely to be produced. Interest seems likely to settle more and more upon aircraft of distant decades. None of us who enjoyed peering over the fence at Feltwell's Harrows, or thrilled to the sight of the first Wimpeys and Blenheims, seem to have considered that one day many people who could only read of such things or delight in the relatively few photographs taken of them would view them with such eager interest. Indeed they did make the pulse of any enthusiast run fast in a manner modern aeroplanes never seem to do. To stand at the end of the runway, as 7 Squadron's Stirlings roared away to some distant town, only a name on a map, in an age when few had travelled, was unforgettable. To gaze excitedly at a formation of slow-moving Harrows or skim the Fens in a Lanc—these were destined to be memories of an Air Force before professionalism had taken over. I, for one, am glad I was old enough to fully appreciate it all.

o

APPENDIX 1: Airframe serial numbers of Royal Air Force bombers, 1937-73

Armstrong Whitworth Whitley I: Prototypes K4586-87. Production: K7183-7216.
Armstrong Whitworth Whitley II: K7217-7262.
Armstrong Whitworth Whitley III: K8936-9015.
Armstrong Whitworth Whitley IV: K9016-9048.
Armstrong Whitworth Whitley IVA: K9049-9055.
Armstrong Whitworth Whitley V: N1345-1394, N1405-1444, N1459-1508, N1521-1528, P4930-4974, P4980-5029, P5040-5065, P5070-5112, T4130-4179, T4200-4239, T4260-4299, T4320-4339, Z6461-6510, Z6552-6586, Z6624-6673, Z6720-6764, Z6793-6842, Z6862-6881, Z6931-6959, Z6970-6980, Z9119, Z9125-9134, Z9140-9168, Z9188-89, Z9200-9232, Z9274-9323, Z9361-63, Z9384-90, Z9419-9443, Z9461-9490, Z9510-15, AD665-714, BD189-238, BD252-296, BD346-395, BD411-422, BD435-445, BD493-512, BD530-560, BD626-639, BD659-674, EB283-313, EB337-367, EB384-391, EB402-410, LA763-793, LA818-856, LA868-899, LA914-951.
Many of the Tiger-engined Whitleys served as trainers during the war, both for bombing and gunnery and for paratroop work, and wore trainer colouring. A considerable number of Mk Vs were converted into glider tugs and some for use by the special operations squadrons.
Avro Anson I: Ansons served in bomber squadrons and at bomber OTUs. Indeed, some of the bomber squadrons of the 1930s had them as primary equipment. In OTUs they were generally used for navigational training. Some later served with Training Command. Immediately prior to the war some bomber squadrons specialising in training had Ansons as part of their main equipment, again for navigational training purposes. Finish of the aircraft with 'K' serials was mostly silver, whereas the 'Ns' had Dark Green-Dark Earth-Night camouflage with grey codes. Some of the OTU Ansons featured this finish well into the war, whereas others wore standard yellow under surfaces. Codes were usually red on the bomber OTU aircraft, but there were many anomalies. Representative Ansons, and the squadrons with which they served, are as follows:
7 Sqn: N5005, 5006, 18, 25-26. **35 Sqn:** N5264-65. **44 Sqn:** N4988-89, N4995, N4997-5001. **49 Sqn:** N5093-94, N5096-97. **50 Sqn:** N5079, N5192-94, N5196. **51 Sqn:** K6271-6283. **52 Sqn:** N5027-34, N5074-75. **58 Sqn:** K6270-6283. **61 Sqn:** K6263-66, K6269, K6303-6309. **63 Sqn:** N5035-37, N5070-73, N5076-77, N5103. **75 Sqn:** K6322, N5010, N5012-14, N5017, N5019-24. **83 Sqn:** N5082, N5182-84, N5186. **97 Sqn:** N5002, N5004-5011. **104 Sqn:** N5114-17, N5156-59. **106 Sqn:** N5152-54, N5166. **108 Sqn:** N5115-16, N5156-58, N5167-69, N5171-74, N5176-77. **144 Sqn:** K6263-6269, N5080, N5187-89, N5191. **148 Sqn:** N5078-5085, N5186, N5188, N5194, N5209. **207 Sqn:** N5266-67. **215 Sqn:** K6290-6302.
A very considerable number of Ansons served at bomber OTUs, the following list merely giving some examples used: **10 OTU:** N5142. **11 OTU:** N5115. **12 OTU:** N5013. **14 OTU:** N5259. **15 OTU:** N5020. **16 OTU:** N5113. **17 OTU:** N5112. **19 OTU:** AX290. **22 OTU:** N5111. **24 OTU:** AX260. **25 OTU:** N5176. **26 OTU:** N5152.
Avro Lancaster I: Prototypes: BT308, DG595. Production: L7527-49, L7565-84, R5482-5517, R5537-76, R5603-40, R5658-5703, R5724-63, R5842-68, R5888-5917, W4102-40 (W4114 converted to Mk III prototype), W4154-4201, W4230-79, W4301-40, W4355-84, W4761-4800, W4815-64, W4879-4095, W4918-67, W4980-82, DV277-282, DV291-97, DV299-309, DV311-12, DV324-345, DV359-382, DV385-94, DV396-407, ED303-334, ED347-396 (except Mk IIIs DV362, 371, 378, 383, 387, 388, 390, 393, 395, 396), HK535-579, HK593-628, HK644-664, HK679-710, HK728-773, HK787-806, LL740-58, LL771-813, LL826-67, LL880-923, LL935-977, LM100-142, LM156-92, LM205-43, LM257-96, LM301-310, ME554-96, ME613-650, ME663-704, ME717-759, ME773-814, ME827-868, NF906-939, NF952-99, NG113-49, NG162-206, NG218-59, NG263-308, NG321-67, NG379-421, NG434-69, NG485-503, NN694-726, NN739-786, NN798-816, NX548-589, NX603-610, PA158-98, PA214-39, PA252-88, PA303-51, PA365-96, PA410-52, PA473-78, PA509, PD198-239, PD252-

296, PD309-49, PD361-404, PD417-44, PP663-95, PP713-58, PP772-92, RA500-47, RA560-607, RA623-27, RA787-806, SW296-297.

Avro Lancaster B.1 (FE): TW647-671, TW858-873, TW878-911, TW915-29, SW298-316.

Avro Lancaster B.1 (Special): PB995-998, PD112-139.

Avro Lancaster II: Prototypes: DT810 and DT812. Production: DS601-635, DS647-692, DS704-741, DS757-797, DS813-852, LL617-653, LL666-704, LL716-739.

Avro Lancaster III: W4983-5012, DV155-202, DV217-47, DV263-76, DV283-90, DV298, DV310, DV383-84, DV395, ED408-33, ED467-504, ED520-69, ED583-631, ED645-68, ED688-737, ED749-83, ED799-842, ED856-88, ED904-53, ED967-99 (except for Mk I ED series: 409, 411-12, 414, 418, 420, 422, 425, 430, 436, 439, 443, 446-47, 451, 498, 521-22, 525, 528, 533, 537, 548, 550, 552, 554, 567, 569, 586, 588, 591, 594, 600, 601, 604, 610, 615, 622, 631, 650, 661, 692, 703, 715, 732, 735, 749, 751, 754, 755, 757-58, 761-63, 766, 769, 770, 773-74, 777-78, 780-82). Modified for Dams raids: ED765, 817, 825, 864, 865, 886, 887, 906, 909, 910, 915, 918, 921, 924, 925, 927, 929, 932, 933, 934, 936, 937. JA672-718, JA843-76, JA892-941, JA957-81, JB113-55, JB174-91, JB216-43, JB275-320, JB344-76, JB398-424, JB453-488, JB526-67, JB592-614, JB637-84, JB699-748, LM311-346, LM359-95, LM417-48, LM450-93, LM508-52, LM569-99, LM615-58, LM671-97, LM713-56 (of which LM448, 485, 489, 492, 695 were converted to Mk I), ND324-68, ND380-425, ND438-79, ND492-538, ND551-97, ND613-58, ND671-715, ND727-68, ND781-826, ND836-82, PA964, PB112-58, PB171-213, PB226-67, PB280-308, PB341-85, PB397-438, PB450-90, PB504-42, PB554-96, PB609-53, PB666-708, PB721-68, PB780-823, PB836-81, PB893-936, PB949-94. RE115-40, RE153-188, RE200-222, RE225-26 (some conversions to GR III), SW283-295 (all converted to ASR III and all except SW290-92 subsequently converted to GR III), SW319-45, SW358-77 (of which SW319-320, 324-27, 329-30, 334, 336-38, 344, 361-77 were converted to ASR III and most later to GR III), TX263-273.

NB: The listing here by Mks I/III is based upon the state of the aircraft when they were delivered. In service many engine changes were made thereby converting aircraft from Mk I to III and vice-versa. In some cases Lancasters are known to have been flown with mixed versions of the Merlin.

Avro Lancaster VI conversions: DV170, DV199, JB675, JB713, ND418, ND479, ND558, ND673, ND784, NG465.

Avro Lancaster I (VII interim): NX548-610.

Avro Lancaster B.VII (FE): NX611-48, NX661-703, NX715-58, NX770-94, RT670-699. Prototype Mk VII: NN801 (normal bomber finish).

Avro Lancaster B.X: FM100-299, KB700-999. (Some returned to Canada and modified into maritime reconnaissance aircraft.)

Avro Lincoln B.I: RA628-655, RE227-268, RE281-288.

Avro Lincoln B.II: RA656-658, RA661-693, RA709-724, RE289-325, RE338-370, RE393-424, RF329-332, RF335-370, RF383-427, RF440-485, RF498-539, RF553-577, SS715-718, SX923-958, SX970-993, WD122-133, WD141-149.

Avro Manchester: Prototypes: L7246, L7247. Production: L7276-7325, L7373-7402, L7415-7434, L7453-7497, L7515-7526, R5768-5797, R5829-5841.

Avro Vulcan: Prototypes: VX770 and VX777; Mk I XA889 et seq, XH475 et seq (conversions to B. Mk 1A, eg, XH481, XH483). Vulcan B. 2/2A from XH533. Others from XJ782, XL317, XM569.

Boeing Fortress I: AN518-537 (marked AM518-537 in error).

Boeing Fortress IIA: SR376-389 ex USAAF, eg, SR376 (ex 42-3177), SR378 (ex 42-30241), SR385 (ex 42-30986).

Boeing Fortress III: HB761-793, HB795-796, HB799-803, HB805, HB815-820, KH998-999, KJ100-127.

Boeing Washington B.I: WF434-448, WF490-514, WF545-574, WW342-355, WZ966-968.

Bristol Blenheim I: All built and delivered as bombers, but many converted to Mk IF fighters with the exception of these aircraft: K7033-43, 45-47, 49-50, 52-58, 60-64, 66-82, 84, 86, 89, 93-103, 105-13, 115-16, 119, 121, 127-129, 131, 134, 137-138,

141-142, 144-155, 157-158, 161-164, 167-168, 170-171, 173-174, 176-182; L1097-
1101, 103-104, 107-108, 111-112, 114, 116, 118, 120, 126-127, 129, 131-134, 136-137,
171, 174, 176, 180, 182, 184, 187, 199, 1201-1205, 208-211, 213-221, 225, 227-228,
230-231, 234, 238-239, 242-247, 249-250, 252, 254-255, 258-260, 262-264, 266-268,
271, 273-276, 280, 282-283, 287-288, 293-294, 298, 1301-304, 306-307, 309-319,
321-323, 325, 329, 331-333, 338-339, 341-355, 358-359, 362-366, 368-369, 376, 378-
396, 1400, 1402, 1405, 407, 410-417, 421, 425, 427, 430-432, 434-435, 437, 441-446,
479-483, 486-487, 490-492, 495-496, 498-499, 1520, 1526-546. **NB:** From L1447
fighter conversions were delivered as such and not as bombers. (L1484, 85, 88-89,
93, 97 were diverted to Turkey.) L4817-4824, L4903, L4909-928, L4931, 32, 34,
L6594, 96, 98, 600, 606, 620-625, 627-635, 647-650, 653-670, 72, 74, 92-95, L6746-
749, 6751, 753-54, L6757-773, 775, 783-785, 793-796, 800, 809-811. (L6696-6708 and
L6713-6718 to Roumania; L6813-814, L6817-819, L6821-834 to Yugoslavia.)
L8362-366, 374-399, 401-406, 433-437, 440-449, 452-469, 471-482, 8500-507, 510-514,
516-548, 597-612, 615, 618-619, 662-664, 666-668, 671, 673, 682, 683, 689, 721
(L8619-20, L8622-230, L8632, L8652-54 to Roumania).
Bristol Blenheim IV: Aircraft as bombers (ie, not converted to Mk IVF fighters):
L4825-4902, L8732-761, L8776-8800, L8827-839, 843-876, L9020-024, L9027,
L9029-9044, L9170-175, L9177-188, 190-194, 204-218, 237-251, 253-258, 263-273,
294-298, 300-301, 303-312, 314-323, 325-336, 338-342, 375-391, 398-400, 402-
403, 410-422, 458-477; N3522, 532, 535, 536-538, 544-545, 551-575, 578-594,
598, 3613-3631; N6140-174, N6176-6220, N6223-6232, N6234-6342; P4826-828,
838-864, 898-901, 903-909, 912-914, 917-920, 923-927; (P4810-11, 15-16, 21-22
diverted to Greece.) P6885-890, 893-896, 899-902, 905-934, 951, 954-955, 959-961;
(P6891-92, 97-98, 903-04 to Greek Air Force. P6961 used as TI aircraft for ventral
nose gun turret.) R2770-703, 778, 780-796; R3590-622, R3631-3709, R3730-3779,
R3800-3825, R3828-3838, R3840-3849, R3870-3877, R3879-3885, R3889-3919;
T1793-1802, T1813-1832, T1848-1868, T1871-1897, T1921-1940, T1956-1960,
T1985-1996, T1998, T2002-2004, T2031-2080, T2112-2119, T2122-2126, T2132-2134,
T2137-2141, T2161-2190, T2216-2255, T2273-2292, T2318-2357, T2381-2400,
T2425-2444; V5370-5399, V5420-5428, V5435-5446, V5449, V5455-5469, V5490-
5539, V5560-5566, V5568-5570, V5572-5599, V5620-5659, V5680-5699, V5722-5727,
V5731-5733, V5739-5740, V5742-5751, V5755-5759, V5762-5763, V5766-5769,
V5790-5798, V5800, V5804-5815, V5817-5829, V5850-5895, V5897-5899, V5920-
5969, V5990-6039, V6060-6077, V6079-6099, V6120-6149, V6170-6199, V6220-
6259, V6260-6269, V6290-6339, V6360-6399, V6420-6469, V6490-6529; Z5744,
Z5749, Z5756-5758, Z5761, Z5763-5770, Z5794-5818, Z5860-5909, Z5947-5951,
Z5958-5962, Z5977-5991, Z6036-6050, Z6146-6147, Z6149-6173, Z6176, Z6185-6186,
Z6188-6191, Z6239-6243, Z6246-6253, Z6255-6278, Z6280-6283, Z6334-6341, Z6344-
6382, Z6416-6455, Z7271-7320, Z7340-7374, Z7406-7455, Z7483-7522, Z7577-
7596, Z7610-7654, Z7678-7712, Z7754-7803, Z7841-7860, Z7879-7928, Z7958-7992,
Z9533-9552, Z9572-9621, Z9647-9681, Z9706-9755, Z9792-9836.
Bristol Blenheim V: Mostly delivered as Mk VD (commonly known as Bisley); some
delivered as trainers, mainly to No 12 (P)AFU: AZ861-905, AZ922-971, AZ984-999,
BA100-118, BA132-172, BA191-215, BA228-262, BA287-336, BA365-409, BA424-
458, BA471-505, BA522-546, BA575-624, BA647-691, BA708-757, BA780-829,
BA844-888, BA907-951, BA978-999, BB100-102, BB135-184, EH310-355, 371-420,
438-474, 491-517.
Bristol Brigand B.1: Initial range of Brigand production was RH742-851, most aircraft
being built as B.Mk 1 and many converted to T.4/T.5. Those which at some
time were B.Mk 1 were RH755, 756, 757-73, 775-777, 792-796, 797 (prototype conversion to T.4), 798-832, 850-851. Second batch: VS812-816, 833-839, 854-869.
Bristol Buckingham: Prototypes: DX249, 255, 259, 266. Production: KV301-337,
remainder built as C.Mk I and some early aircraft converted to C.Mk I or into
trainers.
Consolidated Liberator II: AL505, 506, 509, 510, 511, 520, 525, 526, 534, 538, 540, 542,
544, 546, 548, 549, 554, 560, 561, 564, 565, 566, 574, 577, 579, 581, 582, 585, 588, 595,
616, 624, 635. These aircraft are known to have been used in bombing rôles. Some

were converted to C.Mk II, and many in the 'AL' range were used in a GR rôle.

Consolidated Liberator B.IV: TS519-20, 525-26, 528, 531-32, TT336, TT340.

Consolidated Liberator B.VI: BZ960, 962, 965, 976-78, 980, 982-83, 989-90, 992-93, 996-98; EV812-17, 820, 822, 825-26, 828, 838-39, 841, 843-47, 849-52, 954-55, 857, 859-60, 862, 865, 867-68, 870, 875-76, 900-18, 920-32, 934, 937-38, 940-41, 944, 946, 949, 951-52, 957-71, 973-84, 989-91, 993, 999; EW138-207, 215, 219-250, 253-87; KG823-46, 871-94, 919-31, 933-34, 937-42, 967-78; KH100-22, 147-51, 155-76, 203-18, 239-58, 269-84, 309-20, 323, 325-28, 349-68, 386, 389-408; KK229-36, 243-48, 269-88, 301-20, 343-62; KL352-88, 391-93, 473, 475-76, 478-79, 481-89, 491-92, 494-95, 499, 501, 512-13, 515-16, 521, 523-31, 534, 536-38, 540-41, 545-49, 552, 556-57, 560, 563-64, 569, 571-601, 603, 611-17, 619-30, 632-33, 635-39, 641-42, 644-52, 654-55, 657-58, 663-67, 672-73, 676, 679, 681-83, 685-89.

Consolidated Liberator B.VIII: KG848, 943-58, 960; KH238, 367-76; KL608-10, 618, 631, 634, 640, 643, 653, 656, 659-62, 668, 671, 674-75, 677-78, 680, 684; KP126, 128, 130, 132, 134, 136, 138, 140.

de Havilland Mosquito prototype: W4050.

de Havilland Mosquito PRU/Bomber Conversion Type (or B.Mk IV srs i): W4064-72.

de Havilland Mosquito B.IV srs ii: DK284-303, DK308-333, DK336-339; (DK324 became PR VIII then B.Mk IX.) DZ311-320, 340-388, 404-442, 458-497, 515-559, 575-618, 630-652, except for PR VIII DZ342, 364, 404, 424 and NF XVs DZ366, 385, 409, 417. Conversion to PR IV: DZ411, 419, 431, 438, 459, 466, 473, 480, 487, 494, 517, 523, 527, 532, 538, 544, 549, 553, 576, 580, 588, 596, 600, 604. Modified to carry 4,000 lb bomb: DZ534, 594, 599, 606, 608, 611, 630, 631, 632, 633, 636, 637, 638, 639, 640, 641, 642, 643, 644, 646, 650. DZ540 converted into PR XVI prototype.

de Havilland Mosquito B.V: W4057 (also served as bomber prototype).

de Havilland Mosquito B.IX: LR475-77, LR495-513; ML896-920, ML921-924; MM237, 238, 241.

de Havilland Mosquito B.XVI: ML925-942, 956-999; MM112-156, 169-179, 181-205, 219-226; PF379-415, 428-469, 481-511, 515-526, 538-579, 592-619; RV295-326, 340-363. (Some conversions to TT 39.)

de Havilland Mosquito B.35: RS699-723; RV363-367; TA617-618, 633-670, 685-724; TH976-999; TJ113-158; TK591-635, 648-656; VP178-202; VR792-806. (Many conversions to TT 35.)

Douglas Boston I: AE457, 464, 470, 472 (remainder converted to fighter/intruder rôles); AX850; BB890, 905-906, 910.

Douglas Boston III bomber: W8252, 61, 71, 73, 83, 85, 87, 93, 95, 97, 8302, 15, 19, 20, 29, 30, 32, 34, 37, 47, 54, 55, 63, 68, 71, 73, 87, 88, 91 (others in range converted to intruders and Turbinlite aircraft); Z2156-59, 61-64, 66-68, 70, 72, 74-83, 87, 90-93, 95-2206, 08-09, 11-13, 15-25, 27-39, 42, 44-45, 47-69, 71-79, 81-89, 91-98, 2300-04; AH740; AL263-64, 66, 68-70, 75-76, 79-80, 84-86, 88-91, 96. Many diversions to USSR and some to SAAF in these ranges. AL668-74, 76-94, 96-706, 708, 710-31, 33-57, 59, 61-62, 65-68, 70, 73, 75, 76-83, 85-87, 90-91, 94, 97, 800-801, 05, 07-10, 12, 18 (many to USSR in this range).

Douglas Boston IIIA: BZ196-352, 355-399.

Douglas Boston IV: BZ400-568.

Douglas Boston V: BZ580-699.

Douglas Invader: KL690-691. Trials only.

English Electric Canberra: Prototypes: VN799, 813, 828, 850; VX165, 169, 177, 185.

English Electric Canberra B.2: WD929-966, 980-999, WE111-122, WF886-892, WF907-917, WG788-789, WH637-674, WH695-742, WH853-887, WH902-925, WH944, WH948-984, WJ564-582, WJ603-649, WJ674-682, WJ712-733, WJ751-753, WJ971-995, WK102-146, WK161-165, WP514-516, WV787, XA536. Numerous conversions and sales overseas. Conversion to T.11 included WH903, etc. Further conversions were to T.19.

English Electric Canberra T.4: WE188-195, WH839-850, WJ857-881, WN467 prototype, WT475-492, XH583-584, XK647, XK650. Conversions to T.Mk 4 from B.2 included WE111, WE118, WH637, WJ564, WJ679.

English Electric Canberra B.6: WJ754-784, WT205-213, WT303-325 (these B(I)Mk 6),

WT369-374, XG554, XH567-570, XK641. Conversions to B.15 and B.16 included: to B.15—WH947, WH955, WH971, WH977, WH984; to B.16—WJ773, WJ777, WJ781, WJ782, WT302 (prototype), WT372.

English Electric Canberra B(I)8 (alternative designations B.F.8 and B.L.8): WT326-348, WT362-368, XH204, XH206-226, 228, 231, 234, 241-244, XK951-952, XM244-247, XM261-279, XM936. (Some British orders diverted to foreign air forces.)

Fairey Battle: Marks were allocated according to the mark of Merlin engine fitted, but mark state differed as engine changes took place. Battles Mks II and III were the commonest variants. Prototype: K4303. Production: K7558-7712 (delivered as Mk I to K7694 then as Mk II), K7559 dual control, K7687 first to have a Merlin II, K7604 to Mk III. K9176-9675 delivered as Mk II, various conversions following. L4935-5797 batch designated Mk I but many were converted or delivered with other engines. L4935, 37, 41, 58, 59, 62 soon converted to Mk II, L4961 to Mk III. Typical delivery for later aircraft—L4991-93 Mk II, L4994 Mk III, L4995-98 Mk II, L4999 Mk III, L5500-03 Mk II, L5504-25 Mk III, L5526 Mk II, L5527-97 Mk III of which L5013, 17, 18, 23, 5135-5140 were converted to Mk V; and L5776, L5797 were converted from Mk III to Mk II. L5598-5797 were all delivered as Battle target towers. In addition there were diversions to fighter squadrons, eg, L5105, 5108-5110 and L5126—all to 253 Sqn, although these aircraft were in reality still bombers. There were from all Battle batches transfers to training organisations and many Battles, before or after active service on squadrons, were shipped to Canada or Australia, Rhodesia, South Africa and in a few cases passed between these countries in the Empire Air Training Scheme. N2020-66 all delivered as Mk II, N2082-2109 Mk II, N2110-2131 Mk III, N2147-2190 Mk III, N2211-2258 Mk III. Conversions in these ranges included N2144-46, 48-49, 53, 56-57 to Mk II, N2118 Mk II to V then III, N2119 to Mk V also N2124, 25, 28, N2176, 77, 79, N2190. P2155-2204, P2233-2278, P2300-2336, P2353-2369 mainly Mk III, with P2157, 58, P2253, 57, P2330 converted to TT aircraft, P2266 to Mk V, P2315 to Mk II and P2277 to prototype Battle (T). P5228-5252 and P5270-5294 mainly Mk III, many overseas, P5277 to Fleet Air Arm. P6480-6509 Mk III almost all overseas, also P6523-6566 and P6567-72. P6596-6615 mixed Mk II and III and remainder of this batch built as Battle (T). R3922-3971, R3990-4019, R4035-4054 built as Mk III, sent mainly to overseas units. V1201-1250 and V1265-1280 delivered as Mk III or V and fitted for bomber training duties. V1280 delivered September 2 1940. AR625 built from parts of K7173, K9439 and N2026.

Handley Page Halifax I: Prototypes: L7244, L7245. Mk I production: L9485-9534, L9560-9584, L9600-9608. L9520 modified to Mk V prototype; L9515 served as a development aircraft.

Handley Page Halifax II: L9609-9624, R9363-9392, R9418-9457, R9482-9498, R9528-9540. R9534 tested rectangular fins, had served as Mk II srs i (Special) prototype with four-gun dorsal turret and later became the Mk III prototype. V9976-9994, W1002-1021, W1035-1067, W1090-1117, W1141-1190, W1211-1253, W1270-1276. Of these V9977 was the first aircraft to fly with H2S radar and V9985 did test drops of the 4,000 lb bomb. Many of the aircraft in this range had Type Z noses—ie, their nose turrets were replaced by a streamlined fairing. W7650-7679, W7695-7720, W7745-7784, W7801-7826, W7844-7887, W7906-7939. (Many modified to have Type Z nose.) BB189-223, BB236-285, BB300-344, BB357-391, BB412-446. Basically Mk II srs i (Special) with Type Z nose, as fitted, for example, to BB202, 209, 217, 219, 220, etc. Some aircraft in the batch appear to have been modified to Mk II srs ia with transparent nose, for example BB323 sandwiched in a group of Mk II srs i (Special). BB241 also had the transparent nose. DG219-230 Mk II srs i (Special). DT481-526, DT539-588, DT612-649, DT665-705, DT720-752, DT767-808. (Many were Mk II srs i (Special) but some became Mk II srs ia, eg, DT692, DT794.) HR654-699, HR711-758, HR773-819, HR832-880, HR905-952, HR977-988. Believed all built as B.II srs ia, likewise HX147-191 and HX222-225. JB781-806, JB834-875, JB892-931, JB956-974, JD105-128, JD143-180, JD192-218, JD244-278, JD296-333, JD361-386, JD405-421, JD453-476, JN882-926, JN941-978, JP107-137, JP159-207, JP220-259, JP275-301. JP319-338, LW223-246, LW259-301, LW313-345 all basically

B.II srs ia. Conversions to GR II included JD176, 177, 178, 217, 218, 245, JP163-174, JP256, JP258, JP296-301, JP319-320, JP328-330, JP333-338.

Handley Page Halifax B.III: HX226-247, HX265-296, HX311-357, LK747-766, LK779-812, LK826-850, LK863-887, LL543-559, LL573-615, LV771-799, LV813-842, LV857-883, LV898-923, LV953-973, LV985-999, LW113-143, LW157-179, LW191-195, LW346-348, LW361-397, LW412-446, LW459-481, LW495-522, LW537-559, LW572-598, LW613-658, LW671-696, LW713-724, MZ282-321, MZ334-378, MZ390-435, MZ447-495, MZ500-544, MZ556-604, MZ617-660, MZ672-717, MZ730-775, MZ787-831, MZ844-883, MZ895-939, MZ945-989, NA102-150, NA162-205, NA218-263, NA275-309, NA492-531, NA543-587, NA599-644, NA656-704, NP930-976, NP988-999, NR113-156, NR169-211, NR225-258, NR271-290, PN167-208, PN365-406, PN423-460, RG345-390, RG413-446. Some became A. Mk III, and LV838 was first with a ventral pannier. 'Rounded' wing tips were featured by some aircraft from the LV et seq ranges. Examples of such aircraft are LV917, LV922, LW193, LW201, LW469, MZ294, MZ296, MZ359, MZ710, etc. There seems little doubt that some aircraft were modified to have the extended span. Aircraft on the production lines seem to have been completed at times with either style of wing tip, eg, NA126-129 square tips, NA130 'rounded', NA131-136 'square', NA137 'rounded', NA169 'rounded', NA170-175 'square', NA178-180 'rounded', etc. The list of aircraft used by airborne squadrons is too lengthy to incorporate here, but some such machines were these ('rt' following the serial denoting 'rounded' wing tips): NA104, NA126, NA129, NA130(rt), NA135, NA248, NA282, NA286, NA295(rt), NA314(rt), NA319(rt), NA336(rt), NA338, NA340, NA341, NA342(rt), NA346(rt), NA348, NA349(rt), NA351(rt), NA353(rt), NA354, NA366, NA379(rt), NA380, NA388, NA395(rt), NA397, NA399-401(rt), NA406-410, NA425 (built with square wing tips, modified to rounded tips). There were also a number of Met Mk IIs evidenced by NA223, NA227, NA229, NA247, NA249, etc.

Handley Page Halifax Mk V: DG231-253, DG270-317, DG338-363, DG384-424, DJ980-999, DK114-151, DK165-207, DK223-271, EB127-160, EB178-220, EB239-258, EB274-276, LK626-667, LK680-711, LK725-746, LK890-932, LK945-976, LK988-999, LL112-153, LL167-198, LK213-258, LL270-312, LL325-367, LL380-423, LL437-469, LL481-521, LL534-542. Numerous examples served as A. Mk V including DG384, 387, 388, 390-393, 396; DJ992-994; DK121-124, 130-131, 197-198; EB130-132, 135, 139, 143, 145, 153, 159, 160, 178; LL129, 146, 149, 270, 271, 273-282, 284, 287, 289-293, 300-312, 325-338, 340-356, 357, 361, 382, 384, 399-413, 440-441. There were also conversions to GR/Met V: DJ995, DK256, LL117, LL123, LL186, LL188, LL195, LL294-299, LL339, LL393-394, LL451-452, LL481-482, LL485-486, LL510-517. Mk V srs i (Special) and Mk V srs ia existed.

Handley Page Halifax Mk VI: NP715, NP752, NP753, NP822-836, NP849-895, NP908-927, LL165-187, PP203-216, RG480-513, RG527-568, RG583-625, RG639-679, RG693-736, RG749-790, RG813-853, RG867-879. ST794-818 all converted to GR VI/Met VI. TW774-796.

Handley Page Halifax B.VII: LW196-210, PN223-267, PN285-327, PN343-344. Some became A. Mk VIIs.

Handley Page Hampden I: Prototype: K4240. Production: L4032-4211 (conversions to TB—torpedo bomber—L4038, 41, 75, 76, 86, 91, 4105, 115, 118, 141, 144, 150, 170, 196, 201, 204). P1145-1189, P1194-1230, P1233-1261, P1265-1305, P1309-1356 (conversions to TB—P1145, 47, 50, 51, 57, 58, 60, 64, 66, 69, 77, 88, 89, 207, 208, 214, 215, 219, 229, 236-238, 243, 245-46, 249-250, 257-58, 273, 82, 84, 86, 96, 1312-1314, 1335, 44-46, 52, 56). P2062-2100, P2110-2145 (conversions to TB—P2064-65, 67, 78, 80, 84, 95, 2113, 19, 26). P4285-4324, P4335-4384, P4389-4418 (conversions to TB—P4304, 06, 12, 15, 47, 69, 73, 95, 401, 418). P5298-5337, P5338-5346, P5386-5400, P5421-5436 (conversions to TB—P5301, 02, 04, 09, 15, 20, 27, 31, 35, 41, 43, 87, 89). X2893-2922, X2959-3008, X3021-3030, X3047-3066, X3115-3154 (conversions to TB—X2976, 3022, 3131; X3115 converted to Mk II prototype). AD719-768, AD782-806, AD824-873, AD895-939, AD959-988, AE115-159, AE184-203, AE218-267, AE286-320, AE352-401, AE418-442 (conversions to TB—AD743, 908, 977, AE194, 231, 307, 310, 363). AN100-167 (conversions to TB—AN123, 25, 27, 37, 46,

48, 49, 51-61, 63-64, 66-67). AT109-158, AT172-196, AT216-260 (conversions to TB—AN109, 14, 17, 25, 35, 45, 50, 84, 93, 232, 241, 44, 51, 53, 56-59).

Handley Page Harrow: Mk I: K6933-6952, Mk II: 6953-7032. Converted to Mk II: K6935, 36, 37, 38, 39. Wartime conversions to transport rôle: K6941, 47, 49, 51, 62, 70, 73, 74, 75, 78, 83, 84, 85, 87, 94, 96, 7000, 7005, 09, 10, 11, 12, 14, 15, 24, 31, 32.

Handley Page Hereford: Prototype: L7271. Production: L6002-6101, N9005-9081, 9084-9106. Conversions to Hampden I: L6011, 18-20, 55, 76, 80, 96; N9062, 64, 65, 70, 80, 86, 90, 96, 101, 105, 106.

Handley Page Victor: Prototypes: WB771, WB775. Mk 1 production: XA917-941, XH587-594, XH613-621, XH645-651, XH667 (converted to Mk 1A: XH587-594, XH613-616, XH618-621, XH645-651, XH667). Many conversions to K. Mk 1, B(K)Mk 1A and K.Mk 1A. Mk 2 production: XH668-675, XL158-165, XL188-193, XL230-233, XL511-513, XM714-718. Conversions to B.2R, S.R.2 and presently to K.2.

Lockheed Vega Ventura Mk I: Deliveries to RAF in UK and intended for bombing rôle—AE660-662, 679-88, 691-92, 695-97, 699, 701-2, 705, 706, 713-17, 719-20, 722-24, 726-27, 730-34, 736-38, 740, 742-45, 748-51, 753, 758-60, 762, 771, 774, 776, 779-81, 784-85, 787-88, 790, 792, 794, 796-98, 806, 811, 819, 821-22, 833, 839, 842.

Lockheed Vega Ventura Mk II: Deliveries to RAF in UK and intended for bombing rôle—AE846-48, 852-56, 873, 876-77, 880-81, 884, 892, 894, 899, 902, 908, 918, 920, 927, 937-41, 945, 947-48, 956-57; AJ163, 167-68, 171, 174, 177-78, 181-82, 188, 193, 196, 198, 199-200, 206, 209, 213, 216, 220, 221, 224, 225-26, 231-32; AJ444, 446-47, 452-54, 456, 458-61, 466, 468, 491. Many diversions from contract, to USAAF, US Navy, SAAF and RCAF.

Martin Baltimore: Mk I AG685-734; Mk II AG735-834; Mk III AG835-999, AH100-184; Mk IIIA FA100-380; Mk IV FA381-674; Mk V FW281-880. Some used in general reconnaissance rôle.

Martin Marauder: Mk I FK109-160; Mk IA FK362-380; Mk II (B-26C) FB400-522; Mk III (B-26F) HD402-601; Mk III (B-26G) HD602-751. Some diversions to SAAF.

Martin Maryland: ex-French Air Force AX689-690, AX692-693, AX696; Mk I AH205-279, AR702-751, BJ421-428, BS760-777—diversions to SAAF and for reconnaissance duties; Mk II AH280-429, also diverted as for Mk I.

North American Mitchell I: FK161, 162 trials aircraft; FK163-64, 66, 69-77, 79-83 all served at No 111 OTU Nassau; FK165 brief service trials; FK168 remained in Canada.

North American Mitchell II: Delivered to UK—FL164-179, 181-186, 188-198, 201-207, 210, 212-218; FL671-691, 693-696, 698-701, 703-709; FR141-147, 149-152, 156-186, 188-202, 204-209; FR367, 370, 373, 396-397; FV900-916, 918-945, 947-948, 950, 955-989, 991-993, 995, 996, 998, 999; FW100-103, 105-122, 124-131, 133-137, 139-144, 146, 151-153, 155-158, 160-164, 166-175, 177-178, 180-219, 221-232, 234-236, 238-245, 247-250, 252-258, 261-271, 275-277; HD302-307, 316, 321, 328-329, 336. Aircraft not listed, mainly to 111 OTU, Nassau. Conversions to Mk II srs 2 and 3 feature armament modifications such as beam guns and revised window arrangements. Mk II srs 3 had rear gunner's station as on Mitchell Mk III, but with dorsal turret amidships.

North American Mitchell III: Delivered to the RAF in the UK—HD346-351, 353-400, KJ561, KJ563-579, KJ585-587, KJ589-649, KJ651-667, KJ672-694, KJ696-715, KJ720, KJ723-734, KJ736-750, KJ752-755, KJ757-774.

Short Stirling: Prototypes: L7600, L7605.

Short Stirling I: Production: N3635-3684, N3700-3729, N3750-3769. N3645, N3647-51 destroyed by bombing; N3640, N3657, N3711 converted to Mk II trials aircraft. N6000-6049, N6065-6084, N6085-6104, N6120-6129. (N6025-28 and 31 were destroyed by bombing.) R9141-9171, R9184-9203, R9241-9290, R9295-9334, R9349-9358. (R9188, 9309 were converted to Mk III.) W7428-7475, W7500-7539, W7560-7589, W7610-7639. (W7432, 7454 were converted to Mk III.) BF309-358, BF372-416, BF434-454. (BF355 was converted to Mk III.) BK592-628, BK644-647, DJ972-977, EF327-369, EF384-400, EF413.

Short Stirling Mk III: BF455-483, BF500-534, BF561-580. (BF464, 468, 532, 575, 580 converted to Mk IV.) BK648-667, BK686-727, BK759-784, BK798-818. EE871-918, EE937-975, EF114-163, EF177-217, EF231-277, EF289-316. (Converted to Mk IV: EE889, 900, 962, 966; EF213, 214, 234, 241, 242, 243, 244, 248, 260, 261, 263, 264, 265, 267-270, 273-277, 293, 295-298, 303, 305-306, 309, 311, 314 316, 320-323.) EF401-412, EF425-470, EF488-518. (Converted to Mk IV: EF404, 429, 435, 446, 506.) EH875-909, EH921-961, EH977-996, EJ104-127. (Converted to Mk IV: EH897, 950, EJ116.) LJ441-460, 462-474, 476-483, 501, 504-529, 531, 533-544, 558-562, 565, 567-568, 570-571, 573-574, 577-582, 584-587, 589, 592-595, 611, 614, 617, 619, 621, 623-626, 628, 630, 632, 634-635, 637, 639-642, 644-646, 648-649, 651, 653, 670. LK375-411, LK425-466, 479-521, 535-576, 589-624. (Converted to Mk IV: LK389, 405, 428, 431, 439, 440, 486, 498, 505, 509, 510, 512, 513, 542, 543, 548, 549, 551, 553-555, 558, 559, 560, 562, 566, 567, 573, 589, 606.) MZ260-264.

Vickers-Armstrongs Warwick: Prototypes: K8178 (Vulture), L9704. B.Mk I production: BV214-215, 217-222, 224, 228-230, 291, 293, 295-296. B.Mk II prototype: BV216.

Vickers-Armstrongs Wellesley: Prototype: K7556. Production: K7713-7791, K8520-8536, L2637-2716.

Vickers-Armstrongs Wellington: Prototypes: K4049, L4250 Mk II, L4251 Mk III, R1220 Mk IV, R3298 and R3299 Mk V, W5795 Mk VI, P2522 Mk IX, DF609 Mk X.

Vickers-Armstrongs Wellington I: Production: L4212-4311, L4316-4391. L7770-7772, R2699-2703. (Converted to D.W.1 L4212, 21, 27, 4356, 4358, 4374, L7771, R2701.)

Vickers-Armstrongs Wellington IA: Production: L7773-7789, N2865-2914, N2935-2964, N2980-3019, P2515-2532, P9205-9236. (Conversions to D.W.1 P2516, 2518, P9223. Conversions to Mk XV N2871, 77, 80, 86, 87, N2909, 944, 47, 54, 55, 58, P2519, 21, 28, P9209, 9222, 9231. Conversions to Mk XVI N2875, N2990.)

Vickers-Armstrongs Wellington IC: L7790-7819, L7840-7874, L7885-7899, N2735-2784, N2800-2829, N2840-2859, P9237-9250, P9265-9300, R1000-1049, R1060-1099, R1135-1184, R1210-1254, R1265-1299, R1320-1349, R1365-1414, R1435-1474, R1490-1539, R1585-1629, R1640-1669, R1695-1729, R1757-1806, R3150-3179, R3195-3239, R3275-3297, T2458-2477, T2501-2520, T2541-2580, T2606-2625, T2701-2750, T2801-2850, T2873-2922, T2951-3000, W5612-5631, W5644-5690, W5703-5735, X3160-3179, X3192-3221, X9600-9644, X9658-9707, X9733-9767, X9785-9834, X9871-9890, X9905-9954, X9974-9993, Z1040-1054, Z1066-1115, Z1139-1181; Z8704, 09, 14, 16, 18, 20, 22, 24, 26, 28-36, Z8761-8810, Z8822-8871, Z8891-8901, Z8903-8910, 8942-8991, Z9016-9045, Z9095-9114, BB455-460, BB462-470, BB472-475, 477-480, 482-484, 497-502, 504-512, 514-516, DF542-579, DF594-608, DF610-613, DF615-642, DF644-658, DF687-700, DF702-709, DF727-729 DF731-739, DF741-743, DV411-458, DV473-522, DV532-579, DV593-624, DV638-678, DV694-740, DV757-786, DV799-846, DV864-898, DV914-953, ES980-985 ES987-995, HD942-991, HE101-134, HE146, HF829-837, HF839-49, 51-53, 55-56, 58-59, 61-62, 64-65, 67-68, 81-82, 84-85, 87-88, 90-91, 93-94, 96-900, HF902-903, 05-06, 08-09, 911-912, 14-15, 17-18, 20-21, HX364-71, 73-75, 77-78, 80, 82 84-85, 87, 89, 90, 92, 93, 95, 97, 99, HX400, 02, 17, 21, 23, 25, 29, 31, 33, 35, 38 40, 42, 45-47, 49, 51, 68, 70, 72, 75, 78, 80, 83, 84, 86, 88, HX506, 08, 10, 14, 16 18, 21, 23, 25, 27, 29, 33, 36, 58, 60, 64, 67, 69, 71, 73, 77, 80, 83, 85, 89, 91 94, 97, HX601, 03, 06, 27, 31, 33, 35, 37, 39, 43, 45, 48, 51, 55, 70, 73, 76, 80, 82 85, 88, HX710, 12, 14, 16, 17, 22, 24, 27, 30, 34, 36, 39, 42, 46, 48, 50, 67, 69, 73 75, 78, 81, 85, LA965, LA968, 973, 978, 984, 988, 994, LB110, LB116, 120, 126 131, 141, 148, 152, 174. (Conversion to Mk II R3221. Conversion to Mk III P9238 Completed as Mk IV: R1390, R1490, R1510, 15, 20, 25, 30, 35, 85, 90, R1610 15, 20, 25, 50, R1655, 95, R1705, 15, 25, 65, 75, 85, 95. Completed as Mk VIII T2919, 2977, 79, 82, 88. Converted to Mk XVI: N2755, N2801, N2856, N2857 P9289, R1032, R1144, R1172, R1409, R1452, R1521, R1531, R1600, R1605, R1649 R1659, R1700, R1710, R1711, R1720, R3217, R3225, R3234, R3273, T2850, T2920 T2969, W5686, W5709, X3193, X3935, Z8709, Z8831, Z8850, DV491, DV594

DV617, DV704, DV738, DV761, DV762, DV822, DV886, DV920, DV921, DV924, DV942.)

Vickers-Armstrongs Wellington II: W5352-5401, W5414-5463, W5476-5500, W5513-5537, W5550-5598, W5611, Z8328-8377, Z8397-8441, Z8489-8538, Z8567-8601, Z8643-8662. Z8416 fitted for trials with Vickers 'S' gun, Z8570 W2B jet engine trials.

Vickers-Armstrongs Wellington III: X3222-3226, X3275-3289, X3330-3374, X3387-3426, X3445-3489, X3538-3567, X3584-3608, X3633-3677, X3694-3728, X3741-3765, X3784-3823, X3866-3890, X3923-3967, X3984-4003; Z1562-1578, Z1592-1626, Z1648-1697, Z1717-1751; AD589-608, AD624-653; BJ581-625, BJ642-675, BJ688-730, BJ753-801, BJ818-847, BJ876-922, BJ958-991; BK123-166, BK179-214, BK234-281, BK295-315, BK330-368, BK385-408, BK426-471, BK489-517, BK534-564; DF542-579, DF594-608, DF610-642, DF664-685, DF687-700, DF702-709, DF727-728, DF731-739, DF741-743; HF112, HF609-613, 615-621, 23-25, 27-29, 31-33, 35-37, 39-41, 43-45, 47-49, 66-68, 70-703, HF718-719, 21-22, 24-25, 27-28, 30-31, 33-34, 36-38, 40-42, 44-46, 48-50, 52-54, 56-58, 60-64, 91-92, 94-96, 798-802, 805-07, 09-10, 12-816; HZ103-04, HZ106-07, 109-10, 12-13, 15-16, 18-19, 27-28, 30-31, 33-34, 36-37, 38-39, 41, 73-74, 76-77, 79-80, 82-83, 85-86, 88-89, 91-92, 94-95, 97-98, HZ200-201, 03-04, 06-07, 09, 242-244-45, 247-48, 250. Some Mk IIIs had Type 423 provisioning, eg, X3479, DF615-638, HF698, HF719, HF814-816.

Vickers-Armstrongs Wellington IV: 25 aircraft in 'R' IC range completed as Mk IV; others were Z1182-1883, Z1202-1221, Z1243-1292, Z1311-1345, Z1375-1424, Z1459-1496.

Vickers-Armstrongs Wellington V: Prototypes and W5796.

Vickers-Armstrongs Wellington VI: W5797, DR471-484, DR528; Mk VIA W5798-5815, DR485-450, DR519-527.

Vickers-Armstrongs Wellington B.X: DF686, DF701, DF730, DF740; HE147-184, HE197-244, HE258-306, HE318-353, HE365-398, HE410-447, HE459-508, HE513-556, HE568-615, HE627-667, HE679-715, HE727-772, HE784-833, HE845-873, HE898-931, HE946-995. HE series built as ordinary Mk X apart from HE272-285, 320-325, 338-344,800-806, 850-851 with Type 423 provisioning to allow carriage of one 4,000 lb bomb. Those between HE272 and HE366 (con nos 2661-2733) were Mk X C.6, also HE800-849 and HE852-860. HF452-495, HF513-545, HF564-606 —all Mk X only. HF614, 622, 26, 30, 34, 38, 42, 46, 50, 69. HF723, 26, 29, 32, 35— all Type 423; HF739, 43, 47, 51, 55, 59, 63, 93, 97, 805, 08, 11. HZ102, 05, 08, 111, 114, 117, 120, 123, 126, 129, 144, 147, 175, 181, 193, 199, 205, 243, 249. Type 423 gear: HZ132, 135, 138, 141. HZ255-273, 277-82, 300-305, 09-14, 53-58, 62-67, 71-76, 98-403, 410-415, 22-27, 34-39, 57-87, 513-521, 23-33, 40-45, 52-54, 70-72, 79-82, 713-720, 809-818, 941-950 (Type 423 gear between HZ467 and HZ521). JA111-113 (Type 423 gear), JA114-140, 185-194, 341-352, 448-481, 497-512, 519-534. LN157-189, 221-248, 261-303, 317-353, 369-409, 423-458, 481-516, 529-571, 583-622, 633-676, 689-723, 736-778, 791-823, 836-879, 893-936, 948-989. (All with LN serials from LN402 built as Mk X C.6, Type 423 gear between 402-441, 701-705, 719-723, 746-751, 759-770, 793-795, 802-806, 815-816.) LP113-156, 169-213, 226-268, 281-314, 328-369, 381-415, 428-469, 483-526, 539-581, 595-628, 640-686, 699-733, 748-788, 802-849, 863-889, 901-930, 943-986. (All B.Mk X C.6 to LP455. Type 423 gear originally fitted to LP333-34, 38-39, 43-44, 48-49, 52-54, 60-63, 65-69, 83-85, 88-89, 93-94, 98-99, 408-409, 411-12, 28-29, 41-42, 45-46, 49-50, 53-54.) LR110-142, 156-, 164, 168-183, 195-210—All B.Mk X. ME870-883, ME951-60, ME972-999, MF113-124, 131-144, 193-202, 236-249, 281-288, 311-316, 346-351, 367-372, 399-404, 420-424, 439-441, 452-459, 468-479, 500-538, 550-572, 583-596, 614-615, 624-635, 644-655, 676-687, 695-706, 728-739. MS470-475 (Type 423), MS476-477, MS478-496 (Type 423). NA710-754, 766-811, 823-870, 893-937, 949-997, NB110-139. (All Mk X C.6, Type 423 gear in NA710-711, 15-16, 20-21, 37-38, 44-45, 51-52, 69-70, 76-77, 85-86, 89-90, 93-94.) NC421-432, 443-452, 472-481, 494-502, 514-517, 529-533, 545-554, 563-570, 592-601, 614-621, 648-655, 664-671, 678-692, 706-740, 748-750, 766-770, 777-784, 789-796, 801-813, 825-827, 836-847, 856-867, 890-901, 908-925, 929, 942-990. PF823-830, 839-846, 855-862, 883-888, 894-901, 912-915, 927-930, 941-948, 959-966, 987-994. PG177-124, 135-138, 149-152, 175-182, 193-196, 207-210, 232-235, 250-

253, 258-265, 286-297, 304-326, 338-348, 357-366, 371-379, 392-394. RP312-329, 336-347, 352-358, 373-391, 396-411, 430-469, 483-526, 538-561, 565-590.

Vickers-Armstrongs Windsor: Prototypes: DW506, DW512, NK136.

Vickers-Armstrongs Valiant: Prototypes: WB210, WB215, Mk 2 WJ954. Production: B.Mk 1 WP199-203, WP204, WP206-216, 218, 220, 222, WZ361-375, WZ377; B(PR)K.1 WZ380, WZ382, WZ389-399; B(K)1 WZ400-405, XD812-830, XD857-875.

Vultee Vengeance I: AN838-AN999, AP100-137, EZ800-818.

Vultee Vengeance IA: EZ819-999.

Vultee Vengeance II: AF745-944, AN538-837, HB300-550. (Known conversions to T.T.Mk IV: HB304, 05, 06, 07, 12, 13, 14, 15, 16, 20, 21, 22, 25, 26, 27, 29, 33, 35, 38, 41, 42, 43, 45, 49, 55, 57, 58, 59, 61, 63, 64, 65, 66-69, 71, 73, 74, 75, 77, 78, 82, 87, 89, 92, 93, 95, 96, 99, 400, 405, 06, 10, 12, 16, 17, 19, 21-26, 28, 30-32, 36, 37, 39, 40, 42, 46, 54, 55-59, 61, 62, 65, 67-69, 71-78, 81, 82, 84, 86, 87, 94-96, 98, 504, 508, 12, 14, 19, 23, 24, 28, 29, 30, 31, 34, 39, 44-46, 48, 49, 50.)

Vultee Vengeance III: FB918-999, FD100-117.

Vultee Vengeance IV: FD118-221 (srs i), FD222-417 (srs ii)—some diversions to USAAF; KG810-820.

APPENDIX 2: Royal Air Force bomber aircraft unit identity letters, September 1939-April 1951

Units were squadrons unless otherwise stated.

AA 75	CF 625	GA 16 OTU
AC 138	CR 162	GB 105
AJ 617	CX 14	GE 58
AK 1657 Con Unit	1C Stn Flt Scampton	GG 1667 Con Unit
AL 429	DD 22 OTU	GL 5 Grp Pool, 14 OTU,
AM 14 OTU	DF Bomber Dev Flt;	185 Sqn
AO 223	CBE	GN 249, CBE
AR 460	DH 1664	GP 1661 Con Unit
AS 166	DK 158	GR 301
AU 148	DT 192	GS 83 OTU
AY 17 OTU	DX 57	GT 156
AZ 627	EA 49	GV 1652 Con Unit
A2 514	ED 21 OTU	6G 233
A3 1654 Con Unit,	EG 487	HA 218
230 OCU	EM 207	HD 466
A4 115 and 195	EN 27 OTU	HS 109
A5 3 LFS	EO 15 OTU	HV 8
BB 27 OTU	EP 104	HW 100
BH 300	EQ 408	H4 1653 Con Unit
BL 40,1656 Con Unit	EU 26 OTU	H7 346
BM 433	EV 180	3H 80 OTU
BQ 550	EX 199	4H 142
BS 1651 Con Unit	EY 78	8H 8 Grp Comm Flt
BT 30 OTU	FB 24 OTU, 35 Sqn	IC 623
BU 214	FD 1659 Con Unit	IF 84 OTU
BY 23 OTU	FH 15 OTU	IG 1668 Con Unit
BZ 82 OTU	FS 148	IK BCIS
4B 5 Grp Comm Flt	FV 13 OTU	IL 115
CA 189	FZ 23 OTU	IP 434?, BCIS
CE 5 LFS, 1668 Con Unit	8F 105 OTU	IQ 150

JA 1652 Con Unit
JE 195
JF 1654 Con Unit
JG 17 OTU
JI 514
JL 10 OTU
JM 20 OTU
JN 150
JO 463
JP 12 OTU
JS 16 OTU
9J 227
KB 1662 Con Unit?
KC 617
KD 30 OTU
KJ 11 OTU
KK 15 OTU
KM 44
KN 77
KO 115
KQ 13 OTU
KU 47
KW 425
KX 311
2K 1668 Con Unit
8K 571
LB 28 OTU
LD 108
LE 630
LF 38
LG 215
LJ 614
LK 578
LN 99
LQ 405
LR 1667 Con Unit
LS XV
LT 22 OTU
LW 75 Signals Wg
L8 347
MA 161
MG 7
MH 51
MP 76
MQ 226
MU 60
M5 128
M8 4 Grp Comm Flt
NA 428
NF 138
NO 320
NP 158
NT 29 OTU
NY 1665 Con Unit
NZ 304
OA 342
OB 45

OF 97
OG 1665 Con Unit
OJ 149
OL 83
OM 107
OO 13, 1663 Con Unit
OP 11 OTU
OW 426
OY 13 OTU
OZ 98?
O5 BSDU
6O 582
PB 26 OTU
PG 619
PH 12
PL 144
PM 103
PO 467
PP 25 OTU?
PT 420
P3 692
9P 85 OTU
QB 424
QF PFNTU
QN 28 OTU, 214 Sqn
QO 432
QQ 1651 Con Unit
QR 61
QS 620
QT 142
RH 88
RK 10 OTU
RT 114
RV 1659 Con Unit
SB 464
SE 431
SH 216
SJ 21 OTU
SL 13 OTU
SM 305
SN 230 OCU
SR 101
SV 1663 Con Unit
SW 1678 Con Flt
SY 613
4S BSDU, RWE
TC 170
TF 29 OTU
TH 418
TK 149
TL 35
TN 30 OTU
TT 1658 Con Unit
TV 1660 Con Unit
TX 11 OTU
TY 24 OTU

5T 223
6T 608
UF 24 OTU
UG 1654 Con Unit
UH 21 OTU
UJ 27 OTU
UL 576
UM 626
UO 19 OTU
UP 605
UQ 211
UV 460
UX 82
UY 10 OTU
VA 113
VE 110
VN 50
VO 98
VQ 28 OTU
VR 419
VT 84
3V 1 Grp Comm Flt
WG 26 OTU
WI 69
WJ 17 OTU
WL 434
WN 75 Wing?
WO 13 OTU
WP 90
WS 9
WY 28 OTU
XD 139
XF 19 OTU
XG 16 OTU
XJ 13 OTU
XL 20 OTU
XN 22 OTU
XT 1657 Con Unit
XY 186
YH 21
YW 1660 Con Unit,
    230 OCU
YZ 1651 Con Unit,
    617 Sqn
ZA 10
ZB 1658 Con Unit
ZG 10 OTU
ZL 427
ZN 106
ZO 196
ZQ BCIS
ZT 20 OTU
ZU 1664 Con Unit
ZV 19 OTU
Z5 462
7Z 105 OTU

APPENDIX 3: Characteristics of British bombers, 1937-70

Type	Manufacturer	Years of service	Crew	Span	Length	Engine (hp)	Maximum speed/ht (mph/ft)	Loaded weight (lb)	Typical range/bomb load (miles/lb)	Defensive armament
Harrow	Handley Page	1937-39	5	88′ 5″	82′ 2″	2×925 Pegasus XXs	200/10000	23000	1250/1500	4×0.303 in Brownings
Wellesley	Vickers-Armstrongs	1937-41	2	74′ 7″	39′ 3″	1×925 Pegasus XX	207/10000	11100	2590/ ?	2×0.303 in Brownings
Battle I	Fairey	1937-40	2	54′	52′ 1¾″	1×1030 Merlin I	243/16200	10900	1050/1000	2×0.303 in Vickers/Brownings
Blenheim I	Bristol	1937-40	3	56′ 4″	39′ 9″	2×840 Mercury VIIIs	265/15000	12500	920/1000	2×0.303 in Vickers/Brownings
Blenheim IV	Bristol	1939-42	3	56′ 4″	42′ 9″	2×920 Mercury XVs	266/11800	14500	1460/1000	4×0.303 in Brownings
Whitley V	Armstrong Whitworth	1939-42	5	84′	70′ 6″	2×1145 Merlin Xs	222/17000	33500	1930/3500	5×0.303 in Brownings
Bombay	Bristol	1939-41	4	95′ 9″	69′ 3″	2×1010 Pegasus XXIIs	192/6500	20000	880/2000	2×0.303 in Vickers 'K's
Wellington IC	Vickers-Armstrongs	1940-42	5	86′ 2″	64′ 7″	2×1050 Pegasus XVIIIs	235/15500	28500	1805/2750	6×0.303 in Brownings
Wellington II	Vickers-Armstrongs	1941-42	5	86′ 2″	64′ 7″	2×1280 Merlin Xs	247/17000	33000	1400/4500	6×0.303 in Brownings
Wellington III	Vickers-Armstrongs	1942-43	5	86′ 2″	64′ 7″	2×1500 Hercules XIs	261/12500	34500	1200/4500	8×0.303 in Brownings
Wellington IV	Vickers-Armstrongs	1941-43	5	86′ 2″	64′ 7″	2×1200 Pratt & Whitney S3C4-Gs	229/13000	31600	980/4500	6×0.303 in Brownings
Hampden	Handley Page	1938-42	4	69′ 2″	53′ 7″	2×1050 Pegasus XVIIIs	254/13800	22500	1200/4000	6×0.303 in Brownings
Hereford	Handley Page	1940	4	69′ 2″	53′ 7″	2×1000 Dagger VIIIs	265/12000	16000	? ?	4×0.303 in Brownings
Stirling I	Short	1940-43	7	99′ 1″	87′ 3″	4×1500 Hercules XIs	260/12000	59400	740/14000	8×0.303 in Brownings
Stirling III	Short	1943-44	7	99′ 1″	87′ 3″	4×1675 Hercules VIs	270/14500	70000	2010/3575	8×0.303 in Brownings
Manchester	Avro	1940-42	5	90′ 1″	70′	2×1760 Vulture IIs	273/17000	50000	1630/8100	8×0.303 in Brownings
Halifax I	Handley Page	1940-41	7	98′ 10″	70′ 1″	4×1280 Merlin Xs	262/18000	59000	500/13000	8×0.303 in Brownings
Halifax II	Handley Page	1941-43	7	98′ 10″	70′ 1″	4×1460 Merlin XXs	260/19000	60000	1900/4000	9×0.303 in Brownings
Maryland	Martin	1940-42	3	61′ 4″	46′ 8″	2×1200 Pratt & Whitney S3C4-Gs	278/11800	16809	1210/1500	6×0.303 in Brownings/Vickers 'K's
Boston III	Douglas	1941-45	3	61′ 4″	48′	2×1600 Wright Double Row Cyclones	318/10500	23000	1240/2000	7×0.303 in Brownings
Ventura	Lockheed	1942-43	5	65′ 6″	52′ 7″	2×2000 Pratt & Whitney R-2800-31s	289/16000	26700	925/2500	8×0.303 in Brownings
Fortress I	Boeing	1941-42	10	103′ 9¼″	67′ 10¼″	4×1200 Wright Cyclone R-1820-G205As	325/29000	30670	1850/7400	1×0.30 in and 6×0.50 in guns
Wellington VI	Vickers-Armstrongs	1942	3	86′ 2″	61′ 9″	2×1600 Merlin 60s	300/32000	31600	1510/4500	4×0.303 in Brownings

Lancaster I	Avro	7	1941-49	102'	69' 6"	4 × 1460 Merlin XXs	266/12500	68000	1660/14000	8 × 0.303 in Brownings
Wellington X	Vickers-Armstrongs	6	1942-45	86' 2"	64' 7"	2 × 1675 Hercules VI/XVIs	255/ ?	36500	1885/1500	8 × 0.303 in Brownings
Blenheim V	Bristol	3	1942-43	56' 4"	44'	2 × 830 Mercury XXXs	230/ ?	17000	? ?	4 × 0.303 in Brownings
Mosquito IV	de Havilland	2	1942-45	54' 2"	40' 9½"	2 × 1280 Merlin 21s	380/14000	21462	990/2000	Nil
Mosquito XVI	de Havilland	2	1944-48	54' 2"	41' 6"	2 × 1710 Merlins	397/26000	23000	1370/5000	Nil
Mitchell II	North American	5	1942-45	67' 6¼"	54' 1"	2 × 1700 Wright Cyclone GR-2600-13s	294/14800	26000	925/4000	4 × 0.50 in and 1 × 0.30 in guns
Mitchell III	North American	5	1945	67' 6¼"	53' 5¾"	2 × 1700 Wright Cyclone GR-2600-13s	303/13000	32000	925/4000	8 × 0.50 guns
Halifax III	Handley Page	7	1943-45	104' 2"	71' 7"	4 × 1675 Hercules XVIs	281/13500	65000	2005/6250	7 × 0.303 in Brownings
Baltimore III	Martin	4	1942-45	61' 4"	48' 5¾"	2 × 1660 Wright Cyclone GR-2600-A5Bs	302/11000	23000	950/2000	4 × 0.303 in and 2 × 0.30 in guns
Vengeance I	Vultee	2	1942-44	48'	40'	1 × 1700 Wright Cyclone GR-2600-A5Bs	279/ ?	12480	? ?	6 × 0.30 in guns
Marauder III	Martin	5	1944-45	71'	57' 6"	2 × 2000 Pratt & Whitney Double Wasp R-2800-43s	305/15000	37000	1200/4000	11 × 0.50 in guns
Liberator VI	Consolidated	8	1944-45	110'	67' 1"	4 × 1200 Pratt & Whitney Twin Wasp S4C4-Gs	270/20000	62000	2290/4000	9 × 0.50 in guns
Lincoln II	Avro	7	1946-55	120'	78' 3½"	4 × 1750 Merlin 68As	305/19000	75000	1470/14000	2 × 20 mm cannon 4 × 0.50 in guns
Brigand 1	Bristol	3	1948-52	72' 4"	46' 5"	2 × 2470 Centaurus 57s	358/16000	39000	2000/ ?	4 × 20 mm cannon
Washington	Boeing	10	1951-54	141' 3"	99'	4 × 2200 Wright Cyclone R-3350s	350/25000	120000	3000/6000	10 × 0.50 in guns
Canberra 2	English Electric	2	1951-	63' 11½"	65' 6"	2 × 6500 st Avon RA 101s	620/30000*	44500*	2000/6000*	Nil
Canberra 6	English Electric	2	1955-	63' 11½"	66' 8"	2 × 7500 st Avon RA 109s	640/35000*	51000*	2500/6000*	Nil
Valiant B(K)1	Vickers-Armstrongs	5	1955-65	114' 4"	108' 3"	4 × 10000 st Avon RA 28s	567/30000*	140000*	4500/*	Nil
Victor 1	Handley Page	5	1957-	110'	114' 11"	4 × 1100 st Sapphire 202s	620/40000*	—	4000/*	Nil
Victor 2	Handley Page	5	1962-	120'	114' 11"	4 × 17250 st Conway RCo 11s	640/40000*	200000*	—	Nil
Vulcan 1	Avro	5	1956-	99'	97' 1"	4 × 1100 st Olympus 101s	620/50000*	—	—	Nil
Vulcan 2	Avro	5	1960-	111'	99' 11"	4 × 20000 st Olympus 301s	640/40000*	190000*	1700/* Low level 21000 lb	Nil
Buccaneer	Hawker Siddeley	2	1969-	42' 4"	63' 5"	2 × 11200 Spey Sp 2s	720/SL*	46000*	—	Nil

Notes: Period of service is only given approximately since some aircraft remained in use after operational retirement in use with training units long after operational retirement. Performance data is mainly based upon results of service trials except in the case of data followed by an asterisk, this denoting likely performance of aircraft whose true performance figures have not been released.

APPENDIX 4: de Havilland Mosquito B.XVIs used 1946-48

a) **Home based:**
109 Squadron (1944-December 1948): HS-A: PF484 (June 1947-September 1948),
B: PF593, C: PF565, D: PF547, G: PF448, H: PF524 (May 1947-September 1948),
J: PF408 (December 1946-February 1948), S: PF448, also PF506, PF511, PF595,
PF614.
139 Squadron (1945-October 1948): XD-A: PF608 (April 1947-August 1948), B: PF448,
C: PF511, D: PF573, F: PF595, G: PF498, H: PF594 (July 1946-July 1948), also
PF516 (February 1945-June 1947), PF524 (September-October 1948), PF578,
PF593.

b) **In Germany:**
14 Squadron (April 1946-July 1948): CX-F: PF544, F: PF616, G: PF612, Y: PF545,
X: PF618, also PF410 (April 1946-August 1947), PF413 (April 1946-November
1947), PF443 (April 1946-August 1947), PF455 (April-August 1946), PF515 (April
1946-August 1947), PF523 (April 1946-April 1947), PF544, PF545, PF555 and
RV354.
69 Squadron (April 1946-November 1947): WI-F: PF544, L: PF551, T: PF612, also
PF397, PF400, PF432, PF441, PF453, PF455, PF515 and PF544.
98 Squadron (September 1945-June 1948): VO-C: RV362 (January 1946-November
1947), E: MM185, M: RV340, R: PF607, T: PF596, Y: PF555, also PF394, PF400,
PF430, PF520, PF509, PF554, PF613 and PF614.
180 Squadron (September 1945-April 1946): EV-B: PF441 (October 1945-April 1946),
C: MM149, C: PF448, L: PF551, U: PF432, V: PF453, W: MM187, X: PF441,
also PF397, PF455 and PF596.

APPENDIX 5: Avro Lincolns used by Bomber Command and in Training Units

Part 1: Lincolns wearing squadron identity letters formed the backbone of Bomber
Command from mid-1946 until spring 1951. The listing here links many of the
bombers with their individual letters during this period. Squadron number is
followed by the dates of the period when Lincolns were in use. Replacements were
made due to changes of equipment, eg, to H2S Mk IVA, for aircraft refurbishing,
accidents, and for PAMPA met recce aircraft (ie, RF362, RF450, RF455, RF480,
RF500 and RF531).
No 7 Sqn (8.49-12.55): MG-A: RE295, B: RE342, C: RE299, C: RF348, D: RF340,
E: RE400, F: RE359, G: RE348, H: RE397.
No 9 Sqn (7.46-5.52): WS-A: RF462, A: SX984, B: RF395, B: RF470, B: SX987,
C: RF474, C: SX970 (also E), D: RF369 (also L), D: SX979, E: RE289, F: RE305,
F: SX977, G: RF383, G: SX958, H: RA664, H: RF477, H: SX954, J: RA675,
K: RF529.
No 12 Sqn (8.46-4.52): PH-A: RA681 (also J), A: RF500, A: SX984, B: RF480,
B: SX978, C: RF455, D: RF362, D: SX979, F: RF335, F: RF355, F: RF531,
F: SX977, G: RF450, J: RE320, J: RE372, K: RA679 (also N), K: RF390, K: RF569,
L: RE369, L: RE398, M: RE344, M: RE371, M: RF558, N: RF521, O: RA666
(also U), O: RF522, P: RA687 (also V), S: RF529.
No XV Sqn (2.47-10.50): LS-A: RF370, LS-AA: RE341, B: RF514, C: RF392,
D: RF532, E: RF395, E: RF512, F: RF500, F: RF503.
No 35 Sqn (9.49-2.50): TL-O: SX957, S: SX983.
No 44 Sqn (10.45-5.46, 12.46-1.51): KM-G: RF445, G: SX949, H: RF419, J: RF410,
K: RF423, K: RF473, L: RF417, M: RF458.
No 49 Sqn (10.49-8.55): EA-J: RE299, K: RE319, L: RE345, M: RE347, O: RE411,
P: RF336, P: RF388, Q: RF565.
No 50 Sqn (7.46-1.51): VN-A: RE394, A: RF407, A: RF450, B: RF513, C: RF384,

C: RF394, C: RF456, C: RF465, D: RE377, F: RF473, U: RF405, V: RF406.
No 57 Sqn (8.45-9.51): DX-A: RE405, B: RF406, C: RE407, D: RE377, D: RF479,
E: RE379, F: RE380, G: RF385, H: RE374, J: RF387, J: RF501, K: RF469,
K: RF473 (also M), K: RF483, L: RF394, L: RF478, M: RF405, M: RF468,
M: SX935, N: RF386, W: RF465, X: RE317, X: RE370, X: RF517, Y: RF386.
No 61 Sqn (5.46-7.54): QR-D: RE377, F: RE380, G: RF358 (also P), G: RF561,
H: RF365, N: RF386, O: RF476, P: RF390 (also Z), P: RF463, Q: RF471, Q: RF510,
R: RF409, R: RF482, S: RF407, T: RE302, T: RE375, X: RE370, X: RF404,
Y: RF502, Z: RF359.
No 83 Sqn (7.46-12.55): OL-A: RF367, A: RF508, B: RA693, B: RF512, C: RF369,
D: RF505, D: RF525, E: RF400, E: RF481 (also F), F: RE358, G: RE316, G: RF504,
G: RF516, G: RA677, H: RE289, H:RF357, J: RF367, K: RF386, O: SX939.
No 90 Sqn (4.47-9.50): WP-N: RF451, O: RF345, P: RF447, Q: RE366, R: RF466.
No 97 Sqn (6.46-12.55): OF-A: RF391, A: RF526 (also Q), C: RE312, C: RF375,
D: RF505, F: RE302, J: RF399, J: SX940, K: RA669, K: RF529, L: RF516,
N: RF574, P: RA713, S: RF413.
No 100 Sqn (5.46-4.54): HW-A: RF507 (also C), B: RF409 (also J), B: RF472 (also
J), C: RF463, D: RE312, D: RF475, D: RF499, F: RE289, F: RF406, F: RF571,
G: RF384, H: RF359, H: RF404, H: RF534, J: RF525, L: SX942.
No 101 Sqn (6.46-6.51): SR-A: RE372, A: RF372, A: RF500, A: SX986, B: RF480,
B: RF521, B: SX985, C: RE323, C: RF455, C: SX950, D: RF362, D: SX981,
F: RE369, F: RE424, F: RF531, G: RE407, G: RF450, H: RA673, H: RF524,
H: SX934, J: RA689, K: RF390 (also M), K: RF398.
No 115 Sqn (9.49-3.50): KO-G: RE347, H: SX953, J: RE361.
No 138 Sqn (9.47-9.50): NF-N: RF417, U: RF426, U: RF456, U: RF459, V: RF395,
V: RF413 (also Y), W: RF361, X: RF440, X: RF483, Z: SX951.
No 148 Sqn (1.50-7.55): AU-S: RE361, T: SX957, U: SX975, V: SX976, W: SX982,
X: SX983, Y: SX987, Z: SX988.
No 149 Sqn (10.49-3.50): OJ-V: RA709, W: RF565, W: SX982, Y: RA688, Z: SX975.
No 207 Sqn (8.49-2.50): EM-C: RE324, E: RE400.
No 214 Sqn (2.50-2.55): QN-AW: RA709, BW: RE296, CW: RE301, DW: RE320,
EW: RE324, FW: RE360, GW: RE423, HW: RF348, HW: RF570.
No 617 Sqn (9.46-1.52): KC-A: RE376, B: RF499, C: RF396, C: RF517, F: RF456,
H: RF477, K: RF386, O: RF507, Q: RE267, U: RA670, U: RF362, V: RF450,
W: RF455, X: RA711, X: RF362, X: RF480, Y: RE366, Y: RF500, Z: RA712,
Z: RF531.
Part 2: Avro Lincolns served with many units other than front-line bomber squadrons.
Notes on some of these follow.
230 OCU was principally employed for the operational conversion of crews for Lan-
casters and later Lincolns. In the early post-war years its aircraft were coded A3,
eg, A3-A: RE338 and A3-N: RF408. Unit letters changed to SN about 1949 and
machines carrying these included SN-A: RE396, SN-F: RE393, SN-M: RE421 and
SN-W (previously A3-W): RF464. Later the unit was reduced in size as the needs
for Lincoln crews lessened and was based at Upwood where the aircraft then wore
enlarged fuselage serials, like RA674 (H on the side of her nose about 1 foot high)
and RE400: P.
Bomber Command Bombing School arose from the Instructors School, its aircraft
soon after the war including WB-H: RF524 and WB-D: RE417. Later its aircraft
wore blue spinners and enlarged serials, like RA715 in use in 1958. An interim
period existed when the Lincolns had grey spinners, eg, RA674, in use September
1952.
Central Bomber Establishment, Marham, was formed in October 1945 from the wartime Bomber Development Unit, and was responsible for operational techniques
and special modification programmes. Its aircraft were probably coded GN in 1945/46,
but this changed to DF, carried on many Lincolns, including DF-B: RA672, DF-E:
RA722 and DF-Q: RF399.
Bombing Trials Unit operated an assortment of aircraft, including Lincolns with BTU
in yellow aft of the roundels and individual letter ahead, like SX930: B-BTU,

in use June 1957. BTU-A: RF394 and BTU-B: SX972 had similar markings.

The Central Navigation and Control School had a few Lincolns in grey-black finish with grey spinners and white code letter on the sides of the nose. They also had rear fuselage and wing trainer bands, like RE321: A, RE304: B and RE309: D.

Central Gunnery School Lincolns wore standard bomber finish with white letters, like FJS-A: RF386.

Royal Air Force Flying College had a few Lincolns, some like SX935 with an assortment of Arctic red panels on the wing tips and tail unit.

Armament Division, Technical Training Command operated some Lincolns from Debden from the autumn of 1950. At first, they merely carried an individual letter in white; then TDE was added and finally the unit came into line with training units by having a single letter identity, from 1952. RE416 was S-G and RF341: S-D.

Part 3: The final stage in Lincoln markings was the application of enlarged fuselage serials and coloured spinners for squadron identity. Some aircraft also had their squadron badge on the side of the nose. There was a period when some squadrons merely had grey spinners on their machines, and finally the spinners were glossy black. From about 1952 some aircraft also had matt black anti-dazzle panels ahead of the cockpit, but as is usual there was never any complete style covering all aircraft in use at one time. Lincolns with large serials and coloured spinners, etc, included the following:

7 Sqn (Blue spinners—later some aircraft had black spinners): RA664, RE301, RE322, RE340, RE347, RE348, RE362, RE398, SX982, SX983, SX988, etc.

12 Sqn (Yellow spinners): RE322, RF343, RF355, RF388, RF558, etc.

49 Sqn (White spinners): RA664, RA666, RA686, RE322, RE323, RE340, RE399, RE423, RF348, RF444, SX958, SX976, SX984, SX986, etc.

61 Sqn (Colour uncertain; grey spinners were in use in 1953): RE320, RE359, RE366, RE417, RF348, RF349, RF444, SX986, etc.

83 Sqn (When coloured spinners were in vogue the unit had some red, but most were grey): RA662, RA672, RA677, RA693, RE296, RE358, RE415, RF414, RF539, RF574, RF575, etc.

97 Sqn (Red): RA668, RA669, RA693, RE323, RE348, RF414, RF459, RF460, RF488, RF510, RF539, SX925, SX977, etc.

100 Sqn (Green): RA714, RF409, SX937, etc.

148 Sqn (Red): RA666, RA673, RE310, RE345, RE347, RE357, RE397, RE400, RE407, RF345, RF423, SX958, SX982; some machines had a small white identity letter on the nose, like RE397: N.

199 Sqn (Blue and white spinners): RA665, RA721, RF337, RF350, RF360, RF421, RF448, RF510, RF557, SX926, SX945, SX951, etc.

214 Sqn (Yellow): RA664, RA686, RA709, RE322, RE324, RE360, RE400, RE423, RF336, RF344, RF423, SX958, SX975, SX982, etc.

617 Sqn (Red): RA656, RA665, etc.

Lincolns were withdrawn from the last three squadrons (Nos 7, 83 and 97) at the end of 1955.

APPENDIX 6: Canberra squadrons, their aircraft and markings

1) Home-based:

No 9 Sqn based at Binbrook, 5.52-6.59; Coningsby, 6.59-8.61. Flew B.Mk 2, 5.52-11.58 and B.6, 9.55-8.61; extended period of B.2 use resulting from temporary withdrawal of Mk 6s for LABS bombing gear modifications. Canberras initially wore a blue lightning flash on nose sides. Grey-green bat later painted on fins of Mk 6s, as on WH955 and WH959 which wore 'Suez stripes'. Then came a period of light blue tip tanks (WJ756 and WH774 in 8.59). B.6s subsequently had blue nose flash and blue fin panel with white disc carrying grey-green bat with IX in yellow or red above. WH984 in 1.58 had grey-green bat on fin with IX above in red, and blue nose flash and squadron badge on starboard side of nose. WT205 in 4.58 had grey-green bat on a pale blue fin disc on dark blue fin panel, and had nose flash in dark blue. Some B.6s had pale blue tip tanks with '9' flanked by grey-green bat's wings.

No 10 Sqn based at Scampton, 1.53-5.55; Honington, 5.55-1.57. Flew B.Mk 2 only. Initially wore red Scampton 'speedbird' motif on nose (eg, WH667). Nose emblem retained when aircraft acquired white pheasant marking outlined black, on moving to Honington (eg, WH665). By 9.54, some aircraft had a red bow and black arrow on tip tanks, based on squadron badge (eg, WH674). Tank and fin marking worn by WH667, which also featured yellow-black 'Suez stripes'. An unusual machine seen 7.56 was WH853 in that it had silver engine nacelles. All aircraft mentioned had grey-slate grey-blue finish.

No 12 Sqn based at Binbrook, 4.52-7.59; Coningsby, 7.59-7.61 with overseas detachments. Flew B.Mk 2, 4.52-3.59 and B.Mk 6, 5.55-7.61, extended period of B.2 use resulting from temporary withdrawal of Mk 6s for LABS bombing gear modifications. Canberras initially wore a gold lightning flash on nose sides (eg, WD990—grey-slate grey-blue finish). No nose flashes worn by B.6s which acquired a red running fox marking (eg, WH970 and WJ760, in use 8.57). Some foxes had white tail tips. In 10.57 the fox on the tail of WH970 was seen to have been outlined black with XII in red under the motif. In 1958 dark green leading fin panels were used as unit identity, and carried a brown-white-black trim fox's face head-on on a white disc (eg, WH958 and WH963). Marking carried until replacement.

No XV Sqn based at Coningsby, 5.53-5.54; Cottesmore, 5.54-2.55; Honington, 2.55-4.57. Flew B.Mk 2 only. WH723 (silver, no special markings, small fuselage serial) in use 1953 was typical. By 1954 a red hunting horn and horseshoe, based on Cottesmore station badge, were being worn, as on WJ976 and WJ972. After arrival at Honington that station's white pheasant fin marking was applied outlined red, as on WK107, a silver machine with black and yellow 'Suez stripes'.

No 18 Sqn based at Scampton, 8.53-5.55; Upwood, 5.55-1.57. Used B.Mk 2 only. Initially wore the Scampton 'speedbird' on the nose in black (eg, WF908). By 1954 this aircraft was wearing the red Pegasus badge on tip tanks. The black speedbird retained on nose after move to Upwood, as on WH919 (silver). Upwood shield applied to fins in 1956 with red Pegasus on tip tanks (eg, WH708 and WH920) and retained until withdrawal.

No 21 Sqn based at Scampton, 9.53-6.55; Waddington, 6.55-6.57. Disbanded then re-formed and at Upwood, 10.58-1.59. Used B.Mk 2. Early markings not known, but before leaving Scampton aircraft acquired a crossed keys motif on the nose above XXI, as on WJ609 and WJ715. Motif painted ahead of squadron badge. At Waddington acquired the Station's white shield with red cross, as on WJ723 which had the crossed keys emblem on tip tanks.

No 27 Sqn based at Scampton, 6.53-5.55; Waddington, 5.55-12.57. Used B.Mk 2. Aircraft for overseas tour in 6.54 were silver, wore 8-inch fuselage serials and had a narrow cheat line in red from nose to tail, as on WH728 and WH729. Marking retained in 1955, as on WK112 with enlarged serials.

No 35 Sqn based at Marham, 4.54-7.56; Upwood, 7.56-9.61. Used B.Mk 2. First squadron marking was blue tip tanks, introduced 9.54, as on WK133. Yellow wings from black horse's head were applied to fins in 1956 as in use 9.56. Similar motif added to wing tip tanks in 1957. Later the squadron motif, flanked by yellow lightning flashes outlined black, was applied to forward base of fins and sometimes on tip tanks. During time at Upwood, squadron wore Upwood tail badge and winged black and yellow horse's head on tip tanks, as on WJ719, in use 9.58 and WH918 in 9.61.

No 40 Sqn based at Coningsby, 10.53-2.54; Wittering, 2.54-10.56; Upwood, 10.56-12.56. Used B.Mk 2. No squadron identity whilst at Coningsby. At Wittering had yellow and blue checks on fin (Wittering Wing identity) upon which a red disc was centred, as on WH872 in use 8.55 and WH740 in 7.56. Became part of 50 Sqn at Upwood before markings were evolved at new station.

No 44 Sqn based at Coningsby, 4.53-5.54; Cottesmore, 5.54-2.55; Honington, 2.55-7.57. Wore the Cottesmore hunting horn motif in yellow on fins, then the Honington white pheasant, as on WH856 and WH857 in 1956.

No 50 Sqn based at Binbrook, 8.52-1.56; Upwood, 1.56-10.59. Used B.Mk 2. Orange Binbrook flash on nose (eg, WH654, grey-slate grey-blue, and WH880, silver, in 1.56). At Upwood in 1957 acquired Station badge—red lion rampant on white shield— and on tip tanks had '50' in red, and a light blue sword with yellow handle, as on WH731 in 7.57 and WJ723 in 9.58.

No 57 Sqn based at Coningsby, 5.53-5.54; Cottesmore, 5.54-2.55; Honington, 2.55-11.56; Coningsby, 11.56-12.57. Used B.Mk 2. Had yellow hunting horn and horseshoe at Cottesmore, as on WH878. At Honington wore the white pheasant motif outlined green, as on WH720 and WH725 in 7.56. After moving to Coningsby the squadron applied its red and blue Phoenix motif to the fins of its aircraft backed by a white shield, as on WK131 in 9.57. An interesting aircraft held then was WD996 in grey-slate grey-blue finish retained after it had been modified into a T.Mk 4. Previously this machine had worn 27 Squadron's red cheat line which was still being worn in 12.57 along with the Phoenix on the fin.

No 61 Sqn based at Wittering, 8.54-7.55; Upwood, 7.55-1959. Used B.Mk 2. Blue and yellow fin checks at Wittering bearing a disc of unknown colour. At Upwood first wore a large red Lincoln Imp on the fin, as on WH923, replaced by the Upwood shield badge with a red Lincoln Imp trimmed red on tip tanks, as on WH907 and WH922 in 9.58.

No 76 Sqn based at Wittering with numerous overseas detachments. Fin marking was a white rose bearing a black lion passant, as on WH980 (silver). Believed to have worn blue and yellow fin checks previously. Flew some all-white Canberras, like WH962 in use 11.58. During 1958, the Scorpion Canberra, white with black under surfaces, was among its aircraft. Rose motif retained during stay at Upwood.

No 90 Sqn based at Marham, 1.54-5.56. Used B.Mk 2. White tip tanks introduced 9.54, as on WK104. By 12.54 some aircraft were wearing a yellow hind's head on fins (eg, WF886 in use 1.56). WJ632 was wearing the tail motif and white tip tanks in 1.55, these markings being retained until disbandment.

No 100 Sqn based at Wittering, 4.54-8.59. Used B.Mk 2. Aircraft had blue and yellow Wittering Wing tail checks with a green central disc, this colour inherited from Lincoln days, as on WH913 in use 10.55. WD986, similarly attired, wore 'Suez stripes', still being carried in 8.58. Squadron operated a few B.8s later (eg, WT347) without squadron markings.

No 101 Sqn based at Binbrook, 6.51-1.57. Used B.Mk 2, 6.51-2.57 and B.Mk 6, 1.55-1.57. First squadron marking consisted of a black and white nose lightning flash, as on WD949. By 1955 had added a CI and lion motif to fins (eg, WH948, silver with 'Suez stripes'). B.6s with similar markings included WJ765 and WJ766.

No 109 Sqn based at Hemswell, 8.52-1.56; Binbrook, 1.56-2.57. Used B.Mk 2, 8.52-12.54 and B.Mk 6, 1955-1.57. Squadron identity was a yellow triangular fin flash outlined black, as on WH645 and WH868 in use 8.53 and WH741 in use 10.54. This was also included on B.6 WJ768, in use 9.56, and WJ782 which bore black and yellow 'Suez stripes'.

No 115 Sqn based at Marham, 2.54-5.57. Used B.Mk 2. Initial marking was black tip tanks, as on WH905 in 9.55. A few months previously, aircraft of the squadron had green tip tanks, like WH880 in use 7.55. Markings retained until disbandment.

No 139 Sqn based at Hemswell, 11.53-1.56; Binbrook, 1.56-12.59. Used B.Mk 2, 11.53-56 and B.Mk 6, 2.55-12.59. Squadron identity was a red triangular flash, usually outlined white, on fins as on WH741 in 9.53, WJ971 in use 9.53 and on B.6s WJ767 and WJ776, the latter having worn 'Suez stripes'.

No 199 Sqn based at Honington, 1956-58. Partially equipped with Canberra 2s bearing a white fin disc with blue waves and two yellow swords. WJ616 (silver) had this marking in 1956 and WH695 (camouflaged) in 9.57.

No 207 Sqn based at Marham, 3.54-2.56. Used B.Mk 2. Initially had red tip tanks, as on WH876 in 9.54. Possibly wore the squadron's red lion winged yellow, although this is uncertain. WK106 at the time of disbandment had only red tanks.

No 617 Sqn based at Binbrook, 1.52-12.55. Used B.Mk 2 with dark blue nose lightning flash. There is some evidence that some aircraft of the squadron also wore a red flash like WH706, in use 6.53. WJ980, in use 9.53, had a blue flash.

2) Squadrons based outside the United Kingdom

No 3 Sqn based in Germany. Used B.(I) Mk 8. Fin marking was a red and grey cockatrice on a white disc, as on XM271 and WT364. Later the squadron painted a rich green stripe across the fin flanking the disc. At one time white individual letters were painted on the matt black nose anti-dazzle panel, eg, WT366: N in use 5.61 and XM276: H in use 8.63.

No 6 Sqn based at Akrotiri, Cyprus. Equipped with B. Mk 2, 8.57-1960; B.6, 12.59-1963; and B.16, 1.62-1969. Wore the pale blue and red gunner's stripe across the fin from 1958 and a red can-opener motif on tip tanks, as on WJ614 in use 9.59. B.6s included WJ777 and WJ778 in use with similar markings in 11.60. B.16s were camouflaged Dark Sea Grey-Dark Green-Silver, eg, WJ771 in use 5.62 with WJ780. These latter aircraft wore the red can-opener on a white fin disc and later the gunner's stripe flanking the can-opener, then of reduced size. Later the can-opener was applied on a large white disc on the fin.

No 14 Sqn based in Germany. Used B(I)Mk 8 from 12.62. Had a winged cross and disc motif on the fins of its aircraft, and the blue-white checks, inherited from the days when it was a fighter squadron, were painted on the nose flanking the squadron badge, as on WT336 in 1.63.

No 16 Sqn based in Germany. Used B(I)Mk 8 from 3.58. Squadron applied yellow-black crossed keys on a white disc on noses of its aircraft. A black band outlined yellow was painted around the fuselage at the roundel position, as on XM267 in 3.59 and WT345 in 6.67. In the early 1960s white individual letters were painted on the black nose anti-dazzle panel, WT340 having 'H' in 1.60.

No 32 Sqn based at Akrotiri, Cyprus. Used B.2, 1.57-8.61 and B.15, 7.61 *et seq*. Initial squadron marking was a blue fin panel with diagonal white stripes, as on WK111 in 7.58. Similar markings were in use on WH872 in 9.59 and WH866 in 8.61. In 1961, a small blue rectangle with blue diagonals was painted on the fin, and at some time a squadron badge was positioned centrally upon this, as on WH870. Final marking on some B.15s consisted of blue and white stripes flanking the fuselage roundel.

No 45 Sqn, based in the Far East, used B.Mk 2 and B.15. Basic marking was a white fin disc outlined blue bearing a blue camel with red wings, although on some aircraft these markings are said to have been used in reversed colour. WH646 and WH665 were in use in standard marking in 1.59 and a camouflaged machine was WJ981.

No 59 Sqn based in Germany, 8.56-12.57. Initially used B.Mk 2 like WH658 (silver) and WJ569 (camouflaged) in 1956. Mk 8s had a red and white road sign motif on the tail bearing an exclamation mark, as on WT364 in 9.56.

No 73 Sqn based in Cyprus. Used B.Mk 2 and, from mid-1962, B.15. For a time wore black and light blue or dark blue and yellow flashes on tip tanks. One with the former was WH886 which had a grey demi-talbot on a white shield on the fin. WK111 had a red demi-talbot on the fin with blue and yellow tip tank stripes. A third variation was a dark blue-light blue flash with a white disc bearing the squadron badge, as on WH983. A further variation seen on T.Mk 4 WJ566 was a white shield bearing a mauve demi-talbot, in use 1957. The squadron's markings varied many times and finally on the B.15s it appeared as a yellow fin disc with the blue talbot and a yellow arrow on a blue tip tank.

No 88 Sqn based in Germany. Received Canberra 8s in 1956. Initially these carried the squadron badge on the fin. For a time some wore an inter-twined 88 in yellow on the tail (eg, WT344) as in 1958. A later squadron marking was a black and yellow rattlesnake with red and yellow tongue, as worn by XM270.

No 102 Sqn based at Gutersloh, 10.54-8.56; became 59 Squadron on 20.8.56. Used B.Mk 2 including WJ611. Adopted a red lion holding a blue bomb on a fin shield, as on WK124, which wore on its nose the atomic flash and lightning stroke of No 551 Wing.

No 103 Sqn based at Gutersloh. Operated B.Mk 2, including WJ612 and WJ781. No special markings were apparently carried.

No 104 Sqn based at Gutersloh, 1955-56. Operated B.Mk 2, including WH903, but no special markings were apparently carried.

No 149 Sqn based at Gutersloh, 1955-56. Operated B.Mk 2, but no special markings were apparently carried.

No 213 Sqn based in Germany. Used B(I)Mk 6 from 3.56. Aircraft originally silver like WT319, but later camouflaged Dark Sea Grey-Dark Green-Silver. Squadron markings applied to fins in 1961 consisted of the unit badge (a hornet) on a white disc superimposed upon a yellow and black arrowhead. Camouflaged aircraft, which were in use from 1957, had a yellow and black hornet on the fins with this repeated on the nose, where it was flanked by the squadron's black and yellow stripes, as on WT312 in use in 12.57. Early aircraft had belly gun pack, later deleted, as on WT325 (camouflaged) in use 9.61.

No 249 Sqn based in Cyprus. Received B.Mk 2 in 8.57 and used B.6, 11.59-1962 and B.16 subsequently. First unit marking was a version of the Akrotiri Station badge, a pink flamingo on a white shield, or a grey elephant on a white disc. Tip tanks were yellow and bore a red assegai spear with a white disc on its head bearing an elephant, as on WH655. Later marking comprised yellow tip tanks with yellow fin flash outlined black, as on WJ783 in use 7.61. Individual nose identity letters were then carried. A B.Mk 6, used in Dark Green-Dark Sea Grey-Silver finish with a yellow tail flash, was WT374 in use 1960-61. On the camouflaged B.16s, tails bore a pink elephant on a yellow disc outlined white and flanked by yellow and blue diagonal bars outlined white. Finally, B.16s had either a yellow fin disc with black elephant, or black disc with a pink elephant. No 249's markings varied more than any other Canberra squadron.

Notes on illustrations appearing on front and rear end papers

Avro Lancaster tail markings, 1944-45 (front end paper 1):

Between the summer of 1944 and the end of the war in Europe, Lancasters flown by formation leaders carried coloured tails. They served in two distinct ways, either as formating leaders for Lancaster gaggles on daylight operations or as G-H radar leaders. It is certain that they were quite widely used in a profusion of styles and colours. It was relatively easy to record the colours when seen, but if the aircraft was high or distant the unit letters were often impossible to read. Those noted by the author, by Alf Alderson and E. Rhodes form the basis of the drawings reproduced here. Clearly, there is much room for further research in connection with coloured Lancaster tails.

V-Bomber fin markings (front end paper 2 and rear end paper 1):

No 7 Sqn	White stars on bright blue disc	eg, Valiant XD826
No 9 Sqn	Two shades of olive green	eg, Vulcan XM601
No 10 Sqn	Pale red (anti-flash shade)	eg, Victor XA932
No XV Sqn	Colours applied to aircraft with anti-flash markings: Pink wings, pale blue hind head with black trim, pink XV with pale blue shading	eg, Victor XH620
No 18 Sqn	Pale blue disc, red pegasus	eg, Valiant WP211 (white)
No 35 Sqn	Pale grey horse's head, straw-coloured wings with slightly darker trim (anti-flash shades)	eg, Vulcan XH562 with anti-flash roundels
No 27 Sqn	(a) Dull green elephant	eg, Vulcan XJ824 with anti-flash roundels
	(b) Bright green dumbo. Yellow feet, mouth, headband. Black and white trim. All on white disc	eg, Vulcan XM595 camouflaged
No 49 Sqn	Pink greyhound (anti-flash shades)	eg, Valiant XD818 (white, anti-flash roundels)

No 55 Sqn	Dark blue hand and spear outlined white, some aircraft grey hand and spear with blue tip. All outlined white	eg, Victor XH615 camouflaged, second finish
No 83 Sqn	Dark brown antler with lighter trim	eg, Vulcan XL425, pale roundels; white
No 138 Sqn	Yellow sword and rope on green disc	eg, Valiant XD875 (white)
No 90 Sqn	Green pennant, yellow 'XC'	eg, Valiant XD830 (white) pale roundels
No 100 Sqn	White skull and cross bones on pale blue disc (anti-flash shade)	eg, Victor XL192 (pale roundels)
No 100 Sqn	Golden lion (Wittering Wing marking also carried by aircraft of 139 Sqn)	eg, Victor XL192 (camouflaged)
No 139 Sqn	Pale blue disc and JAMAICA, pink and white fasces with white blade and crescent (anti-flash shade)	eg, Victor XL191 (pale roundels)
No 199 Sqn	Blue and white waves, yellow swords	eg, Valiant WP213 (white)
No 207 Sqn	Red lion, yellow wings	eg, Valiant WZ404 (white)
No 214 Sqn	Dayglo red on white base/outline	eg, Victor XA937 (camouflaged)
Finningley badge	White rose with pink centre on pale blue shield (anti-flash shades)	eg, Vulcan XH558 (white, pale roundels)
Lincoln Arms	Yellow-gold Fleur-de-Lys on red cross on white-pale blue-grey shield with black outline	eg, Vulcan XH480 (white)
No 617 Sqn	(a) Pink lightning flashes	eg, Vulcan XL321 (white, anti-flash colours)
	(b) Dayglo red lightning flashes	eg, Vulcan XL427 (camouflaged)
	(c) White diamond with pale blue outline, red flashes, yellow dam walls, black waves. In use 1972.	eg, Vulcan XL392 (camouflaged)

Canberra fin markings (rear end paper 1 and 2):

No 9 Sqn	Pale blue disc, red IX, olive grey-green bat with dark grey-deeper olive green shading	eg, B.Mk 6 WH977
No 12 Sqn	(a) Red fox (some had white tail tip)	eg, WJ764
	(b) White disc, brown and white fox head	eg, WH960
No 4 Sqn	White disc with red cross, gold wings and top, blue nose diamonds on two white rectangles	eg, B(I)8 WT362 (black under surfaces)
No 6 Sqn	Light blue or roundel blue fin stripe with red zig-zag with dark blue outline to stripe on some aircraft. Red can-opener on tip tanks	eg, WK109
No 16 Sqn	White disc with yellow outline on nose with yellow-black crossed keys	eg, B(I)8 XH234 with silver under-sides
No 3 Sqn	Green band, red outline, grey and red cockatrice on white disc	eg, B(I) 8 XM936 with black under-sides

No 32 Sqn	Blue fin panel, white stripes	eg, WH947 (camouflaged, silver undersides)
No 35 Sqn	(a) White shield outlined black, black horse's head with yellow wings, yellow lightning flash. On fin base, tip tanks	eg, WK130
	(b) Black horse's head, yellow rings, red tongue	eg, WH910
No 40 Sqn	Yellow and blue fin checks, red disc	eg, WH740
No 45 Sqn	White disc, pale blue outline. Blue camel, red wings—some probably had reversal of this colour	eg, WH667
No 50 Sqn	Light blue sword, yellow handle, '50' in red	eg, WJ727
No 61 Sqn	61's badge as a Lincoln Imp. Red, black, white trim	eg, WH923
No 59 Sqn	Red triangle, white centre, black marking	eg, WT366 (black undersides)
No 73 Sqn	White shield—hound varied in colour	eg, WD988 (white)
No 76 Sqn	White rose, black lion, red outline and points	eg, WT206 (silver)
No 88 Sqn	Yellow and black snake, red and yellow tongue	eg, XM272 (black undersides)
No 100 Sqn	Blue and buff checks, green disc, white skull with black trim. Current markings	eg, WH739 (light grey)
No 101 Sqn	Black disc, red lion and CI, yellow crown	eg, WJ756
No 213 Sqn	Yellow and black hornet, white wings	eg, WT312
No 249 Sqn	Yellow and blue stripes outlined white, grey elephant on yellow disc	eg, WJ774 (white serial on fuselage, camouflaged with silver underside)

JAMAICA
139 Sqn.

199 Sqn.

207 Sqn.

214 Sqn.

Finningley

Waddington

617 Sqn.

617 Sqn.

.617 Sqn.

V · BOMBER FIN MARKINGS

9 Sqn.

12 Sqn.

12 Sqn.

4 Sqn.

NOSE

TIP TANKS

6 Sqn.

16 Sqn.

CANBERRA FIN MARKINGS